KT-491-141

Vocational A-level
Travel and Tourism Options

Vocational A-level
Travel and Tourism Options

Second Edition

Ray Youell MSc MTS MSA

Longman

An imprint of **Pearson Education**

Harlow, England · London · New York · Reading, Massachusetts · San Francisco
Toronto · Don Mills, Ontario · Sydney · Tokyo · Singapore · Hong Kong · Seoul
Taipei · Cape Town · Madrid · Mexico City · Amsterdam · Munich · Paris · Milan

In this book you will find helpful icons showing which Key Skills the Activities can be used for:

 Communication

 Application of number

 Information technology

 Working with others

 Problem solving

 Improving own learning and performance

Pearson Education Limited
Edinburgh Gate
Harlow
Essex CM20 2JE
England

and Associated Companies throughout the world

Visit us on the World Wide Web at:
http://www.pearsoneduc.com

© Pearson Education 2001

The right of Ray Youell to be identified as the author of this Work has been asserted by him in accordance with the Copyright, Designs and Patents Act 1988.

All rights reserved; no part of this publication may be reproduced, stored in a retrieval system, or transmitted in any form or by any means, electronic, mechanical, photocopying, recording or otherwise without either the prior written permission of the Publishers or a licence permitting restricted copying in the United Kingdom issued by the Copyright Licensing Agency Ltd, 90 Tottenham Court Road, London W1P 0LP.

First edition published 1996
This edition published 2001

ISBN 0 582 40446 0
British Library Cataloguing-in-Publication Data

A catalogue record for this book is available from the British Library.

10 9 8 7 6 5 4 3
06 05 04 03 02

Set by 35 in Humanist, Rotis Serif, Caslon
Printed in Malaysia, PJB

Contents

Introduction

Vocational A-level Travel and Tourism Options has been written specifically for the Vocational A-level Travel and Tourism courses starting in September 2000. It follows exactly the structure of 12 of the new travel and tourism optional units developed by Edexcel, including all the units that are externally assessed. The book will also be invaluable to students and staff following the Vocational A-level Travel and Tourism courses offered by the AQA and OCR awarding bodies. This book is a companion volume to my *Vocational A-level Travel and Tourism* book published by Pearson Education in June 2000.

It builds on the success of my previous best-selling Longman books – *Advanced GNVQ Leisure and Tourism* (1994), *Advanced GNVQ Leisure and Tourism* 2nd edition (1995) and *Advanced GNVQ Travel and Tourism Optional Units* (1996). Together, these have set the standard for the study of leisure and tourism at GNVQ level in schools and colleges across the UK.

This book includes many of the popular features found in my previous editions – case studies, realistic activities and up-to-date statistics. Most of all, it offers something many of you have told me that you have appreciated in my previous books, namely an *in-depth* study of travel and tourism, the industry that I have been involved with for more than 20 years.

However, just like the travel and tourism industry, nothing stands still for long! So there are extra features in this new book, including links to Internet websites and realistic industry examples. You will find these throughout the book, helping to turn theory into practice and giving you ideas for further research.

I hope you find the book a useful companion in your studies. Good luck with your course and future career!

Ray Youell
Aberystwyth
September 2000

Acknowledgements

I am indebted to the many individuals and organisations that have helped with the project. Those who have provided valuable information and illustrations are acknowledged in the relevant section of the text. I am grateful to them all for their co-operation and helpful comments. Thanks are also due to Judith Harvey, Sonia Wilson, Eva Martinez, Kay Spragg and the rest of the team at Pearson Education for their usual professional approach. Peter Carr and Julie Gibson have provided valuable advice throughout the project. As always, the biggest thanks go to Sue, Megan and Owen.

Whilst every effort has been made to trace the owners of copyright material, in a few cases this has proved impossible and we take this opportunity to offer our apologies to any copyright holders whose rights we may have unwittingly infringed.

UK travel destinations

7

Destinations have a very important part to play in the UK travel and tourism industry, since it is often the destination, and its associated features, such as climate, leisure facilities, accommodation and entertainment facilities, that attract visitors in the first place. Having a good knowledge of popular UK destinations and what they can offer visitors is very important for anybody working, or hoping to work, in travel and tourism, so that staff are able to provide the correct information and advice to travellers. In this unit you will investigate the location and features of popular UK travel destinations, as well as main travel and tourism routes. You will also learn about the factors that influence the popularity and appeal of UK destinations, such as the types of facilities provided and how destinations are managed. The unit concludes with details of the types of sources that can be used to gather information on UK destinations.

This unit is divided into five main areas:

- **The location of popular UK travel destinations**
- **The features of popular UK travel destinations**
- **Popularity and appeal of UK travel destinations**
- **Main travel and tourism routes in the UK**
- **Information sources**

We guide you through each of these areas using examples and case studies from the travel and tourism industry. At the beginning of each of these sections you will see a list of key topics to help you fully understand what you need to learn. Look out for the links to websites so that you can learn more about a particular destination, travel and tourism company, organisation or topic.

The location of popular UK travel destinations

Key topics in this section

- **Types of travel and tourism destinations**
- **Characteristics of destination types**
- **Locating popular UK travel and tourism destinations**

Types of travel and tourism destinations

Before we look at the different types of destinations in the UK, it is important that you understand the meaning of the following terms:

- ✪ **The United Kingdom (UK) refers to Great Britain and Northern Ireland**
- ✪ **Great Britain (often shortened to just Britain) consists of England, Scotland and Wales**
- ✪ **The British Isles refers to the United Kingdom and the Republic of Ireland**

This unit concentrates on UK travel and tourism destinations, but you must be familiar with these other terms.

Activity 7.1

With reference to an atlas, draw one map of the UK, one of Great Britain and one of the British Isles. Make sure all the country boundaries are included on your maps.

The UK has a wide variety of destinations that can be grouped as follows:

- ✪ **Towns and cities** – e.g. London, Edinburgh, Belfast, York, Shrewsbury (see Case Study on page 4), Chester, Cardiff
- ✪ **Seaside resorts** – e.g. Brighton, Blackpool, Rhyl, Torquay, Cleethorpes

- ✪ **Purpose-built resorts** – e.g. Butlins, Center Parcs, Forest Enterprise parks
- ✪ **Countryside areas** – e.g. National Parks, Areas of Outstanding Natural Beauty, Heritage Coasts, forests, mountain areas, lakes and waterways
- ✪ **Historical/cultural destinations** – e.g. Stratford-upon-Avon, Bath, Ironbridge (see Figure 7.1), Stonehenge
- ✪ **Business travel destinations and conference venues** – e.g. London, Manchester, Birmingham, Leeds, Cardiff, Edinburgh, Glasgow, Belfast

It is possible for a travel and tourism destination to fall into more than one of these categories. For example, Bournemouth is a typical English south-coast seaside resort as well as being an important business tourism and conference destination.

The following case study on Shrewsbury shows the wide range of attractions on offer to different types of visitors.

Figure 7.1 *Ironbridge Gorge World Heritage Site*
Courtesy of Ironbridge Gorge Museum Trust, Ironbridge, Telford

Case Study
Shrewsbury – a destination in the Heart of England Tourist Board region

▶ **INTRODUCTION**

Shrewsbury is located in the heart of the countryside of Shropshire, yet is within easy reach of Birmingham and the West Midlands conurbation. It is a town steeped in history, with its 'black and white' Tudor architecture, annual Flower Show and associations with Brother Cadfael drawing visitors from home and abroad. It is located in the English Marches and commands an imposing position in a horseshoe meander of the River Severn.

▶ **RANGE OF ATTRACTIONS**

Shrewsbury has a wide range of attractions used both by local people and visitors to the town. The following is a list of some of the most popular attractions, with details of ownership and appeal to different visitor types.

The Shrewsbury Quest
Description: a heritage attraction that re-creates monastic life in early medieval Shrewsbury through mystery, activity and authentic medieval gardens. Illustrates the period and world of Brother Cadfael, the fictional detective monk who features in Ellis Peters' best-selling mystery novels.
Ownership: owned and operated by a private company on a site and buildings owned by, and leased from, Shrewsbury and Atcham Borough Council.
Visitor types: caters for individuals and groups, and is particularly attractive to families and readers of the Cadfael books. Also has facilities to cater for education groups. Fully accessible for disabled people, with tactile maps, information and games in Braille and large format print. Also has facilities for visitors with hearing difficulties.

continued

continued

Rowley's House Museum
Description: sixteenth-century timber-framed warehouse and stone mansion of 1618. Exhibits include information on the Romans in Shropshire, life in medieval Shrewsbury, Shropshire wildlife, geology, costume and prehistory.
Ownership: operated by Shrewsbury Museums Service, Shrewsbury and Atcham Borough Council.
Visitor types: welcomes all visitors to Shrewsbury, individuals and groups. The nature of the building means that there is limited access for visitors with mobility problems.

Clive House Museum
Description: museum that evokes eighteenth- and nineteenth-century life in Shrewsbury. Taking its name from Clive of India, Mayor and MP for Shrewsbury in the 1760s, the house has exhibits featuring social and domestic life, fine and applied arts and the Victorian kitchen.
Ownership: operated by Shrewsbury Museums Service, Shrewsbury and Atcham Borough Council.
Visitor types: welcomes all visitors to Shrewsbury, individuals and groups. The nature of the attraction means that there is access to the ground floor only for visitors with mobility problems.

Coleham Pumping Station
Description: a steam restoration project in progress. Open days are held during the summer months to view the Victorian sewage pumping house and the two beam engines.
Ownership: owned and managed by Shrewsbury Museums Service, Shrewsbury and Atcham Borough Council, with assistance from the Shrewsbury Steam Trust.
Visitor types: welcomes individuals and groups on the open days. There is ramped access for people with disabilities.

Shrewsbury Castle and Shropshire Regimental Museum
Description: red, sandstone castle guarding the northern approaches to Shrewsbury. Castle grounds include the

continued

continued

motte, site of the first Norman castle. Regimental Museum houses collections from the eighteenth-century to the present-day campaigns.

Ownership: owned and managed by Shrewsbury Museums Service, Shrewsbury and Atcham Borough Council. Collections displayed and managed by Shropshire Regimental Museum Trust.

Visitor types: welcomes all visitors to Shrewsbury, individuals and groups. Good access to much of the site and buildings for visitors with mobility problems. There is a coach drop-off point.

Quarry Park

Description: a town park on the banks of the River Severn and the location for the famous Shrewsbury Flower Show every August. The park has a wide range of play facilities for children, including boat hire on the river.

Ownership: under the control of Shrewsbury and Atcham Borough Council.

Visitor types: used by local people throughout the year and visitors to the town. Most areas are accessible to those with mobility problems. The park appeals to all ages.

Meole Brace Golf Course

Description: a 9-hole municipal course on the outskirts of the town.

Ownership: operated by Shrewsbury and Atcham Borough Council.

Visitor types: used by casual visitors to the town, as well as keen, local golfers. No membership is required. The course is used by young and old alike.

Sports and Leisure Centres

Description: a range of purpose-built facilities, including:

★ *The Quarry Swimming and Fitness Centre* – swimming pool, flume ride, gymnasium, aerobics studio, sauna, steam room, spa bath and solarium suite.

continued

continued

★ *London Road Sports Centre* – six-court facility, gymnasium and outdoor multi-sport area.

★ *The Grange Sports Centre* – six-court facility, general hall and outdoor tennis courts.

★ *Roman Road Sports Centre* – three-court facility and regional standard floodlit synthetic surface.

★ *Monkmoor Recreation Centre (Outdoor)* – floodlit synthetic surface, tennis courts, multi-sports area, croquet lawn, bowling green, children's play area, football pitches and skateboard park.

Ownership: under the control of the Department of Health, Leisure & Tourism, Shrewsbury and Atcham Borough Council.

Visitor types: club and public access is available at all centres, no membership required. Extensive sports development and children's activity programmes available. 'Passport to leisure' discount scheme is in operation for all centres.

Guided Tours

Description: a range of guided walking and coach tours of the town and surrounding areas, some themed, e.g. based on the Brother Cadfael mysteries.

Ownership: operated by Shrewsbury and Atcham Borough Council using official Green (local) and Blue (regional) Badge Guides.

Visitor types: available to individuals and groups, with foreign language tours available in French, Italian and Welsh. Advice available on guided tours for people in wheelchairs or with impaired mobility.

Shrewsbury Abbey

Description: the heart of the Brother Cadfael stories, the Abbey was founded in 1083 and became a large and powerful Benedictine monastery. The Abbey Church

continued

continued

survived the Dissolution and is still a place of worship today.

Ownership: Church of England

Visitor types: open to local people and visitors every day, with interesting displays to illustrate its history.

Gateway Arts Centre

Description: an education and arts centre, with exhibition areas, a book shop and coffee shop. Runs a range of continuing education and leisure day, evening and weekend courses.

Ownership: under the control of Shropshire Education Department, Shropshire County Council.

Visitor types: courses and facilities appeal to both local people and visitors to the town, including those with disabilities.

▶ EVENTS IN SHREWSBURY

The town hosts a wide variety of events throughout the year. In a typical year, this includes:

- ★ Shrewsbury Antique Book Fair
- ★ Shropshire and West Midlands Agricultural Show
- ★ Shrewsbury Carnival
- ★ Kite and Boomerang Festival
- ★ International Music Festival
- ★ World Music Day
- ★ Shrewsbury Flower Show
- ★ County of Salop Steam Rally
- ★ Real Ale Festival
- ★ Shrewsbury Abbey Flower Festival

The events are put on by a range of private, public and voluntary sector organisations, and appeal to both local people and visitors to the town.

continued

continued

▶ ACCESS TO SHREWSBURY'S ATTRACTIONS

Shrewsbury's central location in the heart of Britain makes its attractions very accessible by a number of modes of transport.

★ *By car*: The town is a one-hour drive from Birmingham, 3 hours from London and 2 hours from Holyhead. The recent improvements to the A5 road around Shrewsbury have improved access for visitors, with a direct dual-carriageway link to the national motorway network via the M54 (see Figure 7.2).

★ *By train*: Shrewsbury's restored Victorian railway station is right in the centre of the town by the Castle. There are hourly train services from London Euston and good connections to Manchester, Crewe, Chester, Cardiff, Aberystwyth and stations *en route*.

★ *By coach*: There are direct National Express services daily from London Victoria and connections to other UK towns served by the network.

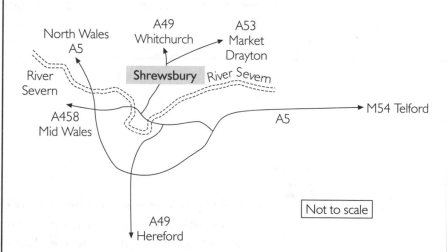

Figure 7.2 *Road access to Shrewsbury*

continued

continued

★ **Buses**: Regular buses serve all main parts of the town, as well as the principal Shropshire towns, with most visitor attractions being accessible by bus.

★ **Park and ride**: This service offers an excellent way for local people and tourists to get right to the centre of the town where many of its attractions are situated. Park and ride facilities can be found to the south, west and north of the main town.

Case study discussion questions

1 Do you consider that the range of tourist attractions given in the case study meets the needs of the majority of visitors to a town such as Shrewsbury?

2 Are there gaps in the provision of attractions and, if so, what other attractions would you suggest?

3 Why are some of the attractions not wholly suitable for visitors with disabilities?

4 What particular marketing and promotional techniques would you implement to give a town such as Shrewsbury maximum national exposure, given the limited resources available?

5 How could the events listed in the case study be best promoted to attract overnight visitors to the town?

Browse this website

www.shrewsbury
tourism.co.uk

Activity 7.2

Carry out some research into the attractions, events and transport access to another popular tourist destination in the UK. Present your information in the same way as the case study on Shrewsbury above. Include a location map in your case study.

Characteristics of destination types

Using the grouping of travel and tourism destinations shown earlier in this unit, we can describe the characteristics of different UK destination types as follows:

- ✪ **Town and cities**: These destinations have a wide variety of tourist facilities, including accommodation, attractions, entertainment and information services, within a relatively small area. They tend to be popular with overseas visitors to the UK, particularly those who are making their first trip to this country. They are well served by public transport, including rail, bus, air, coach and tram services.

- ✪ **Seaside resorts**: These have been part of the UK travel and tourism scene since Victorian times, although today many are experiencing difficulty in attracting visitors. This is due to the increasing competition from tour operators offering overseas package holidays with 'guaranteed' sunshine and good value prices. Many seaside resorts in the UK are investing in new facilities for tourists in order to hold on to their market share, for example by providing 'wet weather' facilities, extra entertainment and upgraded holiday accommodation.

- ✪ **Purpose-built resorts**: Companies such as Butlins, Oasis and Center Parcs offer purpose-built facilities for their visitors, where accommodation, entertainment, activities, catering, parking and information services are all provided on site, often grouped around a central, undercover leisure pool complex.

- ✪ **Countryside areas**: The great outdoors is a magnet for UK and overseas visitors (see Figure 7.3). Protected areas, such as the National Parks and Areas of Outstanding Natural Beauty, and other areas of scenic beauty offer people fresh air, peace, quiet and an escape from the bustle of everyday life. Increased interest in activities and sports, such as mountain biking, climbing and walking, means that the environment in countryside areas is coming under increased pressure.

- ✪ **Historical/cultural destinations**: Britain's heritage is one of the main reasons why overseas visitors come to these shores and why UK tourists enjoy day trips. Destinations such as York, London, Chester, Oxford, Edinburgh and Cambridge welcome millions of UK and foreign tourists every year.

- ✪ **Business travel destinations**: Business people need accommodation, conference, exhibition and meeting facilities throughout the UK. Many towns and cities see business tourists as an important sector of the market for tourism, since they often require better quality facilities for which they are willing to pay higher prices.

Figure 7.3 *The Trossachs and Loch Katrine*
Courtesy of Antonio Martinez

Locating popular UK travel and tourism destinations

Although it would be impossible to be able to locate on a map every travel and tourism destination in the UK, you must be familiar with some of the more popular areas, as well as knowing where to look to find the destinations that you are not familiar with.

The majority of this section on locating popular UK travel and tourism destinations will involve you in researching areas using an atlas and other information sources. You will be asked to mark particular destinations and features on outline maps of the UK that your tutor will provide for you.

Carry out some research, and on an outline map of the UK, locate the following popular travel and tourism destinations and features:

★ *Towns and cities* – the 20 most visited towns and cities in the UK (see Table 7.1), plus Belfast, Shrewsbury, Chester, Norwich, Plymouth, Portsmouth, Exeter, Keswick, Hull, Aberystwyth, Swansea, Londonderry, Aviemore, Inverness, Aberdeen, Fort William and Perth

★ *Seaside resorts* – Blackpool, Rhyl, Torquay, Cleethorpes, Newquay (Cornwall), Bude, Scarborough, Margate, Southend-on-Sea, Clacton, Great Yarmouth and Southport

★ *Purpose-built resorts* – Oasis Village in the Lake District and the three Center Parcs villages at Sherwood Forest, Longleat and Elveden Forest near Newmarket

★ *Countryside areas* – the 10 National Parks in England and Wales (plus the New Forest in Hampshire and the Broads in East Anglia) and the highest mountain in England, Wales, Scotland and Northern Ireland. Also, the Forest Parks in Scotland and the route of the National Cycle Network.

★ *Historical/cultural destinations* – Stratford-upon-Avon, Bath, Ironbridge, Stonehenge, Lincoln and Canterbury

★ *Business travel destinations and conference venues* – London, Manchester, Birmingham, Leeds, Cardiff, Edinburgh, Glasgow, Swindon, Southampton, Northampton, Coventry, Warwick and Belfast.

Browse these websites for information on UK travel and tourism destinations

www.visitbritain.com

www.englishtourism.org.uk

www.tourism.wales.gov.uk

www.ni-tourism.com

www.visitscotland.com

Town	Number of nights (millions) spent in 1998
London	91.7
Edinburgh	5.7
Oxford	4.0
Cambridge	3.7
Glasgow	3.7
Birmingham	3.5
Manchester	3.2
Brighton/Hove	2.9
Bournemouth	2.5
Newcastle-upon-Tyne	2.1
Bristol	2.0
Nottingham	1.7
Eastbourne	1.5
York	1.5
Bath	1.4
Leeds	1.4
Liverpool	1.4
Reading	1.3
Sheffield	1.2
Cardiff	1.1

Adapted from BTA data

Table 7.1   *The 20 most visited towns and cities in the UK, 1998*

The features of popular UK travel destinations

Key topics in this section

- **Climate**
- **Landscape**
- **Natural attractions**
- **Built attractions**
- **Events**
- **Food, drink and entertainment**
- **Types of accommodation**
- **Transport services and links**

Each of the destination types described in the previous section of this unit has its own particular features that appeal to visitors, including:

✪ **Climate**

✪ **Landscape**

✪ **Natural attractions**

✪ **Built attractions**

✪ **Events**

✪ **Food, drink and entertainment**

✪ **Types of accommodation**

✪ **Transport services and links**

It is important to remember that different features of a destination will appeal to different types of visitors. Some people will prefer the peace and quiet of the countryside while others will look for more excitement and entertainment that is often found in city destinations.

Climate

The British Isles has a temperate climate, with warm, wet summers and cool, wet winters. Western areas receive the most rainfall since the prevailing wind is from the west. The east coast of England and Scotland tends to be colder and windier than the west coast, which is warmed by the Gulf Stream. The south-east corner of England is the sunniest region of the UK, whereas the south-west has, overall, the mildest climate. Scotland is generally colder than the rest of the UK, especially in the more northerly regions. In upland areas of England, Wales and Scotland snow is common in winter, and fog and mist may occur at any time of the year.

Given this overview of the UK climate it is clear that overseas tourists visit Britain for something other than its climate! The cool temperate climate is also an important factor in the recent growth in sales of overseas holidays to British people, to destinations such as Spain, Greece and Florida. Within the UK, the West Country is the most popular holiday region, a reflection of its relatively warm summer weather. Britain's unpredictable weather is the reason for the development of 'all weather', undercover facilities at such places as Center Parcs and Oasis Village in the Lake District.

Landscape

Although the UK is relatively small in comparison to other countries of the world, it has an abundance of fine landscapes, from Land's End in Cornwall to John O'Groats on the northern tip of Scotland. Visitors are attracted to its rugged mountains, beautiful coastline, picturesque dales, desolate moorlands, woodlands, lakes, rivers, estuaries and many other features completing the scene. The landscape in the UK is a major selling point for travel and tourism (see Figure 7.4).

Figure 7.4 *Walking on the South Downs Way*
Courtesy of Sonia Wilson

Locate the following landscape features on an outline map of the UK:

★ The Cambrian Mountains

★ The Pennines

★ The Yorkshire Dales

★ Bodmin Moor

★ Dartmoor

★ Exmoor

★ The South Downs

★ The North Downs

★ Salisbury Plain

★ The Cotswold Hills

★ The Vale of Evesham

★ The Wye Valley

★ The Chiltern Hills

★ The Lake District

★ The Peak District

★ Snowdonia

★ The Cheviot Hills

★ The Cairngorm Mountains

★ The Scottish Highlands

★ The Fens

★ The Trossachs

★ The Yorkshire Dales

★ The National Forest

★ The Forest of Dean

★ The Forest of Bowland

★ The Mourne Mountains

★ Lough Neagh

★ Giant's Causeway

Natural attractions

The eighty per cent of the UK population that work in urban areas use the countryside as a leisure resource, for day trips, at weekends and for longer holidays. Tourists visit the countryside for many reasons, such as to walk, view wildlife, take part in active pursuits or simply to enjoy the peace and quiet. They are drawn to the natural attractions that it offers, including mountains, rolling hills and dales, rivers, lakes, forests and gardens (see Figure 7.5).

Figure 7.5   *The palm house at Kew Gardens*
Courtesy of Sonia Wilson

Locate the following rivers, lakes, etc. on an outline map of the UK:

★ The River Thames

★ The River Severn

★ The River Wye

★ The River Avon (running through Stratford-upon-Avon)

★ The River Trent

★ The River Tay

★ The River Tamar

★ The River Test

★ The Great Ouse

★ The Wash

★ Cardigan Bay

★ Bristol Channel

★ The Solway Firth

★ The Moray Firth

★ Loch Ness

★ Loch Rannoch

★ The River Spey

★ Rutland Water

★ Lake Windermere

★ Elan Valley Lakes

★ Lake Vyrnwy

★ Kielder Water

Activity 7.6

Locate the following National Trails on an outline map of the UK:

1 Cleveland Way

2 North Downs Way

3 Offa's Dyke Path

4 Peddar's Way/Norfolk Coast Path

5 Pennine Way

6 Ridgeway

7 South Downs Way

8 South West Coast Path

9 Thames Path

10 Wolds Way

11 Cotswold Way

12 Hadrian's Wall Path

13 Pennine Bridleway

Browse this Countryside Agency website for information on the National Trails

www.countryside.gov.uk

Built attractions

Unit 14 *Visitor attractions* demonstrates that built attractions are an important part of the UK travel and tourism industry. They include heritage attractions, historic buildings (see Figure 7.6), theme parks, cultural attractions, sports facilities, indoor arenas and entertainment venues.

Activity 7.7

Make a list of the popular natural and built attractions within 80 km of your home. Draw a map and mark on it the attractions together with an explanatory key.

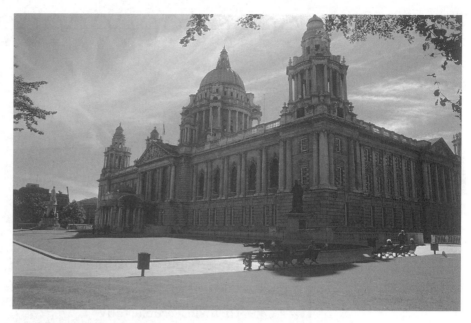

Figure 7.6 *Belfast City Hall*
Courtesy of Antonio Martinez

Events

Visitor attractions are not always permanent. Many tourist destinations stage special events, of national, regional or local significance, as a way of boosting tourism. Indeed some destinations that do not have a large number of built attractions use events as a way of attracting visitors to their area. The themes of events are many and varied, from celebrations of anniversaries and carnivals to sporting events and musical extravaganzas.

Industry example

York, one of Britain's most popular tourist cities, offers an extensive range of events for local people and tourists alike, as the following list of a small selection of its millennium events demonstrates:

★ York Carnival
★ York Early Music Festival
★ Toy and train collectors' fair

continued

continued

* ★ York Radio Rally
* ★ Outdoor concert at Castle Howard
* ★ Last Night of the Proms
* ★ Farmers' market
* ★ Stamp and coin fair
* ★ Yorkshire Day
* ★ Brass band competition
* ★ Festival of Traditional Dance
* ★ Historic vehicle rally
* ★ Great Northern Antiques Fair
* ★ York races
* ★ Lord Mayor's carol service

Browse this website

www.york-tourism.co.uk

Food, drink and entertainment

Food, drink and entertainment play an important part in helping destinations remain successful. Increasingly, visitors expect high standards in what they eat and drink, and the surroundings in which they are served. Restaurants, cafés, pubs, bars, fast-food outlets and nightclubs all play their part in giving visitors a rewarding experience.

Types of accommodation

You will have learned in Unit 1 *Investigating travel and tourism* that tourist accommodation is generally categorised as either serviced or self-catering. Serviced accommodation includes hotels, guesthouses and B&Bs, while accommodation such as cottages, caravans, holiday villages and camping are classified as self-catering. Destinations have to provide a range of accommodation to meet the needs of different types of visitors. In response to higher customer expectations, accommodation providers are upgrading their facilities to provide higher quality standards.

Industry example

The star rating scheme for English hotels, developed by the English Tourism Council in conjunction with the AA and RAC, aims to give customers confidence when choosing hotel accommodation, safe in the knowledge that all accommodation has been inspected and a consistent approach has been taken throughout the country. The categories are as follows:

★ *One star* – high standards of cleanliness. Limited range of facilities and services. Friendly and helpful staff. Restaurant/eating area open to residents and guests for breakfast and dinner. A bar or lounge serving alcohol. Seventy-five per cent of bedrooms with en-suite or private facilities.

★ *Two stars* – all the above plus better equipped and more comfortable accommodation. All bedrooms with en-suite or private facilities and colour TV. A straightforward range of services with a more personal touch. Food and drink is of a slightly higher standard. A wine list is normally available.

★ *Three stars* – all the above plus greater quality and a higher standard of services and facilities. Usually larger hotels with more spacious public areas and bedrooms. A more formal style of service. Room service of continental breakfast. Laundry service. Greater attention to quality of food.

★ *Four stars* – all the above plus superior comfort and quality. All bedrooms with en-suite facilities (both bath and shower) and WC. More emphasis on quality food and drink. Skilled staff anticipating and responding to needs and requests. Room service of all meals. 24-hour drinks and snacks.

★ *Five stars* – all the above plus luxurious and spacious surroundings. The highest international quality of accommodation, services and range of extra facilities. Professional, attentive and highly

continued

continued

trained staff. Superb cuisine. Striking décor. Exceptional comfort. Sophisticated ambience.

There is a similar scheme for guest accommodation other than hotels, e.g. guesthouses, farm accommodation and B&Bs, based on diamonds rather than stars. Accommodation with 5 diamonds represents an excellent overall level of quality and comfort, with ample space and a degree of luxury.

Transport services and links

Whether travelling to a destination by public transport or in their own cars, visitors expect high standards of service and infrastructure, including car parking, park and ride schemes, and travel information services. Later in this unit (see page 28) we investigate the main travel and tourism routes in the UK in greater detail.

Popularity and appeal of UK travel destinations

Key topics in this section

- **Introduction**
- **Image**
- **Facilities provided for tourists**
- **Cost of visiting**
- **Changing customer needs and expectations**
- **Destination promotion**
- **Destination management**

Introduction

UK destinations are popular with both British and overseas tourists. However, the popularity of particular destinations changes over time in response to a number of factors, including:

- **Image**: This is a product of many factors, such as a destination's historical development, the amount of investment in new facilities designed to meet changing customer expectations and the type and extent of media coverage it attracts. As an example, many of the UK's seaside resorts are struggling to maintain their share of visitors; according to BTA data, the number of nights spent at the seaside as a percentage of all domestic tourism fell from 45 per cent in 1991 to 42 per cent in 1997. Relatively cheap overseas holidays with 'guaranteed sunshine', coupled with lack of investment in facilities in the UK resorts, are drawing people away from the traditional two-week seaside holiday in Britain. The government's tourism strategy *Tomorrow's Tourism* acknowledges the difficulties faced by many seaside resorts and suggests that many resorts need to develop far-ranging regeneration plans to stem their decline in visitor numbers, exploiting new market opportunities.

- **Facilities provided for tourists**: UK destinations that have invested heavily in new facilities for tourists have a distinct advantage over those that have not. Resorts such as Brighton (see Figure 7.7) and Bournemouth have successfully diversified into the business tourism sector by investing in conference facilities and associated accommodation.

Figure 7.7 *The seafront at Brighton*
Courtesy of John Ward

Newquay in Cornwall has been successful in gaining National Lottery funding to develop its very popular facilities for surfers. Wet weather facilities are another way of offering visitors an all-year-round experience whatever the weather.

✪ **Cost of visiting**: There is a generally-held belief among British people that it can be just as expensive for a family of four to stay in a hotel in a British resort as it would be to go on an overseas package holiday. While this is open to question, there is no doubt that the cost of accommodation and other tourist facilities in UK destinations is an important consideration when choosing where to go on holiday. Also, rising fuel prices are forcing some people to rethink their travel plans and to consider alternatives to the private car.

✪ **Changing customer needs and expectations**: Throughout your course of study you will have come across this point many times in the context of changes in the travel and tourism industry. Changes in household composition, the ageing of the population, advances in technology and greater concern for the environment, all influence people's travel and tourism choices. Today, tourists have much higher expectations than was the case in the past. People will not tolerate standards of tourist accommodation and facilities that are worse than in their own houses. We all expect high standards of customer service and are not afraid to complain when things are below par. Destinations that fail to adapt to these changing expectations will find it hard to compete in the UK travel and tourism industry.

✪ **Destination promotion**: Effective promotion of a destination will certainly raise an area's profile, e.g. the clever 'English Riviera' slogan adopted by the Torbay area of Devon and Shakespeare's County used to promote the county of Warwickshire. However, good promotion cannot make up for sub-standard accommodation and other tourist facilities. In fact, it can make matters worse, since visitors who have been attracted to an area as a result of an effective promotional campaign will be doubly disappointed if the destination fails to live up to how it was portrayed. Destination managers must develop effective systems to decide on promotion channels, allocate budgets, handle enquiries, carry out market research and develop travel and tourism products that visitors want.

✪ **Destination management**: Factors such as pollution control, transport management, litter control, leisure facilities and investment by the public and private sector will all have a bearing on the popularity of a destination. Handled well, these factors will satisfy existing visitors and portray a positive image to attract more tourists in the future.

It is important to remember that UK travel destinations operate in a very competitive business environment, competing not only with other tourist areas in the UK but also with tourist destinations abroad. Successful UK destinations are those that continually adapt their image, facilities, services and management to meet changing customer needs and expectations.

Activity 7.8

Working with a partner, choose a UK tourist destination and assess its present and likely future popularity on the basis of the following factors.

★ Image
★ Facilities provided for tourists
★ Cost of visiting
★ Changing customer needs and expectations
★ Destination promotion
★ Destination management

Consult a range of sources to gather your information.

Main travel and tourism routes in the UK

Key topics in this section

- **Introduction**
- **Road routes**
- **Rail routes**
- **Air routes**
- **Sea routes**
- **Factors influencing travel decisions**

Introduction

We saw in Unit 1 *Investigating travel and tourism* that the transport sector is a fundamental part of the UK travel and tourism industry. Tourism is all about travelling away from home to visit people and places, using private vehicles and public transport. Leisure and business tourists have a choice of transport routes when deciding how to travel to and within their UK destination. They can choose to travel by:

- ✪ **Road**
- ✪ **Rail**
- ✪ **Air**
- ✪ **Sea**

We will now investigate each of these services in more detail.

Road routes

Road routes include motorways, major trunk routes, secondary roads, scenic routes and cycleways. Motorways are useful for long-distance travel, when speed of travel is important. Not every tourist destination is served by a motorway, but we do have 'A' and 'B' class roads, which cover the country to form an intricate network of routes for those travellers who wish to explore an area more fully or take a scenic journey to their destination. As a general rule, 'A' roads with low numbers, e.g. A1, A2, A3 and A4, radiate from

London, while roads with higher numbers, e.g. A11, A20, A30 and A40, will be close to the A1, A2, A3 and A4 respectively.

Figure 7.8 shows Britain's principal motorways and the destinations they serve.

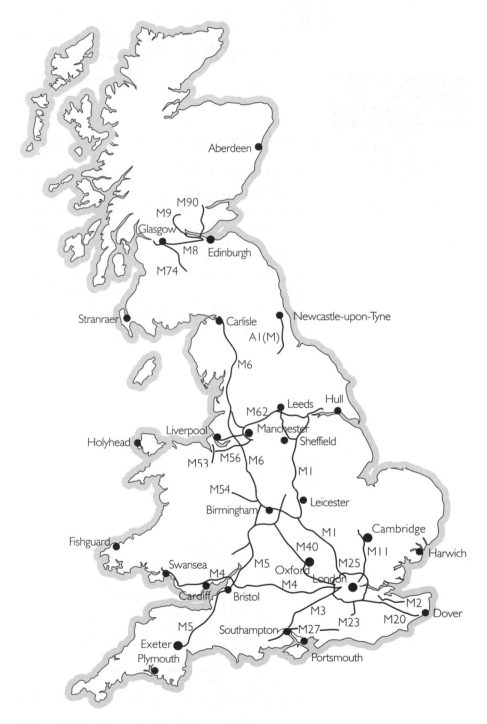

Figure 7.8 *Britain's principal motorways*

Cycling is undergoing something of a revival as a leisure pursuit, particularly since the opening of the National Cycle Network, the subject of the next activity in this unit.

Activity
7.9

Draw the route of the National Cycle Network on an outline map of the UK.

Browse this website for details of the National Cycle Network

www.sustrans.com

Road distances and journey times

It is important for visitors to a destination to know how long their journey will take and the best route to travel. Many UK road atlases and maps have charts showing the distances between major towns and cities by the most direct route. Figure 7.9 gives a simplified example of one of these charts.

The distances in Figure 7.9 are given in miles, but you will sometimes find a combined miles and kilometres chart, so you need to be careful which one you use when giving advice! The chart is easy to use, as the following example shows. To work out the distance in miles between Aberystwyth and London, read vertically down the chart from Aberystwyth and horizontally

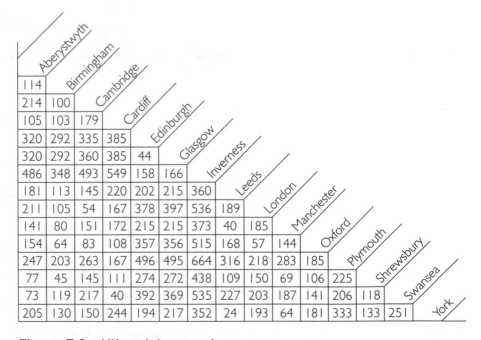

Aberystwyth	Birmingham	Cambridge	Cardiff	Edinburgh	Glasgow	Inverness	Leeds	London	Manchester	Oxford	Plymouth	Shrewsbury	Swansea	York
114														
214	100													
105	103	179												
320	292	335	385											
320	292	360	385	44										
486	348	493	549	158	166									
181	113	145	220	202	215	360								
211	105	54	167	378	397	536	189							
141	80	151	172	215	215	373	40	185						
154	64	83	108	357	356	515	168	57	144					
247	203	263	167	496	495	664	316	218	283	185				
77	45	145	111	274	272	438	109	150	69	106	225			
73	119	217	40	392	369	535	227	203	187	141	206	118		
205	130	150	244	194	217	352	24	193	64	181	333	133	251	

Figure 7.9 *UK road distance chart*

across from London. The point at which they cross is the distance in miles between the two points, in this case 211 miles.

Advising precisely on journey times can be difficult given the number of factors that have an influence on how long a journey takes, such as road works, traffic delays, the time of day, the time of year and the capabilities of the driver. However, as a general rule, the following average speeds can be applied:

- ✪ **Urban areas – 20–30 miles per hour average**
- ✪ **Rural areas – 30–40 miles per hour average**
- ✪ **Motorways – 50–60 miles per hour average**

Activity 7.10

Using the road distance chart in Figure 7.9, calculate the distances in miles between the following destinations:

1 London and York
2 Leeds and Cardiff
3 Aberystwyth and Manchester
4 Birmingham and London
5 Inverness and Plymouth
6 Shrewsbury and Cardiff
7 York and Leeds
8 Plymouth and Glasgow
9 Oxford and Cambridge
10 Edinburgh and Swansea

Having calculated the distances in miles, convert the figures into kilometres.

Activity 7.11

Using the above figures for average speeds, and the road distance chart in Figure 7.9, calculate how long it would take to travel by motorway between the following destinations:

1   London to Leeds
2   Birmingham to London
3   Manchester to Leeds
4   Manchester to Birmingham
5   Swansea to London

Rail routes

Browse these websites for information on UK rail services

www.railtrack.
co.uk

www.thetrainline.
com

Rail offers a convenient method of travel to and between UK tourist destinations. Rail routes in the UK are a combination of high-speed inter-city routes and local/regional services. Many popular tourist cities, such as London, Chester, York, Edinburgh, Manchester, Cardiff and Birmingham, are part of the inter-city network. Smaller tourist areas, including many seaside resorts, historic towns and country areas, are served by local and regional services. Unit 11 *Passenger transport* looks in detail at rail services in the UK.

Activity 7.12

Choose 10 popular UK tourist destinations and draw a map to indicate the rail routes serving each.

Air routes

Travel by air on UK (domestic) routes is increasing rapidly, both for business and leisure travel. The introduction of the low-cost airlines, including Ryanair, easyJet and Go, has led to intense competition on some domestic routes, resulting in lower prices for the travelling public. Airlines now compete with trains for travel to and from a number of UK destinations, such as between London and Edinburgh, Manchester and Aberdeen, and London and Newcastle. Total terminal passengers on domestic routes in the UK increased from 10.9 million in 1988 to 16.8 million in 1998.

Government figures show that the 12 busiest UK airports in terms of domestic traffic in 1998 were (in descending order of terminal passenger numbers):

1 **London Heathrow**

2 **Edinburgh**

3 **Glasgow**

4 **London Gatwick**

5 **Manchester**

6 **Belfast**

7 **Aberdeen**

8 **London Stansted**

9 **Birmingham**

10 **Luton**

11 **Newcastle**

12 **East Midlands**

Activity 7.13

On an outline map of the UK, locate the 12 airports listed above, plus the following UK airports:

Plymouth, Exeter, Bournemouth, Southampton, Bristol, Cardiff, Coventry, Cambridge, Norwich, Liverpool, Leeds/Bradford, Humberside and Teeside.

Include the three-letter international code for each airport on your map, e.g. LGW is London Gatwick. Choose six of the airports shown on your map and make a list of the *domestic* routes they offer, plus the names of the airlines operating the routes.

Sea routes

The UK has a number of important ferry routes from its ports to the continent, Ireland and Scandinavia. These are covered in detail in Unit 11 *Passenger transport*. Ferry routes within the UK are more limited and include services to and from:

- ✪ **The Isle of Wight**
- ✪ **The Isles of Scilly**
- ✪ **The Shetland Isles**
- ✪ **The Orkney Isles**
- ✪ **Northern Ireland**
- ✪ **The Inner and Outer Hebrides**
- ✪ **The Isles of Islay, Jura, Mull, Colonsay, Arran and Bute off Scotland's west coast**

These routes are popular with tourists, since they all serve important tourist destinations.

Activity 7.14

On an outline map of the UK, draw the ferry routes to the islands listed above and make a list of the companies that operate the services.

Factors influencing travel decisions

We have seen that people travelling to UK tourist destinations have a wide choice of transport types and routes from which to choose. People make their travel decisions for a number of reasons, including:

- ✪ **Cost**: Everybody looks for value for money when they are travelling, whether it is a trip to Paris with a budget airline or an expensive cruise across the Atlantic on the *Canberra*. For business people, who often have to travel at short notice and on premium services, cost is not always their main consideration. Increasing fuel costs in the UK have led many people to consider cheaper forms of travel, both for work and while at leisure.

- ✪ **Convenience**: Travel by private car is perhaps the most convenient of all types of travel to UK destinations, except for long journeys. However, travel by car does cause environmental and social problems, which is why the UK government is trying to get more people to travel by public transport. With increased investment, frequency of journeys on offer by public transport operators can be increased and the comfort standards of vehicles improved. The government wants to see a more integrated transport system in the UK, giving people the option of leaving their car at home and travelling to their destination by public transport.

- **Journey time**: This can be important for some people who want to reach their destination as soon as possible. We have already seen that there is competition between the airlines and train companies on some routes, where city centre to city centre journey times by train and plane are comparable. Other people see the journey to their destination as an important part of their holiday and will opt for a longer, but more scenic, route.

- **Range of services provided**: This can vary between the 'no frills' approach of many of the new budget airlines to cordon bleu meals for business and first-class passengers on domestic airline routes in the UK. The price paid for a journey is often a reflection of the range and quality of services provided by the operator.

As these points demonstrate, deciding on how to travel to a UK destination is a complex process, involving a range of economic, social, cultural, political and environmental factors.

Information sources

Key topics in this section

- **Developing your research skills**
- **Sources of UK destination and travel information**

Developing your research skills

Everybody working in the travel and tourism industry needs to develop effective research skills in order to gather information on UK destinations so as to provide accurate and up-to-date information and advice to customers. Developing these skills will not only help in the work situation, but also when it comes to completing activities and assignments as part of your AVCE course. Researching involves:

- ✪ **Being clear about what you are trying to find out**: When responding to customers' enquiries it is important to discover *exactly* what information they need, so as not to waste your time and theirs.

- ✪ **Knowing how to search for information**: Build up lists of useful sources of information, from other work colleagues, your own experiences of destinations, newspapers, magazines, television, the Internet, etc.

- ✪ **Deciding what might be useful**: Match what you find to the customers' needs and discard any information that is not useful (but remember that it may be useful for future enquiries!).

- ✪ **Collecting and presenting relevant information**: Accuracy and reliability are important when collecting travel and tourism information, particularly in relation to timetables, pricing, features of destinations, etc. You should present the information you find in a manner that is appropriate to the customer. This might be in a written letter, included in a brochure, as part of an e-mail, on the telephone, face-to-face over the counter or via a group presentation, for example at a promotional evening to promote your destination.

- ✪ **Drawing conclusions about your findings**: Study the information you find and draw conclusions that are valid in consultation with the customer.

- ✪ **Acknowledging your sources**: If you are compiling a written report it is usual to include details of where you found specific information, so that the reader can go back to the original source to check its authenticity or to get further details.

Browse these websites for information on UK travel and tourism destinations

www.visitbritain.com

www.englishtourism.org.uk

www.tourism.wales.gov.uk

www.ni-tourism.com

www.holiday.scotland.net

www.tourist-offices.org.uk

www.lonelyplanet.com

www.roughguides.com

Having well-developed research skills is particularly important when it comes to advising on travel destinations, since many people will not have visited a particular destination before and will, therefore, be relying on the knowledge and experience of members of staff to provide reliable information. Luckily, you are not expected to know everything about every destination in the UK the minute you start a job in travel and tourism! Knowledge and experience of destinations grows over time. However, what you will be expected to know is where to get hold of information, i.e. the sources of information on UK destinations, which is the topic we look at next in this unit.

Sources of UK destination and travel information

Information on UK destinations is available from a variety of sources, including:

- **Brochures and other publicity information**: At national and regional level the UK tourist boards publish brochures to sell their particular area. Local authorities often take on the role of producing local tourist brochures, distributing them in response to telephone, tourist information centre, postal and e-mail enquiries.

- **Guidebooks and timetables**: Commercially produced guidebooks and 'where to stay' guides are popular with visitors since they tend to give an unbiased opinion of destination areas and the facilities they offer to tourists.

- **Maps, atlases and gazetteers**: These are useful at the planning stage of a UK holiday when tourists may be deciding exactly where to go in a particular region. They are available commercially and are sometimes included in a destination's brochure or 'where to stay' guide.

- **The Internet**: This is an increasingly important tool that visitors use to gather information and opinions on particular UK destinations. Many tourist boards, local authorities, accommodation providers, activity centres and tourist attractions now publicise their areas on the Internet, while direct booking of UK holidays on the Internet is becoming a reality.

- **Textbooks**: Books written specifically for travel and tourism students often include information on UK destinations and background information on their development and management.

- **Newspapers and magazines**: Daily and weekly national, regional and local newspapers include features on UK destinations, sometimes linked to a competition to win a holiday or short break.

- **Radio and television**: Radio and TV programmes sometimes feature UK tourist areas, although they have a tendency to prefer sun-soaked overseas destinations!

Activity 7.15

Working as a group, make a list of all the sources of tourist information on your home area or one nearby that caters for visitors. When you have gathered your information, have a group discussion on whether you consider that the range of sources used to publicise the area to tourists is adequate and likely to be effective in attracting visitors. Give reasons for your comments, making suggestions for future action in the promotion of the area.

Travel agency operations

8

Travel agencies play an important part in the UK travel and tourism industry. They are the 'retail' arm of the industry, selling a wide range of holidays and other travel products and services. In this unit you will investigate the different types of travel agencies found in the UK, from small, independent businesses to the large high street travel shop chains. You will learn about the range of products and services offered by travel agencies, as well as the main legal and financial aspects of running a travel agency. The final section investigates working methods in travel agencies. After completing the unit, you will have a thorough understanding of the skills, practical knowledge and understanding needed to work in a travel agency, allowing you to gain further qualifications and/or experience to progress in a career in retail travel.

This unit is divided into four main areas:

- **Types of travel agencies**
- **Products and services offered by travel agencies**
- **Legal and financial aspects**
- **Working methods in travel agencies**

We guide you through each of these areas using examples and case studies from the travel and tourism industry. At the beginning of each of these sections you will see a list of key topics to help you fully understand what you need to learn. Look out for the links to websites so that you can learn more about a particular travel and tourism company, organisation or topic.

Types of travel agencies

Key topics in this section

- **Introduction – the work of travel agencies**
- **Types of travel agencies**
- **Aims and objectives of travel agencies**
- **Different working methods in travel agencies**
- **Organisational structures in travel agencies**
- **Horizontal and vertical integration**

Introduction – the work of travel agencies

Travel agencies are the retail arm of the travel and tourism industry. In the same way that a clothes shop sells products to shoppers, so travel agencies retail their 'products' to the general public. Indeed, the term 'travel shop' is commonly used to refer to travel agency premises. The one major difference between these two types of retail outlets, however, is that, unlike the clothes retailer, travel agencies do not buy in 'stock' in advance, but rather react to the wishes of their customers before contacting the holiday companies and other travel service providers.

Travel agencies are generally acting on behalf of two parties when they undertake their work. They are agents for the customer, referred to as the client, on whose behalf they are making the travel arrangements. They are also agent for the company that is supplying the product. This company is sometimes referred to as the 'principal', and may include:

- **A tour operator**
- **An airline**
- **A coach company**
- **A hotel**
- **A car hire firm**
- **A ferry company**
- **A train company**
- **A cruise line**
- **A theatre**

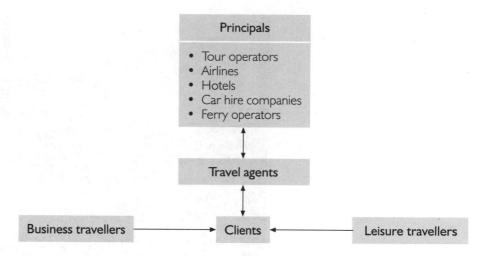

Figure 8.1 *The position of travel agents*

This dual arrangement is shown diagrammatically in Figure 8.1, which indicates that a travel agent's clients may be either leisure or business travellers.

Types of travel agencies

Travel agencies fall into one of three categories:

✪ **Independents** – single, owner-managed enterprises generally with only one retail outlet

✪ **Multiples** – companies that operate a chain of retail outlets under a single brand name, e.g. Lunn Poly, Going Places, Thomas Cook, etc.

✪ **Miniples** – companies with a small number of branches in a particular geographical region

Of the three, the multiple agencies have access to the largest capital reserves and can choose the more expensive high street locations for their branches. Lunn Poly, with 792 branches, is the largest retail travel agency chain in the UK (see Figure 8.2).

Being able to trade in a high street location gives an agency a number of advantages, including:

✪ **Increased visibility**
✪ **Greater opportunities for passing trade**
✪ **A successful image**
✪ **Business from workers in town**

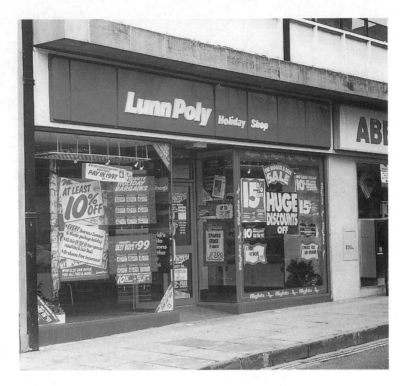

Figure 8.2 *Lunn Poly currently has 792 retail outlets across the UK*

Independent agents, who may not be able to justify the high rent and rates of town centre locations, will nonetheless want to be in a position that is not too far away from the main shopping thoroughfares. Given the particular nature of the products many independent agents sell, their clients are usually more than willing to travel a little further for their specialist advice. Agents located on the outskirts of towns or in city suburbs may have the advantage of easier parking, when compared with high street agencies, a factor of particular importance if older or disabled clients are important customers.

Browse this website

www.abtanet.com

For a travel agency that is setting up for the first time, there are no hard and fast rules about competing with existing agents. Travel agencies operate in a free market and ABTA (the Association of British Travel Agents) does not object to new members joining on the grounds of competition with existing businesses. It must be remembered, however, that anybody opening a new agency close to one that has been successfully trading for some years will find it harder to obtain agency agreements with tour operators, airlines, coach companies and other travel principals, since they will often prefer to continue with a proven enterprise rather than take a risk with a new venture.

Trade sources suggest that, for a new travel agency to have a chance of succeeding, it should not open in an area that offers a ratio of less than one agency to 15,000 population. In other words, if a small market town of 75,000 people is currently served by three travel agencies (1:25,000 ratio), the opening of a new agency would merit serious consideration. If the same town supported six travel agencies (1:12,500 ratio), a new venture is unlikely to be able to survive. Demographics can sometimes come into play when choosing a suitable location for a new agency. Factors such as the age structure of the population, social class of residents and composition of families in an area can have a bearing on success. For example, an independent agent specialising in up-market holidays for couples whose children have left home, the so-called 'empty nesters', may be able to select a suitable location for an agency by careful researching of local demographic data. Choosing to locate in an area that has a higher than average proportion of residents in the A, B and C1 social classes will increase the agent's chances of successful trading, all other things being equal.

Activity 8.1

Carry out some research to find out the number of travel agencies and the total population of your locality. From the figures you find, calculate the ratio of agencies to population. Is your area supporting too many agencies at present?

Aims and objectives of travel agencies

Travel agencies, whether large or small, are in business to make a profit, i.e. profit maximisation is their main objective. However, maximising profits may not be the only objective. The large, multiple agencies will always be working towards increasing their share of the total travel market and keeping one step ahead of their competitors. Agencies will also aim to provide a high standard of service for their customers and offer as wide a range as possible of holidays and other travel products in their local area. Many people who run travel agencies are, not surprisingly, keen on travelling, so access to discounted travel may be an important consideration for some agents.

In striving to maximise its profits, a travel agency will try to generate income from a number of different sources, as the next section of this unit explains.

Travel agency income

A travel agency's main source of income is the commission it earns from the principals whose products it sells. The commission payment is usually expressed as a percentage and varies according to the product being sold and the commission policy of the principal. At present, average commission rates are as follows:

Package holidays	10%
Airline tickets	7.5–9%
Ferry bookings	9%
Travellers' cheques	1%
Travel insurance	35–40%
Coach holidays	10%
Rail ticket	7%
Cruises	9%

These figures should be taken only as a guide, since commission levels fluctuate daily in response to competitor activity. Some principals offer incentive commission, where the amount paid increases as the sales volume rises.

Most tour operators pay 10% commission on package holidays, so that an agent would receive £150 for booking a holiday with a brochure price of £1,500. This figure of £150 is not clear profit for the agent, however, since it does not take account of overheads such as staff costs, heating, postage and telephone charges. Once these costs have been accounted for, most travel agents will make on average only 1% net profit over the course of a year's trading. Put another way, an independent travel agent who has recently set up in business and is hoping to make a net profit which is equivalent to the salary of £18,000 per year that she earned in her last job, would need to achieve sales of £1,800,000.

Although commission is by far the biggest source of income, travel agents can also earn revenue from arranging their own tours. This practice is becoming an increasingly common way of injecting extra income into the business, while at the same time giving clients a more personal service than they might receive on a standard package tour. It is important to remember, however, that such activities fall within the scope of the Package Travel Regulations, since the travel agent is, in effect, becoming the organiser of a tour (see page 73 for more on the Package Travel Regulations).

Another important source of funds for travel agents is the interest gained on any money held on behalf of principals. Deposits and balances paid by clients may stay in the agent's account for some time, thus accruing interest. It is generally in the agent's interest to negotiate a credit rather than cash arrangement with principals. This gives the agent the benefit of simpler administrative procedures and, more importantly, credit agents can hold on to clients' payments longer. Some agents supplement their income in other ways, for example by selling luggage and other travel goods, running training courses or teaching on evening classes, writing a regular column in a local paper, appearing on local radio or selling maps and guide books.

Different working methods in travel agencies

The sales process in travel agencies

Successful selling is a structured activity, not just 'something that happens'. Figure 8.3 shows the six key stages of the sales process in travel agencies.

Raising customer awareness (stage one) relates to the promotional techniques that travel agencies, and the principals whose products they are selling, use to inform customers about products and services. An agency will make full use of its premises to attract custom, with imaginative window displays, a prominent fascia board, late availability notices, posters and other point-of-sale materials. It may also advertise in the local press and on local radio, as well as mailing information to existing clients.

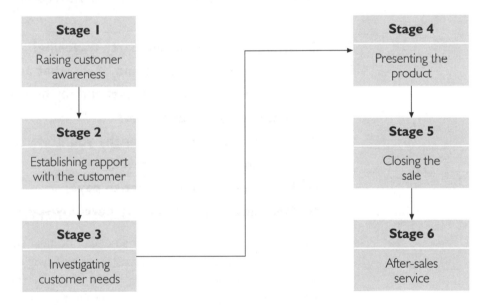

Figure 8.3 *The key stages of the sales process in travel agencies*

Activity 8.2

Thinking of the last two holidays you went on, try to remember how you were made aware of the existence of the holiday in the first place. Are your own findings similar to those of other members of your group?

Once a customer has come through the door of the agency, it is necessary for staff to make an initial contact and establish a rapport (stage two). In order to meet the objective of making a sale, this initial task of engaging the customer in conversation is important, since it gives the salesperson the opportunity to gain his or her trust and to discover the customer's needs. Some customers are suspicious of any attempts to sell them products, often preferring to make their own decisions on product selection and purchase. They may consider sales staff to be 'pushy' or arrogant, but even such reluctant customers can be put in the right frame of mind to buy a particular product or service if they receive a friendly and attentive level of service.

Stage three of the sales process gives the customer the opportunity to state his or her needs clearly, so that the travel clerk has the best chance of presenting a product or service that the client will want to buy. It is important for the member of staff to ask questions, both to solicit the necessary information and to keep the sales interview flowing. Although customers may not be in a position to answer all the questions put to them, the travel clerk will need to build up a picture of the client's requirements by asking such questions as:

- **What is the size of the party travelling?**
- **Are there any children and, if so, what ages are they?**
- **When do you want to travel and for how long?**
- **Where do you want to go?**
- **Is there a particular company you prefer to travel with?**
- **How do you want to travel?**
- **How much do you expect to pay?**
- **Does anybody in the party have any special requirements?**

Having determined the customer's needs, the next stage of the sales process is to present the product to the customer, outlining its features, benefits and advantages. Product knowledge is crucial to the success of this part of the sales process, since the customer may wish to know extra information about the product on offer. Staff may also encounter objections from the customer at this stage, perhaps based on the price of the product or its availability, and must be trained to handle these points in a positive fashion.

Closing the sale (stage five) takes place when all objections have been overcome and the customer seems ready to make a commitment. Helping the customer move from 'I'd like' to 'I'll buy' is what this stage of the sales process is all about. Staff should be continually looking for buying signals from the customer to trigger the process of closing the sale. Statements such as 'that sounds fine' or 'yes, I like that' clearly indicate a desire on the part of the customer to buy. When such signals are evident, the member of staff should begin to finalise the deal, remembering that clients should never be forced into making a decision that they may later regret. Not every sales interview will necessarily end in a sale; what is important from the organisation's point of view is to end up with the best possible outcome to the process. For large purchases, customers may wish to consider the benefits in greater detail or discuss the sale with other people, before making a commitment to buy. In this situation, all sales staff can do is to ensure that the customer has been given excellent customer service throughout, thus increasing the chances of an eventual positive sales outcome.

Stage six, after-sales service, is an appreciation that the sales process doesn't end when the customer has parted with his or her money. Just as we expect an after-sales service for consumer and household items we buy, travel agencies too must offer this service to their customers. Adding customers' details to a database should be the first step in developing a long-term relationship that will hopefully benefit both the travel agent and the customer.

Activity 8.3

Working with a partner, role play the situation of a member of the public who is looking to buy a package holiday to Turkey, but isn't sure which tour operator to book with. Ask another member of your group to evaluate how the person taking on the sales role performed in relation to each of the stages of the sales process.

Processing bookings

Travel agencies sell a wide variety of holidays and other travel products, including package holidays, airline tickets, short breaks, car hire, coach holidays, holiday centres, rail tickets, etc. Travel agencies will have contractual agreements with a range of principals whose products they sell. Each principal will have its own methods of accounting and handling bookings, although there are common elements to the processing of bookings by travel agencies as shown in Figure 8.4.

Figure 8.4 indicates that the process starts with an initial enquiry to the agent from a customer. This may be face-to-face in the agency or over the telephone; a small number of enquiries may also come by e-mail or fax. Except in the case of certain products that an agent can sell without contacting the travel company (known as 'freesale'), e.g. some coach tickets, theatre tickets, rail tickets, etc., the next stage in the booking process will be for the agent to contact the principal to check availability. This may be by telephone, but nowadays more commonly by computer, especially with package holiday bookings and airline flights. Details are next confirmed with

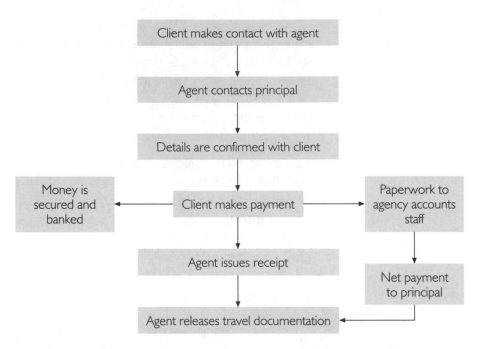

Figure 8.4 *Stages in the processing of customer bookings*

the client who, if happy with the details, makes a payment to the agent. Depending on when the client is due to travel, this may be the full amount or a deposit. Payment may be by cash, credit card, charge card, debit card, banker's draft, money order or cheque accompanied by a cheque guarantee card, for which a receipt is issued by the travel agent. The relevant paperwork is sent for processing by the accounts staff in the agency, while the payment and/or counterfoil is secured for banking. The net payment is sent to the principal, which releases the travel documents to the agent for distribution to the client. Copies of all relevant documentation will be filed for future reference.

Design and layout of travel agencies

When considering the design and layout of an agency, there are two principal issues to be addressed, namely:

- ✪ **External appearance**
- ✪ **Internal layout**

Each of these factors will be investigated further in the next two sections.

External appearance

From the outside, a travel agency should look inviting to the prospective customer, whether it is in a town centre high street location, a city suburb or a small country town. Certain aspects of the external appearance of a travel agency will be 'fixed', for example the size of the overall shop frontage, its position in relation to adjacent shops and any 'street furniture', i.e. lamp posts, fire hydrants, litter bins, etc. Within these constraints, the possibilities for alterations to its external design are limited only by the imagination and the budget of the travel agent, plus any restrictions imposed by local planning authorities or landlords in the case of leased property. A major refurbishment to convert an existing shop into a new travel agency may involve, for example, alterations to the size and style of windows and doors, and the design of fascias.

Two areas where the agency staff and management have some control over the external appearance of the premises are:

1   **Fascia**

2   **Window displays**

In an effort to convey a single corporate identity and image, the multiple travel agency chains adopt the same style of fascia outside all their branches. Independent agents have greater freedom to design a fascia board that says something about the agency and its products. Either way, an effective fascia board is a very important advertising tool for the agent, visible from a long way away. Some fascias are very simple, giving only the name of the agency. Others will include, along with the name, a telephone number, a logo or perhaps a 'strap line', e.g. 'we go further for you' or 'the one-stop-shop'. For maximum effect, and added security, fascias must be illuminated during the hours of darkness, although there may be planning restrictions in certain locations. There may also be local bylaws or planning regulations concerning overhanging signs and fascias on listed buildings. In all such cases, the advice of the local planning authority should be sought.

Window displays are a good way of changing the external appearance of an agency for a short period of time, thereby giving prominence to a particular product or concentrating on different seasons of the year, e.g. city breaks in the autumn and winter, summer sun holidays at the beginning of the main booking season and winter ski scenes. Changing a window display regularly will also generate more interest from passing customers, who may be tempted inside to ask for brochures and information. All travel principals will supply point-of-sale materials for window and shop displays, often in conjunction with brochure launches. What should be avoided at all costs are hand-drawn or hand-written signs, which give a window display an unprofessional look and do little to enhance the image of the travel agent.

Carry out some research on the external appearance of the travel agencies in your local area, noting positive features that attract attention and those that detract from the overall external appearance. Suggest ways that the negative features could be improved.

Internal layout

A well-planned internal layout of a travel agency can do a lot to help achieve the agency's principal aim of selling holidays and other travel products profitably. It will offer staff an efficient environment within which to perform their selling skills, give them greater job satisfaction and allow them to maximise sales opportunities. From the customers' point of view, it will encourage them to consult staff, examine brochures and, hopefully, stimulate them to make a purchase.

As we saw with the design of fascias, the multiple travel agency chains will adopt a 'house style' inside their premises as well, with corporate colours, logos and graphics reinforcing the brand identity.

Independent agents will have greater freedom in finalising the internal layout of their premises, thereby giving more opportunities for individuality.

Any effective internal design of a travel agency should start with an analysis of its main functions, followed by a consideration of how these can best be met through the positioning of furniture and equipment. No two travel agencies are the same, but they nonetheless have similar requirements in terms of internal layout; they all need to incorporate areas for:

- **Displaying brochures and other promotional materials**
- **Conducting sales interviews**
- **Storage for files**
- **Storage of reference materials**
- **Storage of brochure stocks**
- **Secure storage for money, travellers' cheques, foreign currency, tickets, etc.**
- **Staff relaxation**
- **Manager's office**
- **Computer software and hardware, including VDUs**
- **Administrative functions**
- **Toilets and washing facilities**

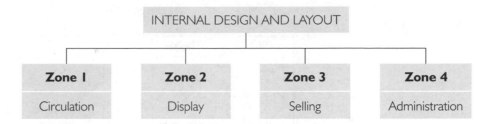

Figure 8.5 *Zoning of functions in a travel agency*

When considering an effective internal layout for a travel agency, it is helpful to group these functions into zones, as shown in Figure 8.5.

Zone 1 is the area concerned with the most important people of all, the customers, and how they circulate around the agency. People like to make their travel purchasing decisions in a relaxed atmosphere, where they are not crowded or overly pestered by staff. The internal design of the agency must reflect these needs with the correct positioning of furniture, fixtures and fittings, which clearly define the circulation routes through the agency. Consideration should also be given to a waiting area for clients when all staff are busy.

Zone 2 is concerned with the display of brochures, timetables, leaflets and other promotional items in the agency. Brochures are crucial to the success of the agency, so time spent on effective display methods will pay dividends. Brochure racks may be fixed to a wall or free-standing, and come in a range of sizes to accommodate different types of brochures. Free-standing racks give greater flexibility, but may not be suitable for large numbers of very heavy brochures. Policies on the racking of brochures will vary between agents, with the multiple agents often directed by their head offices. Some will display large numbers of the same brochure, while others will display a single copy under perspex and instruct customers to ask for a copy from a member of staff. This has the advantage of bringing the customer into contact with a member of staff, but may put some people off, particularly when the agency is very busy. Good use should be made of any available wall space for displaying posters and other point-of-sale materials.

The selling area of the agency (zone 3) is perhaps the most important of all. Staff and customers need a relaxed environment within which the agent has direct access to a VDU, telephone and reference materials, and where the customer can take notes and look at the detail of brochures. Today, many agencies prefer the more informal ambience created by desks and chairs for the selling zone, rather than a high sales counter, which can sometimes create a physical and psychological barrier between the customer and member of staff. Counters do, however, take up less space and may be the only alternative in an agency with a restricted floor area. Agencies that have a quick customer turnover, including some city centre offices selling theatre

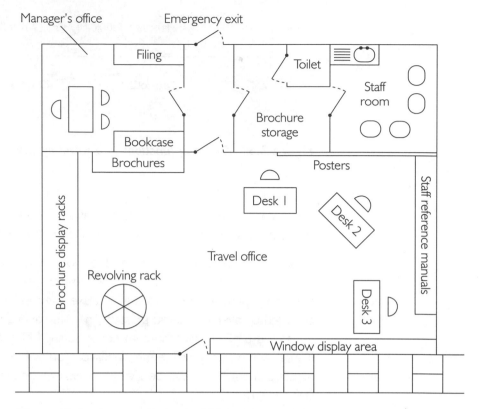

Figure 8.6 *Layout of a typical high street travel agency*

tickets, sightseeing tours, coach tickets, etc., sometimes opt for counters to reduce the length of stay of customers.

Zone 4 focuses on all the administrative functions of the agency, including the storage of brochure stocks and files, secure storage of valuables, a staff relaxation area, the manager's office, toilets and washing facilities. Sometimes referred to as the 'back office', this zone needs to be away from the customer circulation areas for privacy and security.

Taking all these features and functions into consideration, Figure 8.6 gives a simplified example of the layout of a typical high street travel agency.

Activity 8.5

Using the list of travel agency functions given above as a guide, draw your own sketch plan of an 'ideal' travel agency, highlighting the different zones.

Equipment used in travel agencies

The equipment requirements of travel agencies can be grouped under four distinct agency functions, namely:

1   **Sales**

2   **Communications**

3   **Administration**

4   **Safety and security**

Sales equipment

Most travel staff would agree that the most important piece of sales equipment is their computer keyboard and screen. Variously referred to as a VDU (visual display unit), computer terminal or viewdata system, these items are now commonplace in the vast majority of travel agencies in the UK. In the hands of trained staff, the VDU is a powerful selling tool, giving access to the central reservations systems (CRSs) of the major tour operators and airlines. The system allows staff to check availability, confirm prices and ultimately make bookings on behalf of their clients. The computer systems developed by the major tour operators allow agents to offer alternative holidays if the customer's first choice is unavailable. The principals' central reservations systems are accessed through a service provider, such as Fastrak or Istel (see next section on communications equipment). Other equipment concerned specifically with sales of package holidays and other travel products and services includes:

- ✪ **Telephone systems**
- ✪ **Reference manuals and atlases**
- ✪ **Calculators**

Communications equipment

Equipment used in travel agencies for internal and external communication includes:

- ✪ **Central reservation systems (CRSs), e.g. Galileo, Sabre, Worldspan, etc.**
- ✪ **Fax machines**
- ✪ **Telex**
- ✪ **Personal computers (PCs) with access to electronic mail (e-mail) and the Internet**
- ✪ **Viewdata sets, e.g. Istel and Fastrak**
- ✪ **Telephones**
- ✪ **Telephone answering machines**
- ✪ **Postal equipment, e.g. scales and franking machines**

Communication in travel takes place between agents and principals, as well as between agents and their customers, necessitating a range of communications equipment that is both cost effective and reliable.

Administration equipment

Equipment for carrying out administrative functions in travel agencies includes personal computers, typewriters, agency stamps, photocopiers, franking machines, dictating machines, filing cabinets, etc., plus consumables (stationery items, paper clips, rubber bands, pencils, pens, etc.). The agency may use its computer for word processing, spreadsheets and databases, or perhaps a specialist software application concerning payroll or financial accounting.

Safety and security equipment

To ensure the safety and security of staff and customers, travel agencies should take precautions against theft, fire and injury, including keeping a first-aid kit and fire extinguishers on the premises and having smoke alarms fitted (local building regulations may impose conditions in relation to fire protection in the premises). The premises should be inspected by a crime prevention expert who will advise on any security equipment that should be installed, e.g. window and door locks, safes and closed-circuit television (CCTV) surveillance cameras.

Activity 8.6

Carry out an equipment audit of a travel agency with which you are familiar, perhaps while on work placement or when working part-time. Indicate whether each item of equipment is leased, purchased outright or bought on hire purchase.

Organisational structures in travel agencies

More than half of all ABTA travel agencies in the UK are small, family-run businesses employing two or three members of staff under the management of the owner-proprietor. With such an arrangement, there is little room for specialisation by individual members of staff, and all employees, including the owner, will be involved in the many tasks associated with selling holidays and travel products. The organisational structure in an agency such as this is shown in Figure 8.7. Here, the owner-proprietor assumes overall day-to-day control of the agency, with the senior travel clerk deputising in his or her absence. The senior travel clerk will oversee the work of the two travel clerks, one a junior who may be on a training scheme operated by the Travel Training Company.

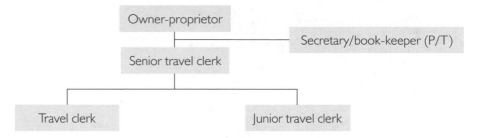

Figure 8.7 *Organisational structure in a small, independent travel agency*

The large travel agency chains have a more complex organisational structure, which is unsurprising given their scale of operations. Data from ABTA shows that, at the beginning of September 2000, the top three multiple travel agency chains had the following number of branches nationwide:

1 **Lunn Poly**   **792**

2 **Going Places**   **771**

3 **Thomas Cook**   **707**

If we take the number one UK travel retailer in terms of number of branches, Lunn Poly, its organisational structure is shown in Figure 8.8.

Figure 8.8 indicates that a sales consultant in a branch of the Lunn Poly chain is one part of a complex business structure. Lunn Poly is an operating division of the Thomson Travel Group, which in turn is part of the multinational Thomson Corporation of Canada. Eleven directors report to the managing director of Lunn Poly, including four sales directors covering the north, east, south and west of Britain. Area managers oversee the work of the branch managers and report directly to their appropriate sales director.

Horizontal and vertical integration

The travel industry is a very complex business! All of the major travel agency chains are part of much bigger travel groups, for example:

✪ **Lunn Poly is part of the Thomson Travel Group**

✪ **Going Places is owned by the Airtours Group**

✪ **Travel Choice agencies are part of First Choice Holidays**

✪ **Thomas Cook agencies are linked with JMC Holidays and Thomas Cook Holidays**

This process, where one company has control over other companies at different levels in the distribution chain, is known as vertical integration. There is further integration when the same company also owns its own airline, e.g.

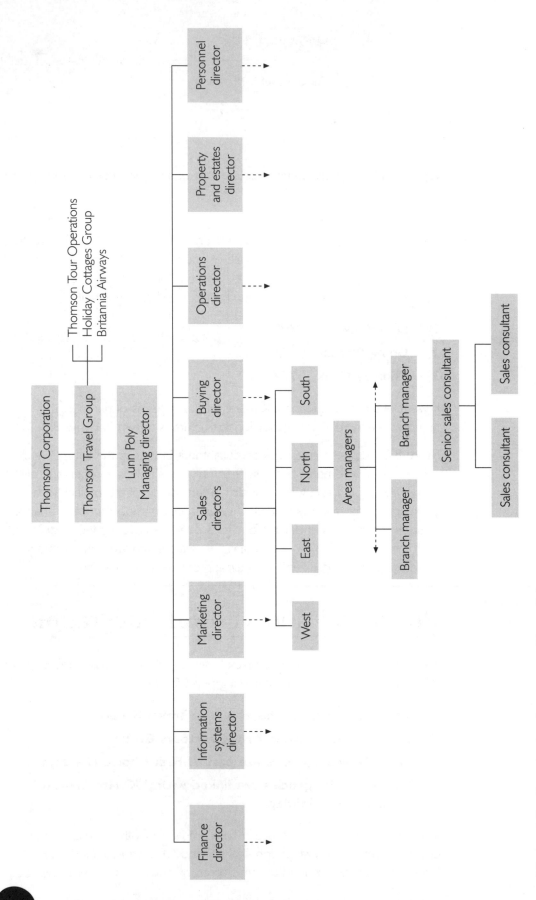

Figure 8.8 *Organisational structure of Lunn Poly*

Thomson owns Britannia Airways and Airtours owns Airtours International. Vertical integration of this sort, when a tour operator controls the sales policy of its own retail travel agencies, is thought by some people to be against the public interest, as it could lead to an anti-competitive environment. In such cases the Competition Commission (formerly the Monopolies and Mergers Commission) can be asked to investigate if the public are indeed being disadvantaged. Also, since October 2000, all vertically integrated travel companies have been obliged to make their links to other travel companies clear for the public to see.

Horizontal integration is when companies in the same level of the distribution chain, or the same industry sector, merge for mutual benefit, e.g. when a large hotel group takes over a smaller independent hotel.

Products and services offered by travel agencies

Key topics in this section

- **Product knowledge**
- **Travel agency products and services**
- **Sources of product information**

Product knowledge

Product knowledge, i.e. knowing the features and benefits of a range of holidays and other travel products, is an essential requirement for travel agency staff. Knowledge is built up over time and comes from a variety of sources, including:

- ✪ **Learning from more experienced members of staff**
- ✪ **Training**
- ✪ **Consulting a range of information sources**
- ✪ **Educational trips to experience travel products first-hand**

Travel agency products and services

Most people associate high street travel agencies with the sale of one particular product, namely overseas package holidays (also known as inclusive tours). An analysis of the work of a typical agency, however, shows that it actually offers a wide range of products and services, including:

- ✪ **Package holidays**
- ✪ **Short breaks**
- ✪ **'Flight-only' sales**
- ✪ **Bookings for hotels and other accommodation (see Figure 8.9)**
- ✪ **Travel insurance**
- ✪ **Theatre bookings**
- ✪ **Car hire**
- ✪ **Ferry bookings**

Figure 8.9 *Hotels are popular with package holidaymakers*
Courtesy of John Ward

- ✪ **Rail tickets and excursions**
- ✪ **Cruising holidays**
- ✪ **Coach tickets and holidays**
- ✪ **Activity and special interest holidays**
- ✪ **Foreign exchange and travellers' cheques**
- ✪ **Visa and passport applications**

As the market for overseas travel becomes even more competitive, travel agencies will be looking for ways of increasing their income from the sale of products other than the traditional package tours.

Sources of product information

All sales staff working in travel agencies must be able to refer to a wide variety of information sources when dealing with package holiday bookings. They will use tour operators' brochures as a starting point for reference when handling enquiries, but will need access to other printed and computer-based information in order to provide a complete service to customers. Although viewdata-based information sources and the Internet are growing in popularity, a good range of travel manuals and timetables is essential for the professional travel agent.

Trade manuals

Manuals provide travel agency staff with general resort information, hotels and travel requirements. Some of the most common in use in agencies are:

- ✪ **OAG Guide to International Travel**
- ✪ **Official Hotel Guide (OHG) – formerly Official Hotel and Resort Guide (OHRG)**
- ✪ **Travel Trade Directory**
- ✪ **World Travel Guide and World Travel Atlas**
- ✪ **Hotel and Travel Index**
- ✪ **Agents' Hotel Gazetteer**
- ✪ **Apartment Gazetteer**

Timetables

Access to timetables is very useful for staff putting together itineraries for clients and can save the time of contacting a number of individual carriers. A basic set of timetables in any travel agency should include:

- ✪ **Thomas Cook European Rail Timetable**
- ✪ **Thomas Cook Overseas Timetable**
- ✪ **UK National Rail Timetable**
- ✪ **OAG Flight Guide**
- ✪ **Individual airline timetables**

Other information sources

The National Tourist Offices (NTOs) of overseas destinations are happy to provide travel agents with country information in the form of brochures, maps, posters and videos. The UK tourist boards too are keen to promote the sale of British holidays through travel agents and produce an annual UK Handbook of Commissionable Holidays. The travel industry press, including *Travel Trade Gazette*, *Travel Weekly* and *Travel Agency*, also has valuable information for agents. As technology develops, it is likely that more travel information will be available on CD-ROMs and via the Internet. Already Thomas Cook is experimenting with CD-ROM screens in a selection of its agencies, giving clients the chance to look inside their 'virtual' hotel bedroom!

Activity 8.7

Make a list of some of the main consumer reference sources that a package holidaymaker could look through before contacting a travel agency to make a booking.

Legal and financial aspects

Key topics in this section

- **Introduction**
- **Consumer protection**
- **Membership of trade organisations**
- **Agency agreements**
- **IATA licensing**
- **Law of contract**
- **Fair trading charters**
- **Package Travel Regulations**

Introduction

Newly established travel agencies, as well as those that have been trading for some time, are faced with an array of licensing and financial requirements, which seek to regulate business practices and ensure a high quality service for the customer. Some of the most important are considered in the following paragraphs, including:

- ✪ **Consumer protection**
- ✪ **Membership of trade organisations**
- ✪ **Agency agreements**
- ✪ **IATA licensing**
- ✪ **Law of contract**
- ✪ **Fair trading charters**
- ✪ **Package Travel Regulations**

Consumer protection

Travel agency staff must be aware of the main legislation that exists to protect the travelling public. In addition to the Package Travel Regulations (see page 73), consumers have protection under the following UK laws:

- ✪ **Trade Descriptions Act**
- ✪ **Supply of Goods and Services Act**
- ✪ **Consumer Protection Act**
- ✪ **Unfair Contract Terms Act**
- ✪ **Fair Trading Act**
- ✪ **Data Protection Act**
- ✪ **Disability Discrimination Act**

Each of these is described in detail in Unit 10 *Tour operations* (see page 113 onwards). In addition, all ABTA travel agency members must take out a bond to compensate passengers in the event of company failure (see below).

Membership of trade organisations

Travel agencies can choose to become members of a number of national and local trade organisations. Alternatively, they can opt not to join any! However, any professional travel agent is sure to consider joining the main UK trade body for the travel industry, the Association of British Travel Agents (ABTA).

Membership of ABTA

The Association of British Travel Agents (ABTA) is the UK's leading trade body for the travel and tourism industry, representing the interests and business practices of both tour operators and travel agents. Although it is not compulsory for a UK travel agent to become a member of ABTA, membership does confer a range of benefits, including:

- ✪ **Commercial** – use of the ABTA logo, bonding schemes, independent arbitration service, etc.
- ✪ **Representation** – lobbying at Westminster and Brussels, plus regular dialogue with other important interest groups
- ✪ **Member services** – an information bureau giving advice to members, legal advisory service, legal seminars, annual receipt of the ABTA Members' Handbook and ABTA List of Members, monthly issues of *ABTA News*, ABTA's own viewdata service ABTEL, regional meetings of the Association, annual ABTA Convention, etc.
- ✪ **Training** – ABTA's wholly owned subsidiary, the Travel Training Company (formerly ABTA National Training Board), offers a range of courses for staff and management and supports the work of the Travel Industry Lead Body

✪ **Charity** – ABTA administers its own benevolent fund for members who need financial assistance

Application for ABTA membership can take up to three months to process. Once an application has been received, and before any decision on its approval or otherwise is taken, the agency will receive an unannounced visit from an ABTA inspector, who will interview staff and inspect the premises. If successful, the applicant will be granted an ABTA licence number, which should be used on all publications and correspondence.

Conditions of travel agency membership of ABTA are contained in its Articles of Association and the Travel Agents' Code of Conduct. The following are some of the current conditions that ABTA travel agents must adhere to:

✪ **Staffing**: There must be at least one qualified person at each travel agent's office. To be considered as qualified, the person concerned must have had at least two years' relevant practical experience, or at least 18 months' such experience plus COTAC Level I (General Section only) or ABTAC (Primary Level), or at least one year's such experience plus COTAC Level II (General Section only) or ABTAC (Advanced Level). 'Relevant practical experience' is judged to be those activities that an average travel agent would expect to acquire in the course of running a non-specialist agency, including procedures concerned with the full range of package tours.

✪ **Premises**: Although there are no specific membership conditions concerning travel agents' premises, the Travel Agents' Code of Conduct makes it clear that no ABTA agent should have any connection with a travel agency that falsely represents itself as a member of the Association.

✪ **Identification**: All ABTA travel agencies must clearly show on their premises, notepaper and other business literature their full company name and all other information required under the Business Names Act of 1985.

✪ **Trading names**: Members of ABTA must not use the name, or an imitation of the trading name, of any former member that has failed to meet its liabilities.

✪ **Acceptability of directors, proprietors, partners and qualifying staff**: ABTA membership conditions state that all persons employed or concerned in the management of a travel agency must be respectable and honest individuals, none of whom is an undischarged bankrupt or is guilty of conduct unbecoming of a member of the Association, as defined by the Travel Agents' Council.

✪ **Financial stability**: All applicants for membership of ABTA travel agency class are required to provide financial protection to the Association in the form of a bond, as well as giving evidence of financial stability. The bond is a formal undertaking from an approved bank or insurance company to pay a sum of money to ABTA in the event of the member's financial failure, primarily for the purpose of reimbursing customers who would otherwise lose the money they had paid. The minimum acceptable financial standards for entry to the Association are currently:

1   **There must be paid-up share capital or capital account balance of at least £50,000. Total net assets after deducting intangible assets should not be less than £50,000. There must be a working capital surplus of not less than £15,000.**

2   **The minimum bond level is £50,000.**

3   **Contribution to the Travel Agents' Bond Replacement Scheme is £400 for each head office and £40 for each additional branch, plus 2.5 per cent insurance premium tax.**

All members are required to submit audited accounts annually together with quarterly turnover statements. Additionally, management accounts must be supplied made up to a date six months after admission to membership.

✪ **Fees and subscriptions**: ABTA currently levies a non-returnable registration fee of £387.75 payable at the time of applying for membership. The entrance fee is £1,175.00 payable upon admission to membership. Basic annual subscription is £500 plus VAT per company plus £120 plus VAT for each additional branch office.

✪ **Code of Conduct**: All applicants for membership of the travel agents' class of ABTA are required to declare their adherence to the Travel Agents' Code of Conduct.

✪ **Change of address and opening of new branches**: All changes of address, plus the opening or acquisition of new branches, must be notified to ABTA within seven days of the event. Fees are charged for this service and members opening or acquiring additional branches are required to provide additional bonding.

We will now look in more detail at the work of ABTA, the principal trade body representing the interests of UK travel agents and tour operators.

Case Study

ABTA – The Association of British Travel Agents

▶ INTRODUCTION

ABTA is the trade body representing over 90 per cent of travel agents and tour operators in the UK. It was formed in 1950 with just 100 members, at a time which coincided with the dawn of a new era for British travellers, when new aircraft technology and greater personal freedom were giving people the means to travel further afield. Foreign travel came to be seen as a temporary escape from the drabness of post-war Britain and the mass market holiday boom was beginning to take shape. Today, holidays are the high point in the year for many millions of UK travellers, with travel for business purposes remaining an important element of the UK travel scene. In our fast-moving society, we have come to take ease of travel for granted, to the extent that some 17.4 million Britons booked an overseas package holiday in 1998. Many millions will also take short breaks, holidays in the UK, trips by rail or ferry, or travel on business.

▶ ABTA'S AIMS

ABTA's main aims are to maintain the high standards of service among its members, as well as creating as favourable a business climate as possible for the industry. Specific objectives of the Association are:

1   To establish an organisation which is fully representative of travel agents and tour operators in the UK

2   To promote and develop the general interests of all members of ABTA

3   To establish and maintain Codes of Conduct between members and the general public, with the objective that membership of the Association will be recognised as a guarantee of integrity, competence and high standards of service

continued

continued

4   To discourage unfair competition without in any way interfering with initiative and enterprise based on fair trading

5   To promote friendly relations with others in the travel industry

6   To provide means for negotiations and liaison with other bodies concerned with the development of travel both in the UK and abroad

HOW ABTA WORKS

The Association is a self-regulatory body run by its membership. A network of Councils and Committees, appointed by member travel agents and tour operators, make up the policy making and enforcing machinery of the Association and help to ensure that ABTA remains in close contact with the whole of its membership. The Association has an education and training function which is carried out by the Travel Training Company (formerly ABTA National Training Board), which liaises with validating bodies such as Edexcel and AQA to ensure that the industry has programmes of education and training that are appropriate to its needs.

Up until the end of 1993, ABTA legally operated a type of 'closed shop' arrangement known as the 'stabiliser', which stated that ABTA travel agents could sell package holidays only from tour operators who were themselves members of ABTA, and vice versa. The stabiliser was introduced 20 years ago to safeguard the public against unscrupulous agents and operators. The arrangement was dismantled in 1993, since it was considered to be a restrictive practice and also because, in theory at least, the introduction of the EC Package Travel Directive rendered the stabiliser obsolete.

MEMBERSHIP OF ABTA

Those granted membership of ABTA are required to adhere to strict rules governing their business practice. These are

continued

continued

contained in ABTA's Codes of Conduct, which regulate all aspects of tour operators' and travel agents' relationships with their customers and which have been drawn up in conjunction with the Office of Fair Trading (OFT).

The Tour Operators' Code of Conduct lays down the minimum standards for brochures, requiring that they contain clear, comprehensive and accurate descriptions of facilities and services offered. It details rules that govern booking conditions in brochures as they relate, for example, to the cancellation or alteration of tours, holidays or other travel arrangements by the tour operator. The Code also contains strict rules concerning the prompt handling of complaints and regulations relating to the business relationships between tour operators and travel agents.

Similar stringent rules apply also to travel agents who are bound by their own Code of Conduct. The Travel Agents' Code of Conduct regulates all aspects of travel agents' relationships with their customers, covering their responsibility with regard to the standard of service they provide and the information they give to clients. It also lays down rules concerning travel agents' trading relationships with tour operators.

In addition, members of ABTA are required to adhere to precise financial specifications, overseen by ABTA's Financial Services Department, which checks all members' accounts at least once a year.

PROTECTION AND REDRESS FOR THE TRAVELLING PUBLIC

In addition to its Codes of Conduct, ABTA seeks to protect the interests of travellers through its Consumer Affairs Department and its own Arbitration Scheme.

Staff in the Consumer Affairs Department offer a service for clients who have booked with an ABTA-registered travel agent or tour operator and who have reason to complain about some aspect of the service they have received. ABTA

continued

continued

will look into the complaint and seek to redress the situation without recourse to law. If the dispute cannot be resolved through conciliation, the client may pursue the claim through ABTA's Arbitration Scheme, for which a fee is charged depending on the amount of the claim. The ABTA Arbitration Scheme, administered by the Chartered Institute of Arbitrators, gives the client the opportunity for redress without incurring high legal costs.

Tour operators and travel agent members of ABTA are required to provide bonds to protect their customers in the event of financial failure. The bond can take a number of forms, but is often an insurance policy for the amount required by ABTA, or a bank guarantee. The financial protection offered by the bonding system enables ABTA, in the event of a member's financial failure, to:

★ Arrange for clients whose holidays are in progress at the time of the failure to continue their holidays, as far as possible as originally planned, and in any event to make certain that customers abroad are returned to the UK; and

★ Reimburse customers whose holidays have not started, the money they paid for their holidays or make alternative arrangements for the holidays to proceed. (Information courtesy of ABTA.)

Case study discussion questions

1   Why has ABTA developed its Travel Agents' Code of Conduct?

2   What is ABTA's principal aim?

3   What benefits are there to travellers who book through an ABTA registered travel agent?

4   Why do ABTA travel agencies have to provide the Association with a 'bond'?

5   What training opportunities are offered by the Travel Training Company?

Agency agreements

All of the business conducted by travel agents on behalf of principals is strictly controlled by individual agency agreements. These contractual arrangements set out the obligations of each party to the agreement, the terms of trade and remuneration details. The most common agency agreement will be that between the travel agent and a tour operator, where the agent undertakes to sell the tour operator's products in return for a commission on sales. Other agreements may be made with coach operators, holiday centres, hotel groups, ferry companies (see Figure 8.10), rail companies, National Express, car hire firms and a range of other travel and tourism companies. A standard written agency agreement between a travel agent and a tour operator will include details under a number of clauses, including:

✪ **Accounting procedures for deposits and balances**

✪ **Commission rates and arrangements for payment to the agent**

✪ **Procedures for issuing tickets, vouchers and other travel documentation**

Figure 8.10 *Many travel agents have agency agreements with ferry companies*
Photograph courtesy of Stena Line Limited

- ✪ **Policy on refunds and cancellation of holidays by the client or tour operator**
- ✪ **Handling of complaints made to the agent about the operator's products**
- ✪ **Racking responsibilities of the agent in respect of the operator's brochures**
- ✪ **Training and promotional support offered by the tour operator**

Such agreements are generally on a non-exclusive basis, i.e. many other travel agents will be selling the same products. It is only in the case of very specialised products that an agent may enter into an exclusive arrangement with an operator, although exclusive agreements in a particular geographical area are not uncommon.

IATA licensing

The International Air Transport Association (IATA) is an international trade body representing the interests of more than 80 per cent of the world's major airlines. Its principal aim is to promote safe, regular and economic air travel. Travel agents in the UK, in common with agents worldwide, can apply for an IATA licence to sell airline tickets and other services of IATA member airlines. Since these airlines pay commission only to approved IATA sales agents, an IATA licence is a much sought after commodity. Applying for an IATA licence has similarities to an application for ABTA membership, in that the applicant has to meet certain minimum criteria and will be subject to an inspection and interview by an IATA representative. The criteria for approval are concerned with a number of factors, including:

- ✪ **Nature of the premises**: The agency must be open for business on a regular basis and clearly identified as a travel agency.
- ✪ **Security of premises**: Premises must be adequately protected and a safe installed for the storage of airline tickets and other valuables.
- ✪ **Staff qualifications**: Staff selling the IATA tickets and services must be permanent employees and have relevant experience and qualifications, e.g. British Airways Fares and Ticketing Courses.
- ✪ **Finances**: Applicants must submit a full set of audited accounts for scrutiny by IATA personnel and meet certain minimum share capital/capital account amounts. Additionally, approved agents are required to submit a copy of their annual report and accounts within six months of the financial year end.
- ✪ **Bonding**: A bank or insurance company bond will be required, based on a percentage of annual turnover.

On payment of a non-refundable application fee and an entry fee, the successful applicant will be granted an IATA licence to sell airline tickets and services of IATA member airlines.

Activity 8.8

Try to find out which travel agencies in your locality have an IATA licence. What do the non-IATA agents do when a client wishes to buy an airline ticket?

Law of contract

Contrary to popular belief, most contracts do not need to be in writing. From a lawyer's standpoint, a contract is any agreement that the law will enforce, whether in writing, verbal or implied, i.e. assumed from the conduct of the parties. Contracts range from the very simple, e.g. buying a drink at a resort complex, to the very complex, e.g. building the Channel Tunnel. The law of contract is principally concerned with promises that constitute part of an agreed exchange. It governs such questions as which agreements the law will enforce, what obligations are imposed by the agreement and what will happen if the obligations are not carried out.

The following conditions must be satisfied if a contract is to be legally enforceable:

1 **There must have been agreement between the parties on all material aspects of the contract**

2 **The parties must have intended to create a legally binding contract**

3 **There must be at least two parties to the contract**

It is an essential requirement of English law that, for a contract to be legally binding, each party must have agreed to provide something of value to the other. For example, when a customer books a package holiday, but the booking has yet to be confirmed, the contract between the customer and the tour operator may still be legally binding even where he or she has not yet paid for it. The important point is that the customer has promised to pay the price for the holiday when required to do so. The tour operator, on the other hand, promises that the holiday is available.

It is important to remember that when a holidaymaker books a package holiday through a travel agent, the contract is between the customer and the tour operator, with the travel agent merely acting as an intermediary. It is against the tour operator that the customer must seek legal redress in the event of a breach of contract, although the travel agent may be liable to you for any other extras that are not part of the brochure holiday, such as currency exchange, airport car parking, etc.

Fair trading charters

Many of the large travel agency chains produce fair trading charters as a way of demonstrating their customer commitment. Trade organisations also publish such charters.

Activity 8.9

Browse through some tour operators' brochures to see if any publish a fair trading charter. From what you have found, make a list of the types of points covered in such charters.

Package Travel Regulations

Unit 10 *Tour operations* has detailed information on the Package Travel, Package Holidays and Package Tour Regulations 1992. The main aim of the Regulations is to give people buying package holidays more protection and access to compensation when things go wrong, while at the same time harmonising the rules covering packages operated throughout European Union countries. In the normal course of events, travel agents are not bound by the requirements of the Regulations, since they are not the 'organiser' of the package, but the 'retailer'. The Regulations define these terms as follows:

✪ '**Organiser**' – the person who, other than occasionally, organises packages and sells or offers them for sale, whether directly or through a retailer

✪ '**Retailer**' – the person who sells or offers for sale the package put together by the organiser.

In the UK travel and tourism industry the 'organiser' will be normally be a tour operator and the 'retailer' a travel agent. There may, however, be occasions when a travel retailer does fall within the scope of the Regulations. This will certainly be the case when the travel agent escorts his or her own tours for clients, since the contract for the holiday is between the agent and the customer, with no tour operator involved. Similarly, a travel agent who uses a range of reference materials to assemble a package for a client is likely to fall within requirements of the Regulations. It is only when the customer enters into a contract directly with the tour operator, or other principal, that the travel agent will not be the 'organiser' as defined by the Regulations. Happily for travel agents, this is the normal situation, and most agents are unlikely to become entangled in the complexity of the Package Travel Regulations. To make sure that the position is clear, the agent should ensure that the customer signs the tour operator's booking form and receives an unaltered confirmation invoice from that party. Travel agents must be careful to ensure that correct documentation is passed from the principal, normally a tour operator, to the client.

Working methods in travel agencies

Key topics in this section

- **Procedures and documentation for selling products**
- **Filing and dealing with correspondence**
- **Security and confidentiality**
- **Dealing with money**
- **Brochure handling, merchandising and displays**

Procedures and documentation for selling products

Booking a package holiday

The starting point for a package holiday booking will be when a client makes contact with a travel agent, either in person or by telephone (see Figure 8.11).

If the client has a definite departure date, holiday company and resort in mind, the agent will quickly be able to check availability on the computer system. If there is availability, the booking can proceed. If not, or if the client is unsure about which resort to choose, some further advice and help will be needed from the agent. The tour operators' reservation systems are designed

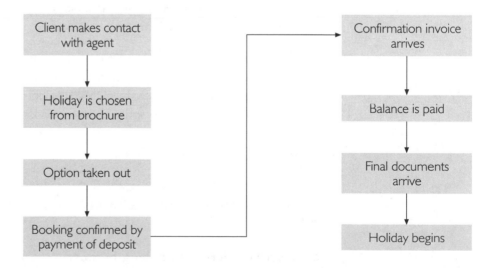

Figure 8.11 *Stages in the booking of a package holiday*

to be able to search by date, resort, hotel, type of holiday, etc., so the client's needs should be satisfied eventually. Once the holiday is chosen, the agent takes out an option, giving the client the chance to think about the choice before committing himself or herself. The option will be entered on the screen and normally lasts for 24 hours, after which time it lapses and the holiday is put on sale again. If the client returns within the 24 hours and pays a deposit, then the booking is confirmed. The client will be issued with a receipt for the deposit payment and a new file started.

Normally within two weeks of making the booking, a written confirmation invoice will be sent from the tour operator, giving precise details of the clients travelling, the booked holiday and travel details. The balance is normally paid eight weeks before departure, but if the holiday is booked within eight weeks of departure the full amount must be paid. Two to three weeks before the holiday starts, final tickets and documentation are received by the agent and passed to the client. This is a good point at which to try some 'cross-selling' by asking clients if they need any foreign currency or travellers' cheques for their holiday.

Documentation used in package holiday bookings

One of the most important documents used in travel agencies is the form that records the details of an initial enquiry from a customer. This may be called the enquiry form, office booking form or option form and it becomes the first item of a client's office file, to which other documentation is added later if the booking progresses. Whether the customer makes contact by telephone or in person, the enquiry form gives a travel clerk the opportunity to record basic client information and holiday details in a logical manner. This will be invaluable when the client wishes to proceed with the booking or the agent needs to contact the client to seek clarification. The form also acts as a reminder to staff, ensuring that the necessary information is obtained and recorded correctly. Figure 8.12 gives an indication of the sort of information that appears on an enquiry form.

The enquiry form shown gives a member of staff the opportunity to record client information, such as name, address and telephone numbers, plus details of their chosen holiday or other travel arrangements. There is space at the bottom for the agent to make some price calculations on behalf of the client.

Confirmation invoice

Once a holiday has been booked, the first document the client receives will be a confirmation invoice (see Figure 8.13) giving precise holiday details, including:

- ✪ **Holiday reference/booking number**
- ✪ **Inclusive dates of the holiday**

Out and About Travel		TEL: 014 682 595	

Client details

Names	Address	Tel. No.
1.		
2.		
3.		
4.		
5.		
6.		

Holiday details

Holiday company:	Thomson ❑	Airtours ❑	First Choice ❑	Other..... ❑
Booking ref.:	Holiday no.:	Option exp. date:	Date confirmed:	Agency ref.:
Resort:	Dep. date:	Duration:	Dep. airport:	Insurance: Y/N
Hotel/Self-cat.:	Accom. details:	Special requests		

Flight details		Airline:		Ref.:		
	Date	From	To	Flight no.	Dep. time	Arr. time
Outward						
Return						

Other travel requirements

Notes/costing		Agency ref.:
		Taken by:
		Date of booking:

Figure 8.12 *Example of a travel agent's enquiry form*

Back Out Travel
Oildrum Lane, Anytown, UK

TEL: 018 759 28762
FAX: 018 759 28763

┌─ **Booking details** ─┐
Booking Nos.   : 12345
Issue date   : 1/2/01
Sales advisor   : JENNY
Holiday type   : VILLA INCLUSIVE
Membership No. : –
Party size   : 2Ad 2Ch 0 Inf

Holiday Details COSTA BLANCA

Provisional Travel Details – subject to alteration – local timings

```
SATURDAY  18-MAY-01 BRISTOL   -ALICANTE  1425 / 1750 AIH707 AIRTOURS
SATURDAY  01-JUN-01 ALICANTE  -BRISTOL   1840 / 2000 AIH708 AIRTOURS
       PROVISIONAL FLIGHT TIMINGS           NON SMOKING AIRCRAFT
```

Accommodation

```
Property:  VILLA PAELLA Reserved: SATURDAY 18-MAY-01 to 01-JUN-01 (14 nights)
                        3 BEDROOMED VILLA FOR UP TO 6. OWN POOL

No. of cots: 0        Overseas taxi transfers to property: 0 From property: 0
```

Car & Boat Hire, Motorail, Hotel, etc.

```
GROUP [A]           18-MAY-01 AIRP 01-JUN-01 AIRP Roof-rack: N Requests-Babyseat:  0
                                              "          "          "
           Notes/Requests
                            INV. DEPOSIT REFUNDABLE ON 16-JUN-01
```

CONFIRMATION & INVOICE TO

```
MR J Brown
10 St. John Street
Anytown
AN1 7HQ
```

We have pleasure in confirming your holiday arrangements. Please check the details carefully and notify us by return if there are any discrepancies. Where special requests have been made, details are shown above.
We will endeavour to fulfil them but no guarantee can be given. If you have any queries or require further information, please do not hesitate to contact us.

Message

Holiday costing

	1	2	3
Basic holiday cost:	389.00	344.00	0.00
Regional airport/port supplement:	0.00	0.00	0.00
Other: SEASONAL SUPPLEMENT	15.00	15.00	0.00
Insurance:	25.00	12.50	0.00
Cost per person	£429.00	£371.50	£0.00
Number of clients (excl. accom.only)	2	2	0
Total columns 1, 2, & 3		£1601.00	
Infant:		0.00	
Other:		0.00	
		0.00	
PROPERTY DEPOSIT		100.00	
Car hire: 2 × 111		222.00	
Reductions: 1 WEEK FREE CAR HIRE		–111.00	

Total	£1812.00
Payment received:	£1812.00
Balance due for payment by:	£ 0.00

Passenger Details Note – Only clients named below may travel or occupy the property

			Age	Sex	Ins				Age	Sex	Ins
1	MR	BROWN		M	Y	2	MRS	BROWN		F	Y
3	MISS	BROWN	13	F	Y	4	MSTR	BROWN	6	M	Y

Registered in England No. 123456789

Figure 8.13 *Package holiday confirmation invoice*

- ✪ **Name and address of lead person**
- ✪ **Names of all clients travelling (including ages of children and infants)**
- ✪ **Details of travel arrangements for the outward and return journeys**
- ✪ **Details of the accommodation booked**
- ✪ **Details of other items booked, e.g. car hire**
- ✪ **Full holiday costing**

The confirmation invoice will also indicate when the balance is due for payment. Any discrepancies noticed by the client or agent should be rectified at this stage.

Final travel information form

Two to three weeks before the holiday begins, the clients will receive their final travel details and documents. This will include their travel tickets, accommodation vouchers, insurance details, car hire details (if applicable), baggage labels, customer satisfaction questionnaire and a printed travel information form that duplicates some of the details on the original confirmation invoice (see Figure 8.14). These are the documents that the clients will need to take with them on holiday as proof of purchase when boarding their flights and checking in to the accommodation.

Filing and dealing with correspondence

Staff in travel agencies must be able to respond quickly to enquiries, whether they are from a client, a tour operator or another principal. This calls for an efficient system for filing client documentation and other information, such as country fact sheets and file copies of brochures, timetables, etc. Most agencies still operate manual filing systems, but the popularity of computerised filing systems based on database software is growing rapidly. A filing system can be arranged alphabetically, numerically or in date order. Information on countries, office copies of brochures, timetables, etc. are best filed alphabetically. Numerical filing is favoured by some agencies for clients' bookings, each being assigned a unique reference number and filed accordingly. The majority of agents, however, prefer to organise their client files in date order based on the date of departure. One drawback of this method is that the peak travel months of July and August generate a great deal of paperwork, making it necessary to devote extra space to these

Back Out Travel
Oildrum Lane, Anytown, UK

TEL: 018 759 28762
FAX: 018 759 28763

Booking details
Booking No.   : 12345
Linked bookings : –
Holiday type   : VILLA INCL.
Party size   : 2Ad 2Ch 0Inf
Insurance status : FULL
Membership No. : –
Issue date   : 26-APR-01

YOUR HOLIDAY DOCUMENTS

Please check the following
information and advise us immediately
if there are any discrepancies.

Lead name: Brown
Holiday from: 18-MAY-01 – 01-JUN-01

Travel information and check-in details

Please check in 120   minutes before departure time at BRISTOL AIRPORT
SATURDAY 18-MAY-01 BRISTOL   -ALICANTE   1425 / 1750 AIH707 AIRTOURS
SATURDAY 01-JUN-01 ALICANTE -BRISTOL   1840 / 2000 AIH708 AIRTOURS
      NON SMOKING AIRCRAFT   BAGGAGE ALLOWANCE = 20K
Airport Representative:
      WILL BE IN THE ARRIVALS AREA BETWEEN 10AM & 5PM.

Accommodation details — COSTA BLANCA

Taxis provided to property: 0   from property: 0   Note: Only the people named on the holiday invoice may occupy the property
Property: VILLA PAELLA
                  3 BEDROOM VILLA, OWN POOL.
Arrival: 18-MAY-01 For 14 nights   No. of cots: 0
Key collection: SEE ENCLOSED DETAILS
Villa/house changeovers: If you arrive at the property before 1600 hrs you may find changeover
                  cleaning still in progress.
                  On the final day of your stay please vacate the property by 1000 hrs.
Overseas   MEET AT AIRPORT
representative

Local assistance
in addition to above

Emergency
contacts

If you have a complaint

Our objective is to provide you with a happy and successful holiday, however things can occasionally
go wrong. In this unlikely event follow the procedure outlined on the **Incident Report Form** enclosed
with your travel documents. If you do not follow this procedure we cannot resolve the matter while you
are on holiday. Comments received after you return home can only be treated as information for the
benefit of future clients.

Car & Boat Hire, Motorail, Hotel, etc.

1 GROUP [A] AIRP 18-MAY-01 1750 AIRP 01-JUN-01 1640
2
3
4
5

Message

Distribution
Top copy is client copy, other
copies to property managers
or hire companies if required.

Registered in England No. 123456789

Figure 8.14 *Package holiday travel information form*

months. Filing by date of departure is, nonetheless, preferred by most travel agencies.

Some agencies further refine their client filing system according to the status of the booking, with separate sections for:

- ✪ **Initial enquiries** – written record of a client's first contact
- ✪ **Options** – details of a client who has taken out an option on a booking
- ✪ **Confirmations** – clients who have paid a deposit
- ✪ **Final payments** – bookings on which the balance has been paid
- ✪ **Awaiting tickets** – clients who are awaiting their tickets and vouchers
- ✪ **Refunds due** – any clients who are due a refund on their payments

With this system, clients' files are moved from one section to another according to their current status. This way, a member of staff can see at any one time the progress of a client's booking. Client files are normally kept for up to two years, although new rules for self-assessment of income tax insist on longer periods of time. Files that are no longer current are referred to as 'dead files' or 'closed files' and are stored in an archive in case they are needed for any claims that may be made.

Storage of files

The most common method of storage is in filing cabinets with suspension files. These are excellent for paper documents, such as copies of booking forms, receipts, options forms, etc. Bulkier material, including maps and country information, is best stored in strong box files on shelving. Contact telephone numbers and addresses of clients are sometimes stored on index cards, filed by client surname. These can be actual cards stored in a box or details entered on a card file on a computer.

Activity 8.10

Carry out some research in a travel agency with which you are familiar and find out what filing systems they use and the types of material stored in each system.

Receiving and distributing correspondence

Travel agencies receive and generate a wide variety of correspondence in the course of their normal trading activities, including:

- ✪ **Brochures**
- ✪ **Other promotional materials, e.g. posters, leaflets, price lists, etc.**
- ✪ **Booking forms**
- ✪ **Invoices**
- ✪ **Letters**
- ✪ **Notifications of special offers, late availability, etc.**

Much of this will arrive via the postal service, although brochure stocks will normally be delivered by specialist courier and distribution companies, such as BP Travel Trade Services. On-screen information, fax transmissions and electronic mail (e-mail) are also popular ways of receiving and distributing information, particularly between agents and principals. All staff should be briefed on current offers and products so that they can provide the best possible service to their clients. The travel supervisor will generally be responsible for distributing information to the relevant members of staff. Correspondence relating to clients' holiday and travel plans will be dealt with accordingly, with copies being placed in the appropriate office files.

Security and confidentiality

Like all commercial enterprises, travel agencies need constantly to monitor their operations in respect of security threats and breaches of confidentiality. It is important for the owners and managers of agencies to address a number of security hazards, relating to the security of premises, systems for handling and storing money and other valuables, the safety of staff and customers, and the security of information. Government legislation on health and safety at work places a duty on the operators of travel agencies to provide a safe environment for staff, customers and all other people visiting their premises.

All retail premises need to be made secure against burglars, and travel agencies are no exception. Attention to external security is very important and may include:

- ✪ **Fitting security locks to doors and windows, and window bars to high-risk areas such as equipment stores and bar areas**
- ✪ **Using closed circuit television (CCTV) or employing security personnel to monitor large areas, including car parks, and staff and public entrances and exits**

- ✪ **Installing invisible beams and pressure pads in passageways and entrances to activate alarms**
- ✪ **Fitting intruder alarms which, for large organisations, should be capable of alerting a central monitoring station that operates 24 hours a day**
- ✪ **Introducing card access control using PIN systems to identify which parts of a building are for staff access only**
- ✪ **Installing security lighting, particularly in high-risk areas**
- ✪ **Providing panic alarms for staff**

Inside the premises, attention will need to be paid to the secure storage of money, passports, travellers' cheques, foreign exchange, travel tickets and other valuables, as well as staff possessions and confidential information about clients, whether held manually or on computer. A strong safe is an essential item of security equipment for all travel agencies and is usually a requirement for the granting of an agency licence with a principal or association, e.g. IATA.

Security of information

All travel agencies carry a variety of sensitive and confidential information about their clients, employees and business operations. In the competitive world of travel and tourism, guarding commercially sensitive business information is an important consideration. No travel agent in a town would want his or her competitors to know about sales performance and revenue. It is for this reason that contracts of employment often contain a clause about not disclosing commercial information to third parties. This point should be reinforced at staff induction sessions.

The two main security hazards associated with client information and business records are fire and theft. Twenty years ago, all business records would have been held entirely on paper. Today, information is held on a variety of other formats, including microfiche, computer disks, photographic materials and audio/video tapes. These are all vulnerable to the twin threats of fire and theft and do not inherently offer any greater security than paper. Computers, however, do give the option of storing information on floppy disks, which can be stored securely away from the main computer terminal, thus reducing the risk of losing information in the event of theft or fire. All computer and other sensitive information should be routinely locked in safes or fire-proof data protection cabinets kept in controlled access rooms.

The storage of information on computers raises the issue of the Data Protection Act, which was introduced to safeguard the public from problems relating to the inaccuracy of any information held about them on computer records (see page 139 in Unit 10 *Tour operations* for more on the Data Protection Act).

Dealing with money

Staff in travel agencies handle cash and other forms of payment on a regular basis. Common methods of paying for holidays and other travel products include the use of credit cards, charge cards, debit cards and cheques, supported by cheque guarantee cards. When handling cash, staff should always follow these simple procedures:

- ✪ **Count the amount in front of the customer**
- ✪ **Take care to give the right amount of change; it is good practice, when a note is given in payment, to leave it outside the till until the change has been given, to avoid claims that a higher value note was tendered**
- ✪ **Check that notes are genuine; some travel agencies have now installed equipment to detect fake notes**
- ✪ **Ensure that tills and cash boxes are not left unattended for long periods**
- ✪ **Make sure that tills are emptied overnight and that cash is locked securely in a safe or deposited in a bank**

When accepting payment by cheque (see Figure 8.15), it is important to reduce the risk of fraud by checking that:

1 **The date on the cheque is correct**

2 **The amount in words and figures agree**

3 **The amount is within the cheque guarantee card limit**

4 **The signature on the cheque matches that on the cheque guarantee card**

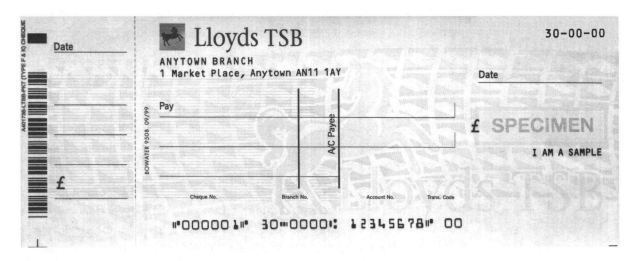

Figure 8.15 *A cheque from a high street bank*
Courtesy of Lloyds TSB Bank

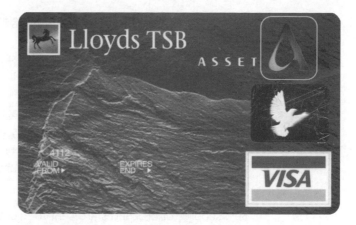

Figure 8.16 *Credit cards are widely used for travel payments*
Courtesy of Lloyds TSB Bank

5   **The code numbers on the cheque and the cheque guarantee card are the same**

6   **The cheque is signed in front of the payee**

7   **The cheque guarantee card has not expired**

Increasingly, customers in travel agencies are using credit and debit cards in preference to cash and cheques, for reasons of security and convenience (see Figure 8.16). Once again, simple procedures should be followed by staff, including checking that:

✪ **The card is one that is accepted by the agency**

✪ **The card has not expired**

✪ **The card is not on a list of stolen or lost cards**

✪ **The card has the same name as the customer**

✪ **Whether the card requires authorisation from the credit/debit card company before use**

✪ **Details on any vouchers completed by staff are correctly entered**

✪ **The customer's signature matches that on the card**

Brochure handling, merchandising and displays

Brochures play a vital role in the promotion and sale of holidays and other travel products sold in agencies. The brochure is the travel agent's prime sales tool and is the mechanism by which a customer's enquiry is, hopefully, turned into a sale. The high costs of designing, printing and distributing brochures means that tour operators and other principals keep firm control on which agencies receive brochure stocks and in what quantities. The agencies with the best track record of selling a company's products will receive regular bulk supplies and command special treatment, including extra incentives for travel agency staff and management to encourage even more sales. Agencies with smaller sales volumes will still be sent brochure stocks, but on a smaller scale. In all cases, the tour operator will ensure that the agency has a file copy of the latest brochure as soon as possible after printing in advance of the bulk supplies being delivered.

Bulk supplies of brochures are sent to agents in a variety of ways. The mass market tour operators generally have their own distribution departments and networks, whereas smaller operators may use specialist distribution firms, such as BP Travel Trade Services. Brochure distribution is sometimes graded on a regional basis, where agencies close to airports used by a tour operator are handled separately.

When bulk brochure supplies arrive at the agency, there is often a problem in deciding where to store them. All agencies will have an area set aside for storage, but at certain times of the year this may be overloaded. An alternative 'overflow' area should be identified, bearing in mind the safety of staff and customers. Either way, there should be a workable method of storing the brochures, using an alphabetical system that will enable staff to locate a particular brochure when required. Brochures should never be left in piles on the floor of the main selling area of the travel agency. Apart from looking very untidy, there are clear issues concerning fire regulations and health and safety legislation.

Agencies sometimes delegate the task of brochure stock control and reordering to a specific member of staff, in order to minimise the chances of running out of supplies. Agencies should, without fail, always keep an office copy of every brochure they sell so that, should the bulk supplies run out, staff will at least have one copy for reference. Nowadays, brochure re-ordering is often handled via the viewdata screens, but brochures can also be ordered by fax and over the telephone.

In-store displays

Point-of-sale materials, such as window displays, free-standing displays in the main body of a travel agency and brochures, play an important role in promoting holidays and other travel products. They should be changed on a regular basis to provide customers with a new 'focal point' and as a way of alerting clients to new products and special offers (see Figure 8.17). Displays should, at all times, look professional and tidy. The use of hand-written signs and posters should be avoided, since they do little to enhance the image of the product being sold or the agency as a whole.

Figure 8.17 *Brochure displays must be kept fully stocked*
Courtesy of John Ward

Activity
8.11

Working in teams of two, visit some travel agencies in your local area and study their window displays. Make a note of any good features you notice and any points that would benefit from improvement. Suggest ways that the improvements could be carried out.

Business travel

9

Business travel has emerged as one of the fastest-growing sectors of the travel and tourism industry. It includes travel for business meetings, conferences and conventions, trade fairs and exhibitions, as well as incentive travel, where holidays, short breaks and other travel products are offered to members of staff as incentives to achieve specific sales targets and work more effectively. In this unit you will learn about the complex demands of business travellers and develop the skills and knowledge necessary to provide an efficient service to this valuable market. Specifically, you will investigate the business travel customer and key characteristics of the business travel market. You will also learn about the structure, size and economic value of the UK business travel industry, before focusing on the skills and knowledge needed to plan a business travel itinerary.

This unit is divided into three main areas:

● **The business travel market – the customer**

● **The structure, size and economic value of the UK business travel industry**

● **Planning a business travel itinerary**

We guide you through each of these areas using examples and case studies from the travel and tourism industry. At the beginning of each of these sections you will see a list of key topics to help you fully understand what you need to learn. Look out for the links to websites so that you can learn more about a particular travel and tourism company, organisation or topic.

The business travel market – the customer

Key topics in this section

- **Introduction – what is business travel?**
- **Organisations and staff involved in business travel**
- **Purpose of travel**
- **Key characteristics of the business travel market**

Introduction – what is business travel?

Business travel is the category of the travel and tourism industry concerned with travel for business purposes, rather than travel for leisure purposes. You will remember from studying Unit 1 *Investigating travel and tourism* that there are three main categories of travel:

- ✪ **Leisure travel**
- ✪ **Business travel**
- ✪ **Visiting friends and relatives (VFR)**

Figure 9.1 shows the relationship of these three categories to each other and to the tourism industry in general.

There is sometimes overlap between the three categories, for example a business trip to the USA being extended by a week to take in a holiday in the Rocky Mountains, a business woman staying overnight with a friend before attending a meeting or a sales manager being given an all-expenses-paid

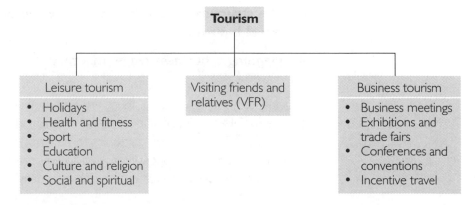

Figure 9.1 *Main categories of travel*

weekend break to Paris for achieving his yearly sales targets (an example of incentive travel).

Business travel is an increasingly important sector of the UK travel and tourism industry, since it is often 'high value tourism', earning hoteliers, caterers, transport providers, travel agents and a host of other service providers significant income. Business travel is considered a high value sector since:

❂ **Clients often have to travel at short notice, meaning that they are not able to take advantage of advance purchase rates**

❂ **Business people often use high quality accommodation**

❂ **Business travel invariably includes an element of entertaining business colleagues**

❂ **Travel is often in upgraded seating, e.g. business class or first class**

Business travellers are able to take advantage of frequent flyer programmes (and even frequent stay schemes in accommodation and frequent use programmes for car hire, etc.), where they earn points when travelling with a particular company and can exchange the points for free or discounted travel. Such schemes help to build customer loyalty to particular companies, as the following industry example of British Airways' frequent flyer programme 'the Executive Club' illustrates.

Industry example

The Executive Club is British Airways' current frequent flyer programme. Business passengers who fly on eligible fares with British Airways, or any of its partner airlines (see below), earn Executive Club points, which allow them to become members of either the blue, silver or gold Club. Travellers with enough points to move into the silver and gold tiers benefit from access to the airline's worldwide network of over 180 Executive Club lounges, all designed to make business travel easier.

While in the UK, Executive Club members have use of the Hewlett-Packard business centre in the Club Europe lounge in London Heathrow's Terminal One. The centre provides business travellers with the following:

continued

continued

★ Use of computers with a full suite of office applications

★ Business centre staff

★ Free Internet access

★ Free black and white, and colour, printing

★ Free faxing

★ Free scanning and copying

★ Free Internet e-mail

★ Modem connections for laptop computers

★ Telephones

Executive Club members also have access to a number of dedicated reservation lines around the world, which give priority over non-members.

British Airways' frequent flyer partner airlines include:

★ Aer Lingus

★ Air Liberté

★ Alaska Airlines

★ America West Airlines

★ American Airlines

★ Cathay Pacific

★ Deutsche BA

★ Emirates

★ Finnair

★ Iberia

★ JAL

★ LanChile

★ Lot Polish Airlines

★ Qantas

Car rental partners include Hertz, Avis and Sixt Rent-a-Car, while hotel partners in the frequent flyer programme include The Savoy Group, Thistle Hotels, Hilton Hotels and Hyatt Hotels and Resorts.

Browse this website

www.british-airways.com/execclub/uk/welcome.shtml

Browse this website for more information on Air Miles

www.airmiles.co.uk

Another well-known loyalty and incentive scheme is Air Miles, where customers earn 'miles' when they use specific services or buy particular goods and trade them in for flights, other travel products and services offered by the Air Miles company.

Organisations and staff involved in business travel

Organisations of all sizes and in all sectors of the economy often need their staff to travel on business. Sole traders, members of partnerships, company directors, public sector staff, junior and senior managers, all travel from time to time on business. This could be in their local area, elsewhere in the UK, to countries in continental Europe or further afield in the world. Business travel operates across all types of industry sectors, from manufacturing, mining and construction to banking, insurance, financial services and even travel itself!

Activity 9.1

Write down six specific examples of UK people travelling on business, two to places in the UK, two to countries in Europe and two to worldwide destinations, indicating their job title, business location in the UK, business destination and purpose of travel, e.g. a sales representative of a pottery supplier in Stoke-on-Trent travelling to Birmingham for the annual sales conference.

A travel agent who has a large number of business travellers may set up a database of their specific travel requirements in order to be able to offer a fast and efficient service to business clients. Figure 9.2 shows an example of a business traveller profile form, which business clients are asked to complete before the information is entered on to the travel agent's database.

Purpose of travel

The main purposes of business travel are:

1   **Attending business meetings**
2   **Visiting exhibitions and trade fairs**
3   **Attending conferences and conventions**
4   **Taking part in incentive travel**

Figure 9.3 gives various examples of these four different types of business travel.

PERSONAL DETAILS

COMPANY NAME _____

TRAVELLER'S NAME _____ TITLE _____

COMPANY ADDRESS _____
_____
_____
_____

TELEPHONE _____
COMPANY CONTACT _____

HOME ADDRESS _____
_____
_____
_____

TELEPHONE _____

NATIONALITY _____ DATE OF BIRTH _____

PASSPORT No(s) _____ EXPIRY DATE _____
_____ EXPIRY DATE _____
WHERE PASSPORT ISSUED _____

VISA DETAILS   COUNTRY _____ No _____ EXPIRY _____
                COUNTRY _____ No _____ EXPIRY _____

CHARGE CARDS   CARD/NUMBER _____ EXPIRY _____
                CARD/NUMBER _____ EXPIRY _____
                CARD/NUMBER _____ EXPIRY _____

VACCINATIONS _____ EXPIRY _____
_____ EXPIRY _____

ANY OTHER RELEVANT MEDICAL INFORMATION _____

TYPE OF CAR _____ REGISTRATION No _____
DRIVING LICENCE NUMBER _____ INTERNATIONAL DRIVING LICENCE NUMBER _____

FOR OFFICE USE ONLY
DATE ENTERED ON TO DATABASE _____

Figure 9.2 *Business traveller profile form*

PERSONAL TRAVEL REQUIREMENTS

	AIR				
SHORTHAUL		LONGHAUL	HOTEL	CAR HIRE	RAIL

PREFERRED CLASSES

SHORTHAUL	LONGHAUL	HOTEL	CAR HIRE	RAIL
☐ FIRST	☐ FIRST	☐ 4/5 STAR	☐ LUXURY	☐ FIRST
☐ BUSINESS	☐ BUSINESS	☐ 3 STAR	☐ STANDARD	☐ STANDARD
☐ ECONOMY	☐ ECONOMY		☐ OTHER	

PREFERRED SUPPLIER

SHORTHAUL	LONGHAUL	HOTEL	CAR HIRE	RAIL
PREFERRED AIRLINE	PREFERRED AIRLINE	PREFERRED HOTEL CHAIN	PREFERRED CAR HIRE Co.	
_____	_____	_____	_____	
_____	_____	_____	PREFERRED HIRE CAR	
_____	_____	_____	_____	
_____	_____		_____	

PERSONAL PREFERENCES

SHORTHAUL	LONGHAUL	HOTEL	CAR HIRE	RAIL
☐ SMOKING	☐ SMOKING	☐ CITY CENTRE	☐ MANUAL	☐ SMOKING
☐ NON SMOKING	☐ NON SMOKING	☐ OUT OF TOWN	☐ AUTOMATIC	☐ NON SMOKING
☐ WINDOW	☐ WINDOW	☐ AIRPORT LOCATION		☐ WINDOW
☐ AISLE	☐ AISLE	☐ MODERN		☐ AISLE
☐ OTHER	☐ OTHER	☐ TRADITIONAL		☐ OTHER
☐ FRONT CABIN	☐ FRONT CABIN			☐ FACING ENGINE
☐ REAR CABIN	☐ REAR CABIN			☐ BACK TO ENGINE
☐ FILM VIEW	☐ FILM VIEW			☐ DINING
☐ FILM NON VIEW	☐ FILM NON VIEW			☐ NON DINING
☐ AIRPORT ASSISTANCE	☐ AIRPORT ASSISTANCE			
DIETARY REQUIREMENTS	DIETARY REQUIREMENTS	DIETARY REQUIREMENTS		
_____	_____	_____		
_____	_____	_____		

MEMBERSHIP DETAILS

AIRLINE CARDS		HOTEL CARDS	CAR HIRE CARDS	
CARD _____	CARD _____	CARD _____	CARD _____	
No _____	No _____	No _____	No _____	
CARD _____	CARD _____	CARD _____	CARD _____	
No _____	No _____	No _____	No _____	

ANY ADDITIONAL INFORMATION

_____

_____

_____

_____

Figure 9.2   (cont'd)

Business meetings	• A British sportswear manufacturer on a two-week fact-finding tour of the west coast of the USA
	• An advertising executive taking a train journey from her home base for a meeting with a client in Belfast
	• A Member of the European Parliament flying to Brussels for the day for meetings with EU officials
Exhibitions and trade fairs	• A representative of the English Tourism Council visiting the Scottish Travel Trade Fair in Glasgow
	• The Gardeners' World exhibition at the Birmingham NEC
	• Visiting the World Travel Market in London
Conferences and conventions	• Lawyers from EU countries attending a two-day conference on new Directives in Copenhagen
	• Attending the TUC Conference in Blackpool
	• Visiting the ABTA Domestic Conference in Llandudno
Incentive travel	• A weekend golfing break at Gleneagles for achieving top monthly sales for your company
	• Free care hire for one week on your holiday for completing an important project ahead of time
	• Two weeks in Florida for you and your family for clinching a new multi-million pound contract

Figure 9.3 *Examples of business travel*

Industry example

The Hilton Belfast Hotel has extensive business facilities, including the following nine conference and dining rooms on its mezzanine floor, with a pre-function area, business centre and private bar:

★ *Lagan Suite* – seats 300 for dinner, 265 dinner dance, 500 reception, 400 theatre style, 200 classroom style (180 with back projection). Area 384 sq. metres, ceiling height 3.55 metres.

★ *Boardroom* – seats 18 boardroom style. Area 58 sq. metres.

★ *Spectra Suite* – seats 100 theatre style and reception, 60 classroom style and dinner, built-in media wall with state-of-the-art projection

continued

continued

equipment. Area 118 sq. metres, ceiling height 3.20 metres.

★ *Brookfield Room, Broadway Room, Glenbank Room* – seat 45 for a reception, 40 theatre style, 32 for dinner. Area of each room is 51 sq. metres.

★ *Ewart Room* – 20 theatre style, 10 boardroom style. Area 32 sq. metres.

★ *Rosebank Room* – 10 boardroom style. Area 29 sq. metres.

★ *Tower Suite* – round room suitable for small dinners and VIP receptions

The hotel offers conference planners easy reservation options, dedicated conference support staff, flexible and creative food service, clear billing and easy departure.

Key characteristics of the business travel market

✪ **The importance placed on price, value for money and effective use of time**: As we saw earlier in this unit, business travel can be 'high value' travel, since business people often have to make journeys at short notice and generally use high quality accommodation. However, this does not mean that they are not concerned about the prices they pay for travel. Just like leisure travellers, business people expect to get good value for money when they travel. In order to make their travel budgets stretch as far as possible, UK business travellers are increasingly making use of low-cost airlines, such as Go, easyJet and Ryanair, when they travel. Organisations that have a large budget for business travel can often negotiate better rates for accommodation and travel when compared with companies with small travel budgets. Many business travellers are prepared to pay extra for travel if the arrangements mean that they can make better use of their scarce time.

✪ **Credit arrangements for travel payments**: Business travel will generally be offered on a credit basis, with the travel company making the travel arrangements setting up credit terms with its business clients.

Smaller businesses may well pay for their travel arrangements by business credit card.

✪ **The need to be able to make reservations or changes to bookings at short notice**: Travel agents making arrangements for businesses must be able to respond quickly to clients' needs, which may change quickly due to unforeseen circumstances such as a cancelled conference or hastily arranged meeting.

✪ **Making bookings out of normal office hours**: In today's global, 24-hour society businesses expect to be able to make their travel arrangements out of normal office hours. Business travel agents are responding by extending their office hours and/or allocating specific members of staff to handle out-of-hours enquiries.

✪ **The particular needs of business travellers**: People travelling on business look for speed, convenience, flexibility and quality when choosing their travel suppliers (see Figure 9.4). Today, there are far more women travelling on business than in the past, meaning that travel companies must strive to meet their particular need for safety and security.

✪ **Type and class of travel and accommodation**: Business people tend to use higher quality accommodation and upgraded travel, particularly when entertaining important clients. However, there is an important sector of the business travel market that uses budget hotel

Figure 9.4 *Air travel is a fast and convenient way to travel long distances*
© Photograph reproduced courtesy of Britannia Airways Limited

accommodation and the new, budget airlines in order to keep travel and accommodation costs to a minimum.

- ✪ **Management information reports**: Large business travel companies, such as Thomas Cook, American Express and Carlson Wagonlit Travel, offer their clients regular management information reports detailing the extent of travel by members of staff and expenditure incurred.

- ✪ **Direct reservations via the Internet**: The dramatic growth in the use of the Internet is beginning to have an impact on the work of business travel agents. The Internet gives business travellers the opportunity of searching for particular travel products and making their own bookings direct with travel companies. However, this can be a very time-consuming process and many companies still prefer to use the services of a business travel agent with their experience and industry knowledge.

The structure, size and economic value of the UK business travel industry

Key topics in this section

- **Suppliers of business travel services**
- **Service requirements in business travel**
- **Economic significance of business travel**
- **Threats to the business travel sector**
- **Types of business travel services**
- **The role of travel industry organisations**

Suppliers of business travel services

There is a wide range of travel agencies that meet the needs of business travel clients, including:

✪ **Business travel agents**: These specialise in serving only business clients, gearing all their operations to this one sector of the travel market. Many are members of the Guild of Business Travel Agents (see page 108) and their staff hold business travel qualifications, such as the Certificate in Business Travel created by the GBTA. Business travel agents vary from single person operations to multinational operations such as American Express Travel.

✪ **Retail travel agents**: Although arranging travel for leisure purposes (holidays, short breaks, flights, etc.) accounts for the bulk of the work of retail travel agents, some may have a business travel specialist or even a business travel department catering exclusively for the needs of corporate clients. These specialist services are offered across the whole range of retail travel types – multiple agencies (e.g. Lunn Poly, Thomas Cook), 'miniples' (small chains in a particular region) and independent agents (predominantly single branch owner-operated agencies).

✪ **Implants**: This is where a travel agency is invited by a business customer to set up a branch within the business premises and organise all the company's travel arrangements. The branch is staffed by travel agency employees who are subcontracted to the business customer. Those working as 'implants' remain the employees of the travel agency, but they work on the premises of the company whose travel they organise.

The levels of business travel services provided by these different suppliers will vary, depending on the nature of business handled in the agency. Business travel agents will devote 100 per cent of their time and resources to business clients whereas a typical high street travel agency will handle a wider range of clients depending on the nature of the surrounding population, e.g. if there is a sizeable business community nearby, the proportion of the agency's work for this sector will be greater.

Browse this website

www.
carlsonwagonlit.
com

Industry example

Carlson Wagonlit Travel is one of the leading business travel and expense management companies in the world. It is owned by the Paris-based Accor Group and Minneapolis-based Carlson Companies Inc. The Accor Group has leading positions in hotels, travel agencies and car rental in 135 countries, representing a yearly sales volume of US$18 billion and employing 124,000 people. Carlson Wagonlit Travel, with executive offices in New York, is a world leader in business travel management, with offices in more than 140 countries and an annual turnover of US$11 billion.

Industry example

Business Travel International (BTI) is one of the world's leading travel management companies operating in nearly 80 countries and with a turnover approaching US$20 billion. It operates more than 3,000 offices throughout Europe, the Americas, Asia-Pacific, the Middle East and Africa, and employs 30,000 staff worldwide. It offers the following services to its business clients:

continued

continued

- ★ Scheduled air reservations
- ★ Executive aircraft and helicopter charter
- ★ Rail tickets and journey planning
- ★ 24-hour reservation service
- ★ Worldwide hotel reservations
- ★ Self-drive and chauffeur-drive car rental
- ★ Car ferry reservations

BTI also offers the following destination management and leisure services:

- ★ Group travel services
- ★ Conference and incentive travel
- ★ Leisure travel services
- ★ Theatre and special event tickets

Browse this website

www.bti-worldwide.com

Service requirements in business travel

You will have heard the saying that, in business, time is money. The business traveller needs to receive a fast and reliable service to meet exacting requirements (see Figure 9.5). For example, a business traveller may need to travel at short notice or undertake complicated travel itineraries taking in several countries. In such a case, the business travel agent will not only be expected to arrange flights and accommodation, but will also be called upon to advise on visa and health requirements, currency, car hire, entertainment options, plus a host of other travel-related details. To meet such exacting requirements, business travel staff have to be very well trained, with access to the latest information and communication technology (ICT).

Figure 9.5 *Eurostar international high-speed passenger trains offer fast and reliable services to the continent from Waterloo International Terminal*
Courtesy of Eurostar Group Ltd

Economic significance of business travel

From the UK perspective business travel can be divided into two categories, as follows:

1   **Outbound business travel** – UK residents making trips abroad on business
2   **Inbound business travel** – overseas tourists visiting the UK on business

Outbound business travel

Table 9.1 shows the contribution that business travel made to all overseas visits by UK residents in 1998. As you can see, business trips accounted for just over 8 million of the total of nearly 51 million visits abroad in 1998. While, at first glance, this may seen a relatively low figure, it is important to remember that business tourism is often high value tourism, yielding higher receipts per head than leisure tourism. This is demonstrated by the fact that, although business travel accounted for just 15 per cent of all trips abroad by UK residents in 1998, it accounted for 21 per cent of all expenditure for the same period.

Region visited	Holidays	Business	VFR	Misc.	Total
North America	2,591	771	690	105	4,157
EU Europe	23,510	5,878	4,129	3,719	37,236
Non-EU Europe	3,058	725	454	78	4,315
Rest of world	3,147	657	1,179	180	5,163
Total world	32,306	8,031	6,452	4,082	50,871

NB: Not all figures total due to rounding
Adapted from ABTA data

Table 9.1 *UK residents' visits abroad (thousands), 1998*

In monetary terms, outbound business travel from the UK in 1998 generated just over £4.1 billion out of a total expenditure of £19.5 billion for all overseas visits by UK residents.

Inbound business travel

The UK is an important destination for business travellers from all over the world, as the data in Table 9.2 demonstrates.

Table 9.2 shows that business tourists accounted for just over 6.8 million of the total of 25.7 million overseas visitors to Britain in 1998. British Tourist Authority (BTA) statistics indicate that overseas tourists on business spent £3.82 billion in 1998 out of a total expenditure of £12.67 billion.

Region of origin	Holidays	Business	VFR	Misc.	Total
North America	2,169	905	1,000	479	4,553
EU Europe	5,815	4,639	3,093	1,665	15,212
Non-EU Europe	544	403	277	205	1,429
Rest of world	1,948	935	1,029	639	4,551
Total world	10,476	6,882	5,399	2,988	25,745

NB: Not all figures total due to rounding
Adapted from BTA data

Table 9.2 *Overseas visitors to the UK (thousands), 1998*

Browse this website

www.culture.gov.uk

Industry example

In its tourism strategy *Tomorrow's Tourism*, the UK government recognises the importance of business travel and tourism and states:

One of the most lucrative, yet least well-acknowledged, components of our tourism industry is business tourism – this embraces meetings, incentive travel, conventions and exhibitions. Business tourists demand high quality standards, yield high receipts and utilise many venues otherwise poorly patronised out of season. Expenditure by business tourists has been growing more quickly than most other kinds of tourism.

Threats to the business travel sector

Travel and tourism is an industry that is constantly changing. New destinations are discovered, hotels are upgraded, new attractions open and airlines introduce new routes. The business travel sector is also in a state of constant change, with new companies being formed, existing companies merging, and new products and services being introduced. The introduction of new technology offers the business travel sector a range of new opportunities, but may also pose certain threats. Direct bookings via the Internet will undoubtedly increase, with smaller companies, individuals and even large corporations handling their own travel arrangements in the future. Business travel agents will need to adapt to this type of change, by developing new Internet-based services of their own and offering support/ advisory services to their existing clients.

Types of business travel services

The business travel sector uses a wide variety of travel products, services and facilities to meet client needs, including:

✪ **Transportation**
✪ **Accommodation**

- ✪ **Conference facilities (see Figure 9.6)**
- ✪ **Stopover packages**
- ✪ **Entertainment**
- ✪ **Car hire**
- ✪ **Ancillary services, e.g. travel insurance, visas, health regulations, foreign currency, travellers' cheques and cultural advice**

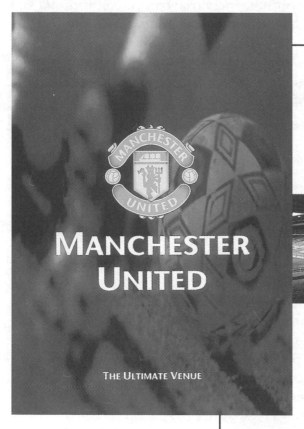

As a football club, Manchester United needs no introductions. Through its successes at home and abroad, it has secured its position as one of the world's most famous football clubs. Yet success is not just confined to the pitch. Within the heart of the magnificent Old Trafford stadium there is an impressive complex of function suites of varying sizes available for business and social use alike.

The ultimate venue for every important event - from a major product launch or sales conference, a corporate dinner dance or an intimate dinner party - we offer nothing less than the ultimate in versatility and flexibility. With 10 different suites of varying sizes, Manchester United offers a truly unique venue, certain to lend extra prestige and excitement to your event.

THERE'S ONLY ONE MANCHESTER UNITED

The facilities at Manchester United have been designed for every type of event for national and international clients alike. From the small syndicate-style meetings with views of the pitch, to a prestigious new car launch in the drive in/drive out presentation suite, every type of function can be catered for.

The complex also contains one of Europe's largest purpose built facilities - the 12,000 sq. ft Manchester Suite - which allows it to compete as a prime events location.

Attention to detail is key to our service with every event held at Manchester United being given the personal touch. Our experienced Events and Banqueting Managers will discuss your particular requirements in-depth to ensure that your event goes smoothly.

And whether it's a prestigious conference or celebratory dinner dance, our brigade of in-house international chefs are able to produce a menu to suit your requirements. On match days alone, they create and serve in excess of 4,000 freshly prepared imaginative meals.

One special extra when staging an event at Old Trafford is that it can be arranged for your itinerary to include a tour of the stadium and a visit to the new Manchester United Museum, organised to coincide with your events schedule. All this, plus free security patrolled parking for over 1,000 vehicles and an easy to find location.

For less formal dining, Red Cafe, the unique Manchester United - themed video restaurant.

Old Trafford is just minutes away from Manchester's city centre and is even handier for the motorway network. So as well as offering easy access from all parts of the country, we're close to all the best hotels and city centre amenities.

Conference & Catering

in the heart of United

Available throughout the year, weekdays and weekends, daytimes and evenings,
MANCHESTER UNITED IS THE ULTIMATE VENUE FOR ALL BUSINESS AND SOCIAL OCCASIONS.

Figure 9.6 *Details of Manchester United's conference facilities*
Trademarks and text used with permission of Manchester United

Activity 9.2

Working with a partner, make a list of all the travel services that a UK business traveller is likely to need in preparing for and attending a one-week sales convention in Shanghai.

The role of travel industry organisations

International Air Transport Association (IATA)

Browse this website

www.iata.org

The International Air Transport Association (IATA) is an international trade body representing the interests of more than 80 per cent of the world's major airlines. Its principal aim is to promote safe, regular and economic air travel. Business and leisure travel agents in the UK, in common with agents worldwide, can apply for an IATA licence to sell airline tickets and other services of IATA member airlines. Since these airlines pay commission only to approved IATA sales agents, an IATA licence is a much sought after commodity. Applying for an IATA licence has similarities to an application for ABTA membership, in that the applicant has to meet certain minimum criteria and will be subject to an inspection and interview by an IATA representative. The criteria for approval are concerned with a number of factors, including:

✪ **Nature of the premises**: The agency must be open for business on a regular basis and clearly identified as a travel agency.

✪ **Security of premises**: Premises must be adequately protected and a safe installed for the storage of airline tickets and other valuables.

✪ **Staff qualifications**: Staff selling the IATA tickets and services must be permanent employees and have relevant experience and qualifications, e.g. British Airways Fares and Ticketing Courses.

✪ **Finances**: Applicants must submit a full set of audited accounts for scrutiny by IATA personnel and meet certain minimum share capital/capital account amounts. Additionally, approved agents are required to submit a copy of their annual report and accounts within six months of the financial year end.

✪ **Bonding**: A bank or insurance company bond will be required, based on a percentage of annual turnover.

On payment of a non-refundable application fee and an entry fee, the successful applicant will be granted an IATA licence to sell airline tickets and the services of IATA member airlines.

Activity 9.3

Try to find out which travel agencies in your locality have an IATA licence. What do the non-IATA agents do when a client wishes to buy an airline ticket?

Association of British Travel Agents (ABTA)

Browse this website

www.abtanet.com

ABTA is the trade body representing over 90 per cent of travel agents and tour operators in the UK, including the majority of business travel agents. Unit 8 *Travel agency operations* has a case study on ABTA's aims and the work it undertakes on behalf of its members.

Guild of Business Travel Agents (GBTA)

Browse this website

www.gbta-guild.com

The GBTA was founded in 1967 when six travel agents sought special attention and better recognition for the needs of business travel agents. From its small beginnings, the GBTA has progressively built up its influence in the business travel sector to the point where it is regularly called upon to advise in every sphere of travel – technical, commercial and political. The stated mission of the Guild is:

> *To be a committed and respected organisation representing the interests and requirements of the business travel market. To be recognised as delivering the best standard of service, quality and value to the business traveller.*

The GBTA is a membership organisation, by invitation only, comprising 37 of the UK's leading business travel agents, including the Portman Travel Group, P&O Travel Ltd, Going Places, Carlson Wagonlit Travel and Ian Allan Travel.

It is the broad sphere of agency membership that enables the GBTA collectively to dominate the business travel market, with some 80 per cent share of UK agents' air travel bookings. The combined turnover of Guild members has risen throughout the 1990s, from £3.5 billion in 1992, £4.34 billion in 1995 to £7.64 billion in 1998. Member agencies employ around 15,000 staff in their businesses.

The Guild of European Business Travel Agents (GEBTA) was formed in January 1990 at the instigation of the GBTA in Britain. There are now 11 national guilds with over 300 members in Austria, Belgium, Denmark, Germany, France, Ireland, Italy, The Netherlands, Portugal, Spain and the United Kingdom.

Planning a business travel itinerary

Key topics in this section

- **Introduction**
- **Using manual information sources**
- **Using computer-based information sources**
- **Planning a business travel itinerary**

Introduction

Business travel agents need to be able to access and process a vast amount of information in order to plan itineraries. As with any sector of the travel and tourism industry, business travel agents are not expected to know the answer to every query immediately, but they must know where to look to get hold of relevant information for their clients. Relevant information is contained in manual and computer-based systems, which offer a wide range of information, including:

- ✪ **General guidance for international travellers**
- ✪ **Details of scheduled air services**
- ✪ **Information on cruise and ferry travel**
- ✪ **Details of all types of hotel accommodation**

Manual information sources

Trade manuals provide business travel staff with general destination information, hotel accommodation and travel requirements. Some of the most common in use in agencies are:

- ✪ *OAG Guide to International Travel*
- ✪ *Official Hotel Guide (OHG) – formerly Official Hotel and Resort Guide (OHRG)*
- ✪ *Travel Trade Directory*
- ✪ *World Travel Guide* and *World Travel Atlas*
- ✪ *Hotel and Travel Index*
- ✪ *Agents Hotel Gazetteer*
- ✪ *OAG directories and gazetteers*

Access to timetables is very useful for staff putting together itineraries for business clients and can save the time of contacting a number of individual carriers. A basic set of timetables in any business travel agency should include:

- ✪ *Thomas Cook European Rail Timetable*
- ✪ *Thomas Cook Overseas Timetable*
- ✪ *UK National Rail Timetable*
- ✪ *OAG Flight Guide*
- ✪ **Individual airline timetables**

Browse this website

www.oag.com

Industry example

OAG is one of the world's leading suppliers of travel information products and services, offering business travellers, corporations and the global travel industry the information necessary to make effective travel planning decisions. Best known for its flight guides (OAG stands for overseas airways guides), OAG offers travel information for use in the office and on the road. Customers can access the information through a variety of media, ranging from printed guides to wireless mobile applications, or through a customised travel information system for use on a company's intranet or LAN (local area network). OAG's information databases are the core of its business and are the basis for all its publishing activities. OAG also supplies airline data to the world's global distribution systems (GDS) used by travel agents, corporations and airlines throughout the world.

In addition to its publishing activities, OAG offers travel training courses to travel agents, corporations and students, covering such items as travel planning, making reservations and understanding air tickets.

Computer-based information sources

Increasingly, information needed by business travel agents is available on computer-based systems, offering speed, convenience and reliability. The main electronic sources of information for business travel specialists are the global

Browse these websites

www.galileo.com

www.sabre.com

www.worldspan.
com

distribution systems (GDS) developed by the world's airlines, for example Galileo, Sabre and Worldspan. In addition to airline information, these systems offer a bewildering range of travel-related information, from destination data and passport requirements to theatre tickets and car hire.

The Internet is developing rapidly as an excellent tool for business travel agents, offering similar features to the GDS systems, including accommodation, destination and travel services, plus on-line reservations.

Other information sources

The National Tourist Offices (NTOs) of overseas destinations are happy to provide travel agents with country information in the form of brochures, maps, posters and videos. The UK tourist boards too are keen to promote the sale of British holidays through travel agents and produce an annual *UK Handbook of Commissionable Holidays*. The travel industry press, including *Travel Trade Gazette*, *Travel Weekly* and *Travel Agency*, also has valuable information for business travel agents.

Planning a business travel itinerary

The remainder of this unit will give you experience in planning an itinerary for a business traveller. In planning the itinerary, you will need to consider a range of factors, including:

- **Types of transport**
- **Details of the carrier(s)**
- **Fare type(s)**
- **Departure and destination points**
- **Dates and timings of travel**
- **Joining instructions**
- **Baggage allowances**
- **Route transfers**
- **Stopovers**
- **Accommodation**
- **All relevant documentation**

Activity 9.4

Mr Black, a sales manager from Kent, is embarking on a 10-night sales trip to Switzerland and France. You are to plan an itinerary for Mr Black based on the following requirements:

1   Depart London a.m. on Wednesday 6 March 2002

2   Travel by air to Geneva (business class)

3   Spend 2 nights in hotel accommodation in Geneva

4   Pick up a hire car (medium size with air conditioning) from Geneva on 8 March and drive to Lausanne, where he will spend three nights in hotel accommodation (retaining the hire car for the rest of the trip)

5   Drive to Lyon, where he will spend four nights in hotel accommodation

6   Drive to Bordeaux, where he will spend one night in hotel accommodation (drop off hire car at the hotel in Bordeaux)

7   Return by air to London p.m. on Saturday 16 March 2002 (business class)

Your itinerary should include all timings and a breakdown of all costs. Mr Black's budget for accommodation is approximately £50 per night.

Tour operations

10

Tour operators play an important role in the travel and tourism industry. They assemble the holidays that are such an important feature of life in the twenty-first century, by working with airlines, hoteliers, car hire companies and a variety of other travel service providers. This unit introduces you to the business of tour operations, starting with an overview of the sector and a review of the growth of the 'package holiday' in the UK. You will also learn about the legal and financial side of tour operating and the different functions carried out by tour operating companies. In the final part of the unit you will investigate the UK and overseas operations of a typical holiday company. The unit will help you to identify the skills, knowledge and experience needed to work in tour operations.

This unit is divided into five main areas:

- **An overview of UK tour operations**
- **The package holiday**
- **Travel legislation, trade body membership, licensing and bonding**
- **The functions of tour operating**
- **UK and overseas operations**

We guide you through each of these areas using examples and case studies from the travel and tourism industry. At the beginning of each of these sections you will see a list of key topics to help you fully understand what you need to learn. Look out for the links to websites so that you can learn more about a particular travel and tourism company, organisation or topic.

An overview of UK tour operations

Key topics in this section

- **Links with other organisations**
- **Horizontal and vertical integration**
- **Categories of tour operators**

Links with other organisations

Unlike travel agents, who sell holidays and a range of other travel products, tour operators actually assemble the component parts of a holiday, i.e. the means of travel, accommodation, facilities, transfers, excursions and other services. If we consider that travel agents are the retail arm of the travel business, then tour operators can be likened to wholesalers, since they buy in 'bulk' from the providers of travel services, such as the hoteliers and airlines, break the bulk into manageable packages and offer the finished product, the package holiday (or inclusive tour), for sale via a travel agent or direct to the consumer. The package is sold for an all-inclusive price, which is generally lower than if the component parts of the holiday had been booked individually by the holidaymaker. Figure 10.1 shows the role of tour operators and their position as intermediaries between the suppliers of travel products and travel agents.

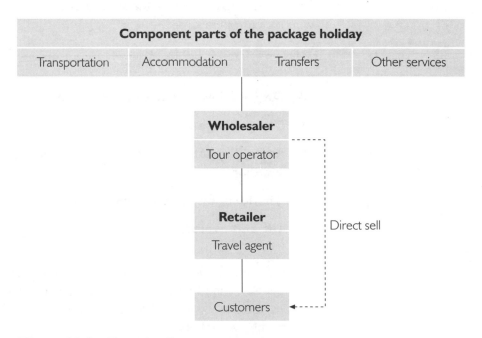

Figure 10.1   *The role of tour operators*

Figure 10.1 also shows that some tour operators deal direct with their customers rather than selling through travel agents. In the case of foreign package holidays booked by British people, 75 per cent of customers use the services of a travel agent rather than booking direct with the operator. There are, however, a number of high volume 'direct sell' operators, such as Portland Holidays and Eclipse, plus many smaller, specialist tour operators who prefer to deal directly with their clients, advertising their holidays through newspapers and other media. Direct sell operators stress that, since they do not have to pay a commission to a travel agent, they are able to pass this saving on to the client who should benefit with a cheaper holiday. The more specialist the product on offer, the more likely it is that the customer will deal direct with the operator, for example skiing holidays and mountain exploration tours.

Horizontal and vertical integration

As competition in the outbound travel industry has intensified, tour operators have sought alliances and mergers with other travel and tourism businesses as a way of maintaining or increasing their market share and maximising profitability. This is most noticeable in the tour operator/travel agent relationship, where:

- ✪ **Thomson owns the Lunn Poly travel agency chain**
- ✪ **Airtours owns Going Places travel agencies**
- ✪ **First Choice Holidays owns Travelchoice agencies**
- ✪ **JMC Holidays is part of the Thomas Cook Group**

Browse these websites

www.airtours.co.uk

www.thomson-holidays.co.uk

www.thomascook.com

www.firstchoice.co.uk

These are all examples of vertical integration in the travel industry, when a company has control over other companies that are at different levels in the chain of distribution. Some of the largest tour operators also own their own airlines, giving even greater control over the component parts of package holidays, e.g. Airtours plc owns Airtours International (see Figure 10.2).

The structure of the travel business is further complicated since the large tour operators trade under different holiday brands, with products aimed at different types of customers (see Table 10.1).

Table 10.1 shows the complex structure of the four biggest UK tour operators, Thomson Holidays Ltd, Airtours, Thomas Cook and First Choice, each with its own range of holiday brands, travel agencies and airlines.

Horizontal integration occurs when companies at the same level in the distribution chain, or in the same industry sector, merge voluntarily or are the subject of a takeover bid. In the airline sector, for example, British Airways is seeking to achieve its ambition of becoming the world's biggest airline by

Figure 10.2 *Vertical integration in the travel and tourism industry*

mergers and take-overs with other operators, including American Airlines, Qantas and TAT, a French domestic airline. It also took over the former British charter airline Dan Air and has interests in Germany with Deutsche BA. Horizontal integration is also common in the hotels sector, where companies such as Forte and Bass achieve economies of scale by controlling the operation and marketing of large numbers of individual hotels, for example:

❂ **Forte Hotel Group has the following hotel 'brands' under its control – Le Meridien, Posthouse, Heritage Hotels and Travelodge**

❂ **Marriott Lodging operates the following – Marriott Hotels, Resorts and Suites, Ritz-Carlton, Renaissance Hotels, Resorts and Suites, Ramada International Hotels and Resorts, Residence Inn by Marriott and Marriott Vacation Club**

❂ **Starwood Hotels and Resorts has the following 'brands' – Sheraton Hotels and Resorts, Westin Hotels and Resorts, Four Points and St Regis Luxury Collection**

❂ **Bass Hotels and Resorts operates the following – Inter-Continental Hotels and Resorts, Crowne Plaza Hotels and Resorts, Holiday Inn, Express by Holiday Inn, Forum and Holiday Inn Garden Court**

Thomson Travel's acquisition of Country Holidays in 1994, and their takeover of Blakes Country Cottages and English Country Cottages in 1995, is evidence that the major tour operators are actively engaged in both horizontal and vertical integration within the travel and tourism industry, as a way of securing competitive advantage.

There is growing concern among consumer groups and the public generally that the concentration of ownership through vertical and horizontal integration

Table 10.1 Structure of the 'big four' tour operators

	Thomson Holidays Ltd	Airtours	Thomas Cook	First Choice
Tour operations	Thomson Holidays Portland Direct Budget Travel (Ireland) Skytours Freestyle Thomson Breakaway Crystal Travel Ausbound Austravel Jetsave Jersey Travel Service Tropical Places Greyhound International American Holidays Thomson Independent Holidays Group Holiday Cottages Group Something Special Holidays Spanish Harbour Holidays Chez Nous Blakes Holidays Boating Magic Travel Group Simply Travel Headwater Holidays	Airtours Holidays Panorama Bridge Travel Cresta Eurcsites Tradewinds Jetset Vacation Canada Freedom Breaks Jetset Flights Airline Consolidation Centre Direct Holidays Escapades	JMC Holidays Thomas Cook Holidays Neilson Club 18–30 Time Off Style Holidays Cachet Travel Skiers World	First Choice Holidays Eclipse 2wenties Sovereign First Choice Ski, Lakes & Mountains Unijet Viking Aviation Hayes & Jarvis Meon Travel Suncars Rainbow Holidays Sunsail Globesavers Falcon (Ireland) JWT (Ireland) Flexiski
Travel agencies	Lunn Poly Callers-Pegasus Sibbald Travel Travel House Team Lincoln Manchester Flights Budget Travel Thomson Preferred Agents	Going Places Travelworld Advantage Travel Centres Late Escapes Go Direct Space Flightdeck	Thomas Cook ARTAC Worldchoice Thomas Cook Direct Orchid Travel	Travelchoice Travelchoice Express Travelchoice Direct Bakers Dolphin Holiday Hypermarkets Hays Travel Holiday Express
Airlines	Britannia Airways	Airtours International	JMC Airlines	Air 2000

is against the public interest, since it may limit choice and reduce competition in the industry. For example, it would not be surprising for Lunn Poly travel agencies to favour selling Thomson holidays since they are part of the same group. It is for this reason that any large-scale merger between travel and tourism companies is often referred to the Competition Commission (formerly the Monopolies and Mergers Commission) and sometimes the European Commission for investigation. Also, from October 2000, new government legislation in the UK made it compulsory for travel agencies and tour operators to display their links to the public, as the following industry example explains.

Browse this website

www.competition-commission.org.uk

Industry example

Companies must comply with the following rules from 9 October 2000:

★ Agents must display a prominent notice in the front window of each shop outlining its ownership links.

★ A notice must be displayed on the front cover of every in-house brochure explaining its links with the agency.

★ The name of every operator that is part of the same group must be listed inside the shop.

★ All company stationery must outline ownership links of the agent.

★ All joint advertisements between a tour operator and an in-house agent must spell out the link between the two. This includes Teletext pages that direct customers to book through a sister company, e.g. a Thomson-owned site that refers people to Lunn Poly Direct must explain the connection.

Categories of tour operators

There are approximately 600 UK tour operators, most of which are small companies specialising in a particular destination or type of product, e.g. family holidays, activity holidays, cruising and special interest. Most operators fall into one of the following four categories:

Figure 10.3 *The wide range of tour operators' products*

- ✪ **Mass market operators**
- ✪ **Specialist operators**
- ✪ **Domestic operators**
- ✪ **Incoming tour operators**

Figure 10.3 gives an indication of the wide variety of products offered by the various categories of tour operators.

The principal product of the mass market operators, such as Thomson, Airtours, First Choice Holidays and JMC, is the package holiday, which combines accommodation, transportation and other services for an all-inclusive price. Figure 10.3 shows us that these can be classified according to the destination chosen (long haul or short haul) and/or the season of travel (summer or winter). Seat-only sales have become a major growth area for mass market tour operators, as more travellers choose to put together their own foreign holidays or take advantage of cheap flights to visit friends and relatives abroad. Specialist operators focus on specific market niches by providing products based on particular themes, destinations or activities, e.g. Eurocamp specialises in self-drive camping holidays in Europe, Saga provides holidays for older travellers and the Paris Travel Service specialises in holidays to the French capital. Domestic tour operators provide a range of products using a variety of accommodation and transportation arrangements, e.g. coach tours, short breaks in city centre hotels, boating holidays on England's waterways and farm holidays. Incoming tour operators specialise in products for overseas visitors to the UK, such as coach tours of England, Scotland, Northern Ireland and Wales, often based on themes, such as castles, historic houses, gardens and industrial heritage.

Mass market operators

These tour operators include some of the best-known names in the travel industry, such as Thomson, Airtours, Thomas Cook and First Choice

Holidays. They organise package holidays (also known as air-inclusive tours) for around 11 million British people each year, thereby dominating the UK outbound tourism market.

At present, four companies together share 56 per cent of the total package holiday market, according to Civil Aviation Authority (CAA) statistics:

Thomson	18 per cent
Airtours	15 per cent
Thomas Cook	13 per cent
First Choice Holidays	10 per cent

As the figures show, Thomson is the market leader in the UK outbound tour operating market, followed by Airtours, Thomas Cook, which operates a number of brands including JMC and Club 18–30, and First Choice Holidays. Table 10.1 demonstrated that the 'big four' tour operators have complex linkages to travel agencies and airlines through vertical integration.

Industry example

Airtours plc is the largest provider of air-inclusive holidays in the world. Airtours and its associated companies carry passengers from 17 countries, with:

★ 1613 travel agency outlets

★ 17 telesales centres

★ 42 aircraft

★ 40+ principal tour operating brands

★ 46 resort properties

★ 10 cruise ships

★ 2 vacation ownership resorts

Airtours employs over 20,000 people worldwide.

Browse this website

www.airtours.co.uk

Activity 10.1

How do you think that the 'products' offered by mass market tour operators might change in the next 10 years? How is the role of the travel agent likely to change over the same time period?

Specialist operators

Although less well-known than the mass market operators, there are literally hundreds of specialist operators in the travel industry, including:

- ✪ **Those that offer holidays and other travel arrangements to a particular geographical region or destination, e.g. Paris Travel Service and Magic of Italy**

- ✪ **Those that cater for a particular segment of the market, e.g. PGL Adventure Holidays for young children and Saga Holidays who specialise in the 'senior' market**

- ✪ **Those that specialise in a particular type of activity, e.g. walking holidays offered by the Ramblers' Association and Susie Madron's 'Cycling for Softies', which offers all-inclusive packages to France**

- ✪ **Those that cater for the special interests of their clients, e.g. wine tasting holidays in the Loire and art history tours to Italy**

- ✪ **Those that specialise in sporting holidays and breaks, e.g. Roger Taylor's tennis holidays in the Algarve and tours to see the motor racing Grand Prix around the world**

- ✪ **Those that use a specific type of accommodation or form of transport, e.g. Eurosites, part of the Airtours Group, which organises self-drive camping holidays on the continent, and operators that offer nostalgic tours on steam railways**

Figure 10.4 *Many specialist tour operators offer ski packages*
Courtesy of First Choice Holidays

A glance at the *Travel Trade Directory* will show that the range of specialist operators is vast, indicating that the travel industry is not afraid to rise to the challenge of meeting the needs of many different types of customers.

Activity
10.2

Select a small number of activities and special interests, and carry out some research to discover if there are any UK tour operators that sell programmes in your chosen areas.

Domestic operators

Although, in general, the British tourism product has not been extensively 'packaged', there are a number of UK operators that put together inclusive tours for the home market. Probably the best-known are coach operators, such as Shearings and National Holidays, which offer value-for-money products geared mainly to the older age groups.

The packaging and marketing of UK short breaks has been something of a success story in recent years. Companies such as Superbreak and Rainbow Holidays have led the development of city and country breaks offered for sale through travel agencies. Some local authorities, keen to boost their visitor numbers, have worked with tour operators to feature their particular destinations in brochures and tour programmes.

Special interest groups are well catered for by domestic operators. Activity holidays are growing in popularity, and operators, large and small, are emerging to cater for the demand, e.g. YHA Holidays and HF Holidays. Companies offering specialist services and facilities, ranging from sketching holidays to ballooning breaks, are being increasingly sought by a public looking for something unusual to do in its leisure time.

Hotel groups and marketing consortia (for example, Best Western Hotels) have created and marketed domestic tours for some time, often in conjunction with coach companies. The competitive situation that has arisen in the hotels sector in recent years, however, has forced some hotel groups to widen their customer base, by developing themed breaks and activity and special interest tours.

Case Study
Hoseasons Holidays

► INTRODUCTION

Hoseasons Holidays is the leading independent holiday booking agency in the UK, with its headquarters in Lowestoft, Suffolk. Although its name is most often associated in the public's mind with boats, two-thirds of its clients actually book holiday homes. All Hoseasons' holidays are self-catering, with the company's boating clients booking self-drive, live-aboard cabin motor cruisers or yachts, while the remaining customers opt for a self-catering holiday in a range of accommodation, from modern chalets, caravans and bungalows, to detached country cottages and Scandinavian-style lodges. Hoseasons staff book around 200,000 holiday-weeks each year; with an average party size of 4.8 persons, this gives a grand total of 925,000 clients per year. The company claims that it is responsible for arranging one in 22 of all paid-for holidays taken in Britain each year.

► COMPANY MISSION AND ETHOS

The company's mission statement is as follows:

Hoseasons Holidays continually aims to be the UK's leading company profitably selling quality self-catering holidays in Western Europe and setting the highest standards of customer service.

We will develop complementary businesses by using our established skills and resources.

We will continue to provide an environment in which staff are encouraged to play a full part in the development of the business and to share in its profitability.

For more than 25 years, Hoseasons has been run on a formal management by objectives (MBO) regime, with impressive results. The company's commitment to its staff and their personal and professional development resulted in it becoming one of the first organisations in the UK to be awarded the 'Investor in People' standard in 1991.

► COMPANY HISTORY

Hoseasons Holidays was founded in 1944 by Wally Hoseason, the father of the present Chairman, James Hoseason OBE. When the business began it was a

continued

continued

combination of a booking agency for boating holidays and a sales agency for boats. In 1945 the agency booked 200 people for a boating holiday on the Norfolk Broads and, from that point on, the business grew and grew.

In the late 1960s, the purpose and style of the business was totally overhauled to keep in line with the social and demographic changes taking place in the UK, not least the dramatic rise in car ownership. In the 1970s, the whole basis of the business was broadened, when the company focused on booking boat holidays nationwide on all the waterways in Britain and booking holiday homes throughout England, Scotland and Wales. During the 1980s, the range of destinations grew to include holiday boats in France and Holland, and holiday homes in France, Belgium, Holland, Germany, Italy and Spain.

► STAFFING THE ORGANISATION

Hoseasons employs just over 90 full-time, permanent staff and around 130 part-time staff who work all the year round. There are also seasonal part-timers who work during the main booking campaign, working either in the mail room, brochure despatch area, the dial-a-brochure operation or in Hoseasons Marketing Systems, an associated business unit of the main company specialising in bureau services as diverse as direct mail and credit card control. The company's organisational structure is shown in Figure 10.5.

► DEPARTMENTAL STRUCTURE

★ *Booking services*: This is the hub of the operation, with specially trained teams of sales staff using the latest computer technology. The department is divided into the two core product areas, namely holiday homes, with more than 60 members of staff, and holiday boats, with four section leaders controlling the work of 14 sales staff.

★ *Marketing*: The company's marketing team designs and produces the company's brochures, as well as controlling the £9.5 million national advertising and promotional campaign. They also handle the arrangements for exhibition stands and are responsible for liaison with the media and PR companies.

★ *Finance and accounts*: Staff in this department pay the wages and ensure that suppliers and principals are paid on time. They also administer the company's insurance and pension schemes. In addition, they prepare

continued

continued

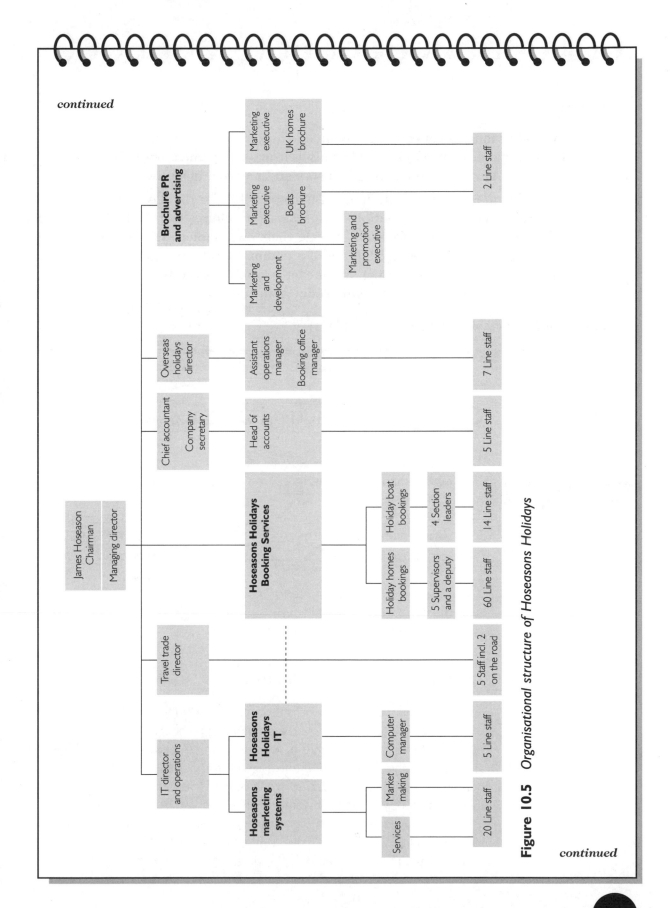

Figure 10.5 *Organisational structure of Hoseasons Holidays*

continued

continued

monthly management accounts, annual statutory accounts, and budgets, forecasts and financial plans. They also ensure compliance with all current regulations concerning VAT, tax and national insurance.

★ *Travel trade*: The travel trade team is responsible for the day-to-day management of the distribution of Hoseasons brochures to travel agents nationwide. They also plan and manage their own annual trade marketing campaign, involving the production of a comprehensive marketing information folder, advertising and media relations in the travel trade press, joint sales promotions and agency staff training.

(Information courtesy of Hoseasons Holidays)

Case study discussion questions

Browse this website

www.hoseasons.
co.uk

1   How does Hoseasons Holidays organise and carry out its marketing function?

2   What are the company's two core products?

3   What techniques does it use to maintain loyalty within its travel trade partners?

4   Who are its main competitors?

5   What internal and external factors are likely to affect the company's performance over the next 10 years?

Incoming tour operators

Incoming, or inbound, UK tourism is concerned with meeting the needs of the increasing numbers of overseas visitors who choose to visit Britain; outbound tourism, on the other hand, deals with UK people taking holidays abroad. Just as we would visit a travel agency to book our annual overseas holiday or business trip abroad, so many overseas visitors do the same in their own country when they want to come to Britain. A travel agent in the USA, for example, who has a client wanting to spend a week in Scotland, has to contact a tour operator to make all the arrangements. This operator, who may be based in the USA or in Scotland, is known as an incoming tour operator, since it is providing a service for overseas visitors to Britain.

There are around 300 incoming tour operators in this country that specialise in dealing with the incoming market. Some are little more than handling agents offering a transfer or 'meet and greet' service on behalf of an agent or operator. Others, such as British Heritage Tours, Frames Rickards and Evan Evans Tours, offer complete package tours of the UK, which are sold through overseas agents. The packages are often themed, including tours based on British heritage, gardens or castles. Approximately 100 incoming tour operators in the UK are members of BITOA (the British Incoming Tour Operators' Association). Founded in 1977, BITOA is an independent organisation that aims to provide a forum for the exchange of information and ideas, to follow an accepted code of conduct and to act as a pressure group in dealing with other bodies in the UK with a common interest in tourism matters.

The package holiday

Key topics in this section

- **Introduction – what is a 'package holiday'?**
- **Growth of package holidays**
- **Elements of a package holiday**

Introduction – what is a 'package holiday'?

At its simplest, a package holiday is one that includes transport to a destination, accommodation, transfer arrangements and the services of a representative for an all-in price. Vladimir Raitz of Horizon Holidays is credited with having organised the first modern package holiday from the UK, when he carried a party of holidaymakers to Corsica in 1950. This first modern inclusive tour included full-board accommodation in tents and travel in a 32-seater DC3 aircraft; things have moved on a lot since those days! Not that package holidays were totally new in the 1950s. The pioneering work of Thomas Cook, who in 1841 organised an excursion from Leicester to Loughborough for his local Temperance Association, was an early indication of things to come. Within 15 years of this first excursion, Cook was running a fully commercial travel company arranging tours and excursions both at home and overseas, including the Great Exhibition in London in 1851 and inclusive tours to the Paris Exhibition in 1855. In 1872, Thomas Cook offered a round the world trip, including stopovers at India, Singapore and Hong Kong, and using a variety of travel methods, including paddle steamer, steamship across the Atlantic, stagecoach and rail. His son, John Cook, took over the business in 1879 and, with his three grandsons, carried on the business into the twentieth century.

Growth of package holidays

The ending of the Second World War heralded the beginning of a positive climate in the UK for the development of travel for leisure purposes in general and package holidays in particular. A number of factors contributed to this situation, including:

- **Increased prosperity once the war had ended**
- **Greater exposure to mass media, including television, creating a desire to travel**

- ✪ **Increased paid holiday entitlements for workers**
- ✪ **Better standards of education**
- ✪ **The end of rationing in 1954**

These factors, coupled with technological improvements in aircraft design and spare aircraft capacity, led to a surge in demand for overseas travel. Much of this demand could not be met initially, resulting in the growth of holidays and day trips in the UK, where holiday camps and seaside resorts prospered. The introduction of the Boeing 707 jet aircraft in 1958, however, led to a surge in scheduled and charter flights, the latter being combined with accommodation and other travel services to form the package holiday that is so familiar to us all today.

From the first modern inclusive tour to Corsica in 1950, the demand for package holidays grew steadily in the 1960s. By 1965, there were more than one million air-inclusive tours (AITs) from the UK to European destinations and this number had risen to more than 3 million at the beginning of the 1970s. There were, however, some casualties resulting from the growth. Fiesta Tours was declared bankrupt in 1964, leaving its clients stranded in Spain, and Omar Khayyam Tours went bust in 1965. In response to the growing problem of company failures brought on by fierce price cutting, a group of the leading tour operators established the Tour Operators' Study Group (TOSG) in 1967 to protect members' interests and discuss matters of common concern. In 1970, the members of the TOSG decided that bonding should be introduced to offer holidaymakers a degree of protection when an operator collapsed (see page 141 for more on tour operator bonding).

The most significant event of the 1970s in the tour operating industry was the collapse of Court Line in 1974, taking the Clarkson and Horizon brands with it. The fact that the number one tour operator of the time had gone into liquidation sent shock waves through the industry and the travelling public alike. The collapse was an early, and stern, test of the bonding system that had recently been put in place. Notwithstanding these company failures, demand for package holidays grew steadily in the 1980s and has continued into the 1990s (see Figure 10.6). The failure of the International Leisure Group (ILG) in 1991, best known for its Intasun tour operating division, was a further stark reminder of the fragility of the ex-UK tour operating industry.

Activity 10.3

Carry out some further research into the reasons for the rapid growth in the number of package holidays taken by British people since the 1980s.

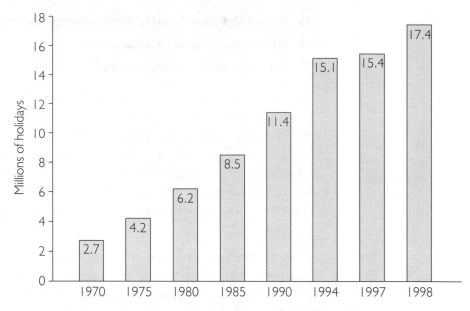

Figure 10.6 *Overseas package holidays taken by UK residents*
Adapted from ABTA data

Elements of a package holiday

The providers of package holidays assemble their constituent components into a saleable product that meets the needs and expectations of the customer. All package holidays will differ in their make-up, but we can identify three distinct components:

- ✪ **Accommodation**
- ✪ **Transportation**
- ✪ **Other travel services, e.g. car hire, transfers and the services of a representative**

Each of these elements will be considered in the following sections.

Accommodation

The accommodation component of the tour operators' package can be either serviced or self-catering. There has been a steady growth in the demand for self-catering holidays in recent years. Serviced accommodation is usually in a hotel that can offer a range of meal arrangements, including:

- ✪ **Full board (sometimes called American Plan), which means that three meals are provided**
- ✪ **Half board (or modified American Plan), which on overseas package holidays usually refers to breakfast plus either a midday or evening meal**
- ✪ **Bed and breakfast (sometimes called Continental Plan)**

An arrangement that is proving popular at the moment is the 'all inclusive' package holiday, where the cost includes drinks, food, sports facilities and entertainment. Hotels in some parts of the world do not include any meals in their standard room rates, an arrangement sometimes known as European Plan. This is common in certain parts of Europe, the USA and the Far East. Customers can usually request a room with extra facilities or a particular aspect for the payment of a supplementary charge, e.g. a room with a sea view or a ground floor room.

Self-catering can be in a wide range of accommodation, such as:

- **Studios**
- **Villas**
- **Apartments**
- **Tents**
- **Caravans/mobile homes**
- **Boats**

Self-catering accommodation will usually come complete with cooking facilities and utensils, although many people often choose to eat out and avoid household chores. Some self-catering accommodation will include a maid service, either included in the price or on payment of a supplement.

Transportation

The transport element of a package holiday can be travel by:

- **Air**
- **Coach**
- **Rail**
- **Ship**
- **Self-drive car**

Whichever type of transport is used, the tour operator will be offered preferential, discounted rates, known as inclusive tour (IT) rates. Depending on the volume of business generated, a ferry company, for example, can offer a tour operator prices that may be discounted by as much as 50 per cent of their standard tariff. It is increasingly common for tour operators to offer their clients free or discounted travel on public transport within the UK to their departure point.

Three-quarters of all package holidays sold in the UK use air travel to transport clients to their chosen destinations (see Figure 10.7). These air-inclusive tours (AITs) use either chartered or scheduled services; package holidays that use seats on charter aircraft are known as inclusive tours by

Figure 10.7 *Holidaymakers being greeted at airport check-in*
Courtesy of First Choice Holidays

charter (ITC), while those based on scheduled services are referred to as inclusive tours by excursion (ITX). Aircraft may be chartered for specific flights or for blocks of time, usually a whole year or for the duration of a season. This is known as time series charter and is financially more attractive than 'ad hoc' arrangements. Many tour operators will charter their aircraft on a flight series basis, contracting for the same time and destination each week, for example. By using flight series charters and setting very high load factors for each flight (the percentage of seats that needs to be filled before the operator starts to make a profit), tour operators have been able to keep prices down and stimulate demand. It is not uncommon for an operator to set a break-even load factor as high as 85–90 per cent.

One disadvantage of flight series charters is that there will inevitably be an empty flight home at the beginning of the season and an empty flight out at the end of the season. These flights are referred to as 'empty legs'. In order to maximise capacity, some travel companies will operate a 'bus stop' arrangement, whereby an aircraft will take off from one UK airport, say Manchester, but stop at another, perhaps East Midlands, to pick up passengers, before flying on to its final destination airport. If bookings from one particular regional airport are low, the tour operator may decide to consolidate, i.e. cancel the flight altogether and transfer the passengers by coach to another departure airport.

Other travel services

Apart from accommodation and transport, package holidays will usually include other services, which may include:

- **Transfers to and from accommodation and point of entry (see Figure 10.8)**
- **The services of a representative**
- **Car hire**
- **Excursions**
- **Equipment hire, e.g. skis, hammocks, bicycles, etc.**
- **Insurance**

Depending on the number of passengers, transfers will be by taxi, minibus or, most commonly nowadays, coach. Operators will schedule flight arrivals so that maximum use can be made of coaches, without undue delay being caused to clients.

Resort representatives ('reps') will provide information and support services for their clients, deal with any emergencies, arrange excursions and generally ensure the smooth running of the holiday while the clients are in the resort. Many reps will be employed only for the duration of the season, either summer or winter, with some returning to work at head office out of season.

Figure 10.8 *A Unijet rep in charge of a transfer coach*
© Unijet Travel Limited

Carry out a small-scale survey to find out what people like and dislike about package holidays.

Based on the results of your survey, how might the component parts of overseas and domestic package holidays be improved?

Travel legislation, trade body membership, licensing and bonding

Key topics in this section

- **Travel legislation**
- **Licensing and bonding**
- **The work of trade organisations**

Travel legislation

In addition to carrying out their business within the standard requirements of UK and European legislation, tour operators have a number of specific legal and regulatory requirements to take into consideration, including:

- ✪ **Package Travel Regulations**
- ✪ **Trade Descriptions Act**
- ✪ **Supply of Goods and Services Act**
- ✪ **Consumer Protection Act**
- ✪ **Unfair Contract Terms Act**
- ✪ **Fair Trading Act**
- ✪ **Data Protection Act**
- ✪ **Disability Discrimination Act**
- ✪ **Contract Law**

We will now consider each of these in more detail.

Package Travel, Package Holidays and Package Tour Regulations 1992

The Package Travel, Package Holidays and Package Tours Directive was adopted in June 1990 and came into operation on 1 January 1993 in the then 12 member states of the European Union (the number of countries in the EU rose to 15 in 1995) as the Package Travel, Package Holidays and Package Tour Regulations. The main aim of the Regulations is to give people buying package holidays more protection and access to compensation when things go wrong, while at the same time harmonising the rules covering packages operated throughout European Union countries. The provisions of the Directive did not replace national laws and, in the case of the UK, simply consolidated existing legislation and industry codes of conduct. The Package Travel Directive has, nonetheless, caused something of a stir in the UK travel and tourism industry, given its wide-ranging powers and scope. Up to the introduction of the Regulations, tour operators had been able to disclaim responsibility when holiday arrangements went wrong, for example overbooking at a hotel or the failure of a coach transfer to arrive, on the grounds that they had no control over these unfortunate events. Under the terms of the Package Travel Regulations, tour organisers must accept legal responsibility for all the services they offer to travellers. Exceptions would be made in circumstances which could neither have been foreseen nor overcome, although in such circumstances, organisers must give all necessary assistance to consumers.

What is a 'package'?

This may seem a relatively easy question, but the precise interpretation of the word 'package' has caused problems in some cases where the organiser of a trip has questioned whether his or her activity falls within the scope of the Regulations. The Regulations do not define a package as, for example, a two-week holiday to Spain with a major tour operator booked through a high street travel agency. For the purposes of the Regulations, a 'package' is defined as:

> . . . the pre-arranged combination of not fewer than two of the following when sold or offered for sale at an inclusive price and when the service covers a period of more than 24 hours or includes overnight accommodation –
>
> transport;
> accommodation;
> other tourist services not ancillary to transport or accommodation, and accounting for a significant proportion of the package.

This would mean, for example, that:

- ✪ **A hotel with a golf course next door, where rounds can be booked for guests on request, is not a package**
- ✪ **A hotel with a golf course next door, with a guaranteed minimum number of rounds included in the holiday price, is a package**
- ✪ **A hotel with a golf course next door, with golfing instruction included in the holiday price, is not a package**
- ✪ **A hotel with a golf course next door, with golfing instruction and transport to the hotel included in the price, is a package**

These examples indicate the difficult task of Trading Standards Officers, the people given the job of policing the Package Travel Regulations in the UK, when deciding exactly what constitutes a 'package'. Recent cases have shown that their interpretation of the Regulations can be different, depending on where in the country they operate.

Other definitions included in the Regulations are as follows:

✪ **'Organiser'** – the person who, other than occasionally, organises packages and sells them directly or through a retailer

✪ **'Retailer'** – the person who sells or offers for sale the package put together by the organiser

✪ **'Consumer'** – the person who takes the package (the 'principal contractor'), or any person on whose behalf the principal contractor agrees to purchase the package or any person to whom the package is transferred

✪ **'Contract'** – the agreement linking the consumer to the organiser and/or the retailer

The scope of the Package Travel Regulations

While it is easy to see that the Regulations would apply to foreign holidays taken by UK residents, an important feature is that they also apply to domestic operators, including tourist information centres, resorts, conference and event organisers, school trip leaders and voluntary groups, although there are allowances for non-profit-making voluntary organisations operating less than four excursions in any one year. Organisers cannot escape the requirements of the Regulations by billing separately for the various components of the same package.

Where do the Package Travel Regulations apply?

The Regulations apply to packages sold or offered for sale in the UK, regardless of the operator's place of establishment. They do not apply to packages sold in other countries by operators established in the UK, although similar provisions apply in other member states of the European Union and in those countries that are part of the European Economic Area (EEA). The Regulations do not apply to packages sold in the Channel Islands or the Isle of Man, although the regulations do apply to organisers based in these areas, or anywhere else in the world, who sell their packages within the UK.

What do the Regulations cover?

The Package Travel Regulations place a number of duties and responsibilities on the organisers of packages, namely:

✪ **Providing information to customers on who is responsible for the package they have booked. That person or organisation is then liable in the event of failure to deliver any elements of the package.**

- ✪ **Providing clear contract terms.**
- ✪ **Giving emergency telephone numbers.**
- ✪ **Providing proof of the organiser's security against insolvency and information on any available insurance policies.**
- ✪ **Giving immediate notification with explanation of any increase in prices permitted within the terms of the contract.**
- ✪ **Providing a variety of compensation options if agreed services are not supplied.**
- ✪ **Producing accurate promotional material, including brochures.**

The Package Travel Regulations have come as something of a shock to the UK tourist industry since, as we have seen, they cover domestic as well as outbound packages. The travel and tourism industry generally fears that the extra insurance and bonding requirements needed by tour organisers to cover against claims under the Regulations are bound to put up the cost of holidays to the consumer.

Trade Descriptions Act 1968

This Act protects customers against false descriptions made knowingly or recklessly by those who are selling or providing services, including tour operators' products and services. Any description of, for example, a hotel or resort must be truthful at the time it was written (if circumstances subsequently change, then the operator must inform the customer of the nature of the changes). This places a duty on owners and operators of travel and tourism facilities to produce brochures and other promotional materials that are not intended to deceive the customer.

Supply of Goods and Services Act 1982 (as amended by the Sale and Supply of Goods Act 1994)

This legislation states that any contract for a holiday should be carried out using 'reasonable care and skill'. The tour operator and travel agent should ensure that the booking is carried out correctly and that the holiday itself should be of a generally satisfactory standard, complying with any descriptions made. Tour operators must take great care when selecting accommodation, transport and any services they provide as part of their package holidays.

Consumer Protection Act 1987

The Consumer Protection Act makes it a criminal offence for an organisation or individual to give misleading price information about goods, services, accommodation or facilities they are offering for sale. The Act defines a 'misleading' price as one that:

- ✪ **Is greater than the price given in any promotional material**
- ✪ **Is described as being generally available, but in reality is available only in certain circumstances**
- ✪ **Does not fully state what facilities are included in the price and the fact that surcharges will be payable after booking**

The Act has special significance for tour operators, which must ensure the accuracy of any price information in their brochures and other publicity material. This is because it is an offence to include incorrect price information even if the inclusion was innocently undertaken, but is later shown to be misleading.

Unfair Contract Terms Act 1977 and the Unfair Terms in Consumer Contracts Regulations 1994

Between them, these laws allow customers to challenge any terms in a contract that they consider to be unfair or unreasonable, unfairly weighted against them, or that are ambiguous. Standard contract terms should be written in clear, understandable language. It is illegal to have a contract term that attempts to restrict the customers' statutory rights or avoids responsibility for death or personal injury. In some cases, the Office of Fair Trading (OFT) may be able to prevent a company from using an unfair term in the future.

Fair Trading Act

The Fair Trading Act 1973 forbids any unfair or unreasonable conditions or terms being imposed on customers, e.g. tour operators cannot say in their booking conditions that all complaints must be reported within 24 hours of returning from holiday. This is clearly unreasonable since holidaymakers may have suffered injury or distress, thereby making it difficult for them to complain within such a short time period.

Data Protection Act

This government legislation was introduced in 1984 (and updated in 1998) to safeguard the public from problems relating to the inaccuracy of any information held about them on computer records. Under the terms of the Act, all organisations that hold data about individuals on automated systems must register with the Data Protection Registrar and comply with a series of Data Protection Principles, which are a set of good practice guidelines.

Individuals who have computer data held on them have a number of rights in civil law, including right of access to the data, rights to compensation for inaccuracy of data or its wrongful disclosure, and rights to have any inaccuracies in the data rectified. Travel agencies that hold client details on computer databases are likely to fall within the scope of the Act and must abide by the Data Protection Principles. One of the Principles states that the information held on computer must not be disclosed to third parties. This means that a travel agent who holds information on clients on a computer cannot sell the data to another company without being in contravention of the Act (see Unit 19 *Business systems in the travel and tourism industry* for more information on the Data Protection Act).

Disability Discrimination Act 1995

The Disability Discrimination Act 1995 (DDA) was designed to protect disabled people from discrimination in employment and to increase access to goods, facilities and services. The Act defines 'disability' as:

> *A physical or mental impairment which has a substantial and long term adverse effect on a person's ability to carry out normal day-to-day activities.*

Check out this website

www.disability.
gov.uk

The DDA employment provisions and the duty on service providers not to treat disabled people less favourably have been in force since December 1996. From October 1999, service providers have had to make 'reasonable adjustments' for disabled people. From 2004, they will have to consider making alterations to the built environment, e.g. access to buildings and the ability to move freely inside buildings.

Contract law

The principles of contract law are of concern to all UK tour operators, since, in the normal course of business trading, they make contracts with a wide range of individuals and organisations, including:

- ✪ **Suppliers** – e.g. hoteliers, airlines, coach companies, handling agents, etc.
- ✪ **Intermediaries** – e.g. travel agents selling the tour operator's products to the public
- ✪ **Customers**
- ✪ **Staff**

Contrary to popular belief, most contracts do not need to be in writing. From a lawyer's standpoint, a contract is any agreement that the law will enforce, whether in writing, verbal or implied, i.e. assumed from the conduct of the parties. Contracts range from the very simple, e.g. buying a drink at a resort complex, to the very complicated, e.g. building the Channel Tunnel. The law of contract is principally concerned with promises that constitute part of an agreed exchange. It governs such questions as which agreements the law will enforce, what obligations are imposed by the agreement and what will happen if the obligations are not carried out.

The following conditions must be satisfied if a contract is to be legally enforceable:

1 **There must have been agreement between the parties on all material aspects of the contract**

2 **The parties must have intended to create a legally binding contract**

3 **There must be at least two parties to the contract**

It is an essential requirement of English law that, for a contract to be legally binding, each party must have agreed to provide something of value to the other. For example, when a customer books a package holiday, but the booking has yet to be confirmed, the contract between the customer and the tour operator may still be legally binding even where he or she has not yet paid for it. The important point is that the customer has promised to pay the price for the holiday when required to do so. The tour operator, on the other hand, promises that the holiday is available.

It is important to remember that when a holidaymaker books a package holiday through a travel agent, the contract is between the customer and the tour operator, with the travel agent merely acting as an intermediary. It is against the tour operator that the customer must seek legal redress in the event of a breach of contract.

Activity 10.5

Study a current brochure from a well-known holiday company and list the commitments that the operator undertakes to make to the customer and what is expected in return from the customer.

Licensing and bonding

All tour operator members of ABTA must provide a bond securing their liability in respect of all forms of transportation, accommodation, travel and holiday arrangements, whether outside or within the UK. The bond is a formal undertaking from an approved bank or insurance company to pay a sum of money to ABTA or the Civil Aviation Authority (CAA) in the event of the company's financial failure. The bond monies are used primarily for the purpose of reimbursing customers who would otherwise lose money that they had already paid, so that:

- ✪ **Clients whose holidays are actually taking place when a tour operator ceases trading can continue with their holiday as planned or be brought back to the UK**
- ✪ **Clients who have yet to travel on holidays already paid for can get their money back when an operator fails**
- ✪ **Alternative holiday arrangements can be made for clients, who have paid for trips that have yet to take place, when a tour operator ceases trading**

For bonding purposes, tour operators are classed as either 'licensable' or 'non-licensable'. Licensable activities are those that require the operator to hold an Air Travel Organiser's Licence (ATOL); all other tour operations are classed as non-licensable. The CAA bonds provided by ATOL holders provide the first line of defence for licensable activities when things go wrong, whereas ABTA bonds provided by members fulfil the same function in respect of non-licensable activities.

Industry example

An ATOL is a licence issued by the Civil Aviation Authority (CAA) and is required by all individuals and companies selling holidays and seats on charter flights. Applicants must show that they are fit to hold an ATOL, have adequate financial arrangements and must lodge a bond with the CAA. In the event of company failure, the bond money is used to repatriate clients who might otherwise be stranded overseas and to refund, as far as possible, passengers who have paid in advance but have yet to travel. Where the bond is insufficient to meet all claims, the Air Travel Reserve Fund, managed by the CAA, meets the shortfall.

Browse this website

www.caa.co.uk

The Association of Independent Tour Operators (AITO) also operates a bonding scheme for its 150 member companies, under the AITO Trust banner. It is responsible for monitoring the financial performance of AITO members within the scheme, setting bonding levels and collecting premiums. AITO Trust has approved status under the regulations developed out of the 1992 Package Travel Regulations, offering full financial security to the customers of companies bonded via the system, including repatriation to the UK if necessary. The arrangement is designed to bond non-licensable turnover, i.e. holidays including surface transport options such as self-drive, coach or train-based trips.

The work of trade organisations

Trade organisations exist in all sectors of industry to protect and advance the interests of their members. Most trade organisations draw up codes of conduct, which are, in essence, the minimum standards and rules under which members of the organisation are expected to conduct their everyday operations, governing such matters as their trading relationships with customers, promotional practices and financial security. ABTA is the main trade body representing UK tour operators and travel agents. Other trade associations working in the travel and tourism industry include the Association of Independent Tour Operators (AITO), the Confederation of Passenger Transport UK (CPT), the former Bus and Coach Council, and the Passenger Shipping Association (PSA).

In the tour operations sector, companies can choose to become members of a range of trade organisations, three of the most important are:

- ✪ **ABTA (Association of British Travel Agents)**
- ✪ **FTO (Federation of Tour Operators)**
- ✪ **AITO (Association of Independent Tour Operators)**

We will now investigate each of these in more detail.

ABTA

ABTA is the principal trade organisation concerned with UK-based tour operators and travel agents (see Unit 8 *Travel agency operations* for a case study on ABTA). It has developed two codes of conduct, the Travel Agents' Code of Conduct and the Tour Operators' Code of Conduct, which were drawn up by ABTA in association with the Office of Fair Trading. The Tour Operators' Code of Conduct lays down the minimum standards of operators' brochures, requiring that they contain clear, comprehensive and accurate descriptions of facilities and services offered. It details rules which govern booking conditions in brochures as they relate, for example, to the cancellation or alteration of tours, holidays or other travel arrangements by the tour operator. The code also contains strict rules concerning the prompt handling of complaints and regulations relating to the conduct between tour operators and travel agents.

Browse this website

www.abta.com

FTO

Browse these websites

www.airtours.co.uk

www.thomson-
holidays.com

www.baholidays.
co.uk

The Federation of Tour Operators is an independent membership body representing the interests of the leading British tour operating companies, such as Airtours, Thomson Holidays and British Airways Holidays. Formerly the Tour Operators' Study Group (TOSG), the FTO is active in lobbying government for changes to legislation that affects its members' interests.

AITO

The following case study gives detailed information on the aims and work of the Association of Independent Tour Operators and its relationship with the Campaign for Real Travel Agents (CARTA).

Case Study
AITO and the Campaign for Real Travel Agents

▶ **INTRODUCTION**

AITO is an alliance of over 150 smaller, specialist travel companies dedicated to providing a quality product, personal service and choice to the consumer. It was established in 1976, mainly in response to the problems posed for smaller travel companies by a sudden, sharp increase in bonding requirements following the collapse of a number of major tour operators. In recent years, AITO has come to be recognised increasingly as the official voice of the smaller or specialist tour operator, whose views had seldom been represented or given due consideration by those who regulate the travel industry. The majority of AITO members are small, owner-managed companies, giving high standards of personal service and attention to detail.

Membership of the Association has grown significantly since 1990, when it introduced its own bonding scheme, administered by AITO Trust Ltd. Currently, AITO has over 150 member companies, whose individual passenger carryings range from several hundred to just under 200,000, with the majority of members responsible for between 10,000 and 20,000 passengers per year. AITO

continued

continued

members as a whole carried 1.9 million passengers in 1995, which gives the Association a certain degree of credibility in the travel industry. Member companies include Eurocamp, Explore Worldwide, Allez France Holidays and Cox & Kings Travel.

▶ AIMS OF THE ASSOCIATION

AITO's stated aims are:

★ To ensure that the public can book AITO members' holidays with every confidence

★ To inform members of the issues of the day and to encourage higher standards and greater professionalism amongst members

★ To encourage members and their clients to be aware of environmental issues and to promote environmentally sustainable tourism

★ To help members market their wares more effectively to customers

★ To ensure that the views and problems of the smaller, specialist tour operators are understood and that the interests of their clients are protected

▶ THE WORK OF AITO

The Association's work spans a wide variety of travel concerns, including:

★ *A social forum*: AITO acts as a forum for the exchange of ideas and views between its members and the industry in general. It holds regular meetings in the UK and an annual overseas meeting for members, their guests and the travel press.

★ *Lobbying*: AITO has become increasingly important as a political lobbying group in recent years, as a respected body of opinion representing a significant section of the UK tour operating market. Its views

continued

continued

have been sought by the Monopolies and Mergers Commission (now the Competition Commission), Office of Fair Trading, Department of Trade and Industry, etc.

★ *Promotion and public relations*: AITO has worked hard to raise the profile of its member companies with the press and the public in general. It organises press functions for member companies, two main brochure launches each year and a series of smaller press launches throughout the year. The Association's *Directory of Real Holidays*, produced annually with a print run in excess of 75,000 copies, is a major part of its marketing activity. It lists all member companies and is distributed to the public, the press, retail agencies, Trading Standards Officers, MPs, Members of the European Parliament and a wide cross-section of representatives of the travel and tourism industry. There is also a *Ski Directory* and a *Guide to Real Holidays*, racked in over 400 independent travel agencies.

★ *A regulatory body*: All AITO members agree to comply with the Association's quality charter and code of business practice, laying down basic standards relating to the quality of service to customers, accuracy of brochures, financial security and related matters.

★ *Member services*: AITO ensures that its members are kept up to date on all issues that may affect them by providing information, advice and background notes, where appropriate. This includes material on such matters as health and safety, contracting and insurance.

★ *Green tourism*: AITO was involved, in 1990, in the establishment of Green Flag International, a non-profit-making company set up to encourage tour operators to understand the importance of environmentally sustainable tourism. The principles

continued

continued

of 'green tourism' are promoted in AITO's publications and AITO intends to continue backing initiatives relating to tourism and the environment.

▶ THE CAMPAIGN FOR REAL TRAVEL AGENTS (CARTA)

In June 1994, AITO launched a new initiative to link independent tour operators with independent travel agents, with the aim of generating new business for both parties. Originally called the AITO 100 Club, the initiative was expanded in June 1995 and renamed the Campaign for Real Travel Agents (CARTA). To date there are 120 tour operator brands (85 companies) and 442 travel agents in the scheme. Each of the holidays in the Association's *Guide to Real Holidays* can be booked through an independent agent, who can offer advice on product and destination selection and availability. The Guide is designed for racking in travel agencies and the Association has developed a range of point-of-sale materials to accompany the CARTA initiative. Training is an important aspect of the CARTA scheme, as a way of improving links between operators and agents. Public relations activity and local advertising are used to increase awareness among customers, and the campaign has been reported extensively in the consumer and travel trade press.

(Information courtesy of AITO)

Case study discussion questions

1 What were the main reasons behind the formation of AITO in 1976?

Browse this website

www.aito.co.uk

2 If you were the owner of a specialist tour operating company, what benefits would you receive from membership of AITO?

3 How can AITO help the drive for more environmentally sustainable tourism?

4 What benefits does the CARTA scheme offer to both agents and operators?

5 How does AITO help to raise the profile of its member companies?

The functions of tour operating

Key topics in this section

- **Introduction**
- **Research and planning**
- **Contracting**
- **Pricing the package**
- **Marketing and selling**
- **Reservations**
- **Administration**
- **Public relations**
- **Pre- and post-departure customer service**

Introduction

All tour operators have to perform certain functions in order to plan, organise and sell their tours or packages. The same basic functions have to be carried out whether the tour operator is a small enterprise employing just one or two members of staff or a very large, mass market holiday company employing hundreds of people. These functions include:

- ✪ **Research and planning**
- ✪ **Contracting**
- ✪ **Pricing the package**
- ✪ **Marketing and selling**
- ✪ **Rerservations**
- ✪ **Administration**
- ✪ **Public relations**
- ✪ **Customer service**

Each of these topics is covered in the following sections of this unit, based on the work of a large, mass market tour operator.

Research and planning

In large tour operating companies, it is staff employed in the marketing department who are responsible for researching, planning and developing the different holiday products, which will be aimed at particular segments of the market. Product Managers will focus on the selection of resorts, choice of accommodation and selection of regional UK departure airports. Typical segments of the market for which products are developed include:

- **Singles**
- **Families**
- **Couples without children**
- **Disabled travellers**
- **Groups**
- **Business travellers**
- **Youth market**
- **Elderly travellers**

Planning and organising a holiday programme does not happen overnight. Staff in the marketing department will start making plans for a season 12–18 months before the brochures go on sale. The first task is to assess the total number of holidays that will be taken during a season by all UK holidaymakers. Having calculated this total market figure, individual Brand Managers or Product Managers decide what share of the market it is realistic to sell (the programme capacity). Having decided on the capacity of the programme, detailed planning on how many holidays should be arranged in each resort and what accommodation and flights are needed can begin. Marketing staff are also responsible for the key activity of pricing the holidays, which can be very risky given the advance planning necessary before the launch of a programme and the potential for fluctuations in currency exchange rates.

Activity 10.6

Draw a flow chart of the main tasks involved in developing a package holiday product to a new long-haul destination in South America. Include timescales and staff responsibilities in your chart.

Market research

A great deal of background research is undertaken to ensure that the tour operators' products have the best chance of meeting their sales potential. Sources of research data available to market research personnel include:

- **Internal sales data**
- **External sales data (available from commercial sources)**

- ✪ **Analysis of competitors' programmes**
- ✪ **Analysis of customer comment questionnaires**
- ✪ **Financial analysis**

Staff in the market research department work with marketing department personnel to identify potential new market opportunities, as well as assessing the changing needs and tastes of previous customers. This is achieved by studying sales statistics and market research surveys. They particularly look at the feedback collected from existing customers via CSQs (customer satisfaction questionnaires). The staff try to predict what holidaymakers will want, in terms of which resorts, what type and length of holiday, what standard of accommodation, which departure airports and what price they are prepared to pay.

Contracting

Once the structure of the programme is finalised, staff in the contracts department will negotiate with accommodation providers over the number of beds and names of accommodations required. This function is often the responsibility of senior management, under the direction of the Overseas Regional Manager, who may be assisted by specific Product Managers. The staff involved in contracting the accommodation and related services have to negotiate on price, quantity and quality, within a very competitive environment. It is likely that other mass market operators, for example, will be using the same hotels in their programmes. An operator may try to negotiate exclusive use of particular accommodation, but this will involve a financial commitment on behalf of the operator that it may not be willing to risk.

There are three main types of contracts used in tour operating:

- ✪ **Commitment/guarantee** – where the tour operator guarantees to pay for a certain number of bed spaces
- ✪ **Allocation and release back** – where the tour operator agrees an allocation of a certain number of bed spaces with the hotel and agrees to give back any that it has not sold on a certain date
- ✪ **Ad hoc** – this is a more flexible arrangement when a tour operator agrees a contract (discounted) rate with a hotelier and makes bookings as and when required

Flights

At the same time as accommodation contracting is under way, the flight programmes have to be negotiated, either with an in-house airline in the case

Figure 10.9 *A Britannia Airways Boeing 767*
© Photograph reproduced courtesy of Britannia Airways Limited

of the large operators, or with charter or scheduled airlines in the case of smaller operators (see Figure 10.9). In large tour operating companies, teams working on different programmes and products liaise with the flight or aviation department over how many seats they will need, which regional airports are to be used and whether day or night flights are required. The flight department must make optimum use of its resources, which will include selling spare capacity in the seat-only market.

Pricing the package

A tour operator's main source of income is the revenue it receives from its main holiday product, the package holiday or inclusive tour (IT). This revenue may come direct from the customer, if it is a 'direct sell' company, or, more usually, through a travel agent who will sell the holiday on behalf of the operator. A large tour operator such as Airtours may have a number of separate operating divisions, each of which will contribute to overall group profits; Airtours owns its own airline, runs camping holidays under the EuroSites brand and operates a chain of travel agencies under the Going Places banner. Mass market tour operators offer a wide range of holiday products catering for different sectors of the market. Although this range will vary from time to time in response to fluctuating demand, there is likely to be a series of products, which may include:

- ✪ **A main summer programme**
- ✪ **A winter programme**
- ✪ **City breaks**
- ✪ **Flight-only**
- ✪ **Programmes featuring particular countries or regions, e.g. the Caribbean**
- ✪ **Holidays geared to the youth market**
- ✪ **Programmes for 'seniors'**
- ✪ **Budget holidays**
- ✪ **Specialist programmes, e.g. golf or sailing**

Other sources of income to tour operators include:

- ✪ **Interest on money held in account**: Deposits for holidays are sometimes paid up to 12 months before departure and balances settled 6–8 weeks before the start of the holiday. This money accumulates for the tour operator who receives interest on its balances.

- ✪ **Commission on 'extras'**: Commission for items such as car hire, insurance, flight-only and excursions is generally paid direct to the tour operator. Most operators will offer their own insurance and car hire in their brochures, hoping to benefit from the higher commission levels that these two products attract.

- ✪ **Currency dealing**: Large operators may buy foreign currency in advance if rates are favourable to use later for payments to suppliers. Surplus funds can be invested to provide a return.

- ✪ **Vertical integration**: Tour operators that have financial interests at more than one level of the distribution chain can generate income from a greater number of sources, e.g. in-flight sales and hotel bar sales.

- ✪ **Charges**: Tour operators levy charges for cancellations and amendments to holiday arrangements, which are another source of income.

Costing package holidays

Having considered the sources of income available to tour operators, we now have to look at the costs they must bear in order to generate revenue. Like any commercial concern, a tour operator's costs can be categorised as either fixed or variable.

Fixed costs

These are the costs of running a business that do not alter with changes in the level of activity. For example, the rent or rates for a tour operator's premises will be fixed over a period of time, regardless of the number of holidays it sells. Similarly, the insurance and cleaning costs will be the same whether it has a successful or poor season. Fixed costs for tour operators include:

- ❂ **Rates**
- ❂ **Rent or mortgage**
- ❂ **Interest on loans**
- ❂ **Bonding**
- ❂ **Essential maintenance**
- ❂ **Cleaning**
- ❂ **Insurance**
- ❂ **Permanent staff salaries**
- ❂ **Lighting and heating**
- ❂ **Market research**

Variable costs

Variable costs alter in direct proportion to the volume of business generated by tour operators and include:

- ❂ **Postage**
- ❂ **Telephone, fax and telex charges**
- ❂ **Computer time and equipment hire**
- ❂ **Printing and stationery**
- ❂ **Advertising and publicity**
- ❂ **Part-time staff**
- ❂ **Professional fees and charges**
- ❂ **Bank charges**
- ❂ **Transaction charges, e.g. credit cards**

Determining the price of a package holiday

Tour operators have to bear in mind a number of important factors when determining the final selling price of a package holiday, including:

- ❂ **The contracted rates that have been agreed with accommodation providers, car hire companies, transfer services, etc.**
- ❂ **Seasonal adjustments, e.g. low prices for the 'shoulder season' (either side of the peak) and higher prices for peak season demand**
- ❂ **Load factor on the aircraft, i.e. the percentage of seats that need to be filled before the tour operator breaks even and begins to make a profit**

- **Fixed costs,** e.g. the cost of hiring a transfer coach is the same regardless of the number of passengers aboard
- **Variable costs,** e.g. the cost per person for accommodation where the tour operator pays only for accommodation actually booked
- **Indirect costs,** e.g. head office overheads
- **Direct operating costs,** e.g. the cost of accommodation
- **Profit margins,** i.e. the percentage added to the net selling price, covering all indirect costs and allowing for a profit

In the same way that it is important for tour operators to control costs, pricing their products is crucial to overall profitability. Pricing is a very risky business; a mass market tour operator that sets the prices of its main summer programme holidays too high in relation to the competition will not achieve optimum levels of sales. Too low, on the other hand, and it will find it difficult to produce an adequate profit.

There are two basic methods that can be adopted to arrive at the cost of an inclusive tour:

1   **Cost-based pricing**

2   **Market-based pricing**

Cost-based pricing involves calculating all the fixed and variable costs of a tour product, including any commission payments to agents, and setting the price at a level which covers all these costs and allows a profit margin. This is the method adopted by small, specialist operators who are unlikely to be operating in such a competitive environment as the mass market holiday companies and whose products will have a degree of uniqueness. In large tour companies, apportioning all costs to particular cost centres may be a very difficult task; while it will be relatively easy to determine the variable costs of a tour programme, calculating the proportion of fixed operating costs to be allocated to that programme is much more difficult.

Sometimes referred to as 'what the market will bear', market-based pricing sets pricing in a wider context by taking account of what competitors are charging when determining prices. Reissuing brochures with revised prices is now commonplace among tour operators that are constantly checking competitor activity and making adjustments to maintain their market share. Following the market leader's pricing is a risky business, if a company has not fully taken into account its own costs of operation; the collapse of Intasun in 1991 is a good example of this type of 'overtrading'. The hope is that the economies of scale involved in tour operating will enable the larger operators to reduce their costs, but still allow a profit margin at the end of the day.

To show that pricing is often a combination of market- and cost-based approaches, we will look at a simplified example of how the pricing policy for a typical overseas package holiday is worked out.

Industry example
Costing an inclusive tour to the Costa Blanca – 14 nights half-board

	£	£
Flight costs		
26 return flights during the season @ £16,000 per flight	416,000	
Empty leg at beginning and end of the season	16,000	
Total flight costs	432,000	
Cost per occupied flight (£432,000 divided by 26)	16,615	
Cost per seat based on 90% load factor using Boeing 737 with a capacity of 130 passengers		142.00
Hotel costs per person for 14 days		220.00
Transfers and handling fees		10.50
Total costs of tour per person		372.50

Having calculated that £372.50 is needed to cover the direct costs of the holiday, the tour operator will now determine a price which covers these costs plus a mark-up to cover a proportion of fixed costs, the commission payment to travel agents and leaves a profit margin for the operator. The exact amount of the mark-up, and hence the final price of the holiday, will be determined by:

★ Prices of similar holidays offered by competitors

★ The cost of the holiday last year

★ The season in which the holiday is being taken

Assuming a mark-up of 25%, the final brochure price of this holiday to the Costa Blanca will be:

£372.50 + 25% mark-up = £465.62

This figure is known as the break-even point. The operator will sell the holiday at above break-even when demand is high and below £465.62 when demand is low out of season.

We have seen that tour operators rely on obtaining the elements of their inclusive tours at discounted rates, from suppliers such as hoteliers and airlines, which are happy to negotiate a discount in return for releasing an agreed amount of stock. Discounting is also prevalent at the other end of the distribution chain, namely discounted holidays offered for sale in travel agencies. In the past, tour operators have frowned on travel agents that have offered cut price holidays, but in today's very competitive holiday industry, discounts are a common way for a travel agent to attract custom. At the time of writing, high street travel agents are offering up to 10 per cent off the brochure prices of most major tour operators, in return for the clients taking out the agents' or operators' holiday insurance.

Marketing and selling

Marketing staff will plan and co-ordinate a range of activities, including advertising in newspapers, magazines, Teletext and on the Internet, direct mail, product launches and sales promotion, to ensure that the operators' products are given maximum exposure and sales opportunities. This may be long-term brand support or short-term advertising and promotion. It may involve advertising in consumer and trade arenas, or special point-of-sale materials in travel agencies to raise awareness of particular products.

Brochure production

For tour operators, the brochure is their most crucial promotional tool, providing detailed information, images and prices to potential clients, designed to persuade them to make a booking. In particular, brochures aim to:

- ✪ **Accurately present products and services to the reader**
- ✪ **Supply product information to travel agents**
- ✪ **Convey an image of the company**
- ✪ **Offer a means of booking a holiday**
- ✪ **Explain booking and contractual conditions**
- ✪ **Present the information within the bounds of current UK and European Union legislation**

Above all, brochures should be designed in such a way that they have the best chance of converting enquiries into sales. Teams working in the marketing department will liaise with brochure production staff to finalise design, copy and photographs. A lot of brochure printing takes place outside the UK to save on costs. Sales staff will make decisions about how many brochures are required and to which travel agents they will be distributed.

ABTA's standards on brochures

The ABTA Tour Operators' Code of Conduct states that:

Every brochure published by or in the name of any ABTA member shall contain clear, legible, comprehensive and accurate information to enable the client to exercise an informed judgement in making his choice.

The Code goes on to say that, as a minimum, brochures produced by ABTA members must contain the following information:

1 **Government/statutory licensing authority**: All information necessary to comply with the regulations for the time being of the Civil Aviation Authority or any other governmental or statutory licensing authority.

2 **Legal identity**: The legal identity of the member responsible for publishing the brochure containing the tour, holiday or travel arrangement offered, including their registered company number where applicable.

3 **Financial protection**: The means of financial protection attached to the tour, holiday or travel arrangement offered within the brochure, including the ABTA number and ATOL number where applicable.

4 **Means of travel**: The means of travel, e.g. ship, train, coach, motor vehicle, aircraft; the characteristics of the transport, e.g. charter, scheduled; the category of transport used, e.g. economy, business class, first class or class of cabin.

5 **Destinations and/or itinerary** as appropriate.

6 **Date, place and time of departure and return**: The date, place and approximate time of departure and return. Where any or all of these items are subject to alteration by a regulatory body, e.g. Airport Scheduling Committee, reference must be made to same.

7 **Nature of accommodation**: Including its location, category or degree of comfort, its main features and, where the accommodation is to be provided in an EC member state, its approval or tourist classification under the rules of that member state, where such rules exist.

8 **Meal facilities**: The meals that are included in the price, if any.

9 **Additional facilities**: Any additional facilities or special arrangements included in the price.

10 **Changes to brochure details**: The Package Travel Regulations 1992 (see page 73) make the particulars contained within a brochure binding upon the tour operator, unless the brochure contains a clear, express statement that changes may be made to the particulars within the brochure at any time after publication.

11 **Booking conditions**: The procedures for booking and the contractual conditions under which the booking is made must conform with all relevant provisions of the Tour Operators' Code of Conduct and should include details of, for example, payment of deposits and balance due dates, confirmation of the booking, any alteration to a confirmed booking made by the client, cancellation procedures and charges, the tour operator's liability to the client, etc.

12 **Insurance details**: If a tour operator offers holiday insurance, an accurate and sufficiently detailed summary of the cover provided and the associated premiums must be shown in the brochure. Where the purchase of the tour operator's own insurance is compulsory, the relevant premium must be included in the basic price.

13 **Price policy**: The total price, or a means of arriving at the total price, together with a precise statement of the services included therein, must be shown in the brochure. If a tour operator reserves the right to levy a surcharge, a statement to that effect must appear close to the basic price, with an indication of where further information may be found in the brochure. If a price indication becomes misleading while the brochure is still current, the tour operator shall inform all travel agents to whom the brochure has been distributed.

14 **Health matters**: The brochure must contain adequate information relating to both recommended and compulsory health requirements of countries featured or a reference to the Department of Health leaflet *Health Advice for Travellers*, available from their ABTA travel agent or direct from the Department of Health. Clients should also be advised to check with their own doctor before their departure as to which inoculations are available and necessary for specific areas.

15 **Arbitration**: It is recommended that a statement should be included to the effect that any disputes arising may be referred to arbitration under a special scheme, which, although devised by arrangement with ABTA, is administered independently by the Chartered Institute of Arbitrators.

16 **Noise**: Brochures that feature resort-based holidays shall contain adequate information relating to all known sources of noise which exist or might be expected to exist at resorts, and which may reasonably be considered to cause offence to clients. Such sources of noise include, but are not limited to, night clubs, bars, discos, amusement parks and airports.

17 **Building works**: Where it is known, or can reasonably be expected, that building works which are likely to adversely affect the enjoyment of

a holiday will take place during the period covered by the brochure, all specific information must be published on the relevant page in the brochure.

18 **Publication date**: The month and year of publication must be printed in the brochure.

19 **Delays at points of departure**: Brochures must state clearly and unambiguously the tour operator's policy on the handling of clients who are delayed at the outward and/or homeward points of departure. Tour operators are encouraged, but not obliged, to provide refreshments/meals appropriate to the time of day and overnight accommodation dependent upon the length of delay and nature of the holiday.

Agency sales support

Sales representatives will regularly visit travel agencies and offer product training and point-of-sale materials, such as posters and window displays, in order to maximise sales opportunities. The travel agencies that sell the most holidays will receive particular attention, including enhanced incentives for management and staff to continue high volume sales.

Reservations

Reservations staff are employed to handle bookings from travel agents and direct from the public. All large operators, and many small to medium-sized companies, use computerised systems developed by in-house computer operations personnel or outside consultants. Staff in reservations are fully trained on the operation of the reservation systems and briefed on the features of products included in the operator's brochures. Large tour operators will have separate reservations teams handling group bookings and last-minute bookings. Some specialist tour operators use manual reservations systems based on wallcharts or index cards.

Administration

The tour operator's administration department is responsible for producing invoices, receiving payments and issuing tickets and other documentation. Staff will also produce passenger lists, known as manifests, for distribution to airlines, hoteliers, ground handling agents and resort representatives, plus carry out the full range of everyday administrative duties associated with the operation of a commercial concern.

Working as part of a small group, list the main tasks that would be undertaken by staff in the administration department of a major outbound tour operator. Use your list as the basis for drawing up a job description and person specification for the permanent post of Administrative Assistant for a mass market operator based in Manchester.

Public relations

Public relations staff deal with all aspects of the tour operators liaison with the press and outside agencies. They will be responsible for organising press conferences, writing press releases and handling enquiries.

Pre- and post-departure customer service

This department will be responsible for handling complaints and queries from agents and members of the public. They will try to ensure that all matters are dealt with quickly and efficiently in order to retain goodwill. Often part of a major tour operator's marketing department, the customer services teams are increasingly involved in analysing customer feedback. Relevant information is passed to appropriate UK or overseas personnel to ensure that mistakes are not repeated and that overall quality is enhanced.

UK and overseas operations

Key topics in this section

- **Tour operator organisation**
- **UK operations**
- **Overseas (resort office) operations**

Tour operator organisation

All tour operating companies differ in terms of their strategic and day-to-day organisational structures, although as we have seen in the previous sections of this unit the functions they need to undertake are very similar. Organisational differences usually depend on the scale of operations and the management style adopted by senior staff in the organisation. It is quite possible, for example, for a single person to run a small tour operating business, using the latest computer and communications technology. This individual will be responsible for all aspects of the operation, from contracting with accommodation and transport providers, to producing a brochure and selling the packages to the public. It is more usual, however, for UK outbound tour operators to be medium-sized enterprises, handling the travel requirements of perhaps 15,000 or 20,000 customers per year. The largest operators, Thomson (see case study on page 163), Airtours, Thomas Cook (JMC) and First Choice Holidays, between them handle in excess of 10 million passengers per year. These mass market operators will have:

- ✪ **A main UK head office**
- ✪ **Regional offices in the UK**
- ✪ **Overseas offices**

They will employ a wide range of full- and part-time staff. Smaller, specialist operators, with fewer staff on the payroll, will focus their work in their UK office and often subcontract parts of their operation to overseas agents, e.g. ground handling agents and resort representatives.

UK operations

Earlier in this unit (see pages 148–160) we saw that most of the work of major UK tour operators is based in this country and covers:

- ✪ **Research and planning**
- ✪ **Contracting**
- ✪ **Pricing the package**
- ✪ **Marketing and selling**
- ✪ **Reservations**
- ✪ **Administration**
- ✪ **Public relations**
- ✪ **Customer service**

In addition to these functions, tour operators will have a personnel department and a department controlling the finance and legal aspects of the operation. Staff in personnel are responsible for a wide variety of tasks, including all recruitment for the UK and overseas operations, job evaluation, employee appraisal, training, payments to staff and pensions management, plus all administrative matters related to employees and their welfare.

Control over finance is crucial for success in tour operating. Staff in the finance department handle the flow of revenue into the business and payments to suppliers in the UK and overseas. Senior staff will be responsible for meeting planned sales and revenue targets and managing budgets. The legal department advises on a range of matters, such as the content of contracts, accuracy of brochure copy and statutory regulations concerning the company and its relationship with customers and suppliers.

Overseas (resort office) operations

As well as having a general duty to provide a high standard of service to the tour operator's customers while abroad, staff in the overseas office of a major UK tour operator will have a number of specific responsibilities, including:

- ✪ **Producing rooming lists**
- ✪ **Compiling and checking passenger manifests (lists of clients travelling)**
- ✪ **Organising transfers to and from the accommodation and airport**
- ✪ **Selling and arranging excursions and other 'extras' such as car hire**
- ✪ **Finalising contracts with hoteliers and transport operators**
- ✪ **The well-being, training and deployment of representatives**
- ✪ **The handling of complaints and emergencies**
- ✪ **Feeding back to the UK office any formal or informal research findings**

Smaller, specialist UK operators may have a small number of permanent employees based in overseas resorts, but will also use the services of

Figure 10.10 *Overseas reps play a vital role in overseas operations*
© Unijet Travel Limited

seasonal and part-time UK staff (see Figure 10.10). They also rely on the services of specialist individuals and companies in the resorts to provide a range of ground handling services, such as a 'meet and greet' service, coach transfers and welcome meetings for clients.

Case Study
Thomson Holidays

▶ **INTRODUCTION**

Thomson Holidays is part of the Thomson Travel Group (TTG), which in turn is part of the International Thomson Organisation, with interests not only in travel, but also in publishing and oil. The Group's principal businesses are:

★   Thomson Holidays – the largest tour operator in the UK

continued

continued

★ Britannia Airways – the second largest airline in the UK after British Airways

★ Lunn Poly – the UK's largest wholly-owned travel agency network

★ TTG Independent Holidays Group

Table 10.1 on page 117 gives a full breakdown of all Thomson Holidays' brands.

▶ HISTORY

In 1965, Lord Thomson, a Canadian businessman, took the first step towards the creation of the Thomson Travel Group when he acquired Universal Sky Tours, Britannia Airways and Riviera Holidays. In 1974, when the then number one operator Clarksons failed at the height of the holiday season, Thomson Holidays inherited the enviable number one position which it still retains today. The Lunn Poly travel agency chain with 60 retail outlets was acquired in 1972 and the Thomson Travel Group was made even stronger with the founding of Portland Holidays in 1979, now the UK's leading direct-sell operator. In 1988 the Horizon Travel Group was acquired; this brought Orion Airways and Horizon Holidays into the Thomson Group, plus the Horizon brands of HCI, Wings, OSL and Blue Sky, as well as Horizon Travel Centres. In 1989, Thomson Tour Operations was set up as the new company operating all programmes run by Thomson and Horizon. By summer 1991, all brands and products had been realigned to operate separately, but under the Thomson banner. Only Portland continues to operate as a separate company.

▶ THOMSON HOLIDAYS

This is the most familiar of the Thomson Travel Group's companies and is the UK's largest air-inclusive tour operator, selling 4 million holidays in 1998. Its mission is:

continued

continued

To be the leader in terms of quality, profit and volume of the ex-UK tour operating industry.

The company's specific aims are:

1   To have the best team of people in the industry working for the company

2   To provide all its employees with a challenging, rewarding and secure working environment

3   To ensure that the quality of product and service is better, and is perceived to be better by holidaymakers, suppliers and travel agents, than all major competitors

4   To operate within a lower cost base, quality for quality, than all major competitors

5   To be the clear market leader in terms of size of the ex-UK inclusive tour business

6   To achieve a superior level of profitability compared to all major competitors to ensure the long-term viability of the business

7   To carry out all tasks with due responsibility towards the communities in which they operate and towards the environment

▶ THOMSON HOLIDAYS' COMPANY STRUCTURE

★ *Marketing department*: The job of Thomson Holidays' marketing department is to identify and plan to meet holidaymakers' needs; in other words to provide the right holiday at the right price to the right person. The department has staff involved in creating products, providing a customer service function, producing brochures, undertaking market research and liaising with the press and media.

★ *Overseas department*: This is mainly concerned with operations outside the UK and co-ordinates the overseas operation of all holidays. Its

continued

continued

responsibilities include the contracting of all types of accommodation, providing a high standard of service to clients while in the resort and maintaining and improving the standards of accommodation and service on offer. The aviation team draws up the initial flight plans from the capacity requirements, i.e. the number of holidays planned to be sold and the number of aircraft needed.

★ *Personnel services*: This section is divided into two departments, one serving UK staff and the other dealing with staff overseas. The main activities of the overseas personnel department include planning staffing levels, recruitment, job evaluation, salary and benefits administration and staff relations. UK personnel has the task of assisting managers to recruit the right calibre of staff in the most effective way. This may be by internal progression, transfer or external recruitment. Staff training and development is also handled by the personnel department.

★ *Sales department*: One of the main objectives of Thomson Holidays' sales department is to maintain excellent relationships with travel agents in order to create sales opportunities. This is done through the agency sales force which provides agents with sales and market information and trains agency personnel in products and procedures. Another responsibility of this department is co-ordinating a merchandising team that visits the top agents at regular intervals to check on brochure stocks and visibility on shelves.

★ *Systems division*: Staff in this section provide computing services for all areas of the company. The viewdata-based reservation system for travel agents (TOP) is recognised as the standard for the UK travel industry. There is also an automated funds transfer system for payments from agents.

continued

continued

Thomson's computer systems provide the means to hold, change and update all business- and holiday-related information. They handle all reservations on about 28,000 travel agent terminals around the country.

★ *Finance and legal department*: Responsibilities of this department include working with marketing on the pricing of each programme, preparing budgets, reporting actual results against the budgets and analysing any variances. It handles all financial transactions, including credit control and payments to accommodation providers and airlines. Company secretarial and legal matters are also dealt with in this department.

▶ BRITANNIA AIRWAYS

Britannia Airways is the UK's largest charter airline. For the summer 1999 season, the airline's fleet comprised 44 aircraft operating from the UK, Ireland, Nordic region and Germany. In 1998, over 60 per cent of the 7 million Thomson Travel Group holidaymakers flew on Britannia and 91 per cent of Britannia's passengers were from across the Group.

▶ LUNN POLY

Lunn Poly is the UK's largest wholly-owned retailer of air-inclusive package holidays, with some 20 per cent of the market in 1998. The company has a nationwide network of nearly 800 travel agencies, from which it sold around 2.3 million package holidays in 1998.

▶ TTG INDEPENDENT HOLIDAYS GROUP

This separate operating division was established in February 1999 and comprises the Holiday Cottages Group and a portfolio of specialist tour operating businesses

continued

continued

catering for the more independently-minded holidaymaker. The Group's principal activity is arranging UK holiday cottage lettings, in which it is the UK market leader.

▶ THE FUTURE OF THE THOMSON TRAVEL GROUP

At the start of 1991, Thomson Travel Group's Managing Director set out the agenda for the 1990s and beyond. He stressed the following points as the way to ensure that Thomson remained at number one:

★ Diversity

★ Reliability

★ Quality

★ Value for money

★ Efficiency

★ People

★ Environment

Thomson Holidays has successfully maintained the number one spot in UK tour operations throughout the 1990s and into the new millennium. Whether it can hold its prime position indefinitely remains to be seen, in the light of the fiercely competitive environment for outbound tour operations.

Case study discussion questions

Browse this website

www.thomson-holidays.co.uk

1 What are the main functions of Thomson Holidays' marketing department?

2 What are the risks and advantages of having a number of different companies within the Thomson Travel Group?

3 Why do you think the company has entered the UK self-catering holiday sector?

4 What are the main external threats and opportunities facing the Thomson Travel Group in the next five years?

Passenger transport

11

Passenger transport offers leisure and business travellers the means of reaching their destinations and is the 'hub' around which the whole of the travel and tourism industry revolves. In this unit you will investigate the different types of transport available to travellers by land, sea and air. You will learn about the operating methods of these different transport types and the regulatory framework surrounding each of them. You will also assess the impacts that transport has on the environment, the tourism industry and society in general.

This unit is divided into four main areas:

- **Different types of transport**
- **Methods of operation**
- **The regulatory framework**
- **Impacts of transport**

We guide you through each of these areas using examples and case studies from the travel and tourism industry. At the beginning of each of these sections you will see a list of key topics to help you fully understand what you need to learn. Look out for the links to websites so that you can learn more about a particular travel and tourism company, organisation or topic.

Different types of transport

Key topics in this section

- **The development of transport types**
- **Influence of transport on travel and tourism**
- **The main characteristics of travel**
- **The integration of travel systems**

The development of transport types

By its very nature, the travel and tourism industry involves travelling to, from and around destinations in the UK and overseas. Transport, therefore, is a vital component of the travel and tourism industry. Transport in tourism covers a variety of water, air and land-based services, including travel by coach, train, private car, taxi, hired car, bicycle, aircraft, cruise ship, ferry and canal craft.

You will have learned in Unit 1 *Investigating travel and tourism* that throughout history the growth of travel and tourism has been synonymous with developments in transportation. This still applies today, with advances in aircraft technology, passenger shipping, road improvements and high-speed rail travel offering faster, more comfortable and more convenient travel. Travel by air dominates the international tourism scene whereas travel by private car is the most popular form of transport for domestic tourism, offering flexibility, freedom and good value for money. Table 11.1 shows the relative importance of road, rail and air transport in Britain, demonstrating a rising trend across all transport modes.

As domestic and international tourists become more experienced and sophisticated in their travel habits, the transport sector is having to respond by offering a wider variety of travel options, using the latest passenger-carrying vehicles and providing the highest standards of customer care. Competition between and within the different forms of tourist transport is also contributing to the emergence of an international transport sector that is becoming more customer-centred in its approach. It is important to remember that transportation is often an integral and pleasurable part of a total travel experience and not merely a means of getting from home to a holiday destination. The excitement felt by young children on a charter flight to a summer holiday destination or the pleasure given to senior citizens on a coach tour serves to illustrate this point well.

Year	Road	Rail	Air	All modes
1988	594	41	5	640
1989	639	39	5	683
1990	645	39	5	689
1991	637	38	5	680
1992	636	38	5	679
1993	637	36	5	678
1994	643	35	5	683
1995	648	36	6	690
1996	658	38	6	702
1997	666	41	7	714
1998	667	42	7	716

Adapted from DETR data

Table 11.1   *Road, rail and air transport in Britain 1988–98 (billion passenger km)*

The transport sector includes not only the services provided for tourists but also the related infrastructure that supports the means of travel, such as roads, motorway service areas, ferry terminals, airports and railway stations. Much of this infrastructure is provided by public agencies, or by public/private sector partnership arrangements. As demand for travel has grown, many transport terminals have developed into large, integrated complexes offering a range of catering, currency exchange, business, retail and entertainment facilities.

The future of transport services

All types of transport services, by land, sea and air, will continue to evolve to meet the forecast growth in domestic and international tourism, and the changing expectations of passengers. A number of important themes are likely to be important in the future development of transport for tourism, including:

- ✪ **Quality**: Travellers will look for high quality services and facilities from transport operators
- ✪ **Competitiveness**: Transport will continue to be a very competitive sector of the travel and tourism industry, leading to lower prices in real terms and the development of innovative products and services

Figure 11.1 *Sheffield's Supertram*

- ✪ **Technology**: The transport sector will continue to make use of new technology in its products and services, giving passengers greater speed, flexibility, safety and convenience

- ✪ **Environment**: Concerns over the impact of transport services and infrastructure on the environment are likely to grow and lead governments and operators to investigate more environmentally friendly transport options, such as park-and-ride schemes, more fuel-efficient vehicles and alternative public transport systems (see Figure 11.1)

Influence of transport on travel and tourism

From the construction of the first road networks in Roman times, the introduction of the railways in the early nineteenth century, the growth of private motoring throughout the twentieth century to the development of jet aircraft in the 1950s, the growth of the travel and tourism industry has been closely linked to developments in transport. The provision of safe, reliable, comfortable, fast, convenient and accessible modes of transport, plus an adequate transport infrastructure, is a vital prerequisite for successful tourism development.

On the positive side, transport developments have given tourists the opportunity of travelling quickly to faraway places at a relatively low cost in comparative safety. From the negative standpoint, the development of transport has encouraged often inappropriate tourism development around the world, lacking respect for the environment, culture and people of overseas destinations. Just as the travel and tourism industry must work towards greater sustainability, so too must the transport sector on which it relies so heavily.

The main characteristics of travel

Air travel

Travel by air dominates international travel, offering leisure and business travellers the chance to reach destinations quickly. The rapid growth in international tourism since the end of the Second World War has been closely allied to the expansion of air travel services. Advances in aircraft technology have led to increases in aircraft capacity and the development of aeroplanes with a far greater flying range. These two factors, coupled with increased demand for air travel generally, have enabled airlines to reduce prices and provide the stimulus for the growth of scheduled services and inclusive tours to medium- and long-haul destinations. Allied to the growth in air services has been the rapid expansion of the associated infrastructure needed to cope with business and leisure tourists as well as freight traffic, including airport terminals and runways. London-Heathrow alone handles more than 60 million passengers per year and is the world's busiest airport.

International airlines have sought to increase their dominance in global markets through acquisitions and strategic alliances with other airlines. British Airways, for example, in attempting to achieve its ambition of becoming the world's biggest airline, has established links with Qantas in order to establish a presence in the Asia/Pacific region, TAT (a French domestic carrier) and Deutsche BA, and has an alliance with American Airlines.

Industry example

Launched in May 1997, the Star Alliance is an example of horizontal integration between airlines. The founding airlines were Lufthansa, United Airlines, SAS, Thai Airways International and Air Canada. Subsequent members were Varig Brazilian Airlines, All Nippon Airways, Air New Zealand and Ansett Australia. New entrants in 2000 were British Midland, Singapore Airlines, Austrian Airlines,

continued

continued

Lauda Air and Tyrolean Airways. Total yearly revenue of Star Alliance group airlines amounts to £42 billion with annual passenger numbers of 296 million. Alliance members serve a total of 815 worldwide destinations.
Other airline alliances include:

★ Oneworld – British Airways, Aer Lingus, American Airlines, Cathay Pacific, Finnair, Iberia, LanChile and Qantas

★ Qualiflyer – Swissair/Sabena, TAP Air Portugal, Turkish Airlines, AOM, Crossair, Air Littoral, Air Europe, LOT Polish Airlines, PGA and Volare

★ Skyteam – Delta, Air France, Aeromexico and Korean Air

★ Wings – KLM, Northwest Airlines, Kenya Airways and Braathens

Rail travel

Given that the railway was the dominant form of mass transportation in western industrialised societies until the rise in car ownership of the early twentieth century and the later introduction of air travel services, it is surprising that the demise in the use of rail services has been so swift. It is true that passenger and freight rail transportation still has an important role to play in some developed nations and is the principal form of long-distance travel for people living in the developing countries of the world. In western societies, travel by rail still occupies a small share of most countries' domestic tourism transportation statistics. From an international tourism viewpoint, rail travel finds itself unable to compete with other travel types for the mass movement of tourists to their holiday destinations.

The general fall in demand for tourist travel by rail is not just a consequence of the rise in popularity of the private car and the introduction of travel by air. It is also a function of government approaches to rail travel, which vary considerably in different regions of the world. If we compare rail travel in the United Kingdom and France, for example, we see a UK rail transport network that has suffered from insufficient investment in rolling stock, signalling and track upgrading. As such, demand for tourist travel by rail has fallen sharply. The French government, on the other hand, has invested considerable public funds in the rail system, with its 'flagship' TGV (*train de grande vitesse*) network offering a high-speed service across the country. The French rail system is used extensively for tourist travel and the TGV is regarded as a viable alternative to domestic air services for business travel within the country. A similar situation exists in Japan, where the so-called 'bullet' trains link major centres of population. One notable exception to the poorly developed UK rail network is the Eurostar service linking London with Paris, Brussels and other major European cities via the Channel Tunnel, offering a high-speed service to business and leisure travellers. As yet, however, the high-speed line between London and the Channel Tunnel is only at the planning stage and is unlikely to be operational for some time to come. The European Union has recently agreed plans to develop an integrated transport network throughout the continent by 2010, including a trans-European rail network. Rail links to airports are also growing in popularity, allowing travellers to leave their cars at home (see Figure 11.2).

Despite the best efforts of countries such as France, international tourist travel by rail has become a 'niche market' product, serving the needs of two particular categories of travellers, namely young people travelling on cheap discount tickets often over a long period of time and older people who can afford the luxury of nostalgic trips on the great railway journeys of the world, for example the Venice-Simplon Orient Express, the trans-Siberian route and tourist trains operating in the North American Rocky Mountains.

Figure 11.2 *The Stansted Express links the airport to London*
Photograph courtesy of Josep Casaoliva

Sea travel

In the same way that rail transportation was the dominant mode of surface travel up to the time of the twin developments of the growth in car ownership and the introduction of air travel services, so the ocean-going liners were the most popular form of sea transport for long-distance international travel up to the middle of the twentieth century. Passenger shipping services suffered badly when air travel services were introduced from the 1950s onwards. Companies such as P&O, Union-Castle Line and Cunard withdrew their services to the USA, South Africa and the Far East; such routes were to be serviced by the more accessible and affordable scheduled air travel services.

The demise of the ocean-going liners forced the passenger shipping industry to diversify into cruise shipping (see Case Study on page 193). Today, cruising is enjoying something of a revival, with the Caribbean, Florida, the Mediterranean, the Baltic, the Far East and Australasia among the principal cruise destinations of the world. Paradoxically, the introduction of the very same air services that signalled the demise of the international passenger shipping industry has boosted cruising, with the development of the fly-cruise holiday, where tourists combine a charter or scheduled flight to and/or from a port with their sea cruise. Whereas in the past cruising tended to be the preserve of rich and famous senior citizens, today's cruising industry has products geared to all ages and budgets. The arrival of mass market tour operators and new-generation vessels onto the cruising scene has heralded a new era of packaged cruises at bargain basement prices.

In many parts of the world, ferries offer inexpensive and reliable services on short sea crossings. Places as diverse as the Greek islands, Hong Kong harbour, the Scottish Highlands and Islands, the Adriatic Sea and the Baltic coastline all rely on ferry services for everyday travel and tourist business. In places where there is strong competition between ferry operators, such as on the short sea crossings in the English Channel, there have been considerable advances in vessel technology, with the introduction of hovercraft, hydrofoils and jet-foils to compete with the fast, new generation of passenger ships. The opening of the Channel Tunnel in 1994 increased competition on cross-Channel services still further. In addition to operating the faster vessels, ferry companies have responded to this challenge by offering price reductions, enhanced levels of customer service and greater on-board shopping and entertainment facilities on their services.

Road travel

The road transport element within the transport sector of tourism includes travel by private car, bus and coach, taxi, hired car and bicycle. The private car is the world's dominant form of travel for tourist purposes, especially for domestic tourism and intra-continental travel. It offers a degree of flexibility,

Figure 11.3   *One of the National Express fleet of coaches*
Courtesy of National Express Ltd

comfort and convenience that cannot be matched by other forms of transport, but it does bring with it considerable environmental impacts. The high levels of car ownership in the densely populated industrialised regions of the world, particularly in Europe, some Far East countries, South America and the USA, have resulted in sharp increases in the use of cars for long holidays, short breaks and recreational day trips. This has led to problems of pollution, physical erosion, loss of land to car parks and congestion in many popular tourist destinations, especially historic cities, coastal resorts and national parks, where vehicles often spoil the very ambience that attracted the tourists in the first place. Central and local governments are attempting to minimise the impact of vehicles by introducing a variety of techniques, including public transport initiatives, road pricing and pedestrianisation.

Travel by coach is an altogether more environmentally friendly form of tourist travel, transporting large numbers of tourists on scheduled services, on transfer journeys or forming the transport element of an inclusive tour, for example a coach holiday in the Austrian Tyrol. In the UK, National Express provides an extensive network of routes (see Figure 11.3).

The integration of travel systems

Tourists who use public transport to reach their destinations expect to be able to use a transport system that offers integration. Long delays while waiting for a connecting train, bus or coach do little to create a positive tourist image of an area. The government's *White Paper on Integrated Transport Policy*, published in 1998, set out a wide range of measures to improve travel by public transport in the UK, including:

- ✪ **Establishing 'quality partnerships' between local authorities and bus operators that will lead to quicker, more reliable services, use higher quality vehicles, offer greater timetable stability and provide better interchanges and connections**

- ✪ **Giving local authorities powers to require public transport operators to promote and participate in joint ticketing and travelcard schemes**

- ✪ **Proposed powers allowing local authorities to impose road user charges to tackle congestion and spread the load from more congested roads (the proceeds from such schemes must be reinvested in transport improvements)**

- ✪ **Asking local authorities to make places safer and more attractive for walking**

- ✪ **Continuing to help with the development of the National Cycle Network**

- ✪ **Working with local authorities, transport operators, the police and motoring and other organisations on specific measures to reduce fears about personal security on transport**

The travel and tourism industry offers customers a variety of ways of combining different types of transport, for example fly-drive holidays, fly-cruise arrangements and private cars on ferries. Taxi services to and from airports, railway stations and coach depots are now commonplace, allowing travellers to leave their cars at home. The quality of transport interchange facilities, such as luggage loading, assistance for people with special needs and refreshment facilities, is continually improving.

At European level, companies such as Stena Line and DFDS Seaways offer packages linking train and ferry travel, while coach operators like Eurolines combine coach and ferry travel on their continental services.

Methods of operation

Key topics in this section

- **Common methods of operation**
- **Air travel**
- **Rail travel**
- **Sea travel**
- **Road travel**
- **Advantages and disadvantages of transport types**

Common methods of operation

Although each transport system has its own particular operating patterns, there are certain basic requirements common to them all, for example:

- **Marketing** – each type of service needs to be effectively marketed and sold to its target market(s)
- **Resource use** – transport operators must manage their physical, human and financial resources in as efficient a manner as possible to remain competitive
- **Profitability** – linked to the efficient use of resources, transport operators must set their price levels so as to maximise profitability and retain, or even increase, their market share

All of these issues have to be addressed against the changing needs and expectations of customers, rising costs and rapidly changing technology.

We will now consider each type of transport in more detail, starting with air travel.

Air travel

Travel by air dominates international travel and is developing rapidly for domestic tourism trips. Statistics from the International Civil Aviation Organisation (ICAO) show that the number of passengers carried on scheduled world airline services rose from 88 million in 1972 to 452 million in 1998, while usage of scheduled domestic services throughout the world rose from 362 million to 1 billion passengers over the same time period.

Organisation of air transport

For statistical purposes, the International Air Transport Association (IATA) classifies air travel services into one of three categories, namely:

1   **Domestic**
2   **International scheduled**
3   **International chartered**

Domestic services refer to air travel within a country, while international represents travel between different countries. Scheduled services are those that operate to a published timetable, on defined routes and under government licence. These services must run regardless of passenger load and are used primarily by business travellers who are prepared to pay a premium for the extra convenience and flexibility offered. Many governments still fund their national airlines, for example Air France, although there is a general move away from state ownership towards private sector operation, or at least private–public sector partnerships.

Chartered air services evolved to serve the expanding package holiday industry and now represent a significant proportion of passenger traffic in many countries with established outbound tourism sectors. Indeed, seat-only sales are one of the fastest-growing products in air travel. Although some package holidays do incorporate scheduled air services, the majority include a charter flight, known as an inclusive tour by charter (ITC). Charter services are generally cheaper than scheduled flights since their operators aim to fill as many seats as possible, often only offering the flight if they can be guaranteed a minimum number of passengers, known as the break-even load factor. Often this figure will be as high as 85 or 90 per cent, after which the operator begins to make a profit on the flight.

The distribution process

The distribution process for the airline sector includes marketing, sales and reservations. The process varies according to whether the ticket to be purchased is for a scheduled or charter flight. Seats on many charter flights are not sold direct to the traveller, but rather to a tour operator, who combines the flight with accommodation and other services to create the package holiday with which we are all so familiar. Seats on scheduled flights, on the other hand, tend to be sold direct to the traveller via his or her travel agent or direct from the airline. Discount tickets are available from a variety of different outlets, including consolidators and the Internet.

The traditional, and still most common, method of distributing airline tickets is via an agent or in the post. Like many business systems used in travel and tourism organisations, ticketing can be either manual or computerised. It is quite rare nowadays to find ticketing systems that are totally manually operated. If not fully computerised, many organisations will at least print their tickets with the help of a computer system and are likely to keep ticket records on a computer. New technology is changing the way that tickets are sold and distributed. Bookings for many airlines can now be made 'on-line' using the Internet. Indeed, some companies operate 'ticketless' transactions, where all bookings are made electronically and no ticket is issued to the customer at all; the low-cost airline easyJet is a good example of this.

Browse this website

www.easyjet.com

Airport products and services

Airports offer travellers a range of products and services, including:

- ✪ **Lounges**
- ✪ **Shops (including duty-free sales)**
- ✪ **Business centres**
- ✪ **Catering outlets**
- ✪ **Information outlets**

The following case study of Birmingham International Airport shows that airports play a vital economic role in their own regions.

Case Study
Birmingham International Airport (BIA)

▶ **INTRODUCTION**

The airport was opened at Elmdon, Birmingham on 8 July 1939. Owned and operated by Birmingham City Council as a municipal airport, it was designed to meet the needs of the residents and the industry of the city and its immediate surroundings.

Civil aviation ceased on the outbreak of the Second World War when the airport was requisitioned by the Air Ministry. Still under government control, the airport reopened for civil flying in July 1946. The City of Birmingham took over responsibility again in 1960. In April 1974, the newly formed West Midlands Metropolitan County Council took over the running of the airport. The

continued

continued

county council incorporated the seven metropolitan areas of Birmingham, Coventry, Dudley, Sandwell, Solihull, Walsall and Wolverhampton. As international flights became available, the terminal and the runway were expanded to cater for these growing needs. However, it soon became evident that a long-term solution was required. 1984 saw the opening of the Main Terminal, with a capacity of 3 million passengers.

In 1986 after the West Midlands County Council was abolished, ownership of the airport transferred to a newly formed West Midlands District Joint Airport Committee still comprising the seven district councils of the West Midlands administrative area. The Airports Act 1986 introduced legislation requiring municipal airports with a turnover in excess of £1 million to become Public Airport Companies and on 1 April 1987, the ownership of the airport transferred to Birmingham International Airport plc, a public limited company owned by the seven West Midlands district councils.

July 1991 saw the opening of Birmingham International Airport's second terminal, the Eurohub. A concept already developed in the United States for domestic operations, Eurohub took the 'hub and spoke' principle a stage further by solving the complications of customs and immigration control which previously demanded separate terminals. Eurohub was the first terminal in the world to combine domestic and international passengers. As a result, the greatest distance passengers have to walk to, from and between flights is only 250 metres, all within a target transfer time of just 25 minutes. In 1993, government public sector borrowing restrictions meant that future development could only be funded by using private sector finance. The local authority owners therefore decided to reduce their shareholding to below 50 per cent in order to restructure BIA into a private sector company and thereby make it possible to finance its £260 million development programme.

continued

continued

▶ MISSION AND OBJECTIVES

Birmingham International Airport's mission statement is:

To be the best regional airport in Europe

Its stated objectives are:

1 To meet the needs of the region the airport serves, both in terms of the services available and the facilities provided

2 To identify areas of potential route development to serve the Midlands region, providing the region's travellers with more services from their local airport

3 To continue to work closely with airlines and tour operators who provide BIA's core product

4 To continue to work with politicians, businesses, organisations and the local community to maintain and support existing routes in and out of the region

5 To work towards services which contribute to the economic well-being of the region, providing both employment and inward investment opportunities

6 To work closely with the local community on a wide range of issues, including the future development of the airport, environmental initiatives and developing programmes to encourage disadvantaged groups in the workplace

7 To develop proactive programmes with local schools, colleges and other organisations both by representation in the community and by welcoming groups and individuals to the airport

8 To minimise the impact of its operations and activities on the environment

9 To offer secure and rewarding careers to employees

10 To secure successful implementation of the airport's master plan *Vision 2005*, a strategic outline for the

continued

continued

future development of the airport designed to satisfy the forecast demand for air transport whilst being compatible with local planning policies, other modes of transportation and the local environment

EMPLOYMENT AND THE LOCAL ECONOMY

BIA and the companies that operate on the site together constitute a major employer in the region. Currently around 5,300 jobs are based at BIA and a further 1,000 jobs off-site, but directly related to the airport. Two-thirds of airport employees live locally in Birmingham and Solihull. Current plans for expansion have the potential to create another 5,000 jobs in the region by 2005. Many other jobs in the region are sustained by the airport's activities. Other employment depends on the international and domestic links that the airport provides. There was £1 billion foreign investment in the West Midlands in 1998/99, 50 per cent from North America. Over 600 US-owned companies in the region have invested over £5.1 billion into the region since 1991, employing around 76,000 people. Over 10,000 jobs have been created in the region as a result of inward investment. The international stature of the region is enhanced by the strength of the direct international links provided by the airport.

The National Exhibition Centre (NEC), adjacent to the airport, hosts over 100 international events, exhibitions and concerts, and is one of the top 10 European venues with over 4 million visitors per year. The International Conference Centre (ICC) in the centre of Birmingham holds over 350 conferences per year and over 250 concerts at its Symphony Hall, the majority relying on good transport links, including BIA.

The airport continues its collaboration with external agencies in the development and implementation of academic and competence-based programmes and has introduced further opportunities for staff to develop

continued

continued

management and supervisory skills through the Certificate in Management Programme.

▶ THE AIRPORT IN THE COMMUNITY

BIA is a regional organisation with its roots firmly fixed in, and committed to, the local and regional communities it serves. The airport and its partners have an extensive programme of schools' liaison covering approximately 200 work experience placements for pupils and students from local schools and colleges, and a number of teacher placements and careers advice initiatives. Key members of the airport team are encouraged to develop individual links with local groups, such as sporting organisations, local school governorships and technology teaching. The airport also undertakes opportunities to support through sponsorship and through the fund-raising of BIA's Charity Committee which raises approximately £10,000 each year. The airport's visitor centre welcomes approximately 250,000 visitors per year and is the tenth most popular tourist attraction in the Heart of England Tourist Board region.

▶ BIA STATISTICS

★ BIA is the 5th largest UK airport, after London Heathrow, London Gatwick, Manchester and Stansted.

★ In 1998, Birmingham International welcomed 6.6 million terminal passengers.

★ It is the 4th largest UK airport for international traffic, operating flights to some 100 worldwide destinations.

★ Destinations include Amsterdam, Barcelona, Brussels, Chicago, Dublin, Delhi, Frankfurt, Malta, Milan, New York, Paris, Toronto and Zurich.

continued

continued

★ Airlines operating from BIA include Aer Lingus, Air Malta, KLM, American Airlines, British Airways, British Midland, Cyprus Airways and Jersey European.

★ BIA has the best punctuality record of all major UK airports, according to the Civil Aviation Authority figures.

★ BIA has been voted UK Business Airport in the *Business Travel World* Awards.

★ BIA has received a national safety award from the British Safety Council. The award recognises the combined effort of both management and staff in reducing accidents.

► TRANSPORT LINKS

Birmingham International Airport is situated approximately 8 miles south-east of Birmingham's city centre. The airport is easily accessible by a variety of public transport types, including:

★ *Trains* – Birmingham International station links BIA to the rest of the UK through a network of inter-city and regional services

★ *AirRail Link* – this shuttle bus service links the airport directly to Birmingham International station and the National Exhibition Centre (NEC)

★ *Buses* – there is a fully integrated network of local bus services

★ *Coaches* – National Express and private hire coaches service the airport

★ *Taxis* – the airport's taxi ranks are operated by various independent taxi firms and are located outside the main terminal and the Eurohub terminal buildings

continued

continued

The airport also has extensive car parking facilities for long- and short-stay visitors.

▶ AIRPORT DEVELOPMENT

In July 1994 the airport published a draft master plan covering its planning policies and development strategy for the period to 2005. Following an extensive consultation exercise on this plan, during which important amendments were made to the proposals, the final master plan was published in August 1995. It sets the development framework within which the airport company intends to operate BIA. That process has since been taken forward by the submission of an outline planning application for the expansion of the passenger terminal facilities and related infrastructure. The Planning Application was submitted to Solihull Metropolitan Borough Council (the local planning authority) in September 1995, and was approved in July 1996.

▶ WHY IS THERE A NEED FOR AIRPORT DEVELOPMENT?

Birmingham International Airport is the airport for the West Midlands and a wider area within an hour's drive. The airport's intention is to serve this region's demand, bringing economic benefits through inward investment, ease of access and creating jobs. In 1996, annual passenger throughput at the airport was nearly 5.5 million. In 1986, annual passenger levels were 2.17 million, giving an average rate of growth over 10 years of 10 per cent per year.

Continued growth is expected in the air travel industry generally, but, in addition, Birmingham International Airport is expected to meet increasing levels of the region's air travel demand. A further doubling of passenger air traffic is forecast at the airport over the next 10 years. The basis of this in traffic terms is as follows:

continued

continued

Summary of passenger forecasts by terminal (000s passengers)

| | Actual | Forecast | |
	1994/95	2000/01	2005/06
Main terminal	3393	4882	6468
Eurohub	1656	2218	2979
TOTAL	5049	7100	9447

This demonstrates the need for more facilities. In economic terms, the airport is invaluable to the region's business, maintaining its competitiveness in world markets. The airport, therefore, helps to keep the region's industry moving and maintains employment, as well as directly creating more jobs in the region.

Case study discussion questions

1 How would you summarise BIA's mission and objectives?

2 Why does the airport need to expand?

3 What are the likely positive and negative impacts of any airport expansion and how can the negative impacts be minimised?

4 Why does the airport get involved with work in the local communities?

5 What internal and external factors are likely to affect the airport's performance over the next 10 years?

Browse this website

www.bhx.co.uk

Timetables and fares

All airlines publish timetables for their scheduled services and tour operators include details of their charter flights in their brochures. Reference manuals that include flight details of the world's major airlines, such as the *OAG Flight Guide*, allow comparison of timings and routes, and are used extensively in planning travel itineraries. All airports have an international three-letter code, for example London Gatwick is LGW, Madrid is MAD and BOS is Boston in the USA. Details of the codes can be found in the airline guides quoted previously or in the *World Travel Atlas* published by Columbus Press.

Browse this website

www.oag.com

Activity
11.1

Familiarise yourself with one of the airline flight guides used in the travel industry, in terms of routes, timings, airport codes, etc.

Rail travel

The present organisation of the rail industry in Britain is shown in diagrammatic form in Figure 11.4.

Some of the acronyms and relationships in Figure 11.4 need some explanation, as follows:

✪ **SSRA stands for the Shadow Strategic Rail Authority, which was set up by government in 1999 to provide a focus and strategic direction to Britain's railways. It liaises with the RPCs (Rail Passenger Committees and Council), which represent the interests of the travelling public.**

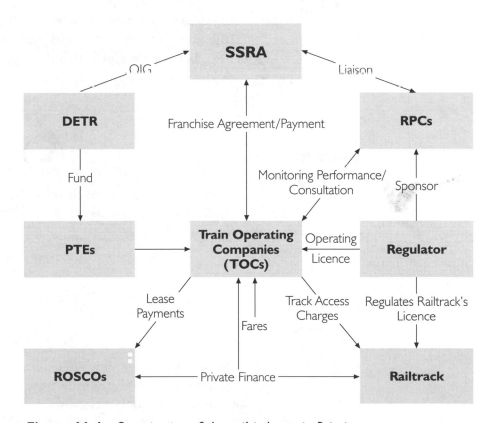

Figure 11.4 *Organisation of the rail industry in Britain*

- ✪ The DETR (Department of Environment, Transport and the Regions) is responsible for government policy on railways and sets objectives, instructions and guidance (OIG) for the SSRA.

- ✪ There are currently 25 train operating companies (TOCs) which are responsible for running the passenger trains.

- ✪ Railtrack owns and operates the national rail infrastructure, i.e. track, signalling, etc., and directly manages 14 major stations.

- ✪ In seven metropolitan areas, PTEs (Passenger Transport Executives) specify the minimum levels of service, administer subsidies and are co-signatories to the relevant franchise agreements.

- ✪ Rolling stock companies (ROSCOs) own rolling stock and lease it to the TOCs for passenger services.

- ✪ The Regulator grants operating licences to the TOCs and regulates the retailing of tickets, information services, competition and monopoly issues.

Browse these websites for information on UK rail services

www.railtrack.co.uk

www.thetrainline.com

Activity 11.2

Familiarise yourself with the National Rail Timetable and use it to work out a selection of journeys between major cities.

Activity 11.3

Carry out some research into the different types of rail fares and rail passes available on rail services in Britain.

Activity 11.4

Browse the Inter Rail website at http://www.raileurope.co.uk/interrail.htm and make notes on the products they sell.

Sea travel

There are many different categories of travel by water, including:

- ✪ **Ferries**
- ✪ **Cruise ships**
- ✪ **Inland waterways (see Figure 11.5)**
- ✪ **Yacht charter**

Ferry routes and fare structures

Sea transport in UK tourism is dominated by the ferry companies, which operate services between the UK and Ireland, Scandinavia and the near continent, principally France, Belgium and the Netherlands. Approximately 9 per cent of all overseas visitors to the UK arrive by car using the many seaports around the coast. If, however, we concentrate on European visitors to Britain, the figure rises to around 20 per cent. Faster, more frequent and more comfortable cross-Channel services, using new-generation 'super ferries', hovercraft and hydrofoils, have given the incoming tourist who wishes to come by car a range of opportunities for travel to the UK. Ferry companies are in fierce competition with Channel Tunnel services to retain their share of the cross-Channel market. It is estimated that approximately 50 per cent of all cross-Channel passenger traffic now uses the Tunnel.

Check out this website

www.eurotunnel.
co.uk

Figure 11.5 *Narrow boats are popular with tourists*
Courtesy of John Ward

Activity 11.5

Locate the following ports on an outline map of the UK:

Folkestone, Ramsgate, Dover, Harwich, Hull, Newcastle-upon-Tyne, Stranraer, Cairnryan, Liverpool, Holyhead, Fishguard, Swansea, Plymouth, Poole, Southampton, Portsmouth

Using a computer word-processing package, make a chart showing all these ports, the destinations to which they offer services and the names of the companies operating these services.

Activity 11.6

Choose one of the major ferry companies operating from the UK and carry out some research on the routes and services they offer, their fleet of vessels, pricing structures, on-board facilities and booking procedures.

Cruise ships

As the following case study demonstrates, cruising has developed into one of the most important sectors of transportation for tourism.

Case Study
Cruising

► **INTRODUCTION**

Cruising is one of the fastest-growing sectors of the travel and tourism industry, showing a 15 per cent increase in demand year-on-year. The growth is clearly demonstrated by the UK market, which tripled in size between 1994 and 2000. Much of this increased demand is due to the arrival of the mass market tour operators into the cruising sector. By utilising their existing programmes of charter flights and accommodation for their cruise passengers, the tour operators have been able to keep prices below those offered by the conventional cruise lines. Consequently, this has opened up the market to a wider clientele and made it more appealing, particularly to first-time cruisers on a tight budget. First Choice entered the fray in 1999 to join Airtours and Thomson, and it is the household reputations of these operators among land-based holidaymakers that have encouraged first-time passengers to take to the seas.

► **TYPES OF CRUISE SHIPS**

Matching the client to the right ship is the fundamental rule of the cruise sector. The types of ships on offer can be categorised as follows:

★ *Mega ships*: These range from 60,000 to 138,000 tons and can be likened to resorts at sea, carrying more than 2,500 passengers. They are most suitable for families and anybody looking for 24-hour entertainment and a lively holiday. The sample price for a seven-night Caribbean cruise on a mega ship starts at around £1,250 per person and includes accommodation, flights, all meals, transfers and taxes. Companies operating in this sector include Royal Caribbean International, Carnival Cruise Line, P&O Cruises and Norwegian Cruise Line.

continued

continued

★ *Traditional ships*: These are more like country manors, with cosy lounges, bars, restaurants and libraries bedecked with antique and plush furnishings. They still have extensive sports and entertainment facilities, but are more discreet. Ship sizes range from 20,000 to 60,000 tons. They are most suitable for clients wanting a cultural experience and who prefer a more intimate holiday away from queues and loud entertainment. The sample price for a seven-night cruise from Athens to Istanbul starts at around £1,600 per person, including flights, meals, accommodation, some shore excursions, port fees and taxes. Companies operating in this sector include Airtours, First Choice, Swan Hellenic, Thomson and Fred Olsen Cruise Lines.

★ *Luxury ships*: These are small but spacious ships where passengers can expect the highest standards of service, plus top quality food and drink. Cabins have elegant bathrooms and restaurants serve à la carte meals. They are most suitable for clients who would otherwise stay in top hotels and travel first class. The sample price for a seven-night cruise from Istanbul to Rome starts at around £2,700 per person and includes flights, transfers, all meals, accommodation, complimentary drinks and taxes.

CRUISE DESTINATIONS

The traditional cruising destinations are facing tougher competition as passengers become more adventurous. Popular destinations include:

★ *UK*: Often overlooked as a cruise destination, the UK offers spectacular scenery, for example along the Irish and Welsh coasts, around the Isles of Scilly and the rugged Scottish Highlands and Hebridean Islands.

continued

continued

★ *Mediterranean*: This remains the number one cruise destination, accounting for half of all UK cruise passengers.

★ *Baltics and Norwegian coast*: Drawn by the scenery of the Norwegian fjords and cities such as Copenhagen, Oslo and St Petersburg, almost 10,000 more UK passengers cruised to Scandinavia in 1999 compared to the previous year.

★ *Caribbean*: The Caribbean is synonymous with cruising, especially during the UK's cold winter months. Most cruises set off from US ports, including Fort Lauderdale and Miami. Fly/cruise is particularly popular with UK travellers to the Caribbean.

★ *Alaska*: The Inside Passage and the Glacier Route are the two main itineraries of an Alaskan cruise, with the primary attractions being the spectacular glaciers and the chance to get close to nature.

★ *The Far East*: This is an ideal cruising area for passengers wanting a cultural experience. Based mainly out of Singapore, many cruise lines take passengers off the beaten track to Vietnam, China, Thailand and Hong Kong.

★ *Around the world*: For clients with money and time on their hands, a round the world cruise is a once in a lifetime experience. Cunard's QE2 sets off on her 21st world cruise from New York to Southampton in 2001.

According to the Passenger Shipping Association (PSA), the top 10 cruise destinations in the world are currently:

1 The Mediterranean

2 Short cruises ex-Cyprus

3 Atlantic islands

4 The Caribbean

continued

continued

5   Scandinavia and the Baltic

6   The Far East

7   West coast USA

8   Alaska

9   Round the world

10 Other destinations

► TARGET MARKETS

In the past, cruising had such a prestigious reputation that most people would never have considered it as a feasible holiday option. Nowadays, perceptions have changed and cruising appeals to a variety of markets, including:

★   Families

★   Single travellers

★   Younger people and first-timers

★   Newly marrieds

★   Business people

► CRUISE TECHNOLOGY

Both the travel industry and passengers can now benefit from the investment made by the cruising sector in new technology. Most of the cruise operators now have Internet sites where it is possible to download information on itineraries, on-board facilities, sample menus, etc. On some sites it is even possible to have a virtual tour of a ship via a web cam. Being in the middle of the ocean doesn't mean being cut off completely. Many ships now offer Internet access and e-mail facilities to passengers.

(Adapted from the *Travel Weekly Cruising Supplement 2000/2001*) www.travelweekly.co.uk

Browse these cruising websites

www.airtours.com

www.cunardline. com

www.fredolsen. co.uk

www.royalcaribbean. com

www.swanhellenic. com

www.pocruises.com

www.festivalcruises. com

Case study discussion questions

1 Why do you think the cruise sector has grown in popularity?

2 What is the world's number one cruise destination?

3 Why is it important to match clients to the right type of cruise ship?

4 How is new technology used in the cruise sector?

Road travel

Major road networks and motorway systems

Britain has a network of motorways (M1, M2, M25, etc.) linked to major 'A' class roads and a large number of secondary 'B' class roads. A map of Britain's principal motorways is included in Unit 7 *UK travel destinations* (see page 29). Many European countries prefix their motorway numbers with 'A', for example France, Italy and Germany. On some road maps of Europe you will also see motorway numbers prefixed with 'E' in addition to the country's own designation, as shown in the map of principal French motorways (autoroutes) in Figure 11.6. The 'E' designation is a move towards the standarisation of road routes across Europe (the 'E' stands for Europe).

Figure 11.6 *Principal French motorways (autoroutes)*

On an outline map of Europe, mark the main motorail routes that are available to UK travellers, marking all origins and destinations of the services.

Advantages and disadvantages of transport types

We have seen throughout this unit that travellers have a wide choice of transport types available to them. How an individual decides to travel is their own personal choice, but it is possible to identify certain advantages and disadvantages of different transport types, for example:

Air travel
Advantages   Speed, refreshments, guaranteed seat
Disadvantages   Luggage restrictions, limited to timetable, limited departure and arrival points, cost

Rail travel
Advantages   Speed, no need to book in advance, refreshments, choice of departure and arrival points, seat reservations
Disadvantages   Limited to timetable, luggage limitations, cost

Sea travel
Advantages   Cars can be taken on ferries, cost
Disadvantages   Limited destinations served, restricted to timetable

Road travel
Advantages   Flexible, 'door to door', cost, no time restrictions
Disadvantages   Environmental, high initial cost, congestion and parking problems

The regulatory framework

Key topics in this section

- **How the transport industry is regulated**
- **Public and social funding of transport**
- **The implications of transport deregulation**

How the transport industry is regulated

Browse this website

http://www.rail-reg.gov.uk/

There are legal obligations on all transport operators to provide safe travel for their paying passengers. The government has a duty to ensure, through licensing and contract agreements, that operators are capable of achieving these aims. We saw earlier in this unit that the rail industry is policed by the Office of the Rail Regulator, which grants operating licences to the train companies and regulates the licence for Railtrack, which has the responsibility for the rail infrastructure.

Browse this website

www.cpt-uk.org

Transport industry trade bodies, such as the Confederation of Passenger Transport UK (CPT), often develop voluntary codes of conduct or codes of practice for their members, so as to ensure safety standards.

The Civil Aviation Authority (CAA) is responsible for all aspects of air travel operation in the UK, including regulation of carriers.

Public and social funding of transport

The government funds, either directly or indirectly, many of the public transport services operating in the UK. Many people would say that the levels of funding have been insufficient in past years to provide the high quality service that everybody expects. Concessionary fares on public transport are made available to certain sectors of society, for example senior citizens and children. Government funding is particularly important in rural areas, where many of the public transport services need a subsidy to keep them operating.

The implications of transport deregulation

Deregulation of transport, i.e. the withdrawal of government control, is intended to increase competition between carriers and, in turn, produce lower fares and higher quality services for passengers (see Figure 11.7). In certain towns and cities in the UK, however, deregulation of bus services has led to an oversupply of vehicles, with resulting pollution and congestion problems. There is little doubt that the deregulation of air travel has increased competition between airlines and helped to keep fares low on an expanding network of routes. Deregulation of coach travel, which occurred in the USA in 1982 and more recently in Europe, has liberalised the market for travel by coach and offered travellers a wider choice of operators. In the case of Europe, EU legislation allows a coach operator from any member state of the Union to offer coach services in any other EU country.

Figure 11.7 *UK bus services are now deregulated*
Photograph courtesy of Josep Casaoliva

Impacts of transport

Key topics in this section

- **Positive and negative impacts**
- **How transport affects the tourism industry**
- **Employment opportunities in transport**
- **Transport systems and society**

Positive and negative impacts

Transport in any form will have impacts on its surroundings and people, some positive and some negative. There has been wide publicity about the damage caused by the construction of new motorways and the extension of airport facilities. Such negative impacts have to be measured against the benefits that new transport developments bring to society as a whole.

As you will have learned from Unit 2 *Tourism development*, the travel and tourism industry can have negative and positive economic, environmental, cultural and social impacts. As the transport sector is so closely allied to the tourism industry, it follows that transport too can have significant impacts. Transport's positive impacts include revenue and job creation, community development and public service provision. Negative impacts of transport include pollution, loss of habitats, noise, air and water quality problems.

Industry example
Birmingham International Airport's environmental policy

In order to achieve its mission of becoming 'the best regional airport in Europe', Birmingham International Airport (BIA) is committed to continually developing and improving its airport facilities. BIA recognises that this objective must be compatible with its commitment to providing the most effective environmental quality management systems and that these systems will enable it to mitigate the environmental impact of its operations. The airport intends to ameliorate community concerns about its operations and those of its airport-based customers by providing progressive environmental protection measures and procedures which will apply throughout the airport, and be available for public scrutiny.

BIA states that it will:

★ *Noise* – ameliorate the noise impact of aircraft and airport operations where possible

★ *Noise insulation* – provide a noise insulation scheme for qualifying residential properties

★ *Air quality* – monitor, report on and improve air quality by reducing emissions where possible

★ *Water quality* – reduce consumption and minimise adverse impact by improvements to surface and foul water drainage systems

★ *Waste management* – minimise waste and recycle where possible. Items purchased will be subject to environmental appraisal

★ *Energy management* – mitigate environmental impact by reducing energy consumption and introducing improved technology

★ *Public transportation* – promote and facilitate the use of public transportation by passengers and staff

★ *Landscape and ecology* – define the effects of airport activity on local ecology, conserve plants and animals, and provide an attractive high quality landscape

Browse this website

www.bhx.co.uk

How transport affects the tourism industry

We saw earlier in this unit that developments in the travel and tourism industry have always been closely allied to developments in the transport sector. Transport continues to affect the travel and tourism industry through, for example, job creation, business expansion and the opening up of new destinations, both in the UK and overseas.

Employment opportunities in transport

The transport sector offers an increasing number and variety of employment opportunities in, for example:

- **Sales and reservations**
- **Marketing**
- **Customer service**
- **Health and safety**
- **Retailing**
- **Operations**
- **Finance and administration**
- **Technical**

Statistics from the Department of Environment, Transport and the Regions (DETR) show that in spring 1999 there were just over 1.2 million people employed in the transport sector in the UK, including 143,000 taxi drivers and chauffeurs, 112,000 bus workers, 42,000 transport managers, 21,000 travel agency managers, 17,000 air traffic planners and controllers, 35,000 travel and flight attendants, and 38,000 railway workers.

Industry example

Air 2000 is the charter airline of First Choice Holidays. It is the UK's second largest charter airline with a fleet of 27 aircraft. It operates 30,000 flights per year from 15 regional airports in the UK and Ireland, carrying nearly 7 million passengers to more than 50 destinations around the world.

Air 2000 currently employs approximately 2,500 staff as follows:

★ Pilots   350
★ Cabin crew   1500
★ Engineering staff   200
★ Ground operations   125
★ Ground administration   325

Browse this website

www.air2000.co.uk

Transport systems and society

As well as being a key component of the travel and tourism industry, transport also plays an important part in society in general. People who own or have access to a car enjoy the freedom and flexibility that this type of transport offers, but, according to DETR figures, there is still nearly 30 per cent of the UK population that do not own a car. These people rely on public transport for their everyday and leisure travel needs. People living in rural areas are particularly dependent on public transport to travel in these remote regions. In its new White Paper *A New Deal for Transport: Better for Everyone*, the government has pledged to work towards an integrated transport system that benefits all members of society, those without cars as well as those who own them.

Working as an overseas representative

12

Overseas representatives play a vital role in the successful operation of a tour operator's programme of holidays. An overseas representative ('rep') is the holidaymakers' first, and probably only, direct contact with the tour company. This unit introduces you to the many overseas jobs available with tour operators and the skills needed to progress in this demanding career. You will investigate the overseas operations of tour operators, as well as the specific roles and responsibilities of overseas representatives. Contact with clients is a vital part of the representatives' job and you will learn about effective communication, administration, presenting local information and personal presentation. You will also consider the employment requirements for working abroad, such as passport and visa requirements.

This unit is divided into seven main areas:

- **Overseas operations**
- **Roles and responsibilities**
- **Communications and relationship with the client**
- **Administration**
- **Gathering and presenting local information**
- **Working overseas**
- **Personal presentation**

We guide you through each of these areas using examples and case studies from the travel and tourism industry. At the beginning of each of these sections you will see a list of key topics to help you fully understand what you need to learn. Look out for the links to websites so that you can learn more about a particular travel and tourism company, organisation or topic.

Overseas operations

Key topics in this section

- **Introduction**
- **Recruitment and placement of resort staff**
- **Managing resort staff**
- **Liaison with UK head office**
- **Administration**
- **Transport**
- **Supplier liaison**
- **Operations**

Introduction

As we saw in Unit 10 *Tour operations*, the division of major, mass market operators into UK and overseas operations means that there are many job roles at home and abroad. Figure 12.1 gives an indication of the main personnel requirements of a major outbound tour operator. Smaller tour operators will need fewer staff, given their smaller scale of operations.

Figure 12.1 shows us that the majority of staff based in the UK are concerned with arranging the package holidays, promoting their sale and controlling the

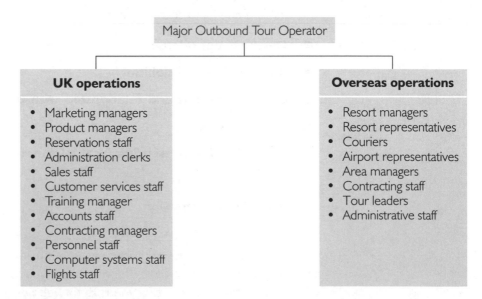

Figure 12.1 *Personnel requirements of a major outbound tour operator*

financial and human resources of the organisation. Overseas staff look after holidaymakers once they are in the resort and handle all administrative duties associated with this function. The UK operation will have a core of full-time, permanent employees, backed up with part-time and contractual staff at peak periods of the season, for example when brochures are distributed, reservations are busy and travel documentation is sent to agents and clients. Many of the overseas staff will be on temporary contracts lasting for the duration of the season, although a small number of staff will be offered all-year-round work either on a summer/winter split season or part UK/part overseas. Fluency in one European language other than English is important for those overseas staff liaising with hoteliers, coach companies, handling agents, etc. Resort representatives tend to be the members of staff who come into contact with holidaymakers the most, making their role as an ambassador for the company very important.

Industry example

Inghams, the specialist ski tour operator, offers a range of overseas appointments throughout the season. These include:

★ *Bar/Brasserie Manager* – responsible for all aspects of running a bar, including staff management and motivation, stock, cash and cost control, maximising profit and sales potential, liaison with suppliers and locals.

★ *Chalet Hotel Host* – responsible for looking after guests, cleaning and the service of meals, wine and drinks.

★ *Chalet Manager* – responsible for all aspects of running in-resort chalet operations, including staff management, budget and menu planning supervision, administration, hygiene, quality control, public relations, sales and problem solving.

★ *Chalet Hotel Manager* – responsible for all aspects of running a chalet hotel, including staff management and motivation, PR and client welfare, budget and menu planning supervision, stock

continued

continued

control, ordering, accounts, general administration, liaising with suppliers and locals.

★ *Head Chef* – responsible for running the kitchen in a chalet hotel, involving menu planning, budget, stock and hygiene control.

★ *Assistant Chef* – responsible to the Head Chef, assisting with preparation and presentation of food and all aspects of kitchen organisation.

★ *Chalet Host* – must be able to cater for 8–10 guests minimum, catering to a very high standard. Duties also include cleaning, looking after guests, menu planning, budgeting and basic administration.

★ *Hostess/Cleaner* – responsible for cleaning rooms, making beds, serving and hosting meals.

Browse this website

www.inghams.
co.uk

As well as having a general duty to provide a high standard of service to the tour operator's customers while abroad, staff in the overseas office of a major UK tour operator will have a number of other specific responsibilities, including:

✪ **Recruitment and placement of resort staff**: A senior representative and/or resort manager will handle the day-to-day deployment of representatives once they arrive in the resort. Recruitment and initial training is likely to have been handled by the personnel department in the UK head office.

✪ **Managing resort staff**: The resort manager will have ultimate responsibility for all aspects of the staff under his or her supervision.

✪ **Liaison with UK head office**: As well as the day-to-day liaison on resort operations, management in the overseas office will feed back to the UK office any formal or informal research findings or customer comments.

✪ **Administration**: Overseas staff are responsible for checking rooming lists and flight manifests (lists of passengers on flights), as well as keeping simple income and expenditure accounts.

✪ **Transport**: Reps are responsible for arranging coach transfers to and from airport and accommodation. They also sell excursions to clients.

- ✪ **Supplier liaison**: Overseas staff will handle initial contacts with hoteliers, car hire firms, coach operators, etc. to smooth out any problems that may arise.

- ✪ **Operations**: Staff have duties in respect of quality control, for example standards of accommodation and catering, plus health and safety issues and dealing with problems of overbooking.

Smaller, specialist UK operators may have a small number of permanent employees based in overseas resorts, but will also use the services of seasonal and part-time UK staff. They also rely on the services of specialist individuals and companies in the resorts to provide a range of ground handling services, such as a 'meet and greet' service, coach transfers and welcome meetings for clients.

Roles and responsibilities

Key topics in this section

- **Introduction**
- **Different categories of overseas representatives**
- **Roles and responsibilities of overseas representatives**

Introduction

Overseas representatives are, to most holidaymakers, the public face of the tour operating company. Clients going on a Cosmos holiday to Torremolinos, for example, will not meet the sales manager based in the UK, nor the head of marketing for the company, but they will have daily contact with their rep, expecting him or her to be the fount of all knowledge about the resort and to be able to help with any problems they may have (see Figure 12.2). How good a rep is at his or her job can have a significant impact on a client's enjoyment of a holiday and the overall image of the company.

From the outside, a rep's job can seem very glamorous, conjuring up images of travel to faraway places, lots of time to explore a resort, endless nightlife

Figure 12.2   *Resort representatives are the public face of the holiday company*
Courtesy of First Choice Holidays

and socialising. This couldn't be further from the truth! Reps work very long hours and are expected to be on call at unsociable hours to answer queries from clients and help in emergencies. Time off in the resort is very limited during the season and the job entails a certain amount of administration and accounting, for example to do with excursions.

Different categories of overseas representatives

There are a number of different types of overseas representatives working for UK-based tour operators in destinations as diverse as Florida, the Gambia, the Caribbean, Paris, Benidorm, Chamonix, the Greek Islands, Hong Kong and Barcelona. Each category of representative has different roles and responsibilities but one thing is constant, every rep needs excellent communication and team working skills, a lot of patience and a great deal of stamina!

We can categorise overseas reps into the following types:

✪ **Resort representative**: This is the type of rep that most of us are familiar with. Resort reps meet and greet clients at the airport, transfer them to and from their accommodation, and act as a source of information and advice throughout their holiday. The job of a resort rep is challenging, varied, responsible and can even be fun! It suits people with a good personality, good organisational and diplomacy skills, plenty of stamina and the ability to sort out problems.

✪ **Children's representative**: This job is ideal for people who like children and like working abroad. An overseas children's rep is responsible for organising activities for groups of children and generally making sure that they enjoy themselves while on holiday (see Figure 12.3). The standard duties of a children's representative working abroad for a holiday camping company include:

  – Providing a variety of activities for children of different age ranges

  – Offering a regular baby-sitting service

  – Visiting newly arrived clients and children to explain the services

  – Maintaining an informative and attractive noticeboard of events

  – Maintaining basic accounts of expenditure

  – Completing a weekly report form

  – Keeping the tents and surrounding area clean and in good order

  – Exercising care and safe practices when planning and delivering activities

  – Liaising with and helping other couriers as required

Figure 12.3 *Children's couriers make lots of new friends!*
© Unijet Travel Limited

Campsite reps will normally be employed for the duration of the season and may be required to work in more than one campsite or resort. Large sites will have a senior representative to control the work programme and delegate duties as necessary. Children's reps need patience, imagination, common sense, energy and good communication skills.

✪ **Campsite representative**: This type of rep typically works for the summer season for a company such as Eurocamp, Sunsites, Canvas Holidays or Eurosites. Full duties of a campsite rep are given in Figure 12.4. Companies look for fit people with good interpersonal skills and the ability to act responsibly in all situations.

✪ **Ski representative and chalet host**: The industry example of Inghams on page 207 shows that the duties of reps and chalet hosts in ski resorts are very varied. Key skills required for these jobs include stamina, good organisational and communication skills, the ability to mix well with clients and plenty of tact!

✪ **Entertainment representative**: Some tour companies employ representatives specifically to entertain their guests while on holiday. This could be singing, dancing, hosting games sessions or something similar. Entertainment skills are needed to be able to do this job effectively, as well as the ability to get on with people of all ages and from different backgrounds.

✪ **Young persons' representative**: Some holiday companies divide the children in their care into different age categories and train some reps in dealing specifically with young people and teenagers. Duties involve arranging discos and other events, water- and land-based activities and

Hours of work and time off

The hours of work of a campsite representative cannot be specified.

You will need to be flexible and adaptable to meet the needs of our customers and therefore it is difficult to specify regular hours of work.

You must remember that whilst on holiday customers may need help at any time and full days off may be difficult, if not impossible, to arrange.

Duties

There are many aspects to a campsite representative's job and although this is not an exhaustive list it is an outline of some of your main duties.

- Montage/demontage duties (erecting and dismantling tents)
- Clean and prepare accommodation for new arrivals (Couriers can expect anything up to 5 hours cleaning per day)
- Welcome new arrivals
- Accompany customers to local doctor/dentist/garage etc. if required
- Act as an interpreter
- Provide advice to customers about local services, i.e. nearest garage if a family has a mechanical problem
- Provide help and support to customers when faced with more serious problems such as road accidents or serious illnesses
- Responsible for arranging the repair/replacement of damaged equipment and replenishment of gas supplies
- Maintain tents and mobile homes as required, or organise external assistance
- Provide current information about local area
- Keep customers up to date about any local events
- Submit regular and accurate reports and basic accounts

Figure 12.4 *Typical duties of a campsite representative*

generally meeting the entertainment needs of this type of holidaymaker. Also, we must not forget that some tour companies now employ older representatives, sometimes called mature couriers or 'golden time hosts and hostesses' in the case of Cosmos Holidays. Older holidaymakers sometimes find it easier to relate to a rep who is closer to their own age.

✪ **Cruise representative**: Demand for cruise holidays has grown dramatically in recent years since some of the major tour operators entered this sector of the travel and tourism industry. This has created opportunities for reps who look after the needs of cruise clients on-board ship and during on-shore excursions.

✪ **Transfer representative**: If a tour operator has a very large number of passengers regularly arriving at a particular airport or airports, they may employ a transfer rep specifically to organise client transfers to and from the airports, thereby releasing the resort reps to carry out their normal duties.

Browse this website

www.cosmos-
holidays.co.uk

Industry example

Cosmos, one of Britain's major tour operators, recruits applicants between the ages of 19 and 27 to be children's representatives in its overseas resorts. The company requires applicants to have a formal childcare qualification, such as NNEB, NVQ 3 in childcare, BTEC in childcare, or similar. Experience of dealing with large groups of children in an open environment is essential. Duties involve organising daytime and evening activities for children's clubs, so musical and artistic talents are an asset, as is a genuine interest in sport.

Roles and responsibilities of overseas representatives

Tour operators often consider that the duties of an overseas representative cannot be fully specified, given the varying nature of the job with its many different aspects. There are, however, a number of principal duties, including:

- **Meeting and greeting customers** – e.g. at the airport, arranging welcome meetings, transferring clients between airport and accommodation at the beginning and end of their holiday, visiting clients in their accommodation

- **Providing information to customers** – e.g. compiling information folders, organising display boards, answering questions during welcome meetings and informally, supplying information during transfers, providing a commentary during excursions

- **Handling groups** – e.g. during transfers to and from the airport, and on excursions

- **Customer service** – e.g. solving problems, dealing with queries and complaints, attending to customers with special needs, selling excursions for which the reps earn commission

- **Contractual and legal aspects** – e.g. ensuring health and safety requirements are met, dealing with suppliers, giving compensation, making refunds

- **Administration and documentation** – e.g. writing reports at regular intervals, handling commission, payments for excursions and currency conversions

- **Personal presentation and company image** – e.g. maintaining a professional approach at all times, even when off duty!

Tour operators look for people who have a responsible and sensible outlook when recruiting overseas reps. Reps need to be tactful, flexible and patient, with a lot of drive, enthusiasm and stamina. They also have to display excellent organisational skills, as the following industry example demonstrates.

Industry example

Thomson, the UK's number one tour operator, offers the following information and advice to would-be overseas representatives in its recruitment pack:

As a member of our overseas team, you will be the face of Thomson. Whether you represent Thomson, Skytours or Portland Holidays, you will be one of the first members of staff that the holidaymaker meets. As such, we will be looking to you to create that excellent first impression and continue to provide the highest quality service throughout their holiday.

We are very aware of the role that our overseas staff play in maintaining our position as the number one holiday company. Although our holidays vary to suit all ages and tastes, our holidaymakers can always rely on receiving a very high quality of service from their resort team.

Working and living in another country is a completely different experience to being at home. The food, the language, the culture and the working hours, to name but a few, will all be new to you. Taking a big step and leaving all your friends and family behind is, therefore, not for the faint-hearted!

The nature of the holiday business also requires a high degree of flexibility. You will work six out of seven days. However, you may be contacted at any time if there is an emergency, so you will need to be willing and able to help if the need arises.

Although leaving your home to work in a different country is a big step, it is also a completely different life experience and on offer is great job satisfaction and excellent career opportunities. So if you want adventure in your life, take a small step towards making a big leap!

Browse this website

www.thomson-holidays.com

Draw up a job description and person specification for the post of resort representative with a major outbound tour operator. The post will be for the summer season only and will be based in Palma Nova, Majorca. You may wish to look at Unit 20 *Human resources* in the travel and tourism industry for more information on job descriptions and person specifications.

Communications and relationship with the client

Key topics in this section

- **Introduction**
- **Face-to-face communication**
- **Group communication and handling skills**
- **Using a microphone**
- **Telephone skills**
- **Handling complaints**

Introduction

Many of the roles and responsibilities of overseas reps are concerned with communicating with customers. This involves communicating in situations associated with decision making and problem solving, assessing situations calmly, empathising with clients and responding to customer needs in the following areas:

- ✪ **Face-to-face communication**
- ✪ **Group communication and handling skills**
- ✪ **Using a microphone**
- ✪ **Telephone skills**
- ✪ **Handling complaints**

Face-to-face communication

By the very nature of the job, being an overseas representative involves a great deal of face-to-face communication with customers, either on an individual basis or in a group situation, for example at welcome meetings, informal talks in the accommodation or on excursions (see Figure 12.5). Important ground rules when dealing with customers face-to-face include the following:

- ✪ **Smile when you greet the customer**
- ✪ **Listen to what the customer is saying**

Figure 12.5 *A rep advising holidaymakers*
© Unijet Travel Limited

- ✪ **Make eye contact but don't stare**
- ✪ **Make sure you look interested**
- ✪ **Address the customer by name**
- ✪ **Don't interrupt the customer**
- ✪ **Keep a reasonable distance from the customer, not too close and not too far away**
- ✪ **Always thank the customer when appropriate**

Face-to-face communication has distinct advantages when compared to other situations when you cannot see the customer. For example, it is the best way of creating a positive impression with the customer, through a welcoming smile, professional manner and smart appearance. Face-to-face communication also allows you to see customers' responses to what you are saying.

Group communication and handling skills

Dealing with groups can be an altogether more skilled task than communicating face-to-face with an individual customer. Handling group situations calls for good organisational and communication skills, so that every member of the group turns up in the right place at the right time! Although the group you are dealing with may be very large, it is important to make every effort to treat the members of the group as individuals by, for example, addressing people by name and taking time to talk to them on a one-to-one basis, particularly those that you feel may need a little more attention or support.

There are certain ground rules that you need to adopt when communicating information to a group of customers, including:

- ❂ **Make sure that members of the group can see, hear and understand you**
- ❂ **Communicate effectively in simple language, using a clear, confident tone of voice**
- ❂ **Make sure that everybody has understood what you have said by allowing time for questions**
- ❂ **Make yourself available afterwards if people want further clarification on a one-to-one basis**

Dealing with groups of clients is an important part of the work of an overseas representative, for example when organising transfers, conducting excursions or on guiding duties. Developing group handling skills will ensure that you can:

- ❂ **Ensure the safety and welfare of groups of clients**
- ❂ **Handle mixed groups, e.g. by age, gender, language**
- ❂ **Handle difficult groups, e.g. rowdy, that are under the influence of alcohol or complaining**
- ❂ **Deal with medical and emergency situations**

Activity 12.2

Take turns at playing the role of a tour guide by taking the rest of your group on a tour of your school/college or the local area. When the tour has finished, the 'customers' should discuss the strengths and weaknesses of each guide, concentrating on communication with the group as a whole as well as with individual group members. You may also like to role play the situation of a group of rowdy holidaymakers to practise some different group handling skills!

Using a microphone

Although daunting at first, most overseas reps need to be able to use a microphone, usually on a tour bus, to communicate with large groups of clients. Many tour operators include developing this skill in their reps' pre-resort training, where staff role play the sort of situations they are likely to find themselves in when abroad. The same general rules that are followed when dealing with groups also hold good when using a microphone, for example making sure that you can be heard by everybody, speaking slowly in a clear tone and giving people time to ask questions or clarify points.

Telephone skills

The telephone is an increasingly important part of daily life, not least in the work of overseas representatives, who increasingly use mobile telephones to keep in touch with each other while in resort. Clients are given contact numbers of the resort office and/or UK head office in case of difficulty or emergency. Some smaller, specialist operators, who may not have a fully staffed overseas office, may also give their reps' mobile numbers to clients. Whatever the circumstances, there are a number of important points to bear in mind when dealing with incoming telephone calls from other members of staff or clients, for example:

- **Answer all calls quickly – leaving a call for more than five rings is considered inefficient**
- **Greet the caller with your name and/or your organisation and ask how you can help**
- **Smile while you are talking! This may sound crazy, but it really does help you to project a welcoming tone to the customer**
- **Listen carefully to what the caller is saying**
- **Always speak clearly and use language appropriate to the caller**
- **Take notes if there is a message for another member of staff**
- **Transfer calls to another appropriate member of staff if you cannot deal with the customer yourself**
- **If you promise to call a customer later, make sure you do it!**

Similar rules apply if you are making an outgoing telephone call.

Handling complaints

Although the great majority of holidaymakers have a trouble-free holiday, there are occasions when reps have to deal with complaints from clients.

This may result from a number of causes, including overbooking, flight delays, accommodation of a poor standard, noise or poor quality food.

The key actions to take when handling complaints are:

- ✪ **Listen attentively so that you get the whole story first time**
- ✪ **Thank the customer for bringing the problem to your attention**
- ✪ **Apologise in general terms for the inconvenience but do not grovel**
- ✪ **Provide support for the customer by saying that the complaint will be fully investigated and matters put right as soon as possible**
- ✪ **Sympathise with the customer and try to see the situation from their point of view**
- ✪ **Don't justify the circumstances that led up to the complaint and go on the defensive**
- ✪ **Ask questions if you are not clear on any points of the customer's complaint**
- ✪ **Find a solution to the problem**
- ✪ **Agree the solution with the customer**
- ✪ **Follow through to make sure that what you promised has been done**
- ✪ **In future, try to anticipate complaints before they happen!**

One step on from somebody who has a justifiable complaint is the customer who is intent on 'causing a scene'. Just like handling complaints, there are tried and tested ways of dealing with these individuals:

- ✪ **Try not to let them get you down or get under your skin; the fact that they wish to cause a fuss may be a sign of their own insecurity**
- ✪ **Never argue with them – it can often get the member of staff into deeper trouble**
- ✪ **Never be rude to the customer, however rude they are being to you!**
- ✪ **Try not to take any remarks personally – you may have had nothing to do with the alleged incident but are simply the nearest member of staff**
- ✪ **Let the customer do the talking and listen to what they have to say**

If a situation appears to be getting out of hand, it is wise to seek help from another rep or senior member of the overseas team.

Administration

Key topics in this section

- **Completing reports**
- **Financial records**

The job of an overseas rep includes a certain amount of basic administration and finance, including:

✪ **Completing reports**: e.g. health and safety reports, customer complaint forms and reports, weekly accommodation reports, incident reports, lost property reports and specific reports at the request of head office

✪ **Financial records**: e.g. petty cash records, expenses sheets, excursion ticketing, commission and sales receipts, records of payments to suppliers, currency exchange records and monthly income/expenditure summary reports

All administrative and financial documentation needs to be completed accurately, concisely, objectively and factually.

Activity 12.3

Calculate the amount of commission (in £ and Greek drachma) that an overseas rep will earn from organising an excursion for 28 adults and 18 children to a water park 19 miles from a holiday resort in Corfu. Prices of the excursion (including admission to the water park) are 10,000 drachma for each adult and 8,000 drachma per child. Assume that the rep will earn 20 per cent commission on all excursion sales. You will need to find out the current £/drachma exchange rate to complete this activity.

Gathering and presenting local information

Key topics in this section

- **Local area**
- **Local and nearby attractions**
- **Hotel and nearby attractions**
- **Local laws and customs**

Many of the responsibilities of overseas reps are concerned with gathering local information and communicating this information to customers, for example:

Browse these websites for information on overseas destinations

www.wtg-online.com

www.travelocity.com

www.tourist-offices.org.uk

www.lonelyplanet.com

www.oag.com

www.roughguides.com

- ✪ **Informing clients about local facilities and attractions at the welcome meeting**
- ✪ **Passing on information during transfers to and from the airport**
- ✪ **Guiding holidaymakers through the resort area and on excursions**
- ✪ **Compiling information books and folders**
- ✪ **Maintaining informative notice boards**

Sources of local information include tourist offices, guidebooks, the Internet, local hoteliers and restaurateurs, as well as other overseas staff. In addition to investigating what local attractions, facilities and events a resort has to offer holidaymakers, reps also need to know about local laws and customs, such as religious codes and festivals.

Activity 12.4

Working as part of a team, choose a popular overseas holiday destination and gather together information on its attractions, facilities and events. Use the information you collect to make a notice board that could be used by British people on holiday in the resort. Use a range of information sources, such as guidebooks, tourist offices and the Internet, to gather your information.

Working overseas

Key topics in this section

- **Passport and visa requirements**
- **Work permits**
- **Employment contracts**
- **Finances**
- **Insurance**
- **Health agreements**
- **Languages**

Passport and visa requirements

Browse this website for information on visa requirements

www.wtg-online.com

It is important that people working overseas have the correct passport and visa documentation. Visas are not generally required by British people travelling to other countries in continental Europe, but may be needed for working in some long-haul holiday destinations. Information on visa requirements for different countries is available direct from embassies of the countries concerned or from travel and tourism directories such as the *World Travel Guide* published by Columbus Press.

For all the countries in Europe, apart from the Irish Republic, people travelling from the United Kingdom need to have a valid passport to comply with immigration and other controls. Some continental European countries have abandoned routine passport checks at their frontiers but they all expect visitors to be able to provide evidence of identity and nationality by way of a valid passport or national identity card while in their country. British travellers must, therefore, have a standard 10-year British passport.

British passports

The standard 10-year British passport is only available to adults over 16 years of age who are in the UK at the time of application and who have one of the following citizenships:

- ✪ **British citizen**
- ✪ **British Dependent Territories citizen**
- ✪ **British Overseas citizen**
- ✪ **British Subject**

At the time of writing, the current fees for passport applications and amendments are as follows:

- ✪ **Standard adult 10-year passport (32 pages)**   **£28.00**
- ✪ **Large size adult 10-year passport (48 pages)**   **£38.00**
- ✪ **Child's passport (0–15 years, valid for 5 years)**   **£14.80**
- ✪ **Amendments (e.g. change of name/photographs)**   **£17.00**

Applications can be made at any one of 2,000 United Kingdom Passport Agency (UKPA) partners (currently post offices and Worldchoice travel agencies) or direct to a UKPA office in Belfast, Glasgow, Liverpool, London, Newport (Gwent) or Peterborough.

Work permits

It is usual for the tour operator to investigate whether a work permit is needed by an overseas representative and to make the necessary arrangements with the appropriate embassy.

Employment contracts

By law, all UK employers are required to give employees, except those taken on for less than a month, a written statement of their main terms and conditions of employment within two months of taking on the employee (or if at an earlier stage the employee is required to work abroad for a period of more than one month, the statement must be given before he or she leaves). Particulars of the following must be included in the statement:

- ✪ **The names of the employer and the employee**
- ✪ **Job title or brief job description**
- ✪ **The date when the employment (and, if different, the period of continuous employment) began**
- ✪ **Wages or salary and the intervals at which they are to be paid**
- ✪ **Hours of work**
- ✪ **Holiday entitlement**
- ✪ **Entitlement to sick leave and sick pay**
- ✪ **Pensions entitlement**
- ✪ **Entitlement of the employer and the employee to notice of termination of employment**
- ✪ **Where it is not permanent, the period for which the employment is expected to continue, or, if it is for a fixed term, the date when it is to end**

- ✪ **Place of work**
- ✪ **Existence of any collective agreements that directly affect the employee's terms and conditions of employment**

The written statement must also include a note giving details of the employer's disciplinary rules and grievance procedures, although employers with fewer than 20 employees need give only the contact name for raising a grievance.

Finances

Most reps have their salary paid directly into their bank account abroad, so establishing a method to withdraw cash overseas is important. In most large resorts, this is relatively easy using a bank cash machine and an appropriate cash card, but, in case of emergencies, it is advisable for reps to set up other arrangements with a local bank in the resort where they are based. Smaller resorts, for example on some Greek Islands and in Turkey, may not have cash machines. In these cases, opening a bank account locally is the most sensible option. From time to time, some countries impose restrictions on the amount of cash that can be taken in or out, in order to protect their own exchange rate and money supply. Details of these can be found in directories such as the *World Travel Guide* published by Columbus Press.

Browse this website for information on currency restrictions in particular countries

www.wtg-online.com

Insurance

Private insurance, covering medical expenses and personal possessions, is recommended for representatives working abroad. Personal and public liability is likely to be covered under the tour operator's own insurance arrangements.

Health agreements

You are probably familiar with the E111 form that gives UK residents access to free or reduced cost emergency health treatment while travelling in Europe. The E111 is valid in all countries of the European Economic Area (EEA), which consists of the 15 member states of the European Union (EU) plus Iceland, Liechtenstein and Norway. Only state-provided emergency treatment is covered by the E111 and visitors will receive treatment on the same terms as the nationals of the country being visited. Form E111 is available from post offices in the UK.

Form E128 is a document which demonstrates that the holder is entitled to free or reduced cost medical treatment for *any* condition during a period

Browse this website
for information on the
E111, E128 and health
advice for travellers

www.doh.gov.uk/
traveladvice/

of study in another EEA member country, or while working temporarily in another EEA country for a UK employer or as a self-employed person. This is the form that overseas reps need for their period of work abroad. Form E128 is available from the Contributions Agency.

Languages

Although not essential for all overseas representatives' posts, fluency in, or familiarity with, another foreign language can be a distinct advantage, particularly for more senior posts that may carry responsibilities for liaison with suppliers in a particular country, as the following industry example demonstrates.

Browse this website

www.cosmos-
holidays.co.uk

Industry example

Cosmos, one of the UK's longest-established holiday companies, recruits a number of Resort Representatives every year to work in its overseas destinations. Applicants need to be between 21 and 30 years of age and possess a minimum of 5 GCSEs or equivalent at grade C or above, including maths and English. Any further education, particularly in travel and tourism, is an advantage, as is a working knowledge of a second language. In the case of Cosmos, they look for people with familiarity in Spanish, Italian, Portuguese or Greek, although other tour operators will have their own language requirements when recruiting.

Personal presentation

Key topics in this section

- **Personal presentation**
- **Uniform requirements**
- **Body language**
- **Appropriate language**
- **Drinking and smoking**
- **Morality**

Personal presentation

First impressions count in any business, particularly in the travel and tourism industry where dealing with people is such an important part of the work. It is vital for overseas reps to understand that the way they present themselves to customers has a direct influence on the clients' enjoyment, as well as the rep's job satisfaction and the future success of the tour company (see Figure 12.6). In particular, reps need to appreciate the importance of the following when dealing with customers:

- ✪ **Grooming and cleanliness**
- ✪ **Personality**
- ✪ **Attitude**

Grooming and cleanliness

This can be a sensitive area, particularly when supervisors and managers have to remind staff about the importance of arriving at work in a clean, hygienic and presentable fashion. All staff working in travel and tourism, but especially those whose work brings them into close contact with customers, must:

- ✪ **Be generally clean**
- ✪ **Have hair that is clean and combed**
- ✪ **Have fresh breath**

Customers will not tolerate staff with poor body odour or bad breath and may well take their custom elsewhere. It is important to remember that the staff are the outward image of an organisation. For example, if you are greeted at an airport by a representative who smells of stale cigarettes or

Figure 12.6 *Personal appearance is very important for reps*
© Unijet Travel Limited

whose hair is unkempt, your first impressions of the company and your holiday are likely to be negative. If, on the other hand, the rep is smartly presented, with a pleasant smile and tidy hair, you are much more likely to be impressed with the tour company from the outset.

Personality

There is a saying in travel and tourism that to get on in the industry you must like people. While this may seem an obvious statement, it cannot be emphasised enough; if you don't like dealing with people, don't get a job as an overseas rep!

It is often said that people with the 'right' personality will do very well in the travel and tourism industry. Employers are always keen to employ staff who are:

✪ **Good communicators**
✪ **Outgoing and confident when dealing with the public**
✪ **Good at relating to customers**
✪ **Able to work under pressure**
✪ **Reliable and trustworthy**

Most of the responsibilities and roles of overseas reps involve dealing with the public, so a pleasant personality and helpful manner are essential. People are on holiday to have fun and relax, and staff play an important part in providing a pleasant experience for customers.

Attitude

It is important to remember that every member of overseas staff is a representative of the organisation and should always have a positive attitude to customers, acting in a professional manner at all times. There are certain ground rules that you must respect when working in travel and tourism. For example, you should *always*:

✪ **Be loyal to the organisation**

✪ **Follow organisational procedures**

✪ **Respect the buildings and equipment where you work**

✪ **Be friendly and courteous with both colleagues and customers**

✪ **Separate your private and professional life as far as possible**

✪ **Respect the views of others**

✪ **Treat both colleagues and customers as you would want to be treated yourself**

✪ **Be honest and constructive**

✪ **Ask if there is anything you are unsure about**

To make sure that you project a professional attitude at work, you should *never*:

✪ **Criticise the organisation to, or in front of, customers**

✪ **Discuss confidential information outside work**

✪ **Argue or swear in front of customers**

✪ **Lose your temper at work**

✪ **Drink alcohol at work**

✪ **Act in a way that could put anybody at risk**

By following these common sense guidelines overseas reps will provide clients with a pleasant and courteous service.

Uniform requirements

Nearly all holiday companies provide uniforms for their overseas staff. Uniforms help to create a positive first impression with customers and make staff easily identifiable if customers need help or advice (see Figure 12.7). The wearing of a uniform also presents a consistent image to the public and helps to build customer loyalty. However, it is important to remember that

Figure 12.7 *A uniform creates a positive first impression*
© Unijet Travel Limited

the word 'uniform' does not necessarily mean a very formal dress code. Overseas reps working on campsites or as children's reps, for example, wear a company 'uniform', but it often consists of a polo shirt, shorts and trainers. The important point about a uniform is that it should be appropriate and functional, i.e. suited to the nature and demands of the job. Overseas staff should be informed at interview about the dress code for the job and what type of uniform is supplied.

Body language

We say a lot about ourselves even without speaking! Non-verbal communication is the way that we send and receive messages without the use of the spoken or written word. Body language is the most common type of non-verbal communication and can be classified as follows:

- ✪ **Bodily contact** – shaking somebody's hand is an example
- ✪ **Physical proximity** – the distance we feel we need to keep between ourselves and other people, for example when queuing at a tourist attraction

- ✪ **Orientation** – where we place ourselves in relation to others, e.g. by tradition, a manager or supervisor running a team meeting will sit at the head of the table
- ✪ **Posture** – whether standing, sitting, lying down, walking or running, there is often something about our body posture that relays a message to those around us
- ✪ **Gestures** – we all make gestures from time to time to signal approval or disapproval, for example a 'thumbs up' to show that all is well or banging on a desk to show that you are not happy with a decision!
- ✪ **Facial expressions** – the face can transmit an enormous variety of messages and emotions, either consciously or subconsciously
- ✪ **Eye contact** – whether we are aware of it or not, we pay a great deal of attention to a person's eyes when they are communicating with us

Overseas staff are often trained in portraying positive body language by, for example, smiling, using appropriate eye contact and maintaining the correct posture.

Appropriate language

Pre-placement training of reps often includes reference to using appropriate language with clients and other members of staff, including not swearing or using slang. A rep's employment contract may well include a clause about respectful behaviour while at work, including the use of appropriate language.

Drinking and smoking

Tour companies have different policies on members of overseas staff drinking and smoking on duty. These are explained to overseas staff on appointment. The overriding concern of all companies is that members of staff are not under the influence of alcohol while at work. Some companies will instantly dismiss staff who are found to be drunk in the workplace.

Morality

Overseas reps must comply with the tour company's policy on relationships with colleagues and customers. As with drinking in the workplace, inappropriate relationships with clients and colleagues, particularly while on duty, are best avoided.

Visitor attractions

14

Visitor attractions are a key component of the UK travel and tourism industry, offering their guests fun, excitement and education. Indeed, the existence of an attraction is often the single most important reason why tourists visit a destination. This unit introduces you to the factors that contribute to the success of a visitor attraction. You will investigate the different types of visitor attractions found in the UK, their appeal and popularity. You will also learn about location and access in relation to attractions and the importance of design and technology in planning and managing attractions. The final part of the unit considers the operation and management of attractions by looking at such matters as managing visitor and traffic flows.

This unit is divided into four main areas:

- **Appeal and popularity**
- **Location and access**
- **Design and technology**
- **Attractions operation and management**

We guide you through each of these areas using examples and case studies from the travel and tourism industry. At the beginning of each of these sections you will see a list of key topics to help you fully understand what you need to learn. Look out for the links to websites so that you can learn more about a particular travel and tourism company, organisation or topic.

Appeal and popularity

Key topics in this section

- **Introduction – what is a visitor attraction?**
- **Types of visitor attractions**
- **The appeal of a visitor attraction**
- **The popularity of visitor attractions**

Introduction – what is a visitor attraction?

This may sound a strange question with which to start an investigation of visitor attractions! We all have our own ideas of what constitutes an attraction; if you live in Birmingham you might think of Cadbury World as an example of a visitor attraction. Those living in the south of England might mention Thorpe Park or Chessington World of Adventures. People living in Wales may include Oakwood theme park or Caernarvon Castle on their list of attractions, while residents of Scotland are likely to mention the Scott Monument in Edinburgh or the Burrell Collection in Glasgow. The people of Northern Ireland would surely put the Giant's Causeway or the Waterfront Hall in Belfast towards the top of their list of visitor attractions.

While all these well-known examples clearly fall within anybody's definition of a visitor attraction, it is important to remember that the majority of attractions throughout Britain are not household names. Small museums, craft galleries, shops, leisure facilities and farm attractions, to name but a few, are crucial to the economic well-being of many areas of the country. Together, they form the 'critical mass' of attractions in a locality that forms the basis for encouraging tourists to explore and perhaps stay overnight. As the following English Tourist Board definition of a 'visitor attraction' shows, such places should be promoted to local people as well as to tourists:

> *A permanently established excursion destination, a primary purpose of which is to allow public access for entertainment, interest or education; rather than being a primary retail outlet or a venue for sporting, theatrical, or film performances. It must be open to the public, without prior booking, for published periods each year, and should be capable of attracting day visitors or tourists, as well as local residents.*

The importance of visitor attractions

Attractions are one of the key components of the UK travel and tourism industry, along with accommodation, destinations and transportation, as shown in Figure 14.1.

Indeed, many people would argue it is the drawing power of an attraction that is the prime reason for making a leisure trip at all and that, without an attraction, tourism in an area is unlikely to prosper. The importance of attractions is demonstrated in the following examples:

✪ **Overseas visitors are attracted to London to see its historic buildings, heritage and monuments, including the Tower of London, Nelson's Column and Buckingham Palace**

✪ **British holidaymakers are enticed by the natural attractions of a variety of European countries, such as the French Alps and Norway's fjords**

✪ **Day visitors look for fun, thrills and excitement at major UK attractions, such as Thorpe Park, Chessington World of Adventures and Blackpool Pleasure Beach**

The British Tourist Authority (BTA) estimates that there were in the region of 396 million visits to UK attractions in 1998.

Figure 14.1 *The structure of the UK travel and tourism industry*

Working with a partner, draw up a list of 10 UK and 10 worldwide destinations and list the principal attractions of each, e.g. York – Jorvik Viking Centre, York Minster; Paris – the Eiffel Tower, the Louvre. Present your findings as a chart, indicating whether each attraction is man-made or occurs naturally.

Browse this website

www.alva.org.uk

Industry example

Member companies of the Association of Leading Visitor Attractions (ALVA) comprise the majority of Britain's biggest and best-known attractions, including Castle Howard, Harewood House, Tate Gallery Liverpool, Chatsworth, Alton Towers, Blackpool Pleasure Beach, Canterbury Cathedral, Thorpe Park, Blenheim Palace, Beaulieu, Tate Gallery St. Ives and Longleat.

In London, ALVA members include the British Museum, Natural History Museum, Buckingham Palace, St Paul's Cathedral, London Eye, London Zoo and the Royal Botanic Gardens at Kew.

Between them ALVA member attractions welcome over 85 million UK and overseas visitors each year, representing some 25 per cent of all the visits made annually in the UK. They seek to provide the highest quality visitor experience.

Types of visitor attractions

Many of Britain's visitor attractions are the products of geology, geography, history and culture, such as its coastline, mountains, museums, monuments and historic buildings. Others are more recent additions to the tourism scene, offering visitors excitement and entertainment, e.g. theme parks, indoor arenas and family entertainment centres (FECs). These examples indicate that visitor attractions can either occur naturally or be built. We will now look in greater detail at the role that each of these categories of attractions plays in the travel and tourism industry.

Natural attractions

On a global scale, the range and variety of natural attractions is immense. Everything from the Sahara Desert and the ice caps in Greenland to the Great Lakes of North America and the foothills of the Himalayas will appeal to particular types of tourists. Closer to home, the natural beauty of the British countryside has been attracting visitors for centuries, with its rugged coastline, majestic mountains and picturesque dales. Many of our natural attractions are of international significance and play a major role in attracting overseas tourists, for example the Lake District, Snowdonia, the Highlands of Scotland and the Mourne Mountains in Northern Ireland. The UK's abundance of natural attractions is also a major motivating force for domestic leisure travellers, whose presence helps to sustain the wide variety of tourist amenities and facilities found throughout Britain. A tourist visiting Cornwall, for example, may initially be attracted by the county's scenic beauty, but will also make use of other tourist support services, such as accommodation, transportation, catering, built attractions and entertainment facilities. The British countryside is a major resource for travel and tourism. English Tourist Board (now the English Tourism Council) figures estimate that there are in the region of 550 million day visits to the countryside each year, a quarter of which take place in July and August. The Countryside Agency suggests that some 18 million people visit the countryside on a fine summer Sunday. In certain parts of Britain, the pressure on the countryside is such that the visitors are in danger of damaging the environment permanently and are certainly guilty of spoiling the very beauty that attracted them in the first place.

It is for this reason that many of Britain's most scenic and fragile areas have been granted special status to help protect their environment and provide facilities for their enjoyment by the public. These include the National Parks and Areas of Outstanding Natural Beauty (AONBs) shown in Figure 14.2, and Britain's Heritage Coasts.

Browse these websites

www.countryside.
gov.uk
(Countryside
Agency)

www.ccw.gov.uk
(Countryside
Council for Wales)

The task of overseeing these protected areas in England lies with the Countryside Agency, whose aim is to conserve and enhance the natural beauty of England's countryside and help give people better opportunities to enjoy and appreciate it. The Countryside Council for Wales does a similar job in the Principality.

National Parks

There are 10 National Parks in England and Wales (see Figure 14.2), covering approximately one-tenth of the land area of England and Wales. They were established under the 1949 National Parks and Access to the Countryside Act (the Broads in Norfolk and Suffolk, and the New Forest are not National Parks as such but have equal status). In October 1999, the Countryside Agency began the process of designating the New Forest as a National Park. In addition, the South Downs are being considered for designation as a

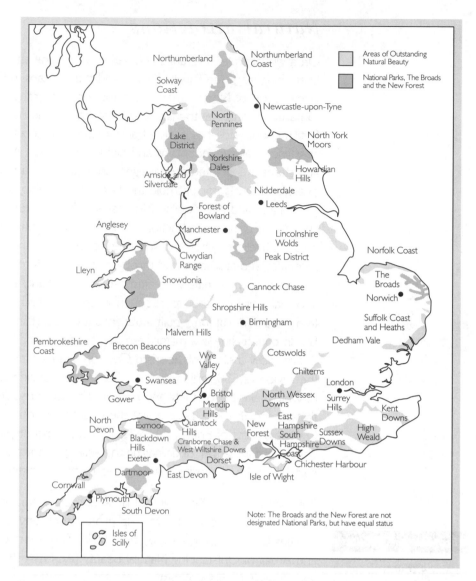

Figure 14.2 *National Parks and Areas of Outstanding Natural Beauty (AONBs) in England and Wales*

National Park. The word 'national' does not mean that the Parks are owned by the government; most of the land within National Park boundaries is privately owned and often under severe pressure from visitors and their vehicles.

The Parks are run by National Park Authorities, set up by law as single purpose local authorities with the twin purposes of:

1   **Conserving and enhancing the natural beauty, wildlife and cultural heritage of the Parks**

2   **Providing opportunities for the understanding and enjoyment of the special qualities of the Parks by the public**

In pursuing these purposes the National Park Authorities also have a duty to foster the social and economic well-being of their local communities. Funds for the National Parks are provided directly by government (75 per cent) and the local authorities (25 per cent) within the Park area. Working in partnership is a very important aspect of ensuring successful policies are developed and implemented within the National Parks for the benefit of the environment, local people and visitors.

Areas of Outstanding Natural Beauty (AONBs)

Thirty-seven of England's most cherished landscapes are protected as AONBs (see Figure 14.2). They range from the wild open moorlands of the North Pennines to the green-belt countryside of the Surrey Hills and the intimate valley of the Wye, which straddles the border with Wales (there are another four AONBs wholly within Wales itself). AONBs can be popular destinations for travel and tourism, although, unlike National Parks, they are not designated for their recreational value. The Countryside Agency has proposed stronger measures for their management and more funding for their upkeep. In total, AONBs in England cover around 15 per cent of the landscape.

Heritage Coasts

There are 44 Heritage Coasts in England and Wales. They are among the most precious assets for wildlife and landscape, as well as for tourism. Concern over the harmful impact of increasing numbers of visitors led to their designation and a plan of action which includes creating and repairing footpaths, cleaning up bathing water and removing litter.

Built attractions

The term 'visitor attraction' generally brings to mind a purpose-built facility, designed to provide a blend of fun, entertainment, activity, stimulation and education. On a national scale, attractions that spring to mind easily include Beamish Open Air Museum, the London Eye and Alton Towers (see Figure 14.3). Internationally, we can think of the Epcot Center at Disney World in Florida or the Pompidou Centre in Paris. Closer to home, your local area is likely to support a number of attractions, perhaps a museum, heritage centre or leisure park. While these built attractions are easily identifiable and provide important facilities for tourists, we must not forget that the natural world also offers visitors a wide variety of sights and experiences.

We will now look at some of the different types of built visitor attractions in more detail.

Heritage attractions

Today, the word 'heritage' is often used to describe a particular type of visitor attraction that aims to depict what life was like at a particular point in time in

Figure 14.3 *Alton Towers*
Courtesy of Alton Towers

the past. Many villages, towns and cities have attached the word 'heritage' to their existing museums as a way of promoting themselves more widely and increasing their visitor numbers. They are part of a trend towards themed attractions, with the Jorvik Centre in York and the Tales of Robin Hood in Nottingham being good cases in point. Certain areas of Britain have established attractions to celebrate their industrial heritage, e.g. Ironbridge Gorge in Shropshire and the Big Pit museum in South Wales.

Cultural attractions

Some destinations attract visitors because of their cultural diversity or associations with music, the arts or famous people. Shakespeare's birthplace in Stratford-upon-Avon is a magnet for UK and overseas visitors alike, while the Cardiff Singer of the World competition attracts visitors from all over the world to Wales. The cultural diversity in cities such as London, Bradford, Leicester and Manchester is used as the springboard for themed events and short breaks, e.g. curry weekends in Bradford and visits to the Chinatown area of London (see Figure 14.4). Cities such as Florence, Leningrad and Vienna attract visitors from around the world to sample their diverse associations with music, the arts and history. Museums and galleries have long been popular places to visit for entertainment and educational purposes. Museums of national importance in Britain are not only located in London, but are also to be found in places as diverse as St Ives in Cornwall (Tate Gallery), Bradford (National Museum of Photography, Film and Television),

Figure 14.4 *London's Chinatown*
Photograph courtesy of Josep Casaoliva

Glasgow (the Burrell Collection), Cardiff (National Museum of Wales) and Birmingham (National Motorcycle Museum).

Theme parks

A theme park is a visitor attraction offering permanent rides and entertainment in a themed setting or range of settings, providing something for the whole family. Most theme parks charge one price for unlimited access to all rides and attractions in a fun environment. Since the first UK theme park opened at Thorpe Park in 1979, there has been a rapid rise in the number of attractions and volume of visitors; the number of theme parks had risen to 7 by 1984 and increased to 10 in 1993. The number of visitors to UK theme parks rose from 5.4 to 10.8 million between 1985 and 1994, with revenues up from £29 million to £130 million over the same time period.

Although each UK theme park has its own particular attractions, there are certain common characteristics that theme parks exhibit, for example:

- **Parks offer a mix of facilities and activities, e.g. 'white knuckle' rides, live entertainment, animals, gardens, events, children's play areas, education centres, corporate hospitality, retail and catering**
- **Most parks operate on a seasonal basis between Easter and the end of October**
- **Most visitors are family groups from the C1/C2 social classes**
- **Group bookings account for between 10 and 25 per cent of all visitors**

Browse these theme
park websites

www.thorpepark.
co.uk

www.alton-
towers.co.uk

✪ Typically, parking for 3,000–4,000 cars is provided

✪ Site areas range from as little as 12 acres to 800 acres plus, with 130–140 acres being a typical size

✪ Parks are generally close to the motorway network, ensuring very large two-hour catchment populations (up to 15 million)

✪ Length of stay on site averages between 6 and 7 hours, presenting park operators with ample opportunities for generating secondary spend, e.g. catering and retail outlets

Activity
14.2

Carry out some research to discover the principal theme parks and major attractions within a two-hour drive time of where you live.

Historic monuments

Browse these websites

www.english-
heritage.org.uk

www.warwick-
castle.co.uk

www.westminster-
abbey.org

www.warwick-
castle.co.uk

www.cadw.wales.
gov.uk

Monuments such as Edinburgh Castle (see Figure 14.5), Westminster Abbey and Warwick Castle have great appeal to UK residents and overseas visitors

Figure 14.5 *Edinburgh Castle*
Photograph courtesy of Antonio Martinez

to Britain. Most historic monuments are in public ownership, with many London properties under the management of the Historic Royal Palaces Agency, a division of the Department for Culture, Media and Sport (DCMS). Many castles and stately homes in Britain are cared for by the National Trust, CADW: Welsh Historic Monuments and English Heritage, who manage the sites and provide facilities and services for visitors. Castles are a particular feature of the attractions scene in Wales, where Caernarvon Castle receives approximately 300,000 visitors per year.

Activity 14.3

Find out which historic monuments in your area are open to visitors, what facilities they provide, what they charge for admission and how they promote themselves.

Entertainment

Facilities such as nightclubs, discos, concert halls, theatres (see Figure 14.6), arenas and opera houses all provide entertainment opportunities for visitors to an area. The bigger the venue, the greater the attraction; arenas such as the NEC Arena in Birmingham and Sheffield Arena, for example, are major

Figure 14.6 *Theatres are a major attraction*
Photograph courtesy of Josep Casaoliva

venues for concerts, attracting people from wide catchment areas. Part of the appeal of UK resorts is the range of entertainment facilities they can offer the visitor. Tourists at seaside resorts such as Blackpool, Brighton and Scarborough, for instance, will be attracted by live shows, concert halls and a range of 'night life' opportunities. Smaller towns and cities will also attract day visitors from their own locality to enjoy what's on at nearby cinemas, theatres and nightclubs.

Sport and recreation facilities

As well as being popular with local people, sport and recreation facilities can also add to the appeal of towns and cities, helping to attract overnight and day visitors. Many local authorities and private operators have upgraded existing swimming pools or built new leisure centres to cater for their needs. Stark, rectangular municipal baths have been replaced with leisure pools boasting such facilities as wave machines, jacuzzis, saunas, flumes, waterslides and splash pools. Many pools are part of larger leisure complexes offering activities such as squash, badminton, tennis, karate, bowls and hockey. On a national scale, sports facilities can help change the image of an area and attract inward investment, e.g. the National Cycling Centre in Manchester and the Don Valley Stadium in Sheffield. Internationally, cities compete to host major sporting events such as the Olympic Games, Commonwealth Games and motor racing Grand Prix, providing the best in sports entertainment for local people and visitors.

The appeal of a visitor attraction

It is clear that not all visitor attractions will appeal to every type of person in the UK. Some people will look for thrills, fun and excitement by visiting theme parks and entertainment venues, while others will prefer the peace and quiet of trips to the countryside, stately homes and gardens. To be successful, any attraction must be clear on precisely which type or types of visitors it is targeting and provide the right facilities and amenities to meet their target markets' needs. Market research is used to gather information on existing and potential visitors to attractions, and is an essential first step in identifying customers' needs.

Having established its target market(s), a visitor attraction must develop a 'product' that its customers will appreciate and enjoy. It will need to give attention to a number of considerations, including:

- **The main features offered by the attraction**
- **Extra features aimed at particular types of visitors, e.g. coach parties, school visits, conferences and corporate hospitality (see Thorpe Park industry example below)**

- Special events and activities, e.g. historic car rallies, balloon festivals, music concerts, etc. (see **Alton Towers industry example below**)

- Catering facilities, e.g. restaurants, pizza parlours, ice cream outlets and links with national chains such as **Burger King** and **McDonald's**

- Other facilities, e.g. baby changing, wheelchairs, buggies, car parking, transport links, etc.

Browse this website

www.alton-towers.co.uk

Industry example

Throughout the season, Alton Towers holds a number of special events aimed at increasing the 'dwell time' (how long they stay on site), and therefore spend, of visitors. Special events include the Fearsome Five Challenge in which visitors have to ride all the attraction's big five rides to claim a free, limited edition T-shirt, and the UK's largest firework and laser spectacular. Alton Towers has also played host to a number of pop concerts featuring Tina Turner, Wet Wet Wet, M People and James.

Industry example

Thorpe Park in Chertsey, Surrey promotes itself as a fun day out with many exciting rides and attractions, but it also markets itself as a venue for corporate (business) functions. Its facilities include:

- ★ *The Dome* – a large single span area for conferences, exhibitions, themed evenings or large dinner/dances.

- ★ *Thorpe Belle* – this is a Mississippi-style paddle steamer catering for up to 200 people. It is used for

continued

continued

Browse this website

www.thorpepark.
co.uk

small conferences, company evenings and company fundays.

★ *Lakeside* – a large, covered hospitality area which is a purpose-built pavilion-style structure covering an area of nearly 558 sq. metres. Over a 3-hour period, Lakeside can comfortably cater for up to 1,000 people.

★ *Peninsula* – a large grassed area located by the lake covering nearly 7,000 sq. metres. It is used for large exhibitions, trade shows, product launches and other corporate events.

★ *The Henley Room/Crown & Anchor Pub* – with a capacity of 50, these facilities are used for cocktail parties, barbeques and business receptions.

The Corporate Services Department at Thorpe Park is responsible for the smooth running of all corporate functions. They supply a co-ordinator to look after each client from initial booking to completion of the function.

The popularity of visitor attractions

All visitor attractions operate within a competitive business environment, with the need to respond to continual changes in consumers' tastes and fashions. There may be direct competition between rival attractions, perhaps between two stately homes in the same part of the country and offering visitors a broadly similar experience. Competition also exists between different facilities in the travel and tourism industry, e.g. a heritage centre, ice rink and cinema in the same town will all be trying to attract customers to their premises, using a variety of promotional techniques. In a wider sense, spending on visits to attractions is in direct competition with other items of household expenditure, such as spending on food, clothing and energy.

It is against this background of competition for visitors that attractions either prosper or fail. Visitor attractions that maintain and even increase their popularity tend to:

- ✪ **Give customer care a high priority**
- ✪ **Be responsive to changes in consumers' tastes and fashions**
- ✪ **Research their markets well**
- ✪ **Be effectively promoted**
- ✪ **Have a professional approach to health and safety**
- ✪ **Have effective management structures**
- ✪ **Invest in staff training**
- ✪ **Have effective financial controls**

Attractions that are professionally managed will have a far better chance of retaining their popularity in the face of increasing local and regional competition.

Trends in popularity of attractions

Like so many aspects of today's consumer society, the popularity of visitor attractions will fluctuate over time. Some of the recent attractions funded through the National Lottery have shown that popularity doesn't always last very long! The popularity of visitor attractions will often reflect fashions and 'fads' seen across society as a whole, for example:

- ✪ **The growth in visits to cinemas has led to the development of multiplex and multi-screen facilities throughout Britain, often with other leisure and retail services on the same site**

- ✪ **The general trend towards making museums appeal to a wider range of visitors has led to the use of new technology exhibits and artefacts to provide a more 'hands on' experience for the visitor**

- ✪ **Increasing concern for the environment has led to the development of attractions focusing on farm life, wildlife conservation, energy, habitat management, etc**

- ✪ **Many attractions have invested in 'all weather' facilities to help extend their use, e.g. indoor arenas, covered leisure pools and 'all weather' sports pitches**

- ✪ **Many natural attractions, such as waterways, nature reserves and forests, have improved access for visitors and offer a wider range of educational and interpretive facilities, e.g. guided walks, self-guided trails and visitor centres**

No matter how an attraction has sought to improve its appeal to visitors, its owners or managers will be only too well aware of the fiercely competitive market in which they operate and the problems often associated with funding and developing a visitor attraction.

Visitor numbers and trends over time

Figures from the English Tourism Council report *Visits to Tourist Attractions 1999* reveal that sightseeing visits in the UK rose by over 1 per cent over 1998, but are still slightly below their pre-1998 level. The trend is based on a constant sample of 3,568 properties. The proportion of attractions reporting an increase in visits in 1999 was 53 per cent, compared with 43 per cent in 1998. *Visits to Tourist Attractions 1999* gives a listing of 2,328 attractions with a minimum of 10,000 visits per annum. Of these, 60 per cent are privately owned, 29 per cent are owned by local authorities and 11 per cent are owned by the government or its agencies. Of the total number of attractions, 38 per cent offered free admission and 73 per cent were open for nine months or more.

The 1999 figures show that outdoor attractions fared better than indoor sites, with farms, gardens, country parks, steam railways, wildlife attractions and leisure parks all experiencing above-average increases in attendance figures. Visits to museums, visitor centres and historic properties showed a small decrease in numbers. Overall, the popularity of national tourist attractions in 1999 remained buoyant.

The popularity of major attractions is shown in Table 14.1, which gives details of the 1999 top 20 UK attractions charging for admission.

		1999 Visits
1	Alton Towers, Staffordshire	2,650,000
2	Madame Tussaud's, London	2,640,000
3	Tower of London	2,422,181
4	Natural History Museum, London	1,739,591
5	Legoland, Windsor	1,620,000
6	Chessington World of Adventures	1,550,000
7	Science Museum, London	1,480,000
8	Royal Academy, London	1,390,000
9	Canterbury Cathedral	1,350,000
10	Windsor Castle, Berkshire	1,280,000
11	Westminster Abbey, London	1,268,215
12	Edinburgh Castle	1,219,720
13	Flamingo Land Theme Park, North Yorkshire	1,197,000
14	Drayton Manor Park, Staffordshire	1,174,448
15	Windermere Lake Cruises, Cumbria	1,140,207
16	St Paul's Cathedral, London	1,076,222
17	London Zoo	1,067,917
18	Chester Zoo	965,721
19	Victoria and Albert Museum, London	945,677
20	Thorpe Park, Chertsey, Surrey	926,000

Adapted from data in Insights, ETC

Table 14.1 *Top 20 UK attractions charging admission*

As Table 14.1 shows, Alton Towers was, once again, UK's most popular attraction charging admission. Its attendance figures remained relatively steady during the 1990s, as the following figures demonstrate:

1994   3.011 million
1995   2.700 million
1996   2.749 million
1997   2.701 million
1998   2.782 million
1999   2.650 million

Visitor attractions, particularly theme parks, must constantly review what they offer their visitors and introduce new facilities in order to retain their market share.

Types of visits

The types of visits to an attraction will be a combination of:

- **Day visits**
- **Repeat visits**
- **Holidays**
- **Short breaks**

Location plays an important part in determining the precise type of visits to any attraction. An attraction close to a centre of population will attract a high proportion of day visits, while one located in a busy holiday region will benefit from tourists on holiday. Some large attractions encourage visitors to stay overnight and spend an extra day at the attraction by offering all-inclusive packages in conjunction with local hoteliers. Alton Towers has gone one stage further by building its own on-site hotel. The growth in short breaks means that attractions are gaining more revenue from this type of holiday experience. All attractions try to encourage repeat visitors, some by offering discounted entry after a first visit and some by running events. Theme parks, museums and other attractions must regularly change what they offer the public in order to tempt back previous visitors.

Types of visitors to attractions

Visitor attractions appeal to different people for different reasons; one family may enjoy a day out at London Zoo, for example, while another might prefer a trip to the nearby Natural History Museum; yet another family may choose somewhere else entirely. Whatever the reasons behind the choice of an attraction, all sites will have a wide range of types of visitors, each with different characteristics. For a typical visitor attraction, these could be:

- **Groups booked in advance**
- **Individuals who pay on arrival**

- ✪ **Family groups**
- ✪ **Young couples**
- ✪ **Special interest parties**
- ✪ **People with disabilities**
- ✪ **Overseas visitors**
- ✪ **Corporate guests**
- ✪ **Local people**
- ✪ **Senior citizens**
- ✪ **School parties**

This list gives an indication of the difficult task of satisfying the needs of each of these different types of visitor, often referred to as 'markets', and stresses the importance of precise market research to identify exactly who visits an attraction and whether they are happy with the 'product'.

Browse this website

www.alton-towers.co.uk

Industry example

Alton Towers in Staffordshire is the most popular paying attraction in the UK, welcoming around 3 million visitors per year. The types of visitors to the attraction can be broken down into:

- ★ Individuals
- ★ Coach groups
- ★ Companies
- ★ School parties
- ★ Group organisers

The age profile of visitors to Alton Towers is as follows:

Age (yrs)	Percentage
Under 7	4.8
8–12	4.0
13–17	19.2
18–24	28.9
25–34	21.1
35–44	14.3
45–54	5.9
Over 55	1.9

Activity 14.4

Choose a local visitor attraction and find out what particular markets it is trying to attract and whether the type of visitors has changed in the past five years.

Location and access

Key topics in this section

● **Factors affecting the location of an attraction**
● **Factors affecting access to an attraction**

Factors affecting the location of an attraction

The location of natural attractions and many cultural heritage sites is pre-determined. Built attractions, however, may be located at sites chosen from a range of factors, including:

✪ **Proximity to major population clusters and markets**
✪ **Transport links**
✪ **Suitable land**
✪ **Other facilities nearby**

Proximity to major population clusters and markets

A visitor attraction that is located close to a large urban area will clearly have a large catchment on which to draw. For example, Chessington World of Adventures, situated 12 miles south of London, has a catchment of 18 million people living within a two-hour drive of the attraction. On the negative side, Chessington has to compete with a wide variety of other attractions located in and around London.

Transport links

All attractions will aim to ensure that it is as easy as possible for visitors to travel to the site either by public transport or in a private car. Promotional leaflets and websites will include travel information, as this example from the Chessington World of Adventures main guide illustrates:

> *Chessington is situated 12 miles from London on the A243, just 2 miles from both the A3 and M25 junction 9. Bus/coaches – Bus 71, Flightline 777, West Link 468 and London Country 465, all stop directly at the main entrance. SouthWest Trains – Chessington South station is a 10 minute walk from the main entrance. Regular services run from Waterloo station,*

also stopping at Clapham Junction and Wimbledon. All coach and car parking is free.

Suitable land

A visitor attraction that is being launched from new will need suitable land or premises on which to be developed. So called 'brown land' is land in urban areas that has been used for another purpose in the past but is now available again for development. The land formerly used for steel working in the Don Valley in Sheffield is a good example of 'brown land' that has since been redeveloped for leisure and sport, with the building of the Don Valley Stadium, Sheffield Arena and various retail/leisure complexes. Although sometimes more expensive to develop than previously undeveloped 'green field sites', 'brown land' is considered a more environmentally friendly option since no new areas of countryside are taken for development. Whether an attraction is considering a 'brown land' or 'green field' site, planning permission will be required from the relevant local authority, whose staff will consult the regional tourist board to gauge trade reaction to the proposed development.

Other facilities nearby

A single attraction in an area that has little in the way of 'tourism infrastructure', i.e. other attractions, hotels and other accommodation, tourist information centres, events, etc., may struggle to attract sufficient visitor numbers to survive. Tourism is an industry where partnerships usually pay dividends. Attractions will carry information on accommodation providers and vice versa. It is sometimes said that an area needs a 'critical mass' of attractions before it can be considered viable in tourism terms. Attractions providers in an area sometimes join together to market their attractions collectively in order to increase visitor numbers.

Factors affecting access to an attraction

In the case of visitor attractions, 'access' is an all-embracing term covering geographical access (transport routes and parking), physical access to the attraction (particularly for people with mobility problems) and access for all sectors of the community, regardless of, for example, their age, gender, race or income level (reflected in the attraction's pricing policy).

Access to an attraction can also have an impact, positive or negative, on the local community and environment. Attractions need to implement measures to make sure that their operations impact as little as possible on local communities.

Browse this website

www.alton-towers.co.uk

Industry example

Alton Towers in Staffordshire works very closely with the local community and as a result has strong ties with the surrounding villages. Members of the management team sit on both the Alton Liaison Committee and the Alton Parish Council. Alton Towers also allocates complimentary guest passes to all households within a 2–3 mile radius. Regular donations are also presented to local schools, charities, sports groups and other organisations. Staff from Alton Towers' Cleansing Department regularly 'litter pick' throughout the surrounding area, helping the local villages of Alton and Denstone to win 'Best Kept Village' awards.

Transport routes to the attraction

Good signposting, both to the locality of the attraction and within its immediate vicinity, is necessary to ensure safe and manageable visitor flows for pedestrians and traffic. Larger attractions are eligible to use the tourist board approved 'brown and white' signs on roads close to their sites, while all attractions can make use of the temporary signposting services offered by the AA and RAC. Local planning and highways authorities need to be consulted before any signs to visitor attractions are erected, since planning permission may be required.

Parking and transfer facilities

Attractions must give careful consideration to how they manage car and coach parking. Statistics show that the great majority of visitors to large attractions outside of cities use their cars for travel. To give you an idea of the scale of provision in two of the UK's major attractions, Thorpe Park has parking facilities for 8,000 cars and 250 coaches, while Alton Towers provides 6,000 car parking spaces and 250 coach spaces. Depending on the design and layout of an attraction, visitors may have to park their cars away from the main site and transfer by bus, model train or even water-driven tramway, in the case of the Centre for Alternative Technology in West Wales.

Opening times and dates

As with other sectors of the travel and tourism industry, seasonality is an issue with visitor attractions. Demand for some high-profile attractions is such that they can afford to open all year round. However, the great bulk of attractions in the UK operate seasonally, often opening at Easter and closing after the October half-term school holiday.

Pricing policy

Attractions and amenities in the non-commercial sector, such as municipal golf courses, leisure centres, museums and sports grounds, will be operated on the basis of providing a service to their local community, as well as welcoming tourists. They will have social and community objectives, often reflected in their pricing and admissions policy. This could involve discounted rates for local Council Tax payers, perhaps via a 'passport' scheme, or cheap rates for senior citizens, single parents and unemployed people at off-peak times. Some facilities will be dual use, where a leisure centre, for example, is used by a school or college between the hours of 9 a.m. and 4 p.m. and by other local people and visitors at all other times.

Private sector attractions will also seek to maintain goodwill with local people by offering them discounted or even free access to facilities at certain times of the year, perhaps the beginning and end of the season. They may also target certain under-privileged sectors of their local community, running special events and promotions for their enjoyment. They will also have a range of concessionary prices for different types of visitor, for example senior citizens and disabled visitors, as the example tariff shown in Figure 14.7 demonstrates.

Oxbridge Leisure Park
2000 Tariff

Prices			
Individuals	**On day**	**In advance**	
		Specified date	**Open dated**
Adult	18.50	16.50	17.50
Child	14.50	12.50	13.50
Senior/OAP	14.00	12.00	13.00
Disabled Adult	11.00	N/A	N/A
Disabled Child	11.00	N/A	N/A
Helper	Free entry if accompanying a guest who could not otherwise visit on their own (i.e. wheelchair bound).		
Family (2 + 2 / 1 + 3)	56.00	52.00	54.00
Moonlight Mardi Gras Adult	9.50	N/A	N/A
Moonlight Mardi Gras Child	8.00	N/A	N/A
Evening Events Adult	9.50	N/A	N/A
Evening Events Child	8.00	N/A	N/A
Season pass			
Season Adult	70.00		
Season Child	70.00		
Family Season Ticket (2 + 2, 1 + 3)	219.00		
Miscellaneous			
Buggy Hire	4.00		

Figure 14.7 *Oxbridge Leisure Park's tariff*

Design and technology

Key topics in this section

- **Introduction**
- **Facilities for visitors with specific needs**
- **Technology in visitor attractions**

Introduction

We mentioned earlier in this unit when considering the changing popularity of attractions that many visitors are looking for an 'experience' rather than simply a day out when they visit an attraction. The design of visitor facilities at both natural and built attractions is aimed at meeting this challenge by satisfying the varying needs of customers and providing an enjoyable leisure experience. The design of an attraction can be described by reference to:

- ✪ **Entrances, exits and car parks**
- ✪ **Main features of the attraction**
- ✪ **Additional features, e.g. information, WCs, first aid, picnic areas, catering and facilities for visitors with specific needs**

Facilities for visitors with specific needs

As well as ensuring good access to a site by both public and private transport, visitor attraction operators will be keen to provide a welcoming, safe and accessible environment on-site for all visitors, including those with impaired mobility or disabilities. It makes good business sense to spend time assessing a site and its facilities from the visitors' point of view, so as to minimise their inconvenience and provide an enjoyable experience for all. Most people's expected 'normal' level of mobility is reduced, temporarily or permanently and to varying degrees at some time in their life, so focusing attention on access to attractions can pay dividends. Injury, illness, pregnancy, ageing or simply walking along with a toddler, all present their own mobility problems. Only a small proportion of the population is in the peak-of-fitness age group and nobody stays there for very long! Back pain sufferers, bifocal wearers and people with slight hearing loss are not uncommon. At any one time, it is estimated that there are 10 million people in the UK in circumstances that affect their mobility. Many would consider themselves 'inconvenienced' rather than 'disabled', but they are nonetheless an important market for visitor attraction operators.

Physical access to an attraction is only one part of the story for those with mobility problems. They will certainly want to feel confident that they will enjoy their visit and not have to struggle to cope, but just as important is that they should feel accepted as valued customers and not treated as a nuisance or an inconvenience.

Providing accessible visitor attractions

In the early 1990s, the Visitor Attractions Advisory Committee of the national tourist boards invited a working group, composed of representatives of the UK tourism industry and disability organisations, to propose a system of assessment and accessibility of attractions, supported by relevant design guidance. Its aim was to continue the work of the Tourism for All Campaign but focus particularly on the attractions sector of the industry.

The results of the working group's findings were published in 1994 as an English Tourist Board report entitled *Providing Accessible Visitor Attractions*. One of the principal assumptions of the report was that attraction operators would want more and happier customers, who would stay longer, spend more on-site, return and recommend the attraction to their friends. The report offered visitor attraction operators an opportunity to:

1   **Appraise the market for visitors with impaired mobility or disabilities**

2   **Understand the disabled visitor's needs**

3   **Examine the best design solutions**

4   **Carry out an initial access assessment**

It contained the information needed to assess, plan and put into action an effective access policy, combining physical design with effective marketing and customer care. The comprehensive report attempted to answer a range of questions concerning access to visitor attractions, such as:

✪   **What are the benefits of catering for visitors with impaired mobility or disabilities?**

✪   **What is it like to be a wheelchair user?**

✪   **How does information on access help to promote an attraction?**

✪   **What signs should be used to welcome and direct visitors?**

✪   **How should staff be trained to communicate with disabled visitors and meet their special needs?**

- ☼ **What size should doors and ramps be so as to give unhindered access?**
- ☼ **How can disabled visitors get the best out of exhibitions, rides, play areas, etc.?**

The report included a useful checklist for visitor attraction operators who wish to carry out an initial assessment of the existing level of accessibility, including recommended standards and criteria for parking, paths, seating, ramps, steps, lifts, handrails, doors, toilets, telephones, communication and marketing.

Activity 14.5

Carry out some research to discover which visitor attractions in your locality have been developed or modified to be able to accept visitors with disabilities.

Industry example

Alton Towers makes every effort to ensure that its attraction is accessible to all guests. On most rides, visitors in wheelchairs and their helpers are allowed to approach via the exit, thereby avoiding queue lines. Throughout the attraction, disabled toilet facilities are available and the Park has its own medical centre where special needs can be catered for, e.g. cold storage of medicines and specialised equipment. Wheelchairs are also available to hire from Guest Services.

Browse this website

www.alton-towers.co.uk

Technology in visitor attractions

Rapidly developing technology has allowed visitor attractions to experiment with a wide range of electronic, laser and computer-generated equipment to enhance visitor satisfaction, including:

- ☼ **Simulation and virtual reality** – e.g. computer-generated images, live action film or 3D film involving visitors in passive or interactive experiences. Special effects are also used to create realistic simulations, for example sound, wind, mist or smell.

✪ **Animatronics** – this is the use of animated figures and remotely operated robots in rides and exhibits.

Good examples of this new generation of visitor attractions are:

✪ **Jorvik Viking Centre in York**
✪ **The Oxford Story**
✪ **The Canterbury Tales**
✪ **The White Cliffs Experience at Dover**
✪ **Techniquest in Cardiff**

Activity
14.6

Choose one of the four attractions listed above and gather some more information on how they operate and the facilities they offer their visitors.

Attractions operation and management

Key topics in this section

- **Introduction**
- **Guiding and interpretation**
- **Health, safety and security**
- **Secondary spending**
- **Managing visitor and traffic flows to and within attractions**

Introduction

The operation and management of attractions involves many topics covered elsewhere in your course, for example in units focusing on business systems, human resource management, financial planning and control, customer service and marketing. We begin this section of the unit by looking at four aspects of attractions management and operation in greater detail, since they are vital to the success of an attraction. First of all we will consider the ownership and objectives of attractions, then investigate funding and finally focus on marketing and promotion.

Ownership of visitor attractions

The ownership of an individual visitor attraction will depend on whether it falls within the private, public or voluntary sector of the industry. However, with the privatisation of many national and local facilities, it is not always easy to tell precisely into which sector an attraction falls. Figure 14.8 shows some of the major UK visitor attractions and indicates into which sector each falls.

As Figure 14.8 shows, private sector organisations operate the major theme park attractions in the UK, with their primary commercial aim being profit

Private sector	Public sector	Voluntary sector
Alton Towers	Buckingham Palace	York Minster
Drayton Manor	Tower of London	Corfe Castle (NT)
Thorpe Park	Edinburgh Castle	Salisbury Cathedral
American Adventure	Cardiff Castle	Jorvik Viking Centre
Madame Tussaud's	British Museum	Ironbridge Gorge

Figure 14.8 *Ownership of major UK visitor attractions*

Figure 14.9 *Big Ben is a major London attraction*
Photograph courtesy of Antonio Martinez

maximisation. Well-known national attractions, such as the Tower of London, the British Museum and Big Ben (see Figure 14.9), are operated and funded through the public purse. Visitor attractions in the voluntary sector, such as York Minster and Salisbury Cathedral, often have charitable status and use part of their revenue for the maintenance of their buildings. The National Trust protects more than 200 historic houses and parks in England, Wales and Northern Ireland, and welcomes some 11 million visitors to its properties each year.

Browse this website

www.nationaltrust.
org.uk

Activity 14.7

Carry out an investigation of the visitor attractions in your local area and find out which fall into the private, public and voluntary sectors of the industry.

Objectives of visitor attractions

The owners and managers of all visitor attractions set themselves objectives or goals in order to provide a framework within which all their resources can be used to best effect and their performance measured. Some objectives may be clearly outlined in a policy document or a mission statement, while other operators prefer an altogether more flexible approach to goal setting, yet still retaining a professional approach to their business activities. Objectives for individual attractions will be very diverse and will reflect the philosophy of the owners or managers, the size of the organisation, its stage of development and whether it is in the commercial or non-commercial sector of the industry. Objectives will be developed and refined by all those who have an interest in the operation of an attraction; sometimes referred to as stakeholders, they may include:

- ✪ **Owners and/or managers** – who will be concerned that the objectives are realistic and achievable, and provide a reward for their effort, skill, investment and management expertise

- ✪ **Staff** – will want to be sure of safe and secure employment, with no discrimination, and will be concerned about their, and the organisation's, future prospects

- ✪ **Visitors to the attraction** – who will expect good value-for-money, high standards of customer care and a safe environment

- ✪ **Shareholders** – will be looking for a growing return on their capital invested in the attraction

- ✪ **Local councillors** – these representatives of the local community will be keen to see that any public funds invested in an attraction are used prudently

- ✪ **Members** (of a charity, club or association) – who will expect to be consulted about changes to the operation or management of an attraction

- ✪ **The local community** – through the planning process, will expect to be informed of the development of new attractions and alterations to existing premises, so as not to adversely affect their quality of life

- ✪ **Society in general** – will expect that statutory agencies will investigate the wider social and environmental aspects of any new visitor attraction development

Objectives of commercial attractions

Many of the largest visitor attractions in the UK are owned and operated by commercial (private sector) organisations. Some of the best-known names in the attractions sector are commercial ventures, such as Alton Towers, Thorpe Park and Madame Tussaud's, to name but a few. The commercial attractions sector is made up of large and small organisations owned by individuals or groups of people whose primary aim is to make a profit. Many individuals rely on the profits generated by commercial organisations for a substantial part of their income. Profit maximisation is an important objective for a number of reasons:

- **In order to provide resources for further expansion of the business**
- **To reward risk taking**
- **To enable the business to respond to the needs of its customers**
- **To encourage efficiency and innovation**

Within an overall global objective of seeking to maximise profitability, private sector attractions will identify specific goals for their businesses, which could include:

- **Increasing the overall number of admissions**
- **Attracting new markets, e.g. more groups**
- **Increasing secondary spend, e.g. on catering and merchandise**
- **Reducing staff turnover**
- **Improving environmental performance**
- **Reducing the level of complaints**
- **Improving standards of customer care**

In very large attractions, objectives may be set out as a hierarchy, as shown in Figure 14.10. The overall objective of the organisation is given in its policy or mission statement, at the top of the apex (Figure 14.11 gives an example of the mission statement for a major UK visitor attraction). This is then translated

Policy or mission statement

Organisational objectives

Departmental/divisional objectives

Team objectives and targets

Individual staff objectives and targets

Figure 14.10 *Hierarchy of objectives for a large visitor attraction*

Alton Towers' mission statement

Alton Towers' shortened mission statement is:

'*to create magic for everyone*'.

The mission statement in full reads as follows:

'*we will create magic for all our guests by exciting them and entertaining them with an experience which is unique and totally themed. We will make AltonTowers a magical place to work by developing individual skills, personal responsibility and work which is fun and rewarding. We will continue to develop a partnership with the local community and to ensure that we both benefit. We will ensure a magical future by beating the competition, improving our financial success and investing to strengthen our position as the UK's number one theme park*'.

Figure 14.11   *Mission statement of a major UK visitor attraction*
Courtesy of Alton Towers

into organisational objectives, which may, depending on the size and structure of the operation, be converted into objectives for particular departments or divisions, e.g. catering, corporate hospitality, merchandising, etc. Targets for individual or team performance will then be developed so that measurement of success or achievement can take place.

Although profit maximisation is the primary aim of most private sector visitor attractions, it is by no means their only objective. Many smaller attractions are run by people who used to work for larger companies, but became frustrated with the high level of bureaucracy they encountered. Operating your own business in travel and tourism can give a great deal of job satisfaction and the feeling that you have control over what decisions are made. Some owners will not seek to maximise profits to the full, but may be content with a level of profit that gives them the type of lifestyle they are happy with; after all, why work in a sector concerned with entertainment and recreation, and have no time to enjoy yourself and have fun!

Objectives of non-commercial attractions

Non-commercial visitor attractions, falling within the public or voluntary sectors of the industry, do not have 'profit maximisation' as their primary objective. They have been developed with wider social objectives in mind. A council-run museum, for example, may well have as a primary aim, 'the provision of an educational and recreational facility for the benefit of local people and visitors to the area'. There are many examples of non-commercial organisations in the attractions sector, including:

✪ **Central government**: This channels funding through the Department for Culture, Media and Sport and other government departments to operate many attractions of national significance, such as the National Gallery, British Museum and the Tower of London.

- ✪ **Local clubs and societies**: These are set up by local people with a specific purpose in mind, will aim to break even on their finances and may apply for some financial help from their local authority. A good example would be a steam railway preservation society that runs excursions in the summer or a wildlife conservation group that opens its nature reserves to the public.

- ✪ **Charitable trusts**: Many trusts are established to conserve or preserve our national and local heritage. One of the best known and respected is the National Trust, which today protects more than 600,000 acres of land in England, Wales and Northern Ireland as well as over 200 houses and parks. The Civic Trust, established in 1957, is a registered charity that aims to uphold high standards of environmental quality and management throughout the United Kingdom.

- ✪ **Local authorities**: Local councils play a major role in the provision of visitor attractions in Britain. Without their involvement, facilities such as recreation grounds, parks, museums, leisure centres, tourist information centres and visitor centres would not exist. The general move towards privatisation, market testing and competitive tendering has meant that local authorities are now functioning much more like private sector operators and the distinction between commercial and non-commercial is becoming blurred.

- ✪ **Quangos**: These are quasi-autonomous non-governmental organisations which are primarily financed from the public purse but which have a high degree of autonomy. Examples in leisure and tourism are the Sports Council, Countryside Agency and the Arts Councils, which, although not directly responsible for the running of visitor attractions, often provide advice and grant-aid for their establishment.

Although profit maximisation is not the primary objective of non-commercial organisations in travel and tourism, those which are part of local government or are agencies of central government (e.g. the quangos) are expected to offer value for money and meet targets and agreed performance criteria. Many local authorities have recruited staff from the private sector and have implemented private sector management practices in their attractions, in order to help achieve their objectives.

Activity 14.8

Choose three local visitor attractions (one private, one public and one from the voluntary sector), and record in detail the objectives of each organisation.

Funding of visitor attractions

The precise funding arrangements of a visitor attraction will depend, to a large extent, on whether it operates in the public, private or voluntary sector of the industry.

Funding of public sector visitor attractions

The funds to run public sector visitor attractions come from a number of sources, including:

- ✪ **National government**: Large public sector visitor attractions such as museums and national monuments receive their funding direct from central government via the Department for Culture, Media and Sport (DCMS). The DCMS allocates approximately 20 per cent of its budget to museums and galleries (approximately £200 million per year). Central government also distributes a proportion of its income from taxation to local authorities, to spend on local facilities and services. Part of this money may be allocated to fund local attractions.

- ✪ **Council Tax**: This is a tax levied by a local authority on people living in its area in order to supplement national government finance for local services. Travel and tourism facilities will be allocated a proportion of Council Tax funds, with some going for the operation and upkeep of local visitor attractions, e.g. museums, theatres, etc.

- ✪ **European Union**: Public sector attractions are encouraged to bid for funding from the European Union for specific tourism projects. Certain parts of the UK have special status when it comes to bidding for funding, e.g. the Highlands and Islands of Scotland, where tourism is seen as a way of injecting extra revenue and employment into the rural economy. The main EU sources for tourism projects include the European Social Fund and the European Regional Development Fund.

- ✪ **National Lottery**: Grants from Lottery proceeds are a relatively new source of income to public sector visitor attractions. Bids are often formulated jointly with private and voluntary sector bodies, and are on the basis of matched funding, i.e. every pound granted from the proceeds of the Lottery must be met equally from other sources.

- ✪ **Uniform Business Rate (UBR)**: In the same way that local residents pay Council Tax, local businesses have to pay UBR to the local authority for services provided. A proportion of these funds may be channelled into the operation of local visitor attractions.

- ✪ **Sponsorship**: The mixing of private and public sector enterprises in travel and tourism means that some public sector attractions encourage sponsorship in order to minimise costs and maximise their revenue. This is particularly the case with attractions concerned with the arts and sport, e.g. sports stadia, art galleries and events.

Funding of private sector visitor attractions

The sources of funding for a private sector visitor attraction usually depend on the size of the operation and its legal identity. A very small attraction, for example, whose owner operates as a sole trader or in partnership, may well be able to finance the enterprise from private savings or gifts from friends and relatives. Government grants and loans for small companies may also be available to these businesses. Larger attractions will normally operate as private limited companies, where the investors in the business are only liable for its debts up to the amount that they have actually invested. The first port of call for financing such ventures is often the high street banks, where the attraction may be offered short-, medium- and long-term loans, commercial mortgages and/or an overdraft facility. The directors of the company may also issue shares to their existing investors or seek out new shareholders, as a way of financing expansion of the attraction. Other examples of funding in the private sector include leasing and hire purchase, where capital items such as vehicles, plant and machinery are not purchased outright, but payments are spread over an extended period of time.

Private sector visitor attractions can also apply to a wide range of public sector bodies for grants or low interest loans to help with expansion or improvements to facilities. These non-commercial sources of finance are offered by a number of agencies, including:

- ✪ **National tourist boards (although the ETC no longer offers Section 4 grants)**
- ✪ **Department of the Environment, Transport and the Regions**
- ✪ **Countryside Agency**
- ✪ **English Heritage**
- ✪ **Forestry Commission**
- ✪ **English Nature**
- ✪ **Arts Councils**
- ✪ **Development agencies, e.g. Welsh Development Agency, Highlands and Islands Enterprise**

As with visitor attractions in the public sector, sponsorship is another important, if uncertain, potential source of finance for private sector visitor attractions.

Some of the very largest private sector visitor attractions in the UK are operated as public limited companies (plcs), although it is interesting to note that the UK's most popular visitor attraction, Blackpool Pleasure Beach, is still run as a private limited company, owned and operated since the early 1900s by one local family. Plcs finance expansion by offering shares to the public, offering their shareholders the same limited liability status that is enjoyed by investors in private limited companies. Plcs sometimes have a parent company acting as the head of a group, with a number of subsidiary enterprises working beneath it. In the visitor attractions sector, a good example of this is the Tussauds Group, which owns or operates a number of attractions, including Alton Towers, Chessington World of Adventures, Madame Tussaud's, Warwick Castle, the London Eye and the Rock Circus.

Funding of voluntary sector visitor attractions

Many visitor attractions in the voluntary sector have charitable status since they aim to promote a cause, conserve the heritage or help individuals, rather than make a profit. There are benefits to being a charity, such as exemption from certain forms of taxation and reductions in business rates. Whether a voluntary sector attraction is very large, as is the case with many National Trust properties, or very small, such as a local craft centre, the funding opportunities and sources open to them are very similar, including:

- ✪ **Sponsorship**: A local conservation trust attraction, for example, may be sponsored by a local company.
- ✪ **Subscriptions from members**: The RSPB, English Heritage and the National Trust receive funds from this source.
- ✪ **Grants from central and local government**: A local council may make a grant to its local museum, while the Arts Councils give grants to individuals and organisations which they consider are advancing the cause of the arts. The Countryside Agency gives grants towards environmental improvement projects, including interpretation and education centres.
- ✪ **Donations and gifts**: Perhaps part of the estate of a deceased person, as is often the case with the National Trust.
- ✪ **Fund-raising events**: Anything from a sponsored walk to a jumble sale can help boost funds for voluntary sector visitor attractions.
- ✪ **Fees**: Fees can be levied for certain services, e.g. hiring out of equipment and entrance fees for special events, such as a motor rally in the grounds of a historic house open to the public.
- ✪ **Retail income**: Larger voluntary sector attractions have set up shops and mail order subsidiaries as a way of generating income, e.g. National Trust shops and the Science Museum in London.
- ✪ **National Lottery**

Revenue funding

The preceding sections of this unit have been primarily concerned with the initial funding to establish a visitor attraction and the identification of sources of funding for capital projects and expansion. Once established, it is vital for attractions to maximise their revenue, while keeping a close check on their expenditure, if they are to survive and prosper. In addition to revenue from entrance charges, many attractions offer catering and retail services in order to supplement their income.

Marketing and promotion of visitor attractions

The marketing of visitor attractions should follow the guiding principles of all marketing activity in tourism, namely that:

- ✪ **Marketing is concerned with helping an organisation meet its objectives**
- ✪ **Identifying customer needs is the starting point for effective marketing**
- ✪ **All departments and individuals in an organisation contribute to overall marketing success**
- ✪ **Marketing is a continuous process, not a 'one-off' activity**

The marketing process in visitor attractions can be explained with the help of Figure 14.12 which shows us that:

- ✪ **Any good marketing strategy (the process by which marketing plans are put into action) should start with the customer as its focus. Knowing who your customers are, where they come from, what they want from your attraction, how much they are willing to pay, whether they are satisfied with the service you offer, and so on, provides an invaluable information base on which to make your marketing decisions.**
- ✪ **Once you know the characteristics of your customers, it is much easier to develop products and services that they will want to use. By giving attention to such matters as pricing and location/accessibility of facilities, you will be able to give the customer what he or she wants, at the right time, in the right place and at the right price.**

Figure 14.12 *The marketing process in visitor attractions*

- There are many ways of promoting visitor attractions to existing and potential visitors, including advertising, direct mail, sponsorship, sales promotions and public relations activity.

- Marketing is not something that the operators of an attraction do once and then forget about. It is a dynamic activity that reflects the ever-changing tastes and fashions of the general public. It is essential, therefore, that all visitor attractions monitor and evaluate what they are doing at each stage of the marketing process, by asking such questions as:

  - Are our customers the same today as they were three years ago?

  - Does our mix of facilities meet their needs today?

  - Is our promotional work reaching its intended target?

  - What are our competitors doing?

Industry example

The Alton Towers marketing strategy is to communicate its strategic brand messages to key target markets, which are teenagers, young adults and families. The main objectives that the attraction aims to achieve through this strategy are:

1 Deliver volume objectives in terms of individual visitors

2 Deliver profit objectives

3 Maintain brand leadership status within the UK

4 Continue to position Alton Towers as a destination resort

The attraction's advertising and promotional strategies are developed as a result of a thorough review of the competitive environment, the current economic climate, market research results, visitor profiles and other internal and external factors influencing the European leisure, travel and tourism market.

Guiding and interpretation

Guiding and interpretation can add an extra dimension to a visit to an attraction. Guiding is the service offered by a guide to enhance the visitors' experience by leading them around an attraction, providing information, answering questions and generally ensuring that the experience is as full as possible. Interpretation is defined by the Centre for Environmental Interpretation as:

> the art of explaining the meaning of sites visited by the public.

It is concerned with offering visitors not only an enjoyable experience, but one that will help them better understand the place they are visiting. Visitor attractions as diverse as farms, ancient buildings, heritage sites, archaeological excavations, coasts, wildlife reserves and urban features can all be interpreted using a variety of techniques, including:

- ✪ **Leaflets**
- ✪ **Signposting**
- ✪ **Cast members – e.g. staff who dress up in period costume and assume the roles of people from a particular period in history**
- ✪ **Self-guided trails – where a visitor uses a set of directions and/or a series of trail marks to follow a route**
- ✪ **Audio-visual trails – where a visitor uses an audio/video guide to move around an attraction**
- ✪ **Guided tours (see Figure 14.13)**

Figure 14.13 *A guided tour of the Tower of London*
© Crown copyright: Historic Royal Palaces

✪ **Demonstrations – e.g. woodland crafts, hedging, dry stone walling, etc.**

Industry example

English Heritage is a public body, funded by the Department for Culture, Media and Sport (DCMS), and is responsible for over 400 historic properties in England (CADW: Welsh Historic Monuments does a similar job in Wales). English Heritage is developing a wide range of visitor services, including site interpretation and publications, in order to enhance visitor satisfaction and increase the likelihood of repeat visits. There are:

★ Defined minimum standards of presentation for all properties

★ Explanatory graphics, audio tours, audio-visual presentations and exhibitions

★ Colour guidebooks and souvenir guides in English, many of which have been revised to be more attractive and readable

★ Children's activity sheets at some sites

★ Guided walks at many sites

★ Brief, plastic-covered guides are provided at some sites where entry is free, designed to be used on site and left for the next visitor

English Heritage is the largest developer and user of audio tours for interpretation of historic properties, with more than 50 sites now offering this service. At Battle Abbey, Stonehenge, Framlingham Castle, Down and Eltham Palace, there are interactive audio tours using the hand-held 'wand' system, which gives visitors the flexibility to choose which information they want to listen to, accessed by a numbered keypad. In addition, English Heritage is working to provide audio tours created specially for visitors with visual impairments, thereby increasing access to its sites.

Browse this website

www.english-heritage.org.uk

As well as adding to the visitor experience, guiding and interpretation can also be used to manage visitors at an attraction. Guides can control where, when and for how long visitors dwell at a site. This is particularly important in the case of small attractions with limited space for large numbers of visitors. For example, visitors to Anne Hathaway's cottage in Stratford-upon-Avon are escorted around the property by fully trained guides to enhance their experience and to control visitor numbers and throughput. Self-guided trails can be planned so as to divert visitors away from environmentally sensitive areas of a site.

Browse this website

www.blue-badge.org.uk

Industry example

The Blue Badge is the British national standard guiding qualification and the internationally recognised benchmark of excellence in tourism guiding. Blue Badge Guides operate throughout the UK and are selected, trained and examined by the official British tourist boards. The training is detailed and comprehensive, the examinations rigorous and registration an achievement for the individual concerned. Training ensures that every Blue Badge Guide has the same background of national core knowledge combined with in-depth local knowledge.

As well as acquiring knowledge, Blue Badge Guides are trained in the selection and presentation of material. This has been so successful that English trainers have trained guides all over the world. Blue Badge Guides have a wide range of languages (40 in total), specialities and interests, and can guide groups or individual tourists on foot, in cars, on coaches, on trains and on boats.

Health, safety and security

We will see in Unit 19 *Business systems in the travel and tourism industry* that health, safety and security are very important considerations for the industry, with the requirements of the 1974 Health and Safety at Work, etc. Act being the main UK legislation at present (see page 411). Under the Management of Health and Safety at Work Regulations 1992 examined in Unit 19, employers have a duty to carry out risk assessments that should highlight potential health and safety risks and lead to positive action to put matters right and so reduce the number of accidents in all leisure and tourism facilities, including visitor attractions. Even the smallest attraction will need to give attention to the health and safety needs of staff and visitors. Bad publicity given to poor (or non-existent) health and safety procedures leading to accidents involving members of the public can have disastrous effects on visitor numbers. For example, the management at Disney resorts believe that accidents and Disney do not mix, and make sure that all staff are rigorously trained in emergency and first aid techniques.

Potential hazards for visitors to attractions include:

- ✪ **Unguarded or unsupervised machinery and equipment**
- ✪ **Fast-moving rides and monorails**
- ✪ **Accidents involving animals**
- ✪ **Slippery or broken walkways**
- ✪ **Loose or broken wiring**
- ✪ **Poor lighting indoors and outside**
- ✪ **Leaks of steam, water, gas or oil**
- ✪ **Blocked aisles and walkways**
- ✪ **Fire hazards**
- ✪ **Water hazards**
- ✪ **Poor signposting**

Activity 14.9

Compile a list of the potential health and safety hazards associated with holding a pop festival at an indoor arena with a capacity of 18,000 people.

Industry example

Alton Towers has the following health and safety codes that it must abide by:

- ★ Fairgrounds and Amusement Parks Guidance on Safe Practice
- ★ The Health and Safety at Work, etc. Act 1974
- ★ The Management of Health and Safety at Work Regulations 1992
- ★ The Provision and Use of Work Equipment Regulations 1992
- ★ The Disability Discrimination Act 1995

Browse these websites

www.alton-towers.co.uk

www.altontowers.com

Industry example

Warwick Castle, part of the Tussauds Group, has a Health and Safety Committee, which is a forum for discussing any issues members of staff wish to raise, via their representative. The committee is chaired by the attraction's Head of Operations, with each department represented by a member of staff and the Health and Safety Officer acting as an adviser. The committee discusses all health and safety issues and minutes of their meetings are distributed to all members of staff at the attraction. To ensure that the attraction's health and safety procedures are correctly implemented, the Health and Safety Officer may seek external advice from a number of sources, including:

★ Architect

★ Police

★ Fire service

★ Ambulance service

★ Health and Safety Executive (HSE)

★ Environmental Health Officer

★ Specialist health and safety external bodies

Browse this website

www.warwick-castle.co.uk

Secondary spending

The revenue from entrance charges are obviously important for visitor attractions, but so too is 'secondary spending', i.e. opportunities for visitors to spend more while in the attraction on items in retail, catering, entertainment and other outlets. Secondary spending is crucial to visitor attractions, hence the number of shops and eating places at major theme parks, for example. Another way of maximising revenue is to diversify into corporate hospitality. We saw in the industry example of Thorpe Park on page 245 that staging hospitality and catering events can contribute significantly to total turnover, while at the same time utilising a facility to the full. Events too can add considerable revenue to an attraction and can help to extend the visitor season if planned carefully.

Choose an attraction that you have visited recently and make a list of all the opportunities it offers for secondary spending.

Managing visitor and traffic flows to and within attractions

Regardless of the size of an attraction, attention will need to be given to how visitors and their vehicles will be controlled on-site and in the immediate vicinity of the attraction in order to ensure maximum safety and convenience for visitors. Management can introduce visitor and traffic management by, for example:

❂ **Controlling the number of visitors** – e.g. timed ticketing (see Alton Towers industry example below), peak and off-peak pricing to encourage/discourage visitors at particular times, restricted marketing to do the same, etc.

❂ **Modifying the behaviour of visitors** – e.g. zoning particular activities, channelling visitor flows, queue control with entertainment to keep visitors occupied while queuing, offering pre-booked tickets, etc.

❂ **Adapting the attraction to meet visitor use** – e.g. new features to diffuse visitor flows, protection of vulnerable objects from damage, amended facilities for visitors with specific needs, etc.

❂ **Techniques used to control traffic flow to and from the attraction** – e.g. size and location of car parks, park and ride facilities, traffic calming measures (humps on roads, bollards), encouraging the use of public transport, etc.

Browse this website

www.alton-towers.co.uk

Industry example

Alton Towers in Staffordshire has introduced a 'virtual queuing system' on two of its most popular rides, Oblivion and Nemesis, to keep queue times to a maximum of 20 minutes. The system is put into operation once visitor numbers reach a certain level. The virtual queue works using time-coded tickets, which state a time after which visitors can return to the ride for their turn. Once guests have reserved their place in the virtual queue, they are free to spend extra time enjoying other rides and attractions in the Park.

UK public sector tourism

16

The term 'public sector' is used to describe a variety of organisations involved in central and local government. The public sector plays a key role in providing tourism services and in the promotion of UK destinations. In this unit you will learn how public sector tourism is structured in the UK and about the various roles involved in managing and promoting tourism at local, regional and national level. You will also investigate the role of local authorities in tourism and how the public sector is funded. You will appreciate the role that the public sector plays in destination management, including promotion of resorts, co-ordination with different tourism industry sectors and carrying out market research.

This unit is divided into four main areas:

- **Structure of public sector tourism**
- **The role of local authorities**
- **How the public sector is funded**
- **Destination management**

We guide you through each of these areas using examples and case studies from the travel and tourism industry. At the beginning of each of these sections you will see a list of key topics to help you fully understand what you need to learn. Look out for the links to websites so that you can learn more about a particular travel and tourism company, destination, organisation or topic.

Structure of public sector tourism

Key topics in this section

- **Introduction**
- **Tourism legislation**
- **Central government involvement in tourism**
- **The structure and function of local government**
- **Non-departmental public bodies in tourism**
- **Regional Development Agencies (RDAs) and Cultural Consortia**
- **Private/public sector partnerships in tourism**

Introduction

The term 'public sector' is used to describe a variety of organisations involved in central and local government. The public sector plays a major role in co-ordinating tourism marketing activities in the UK and, at local level, provides many of the services and facilities that go to make up the 'tourism product', including tourist information centres, museums, leisure centres and other facilities for visitors. In addition, many local authorities provide programmes of events designed to increase the number of visitors to their areas and their planning departments play a significant role in the sustainable development of local tourism.

Figure 16.1 shows the relationships between the various public sector organisations with an interest in tourism in the UK. It demonstrates that the Department for Culture, Media and Sport (DCMS) can be regarded as the 'lead' government department when it comes to tourism matters, although other departments, including the Ministry of Agriculture and the Department of the Environment, Transport and the Regions, undertake activities that are associated with tourism. The emergence of devolution in the UK means that Scotland now has its own parliament, and Wales and Northern Ireland their own assemblies. All three of these new institutions have responsibilities for tourism in their respective countries. Quangos (quasi-autonomous non-governmental organisations) include bodies such as Highlands and Islands Enterprise and the Welsh Development Agency, which have interests in tourism development in their regions. The national tourism organisations (English Tourism Council, Wales Tourist Board, Scottish Tourist Board and Northern Ireland Tourist Board) work with regional tourist boards to develop

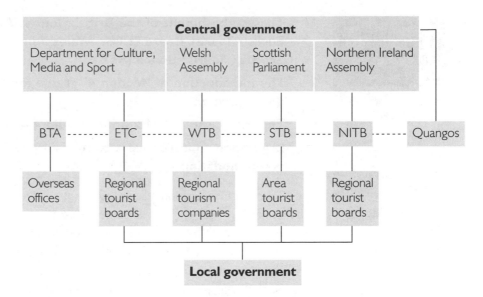

Figure 16.1 *The structure of public sector tourism in the UK*

and market high quality tourism products. The BTA (British Tourist Authority) is responsible for encouraging overseas visitors to the UK by promoting the whole of Britain around the world. Local government plays an important role in the UK tourism scene through providing, maintaining and marketing facilities and services for tourists.

Tourism legislation

There are many laws and regulations that indirectly affect UK tourism, such as consumer protection, health and safety, environmental protection and food hygiene regulations, but the following three topics are directly related to travel and tourism:

- ✪ **Development of Tourism Act 1969**
- ✪ **White Paper on Integrated Transport Policy**
- ✪ **Local Agenda 21**

Development of Tourism Act 1969

Public sector involvement in UK tourism can be traced back to before Victorian times when many 'resorts', both inland and on the coast, benefited from investment in tourist facilities by their local councils. However, central government recognition of the economic significance of tourism was not forthcoming until as late as 1969, with the passing of the Development of Tourism Act. This first piece of tourism legislation, now more than 30 years old, still applies today, although the nature and scale of the industry has changed dramatically. The principal outcomes of the Act were:

Browse these websites for more information on the work of the tourist boards

www.englishtourism.org.uk

www.tourism.wales.gov.uk

www.ni-tourism.com

www.holiday.scotland.net

www.visitbritain.com

1 **The establishment of the British Tourist Authority (BTA), English Tourist Board (ETB), Wales Tourist Board (WTB) and Scottish Tourist Board (STB)**

2 **The introduction of 'section 4' grants for tourist developments**

3 **The establishment of a hotel development grants scheme**

4 **Legislation to introduce a compulsory registration scheme for accommodation**

The Northern Ireland Tourist Board was not included in the Act since it had already been set up in 1948 under separate legislation. The present Labour government has discussed the introduction of a new Development of Tourism Act but, to date, there is nothing on the statute book. However, in 1999 the government recognised the importance of tourism by publishing a new tourism strategy entitled *Tomorrow's Tourism* (see page 289 for more detail on this).

White Paper on Integrated Transport Policy

The UK government published a White Paper (discussion document) on integrated transport in 1998. In chapter 1 of the White Paper, the government states that:

> *We want a transport system that meets the needs of people and business at an affordable cost and produces better places in which to live and work. We want to cut congestion, improve our towns and cities, and encourage vitality and diversity locally; helping to reduce the need to travel and avoid the urban sprawl that has lengthened journeys and consumed precious countryside. We will revise the planning guidance we issue to bring together thinking about better transport and a better environment at the planning stage.*

By 'integrated transport' the government means:

✪ **Integration within and between different types of transport – so that each contributes its full potential and people can move easily between them**

✪ **Integration with the environment – so that our transport choices support a better environment**

✪ **Integration with land use planning – at national, regional and local level, so that transport and planning work together to support more sustainable travel choices and reduce the need to travel**

✪ **Integration with our policies for education, health and wealth creation – so that transport helps to make a fairer, more inclusive society**

The government talks of a 'new deal' for transport that means:

- ✪ **Cleaner air to breathe by tackling traffic fumes**
- ✪ **Thriving town centres by cutting the stranglehold of traffic**
- ✪ **Quality places to live where people are the priority**
- ✪ **Increasing prosperity backed by a modern transport system**
- ✪ **Reduced rural isolation by connecting people with services and increasing mobility**
- ✪ **Easier and safer to walk and cycle**
- ✪ **Revitalised towns and cities through better town planning**

Browse this website

www.detr.gov.uk/
itwp/paper/index

At the time of writing, the White Paper has yet to become law but it is a major influence on public sector thinking, not least in terms of developing transport services for tourism.

Local Agenda 21

Local Agenda 21 (LA21) is a new way for communities, individuals and organisations to move towards a more sustainable way of life. Sustainability is about protecting the environment, involving people in decisions about it, and sharing out social and economic resources more fairly for present and future generations. All kinds of projects are under way, involving local authorities, voluntary organisations, community groups and businesses in new partnerships. Local Agenda 21 has developed out of the first major international conference on sustainable development held in Rio de Janiero in 1992. Known as the 'earth summit', the conference agreed a set of principles for future sustainable development, known as Agenda 21, which has since been interpreted and expanded at national, regional and local level in many countries, including the UK.

Browse this website

www.environment.
detr.gov.uk/
sustainable/la21/
policy/

Although the principles of Local Agenda 21 have yet to become law, it is nonetheless a major influence on public sector thinking, not least in the field of tourism. Local authority tourism departments must strive to incorporate the principles of Local Agenda 21 into their policies and practices by, for example, encouraging tourism businesses to set up recycling schemes, move towards more energy efficient practices and conserve the natural environment and culture. Local Agenda 21 projects are also closely linked to the principles of sustainable tourism that you investigated in Unit 2 *Tourism development.*

Central government involvement in tourism

Figure 16.1 on page 281 showed us that central government has considerable involvement in UK tourism, by providing funding for the Department for Culture, Media and Sport (DCMS), Welsh Assembly, Scottish

Parliament and Northern Ireland Assembly. In turn, these bodies fund the British Tourist Authority (BTA), English Tourism Council (ETC), Wales Tourist Board (WTB), Scottish Tourist Board (STB) and Northern Ireland Tourist Board (NITB). The DCMS also 'sponsors' a number of non-departmental public bodies (sometimes called 'quangos', meaning quasi-autonomous non-governmental organisations), such as the Arts Council of England, English Heritage and the United Kingdom Sports Council. The following industry example and case study illustrate the varied responsibilities of the DCMS, its aims and work in relation to UK tourism.

Browse this website

www.culture.
gov.uk

Industry example

At regular intervals, the DCMS draws up a funding agreement with the organisations for which it provides funding. The agreed levels of grant aid for the British Tourist Authority for the 3-year period 1999–2000 to 2001–2002 are as follows:

1999–2000	£36 million
2000–2001	£37 million
2001–2002	£37 million

The agreed levels of grant aid for the English Tourism Council (ETC) and the English Regional Tourist Boards (RTBs) for the 2-year period 2000–2001 to 2001–2002 are as follows:

2000–2001	£4.475 million (ETC), £5.525 million (RTBs), £1 million (transition)
2001–2002	£4.000 million (ETC), £6 million (RTBs/Mayor of London)

Funding is kept under review and is subject to the organisations that receive funds meeting agreed performance objectives.

Case Study
The Department for Culture, Media and Sport (DCMS)

▶ **INTRODUCTION**

The Department for Culture, Media and Sport (DCMS) was created in July 1997, taking over the work of the former Department for National Heritage, which was established in April 1992. The DCMS aims to improve the quality of life for all, through cultural and sporting activities, and through the strengthening of the cultural industries. It is the youngest government department and is headed by a Cabinet Minister, the Secretary of State for Culture, Media and Sport. The DCMS has responsibility for:

★ Broadcasting
★ The arts
★ Sport
★ Tourism
★ National heritage
★ The film industry
★ The National Lottery
★ Creative industries
★ Museums and galleries
★ Libraries

The Department has seven directorates, namely:

★ Royal Parks Agency
★ Strategy and Communications
★ Education, Training, Arts and Sport
★ Museums, Galleries, Libraries and Heritage
★ Creative Industries, Media and Broadcasting
★ Regions, Tourism, Millennium and International
★ Corporate Services

continued

continued

Ministers		
Secretary of State Departmental strategy, expenditure and organisation National Lottery policy Public appointments Chairman of the Millennium Commission The Millennium	Royal Parks Agency Strategy & Communications	News Communications Departmental Secretariat Statistics and Social Policy
Parliamentary Under Secretary of State Minister for Tourism, Film and Broadcasting Tourism Broadcasting, Film and the Press The Creative Industries (including the music industry) The Millennium Regional and local authority policy issues Environmental issues	Education, Training, Arts & Sport	Arts Sport Education Unit
Parliamentary Under Secretary of State Minister for Sport Sport Support for the Secretary of State on the National Lottery Social policy, access and equal opportunities	Museums, Galleries, Libraries & Heritage	Museums & Galleries Libraries Buildings, Monuments and Sites Government Art Collection
Parliamentary Under Secretary of State Minister for the Arts The arts, crafts and the Government Art Collection Museums, galleries, libraries and archives The built heritage, the Royal estate, architecture and design Education, training and information technology issues European and international issues	Creative Industries, Media & Broadcasting	Broadcasting Media Creative Industries Unit
	Regions, Tourism, Millennium & International	Local, Regional & International Tourism Millennium Unit
Spokesman in the House of Lords		
Parliamentary Private Secretary		
Special Advisers		
Permanent Secretary	Corporate Services	Finance National Lottery Personnel & Central Services Central Appointments Unit Internal Audit

Figure 16.2 *Organisational structure of the Department for Culture, Media and Sport*

Adapted from DCMS data

continued

continued

Figure 16.2 shows the present structure of the Department for Culture, Media and Sport and illustrates its areas of responsibility.

Over 50 public bodies receive funding from the DCMS to deliver direct sporting and cultural support to the public. These include:

★ The Arts Council of England
★ British Film Institute
★ British Tourist Authority
★ English Tourism Council
★ English Heritage
★ UK Sports Council
★ The British Library

DCMS FUNDING

The DCMS budget for 2000–01 is £1 billion, of which 90 per cent goes directly to the service providers in the cultural and sporting sectors. Table 16.1 gives a breakdown of the Department's expenditure and shows that the arts are to receive the greatest amount from the DCMS for 2000–01 (£238 million), while sport is allocated £52 million and tourism £48 million.

DCMS AND TOURISM

The DCMS is the government department that has direct responsibility for funding tourism in the UK. Its key roles in this area are to:

★ Act as tourism's 'champion' in government
★ Facilitate joined-up government in support of tourism
★ Sponsor the English Tourism Council and the British Tourist Authority (BTA)
★ Monitor progress made by the government

continued

continued

Subject area	Expenditure (£ millions)
Museums and galleries	226
Libraries	89
Museums, libraries and archives	19
Arts	238
Sport	52
Historic buildings, monuments and sites	145
Royal parks	22
Tourism	48
Broadcasting and media	104
Administration and research	26
Space for Sport and Arts	15
National Lottery Commission	Nil
European Regional Development Fund	31
Reserve	Nil
TOTAL	1,015

Adapted from DCMS data

Table 16.1 *DCMS expenditure by subject area 2000–01*

The Department provides a lead on tourism issues within government. In terms of its work in tourism, its aims are to promote the interests of tourists and tourism businesses, to champion tourism's potential and to maximise the involvement of the tourism industry in policy initiatives across government.

Within Whitehall, DCMS aims to improve the taxation and regulatory frameworks within which tourism businesses operate. It does this by making, or supporting, appropriate representations to other departments whose policy-making

continued

continued

and regulatory responsibilities affect tourism. In London, the Greater London Authority, established in 2000, has a duty to promote the capital both as a tourist destination in its own right and as a gateway to the rest of the UK.

In the regions, DCMS aims to ensure that the new Regional Development Agencies (RDAs) recognise the importance of tourism in delivering their statutory purposes of economic regeneration, increasing employment, the development of training skills and the encouragement of sustainable development.

In the European Union, it aims to rationalise activity, in line with government objectives, and comment on proposals affecting tourism.

One of the most significant measures completed by the DCMS was the publication of the government's national tourism strategy *Tomorrow's Tourism*, the subject of the following industry example.

Industry example
Tomorrow's Tourism, the national tourism strategy

Tomorrow's Tourism, the government's strategy for the development of tourism in England, was published in 1999. It contains many new initiatives aimed at:

★ Providing a new support structure for tourism in England

★ Developing and promoting quality tourism experiences

★ Providing better information about tourism

★ Promoting improved career opportunities in the tourism industry

continued

continued

★ Promoting the sustainable development of tourism

★ Increasing access to tourism for those with low incomes, families, the elderly and disabled people

Although essentially a strategy for England, the report has clear implications for Wales, Scotland and Northern Ireland. It supports quality, competitiveness and sustainable (wise) growth in the British tourism industry.

▶ FUTURE PLANS OF THE DCMS

Included among the Department's plans for the years 2000–02 are the following initiatives:

1 To make a success of the first Tourism Summit and harness the efforts of the reconstituted Tourism Forum to pursue the tourism strategy

2 To establish a transformed, more effective national strategic body for tourism in England, with more resources for the regional support of tourism

3 To ensure that recommendations from English Heritage concerning the protection of important buildings and archaeological sites are considered within target times

4 To ensure that the English National Stadium is made a success and offers value for money

5 To evaluate the social and economic impact of the National Lottery

Case study discussion questions

Browse this website for more information on the work of the DCMS

www.culture.gov.uk

1 What is the aim of the DCMS?

2 What are the Department's main responsibilities?

3 What are its key roles in UK tourism?

4 What types of initiatives are included in *Tomorrow's Tourism*?

5 What do you think the future holds for the DCMS?

The structure and function of local government

Local government exists to provide facilities and services to people living in a clearly defined geographical area. Local government in England and Wales occurs at different levels:

- ✪ **County councils, e.g. Essex County Council**
- ✪ **District/borough/city councils, e.g. Sheffield City Council**
- ✪ **Unitary authorities, e.g. Telford & Wrekin Council**

In general terms, county councils are concerned with broader issues such as education, social services, highways and strategic planning, whereas district/borough/city councils confine themselves to more local needs such as refuse collection, environmental health, leisure and housing. Unitary authorities were established in 1998 to act as a single point of contact for the majority of services provided in a local area.

At each level there are elected representatives, known as councillors, who implement central government policies at local level. Local government officers, the equivalent of civil servants in central government, carry out the decisions of their councillors, which should, if the democratic system is functioning correctly, reflect the views of the majority of the local people.

Local government's work in the field of tourism can be divided into two main areas:

- ✪ **Providing and maintaining facilities and services for visitors** – e.g. museums, parks, leisure centres, tourist information services (see Figure 16.3) and playgrounds
- ✪ **Destination marketing and promotion** – e.g. in guidebooks, brochures, the Internet and holiday exhibitions

Later in this unit (see page 301) we look in greater detail at the role of local authorities in UK tourism.

Check out this website

www.culture.
gov.uk

Industry example

In its National Tourism Strategy document *Tomorrow's Tourism* (Department for Culture, Media and Sport, 1999), the UK government estimates that local authorities in England invest £75 million per annum in the development and promotion of tourism.

Figure 16.3 *Royal Windsor Information Centre*
Courtesy of the Royal Borough of Windsor and Maidenhead

Non-departmental public bodies in tourism

There are a number of publicly funded bodies that contribute, directly and indirectly, to the development of UK tourism, including:

Browse these websites

www.englishtourism.
org.uk

www.national-
lottery.co.uk

www.english-
heritage.org.uk

- ✪ **British Tourist Authority**
- ✪ **English Tourism Council**
- ✪ **National tourist boards (Wales Tourist Board, Scottish Tourist Board, Northern Ireland Tourist Board)**
- ✪ **English Heritage**
- ✪ **CADW: Welsh Historic Mouments**
- ✪ **The National Lottery**

Activity 16.1

Carry out some research on two of the non-departmental public bodies listed above (with the exception of the National Lottery, which is the subject of the industry example below). Find out their aims, structure, funding and any other important aspects of their work that you discover.

Industry example

The National Lottery was launched in November 1994 to provide extra funding for a range of 'good causes' in the UK, namely:

★ Sport

★ The arts

★ Heritage

★ Charities

★ Projects to mark the new millennium

In 1998, a sixth good cause, covering health, education and the environment, was created; this is the New Opportunities Fund (NOF).

Camelot, a private company, operates the National Lottery on behalf of the Department for Culture, Media and Sport (DCMS). Proceeds from the Lottery go into the National Lottery Distribution Fund, which is divided between the six good causes listed above. There are 12 distributing bodies responsible to the DCMS for giving grants to projects within the good causes. They are:

★ The Sports Councils of England, Wales, Scotland and Northern Ireland (16.66 per cent across all four)

★ The Arts Councils of England, Wales, Scotland and Northern Ireland (16.66 per cent across all four)

★ The National Lottery Charities Board (16.66 per cent)

★ The National Heritage Memorial Fund (16.66 per cent)

★ The Millennium Commission

★ The New Opportunities Fund (33.33 per cent)

Out of every pound spent on the National Lottery, around 28 pence goes to the good causes, in the proportions shown above. The Millennium Commission ceased to exist

continued

Browse this website

www.national-
lottery.co.uk

continued

on 31 December 2000 (it had previously been allocated 20 per cent), when the allocation to the New Opportunities Fund was increased from 13.33 per cent to 33.33 per cent. At the beginning of May 2000 the total donation to good causes stood at £9.3 billion.

Camelot's activities are closely regulated by the National Lottery Commission, whose duties are to safeguard the integrity of the Lottery, to protect players and, subject to these, to maximise the income to the National Lottery Distribution Fund.

A number of tourism projects, large and small, have benefited from National Lottery funding, particularly visitor attractions, e.g. the Dome in Greenwich and the Earth Centre in Yorkshire.

At the time of writing, discussions are taking place about the future operator of the Lottery when Camelot's licence runs out in September 2001. The People's Lottery, headed by entrepreneur Richard Branson, is bidding to take over the running of the National Lottery on a not-for-profit basis.

Regional Development Agencies (RDAs) and Cultural Consortia

Regional Development Agencies

Regional Development Agencies (RDAs) were formally launched in eight English regions on 1 April 1999 (see Figure 16.4). The ninth, in London, was established on 3 July 2000 following the establishment of the Greater London Authority (GLA). They aim to co-ordinate regional economic development and regeneration, enable the English regions to improve their relative competitiveness and reduce the imbalances that exist between regions.

RDAs have the following aims:

✪ **To further economic development and regeneration**

✪ **To promote business efficiency, investment and competitiveness**

✪ **To promote employment**

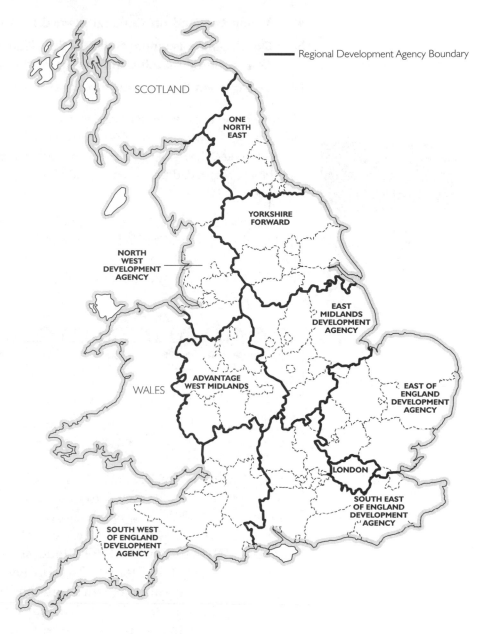

Figure 16.4 *The Regional Development Agencies (RDAs) in England*

✪ **To enhance development and application of skills relevant to employment**

✪ **To contribute to sustainable development**

The Agencies' specific functions are:

1   **Formulating a regional strategy in relation to their purposes**

2   **Regional regeneration**

3   **Taking forward the government's competitiveness agenda in the regions**

4   Taking the lead on regional inward investment

5   Developing a regional Skills Action Plan to ensure that skills training matches the needs of the labour market

6   Taking a leading role on European funding for the region

The government has issued guidance to the RDAs on the formulation of their strategies. Following extensive consultation with regional partners, the RDAs presented their strategies to government on 26 October 1999. The government responded on 12 January 2000, giving a broad welcome to the strategies.

Browse this website for more information on the Regional Development Agencies

www.local-regions.detr.gov.uk/rda/info/index.htm

In some regions, tourism plays a significant role in the economy, creating wealth and employment (see industry example on the South West of England RDA below). It is yet to be seen precisely how the work of RDAs ties in with the role of the regional tourist boards in England.

Industry example
South West of England Regional Development Agency (RDA)

The South West of England RDA was launched in April 1999 as the body designed to co-ordinate strategic investment and development within the region, which stretches from Cornwall in the west, through Devon and parts of Dorset, Wiltshire and Gloucestershire, to major cities like Bristol and Bath. The RDA has a budget of £75 million at its disposal, and tourism, with the region receiving 21 million visitors each year and contributing £3.5 billion to the economy, is sure to feature high on its list of priorities.

The RDA has three key objectives:

1   Increasing prosperity through improving business competitiveness

2   Increasing prosperity through addressing social and economic imbalances

3   Increasing prosperity through improving regional coherence

continued

continued

It identifies four strategic 'drivers' for achieving these objectives:

1   Environment – ensure that the region's cultural and environmental assets are used to attract and develop business potential

2   Innovation and technology – put innovation, creativity and technology at the heart of the region's businesses and institutions

3   Skills and learning – equip people with the skills and adaptability needed to underpin a modern, developing and inclusive economy

4   Partnership – promote greater quality and effectiveness in the ways in which the region works together and organisations operate

A number of tourism projects are seeing the benefit of the RDA's work, with the National Marine Aquarium in Plymouth receiving a £3.3 million grant from the Agency and the Eden Project in Cornwall, an £80 million Millennium project, aided by a £3.9 million grant from the RDA.

Activity 16.2

Find out in which RDA area your school or college is located and what plans exist for tourism development in the region.

Cultural Consortia

The Department for Culture, Media and Sport has established a Regional Cultural Consortium (RCC) in each of the eight English regions outside London. The role of the RCCs is to ensure that culture and creativity have a strong voice in the emerging regional picture in England and that they play a full and coherent part in contributing to increasing prosperity and enjoyment of life in their regions. Currently, the eight RCCs are:

- **East of England Cultural Consortium**
- **East Midlands Cultural Consortium**
- **North East Culture Collection**
- **North West Cultural Consortium**
- **South East Cultural Consortium**
- **South West Cultural Consortium**
- **West Midlands Cultural Consortium**
- **Yorkshire Cultural Consortium**

The boundaries of the RCCs are the same as for the Regional Development Agencies (RDAs) discussed earlier and shown on the map in Figure 16.4.

The Secretary of State in the DCMS appoints the Chairs of the RCCs, following nominations made by regional arts, museums, heritage, tourism and sporting public bodies, library and archive interests, the Regional Development Agency (RDA) and local government. Other interests may be invited to join a Consortium, particularly from the creative industries and also from National Lottery distributors, countryside, recreation and educational interests and the voluntary sector. The major task of each Consortium is to draw up a regional cultural strategy that will set out the future of cultural, creative and sporting activity in the region.

Private/public sector bodies

Partnership is a word that is commonly heard when talking about tourism in the UK. There are many examples of the private and public sectors working in partnership in tourism to make best use of their resources, e.g. regional tourist boards, marketing bureaux and training consortia. The reorganisation of the English Tourist Board into the English Tourism Council has altered the range of services on offer from the regional tourist boards and has created opportunities for further private sector involvement in activities that were traditionally the role of the public sector.

Regional tourist boards

Regional tourist boards play an important role in helping achieve the aims of the government's tourism strategy *Tomorrow's Tourism* (see industry example on page 289). The emergence of regionalism in the UK as a force for economic development and regeneration places new demands on all regional tourist boards, which are encouraged by the government to become 'the voice of tourism' at regional level.

Although partly funded from the public purse, the work of tourist boards at regional level in the UK is altogether more commercial, with close liaison between public and private sector concerns. A typical regional tourist board will have a wide range of members, from hoteliers, restaurateurs and tourist attractions, to local councils, farm guesthouses and education establishments. In order to manage its three designated regions, the Wales Tourist Board has established associated companies, namely 'North Wales Tourism', 'Mid Wales Tourism' and 'Tourism South and West Wales'. The number of English regional tourist boards is now 10, following the demise of the Thames and Chilterns Tourist Board in the early 1990s and the East Midlands Tourist Board in 1996 (see Figure 16.5).

The commercial nature of regional tourist boards is shown by the ways in which they generate revenue, which include:

Figure 16.5 *The regional tourist boards in England*

- Grants from central government sources via the DCMS, Welsh Assembly, Northern Ireland Assembly or Scottish Parliament
- Subscriptions from local authorities
- Subscriptions from commercial members
- Revenue from sales, e.g. selling advertising space in regional publications and letting space on exhibition stands

The main responsibilities of the English regional tourist boards are to:

- Have a thorough knowledge of tourism within their region, as well as the facilities and organisations involved in the tourism industry
- Advise the English Tourism Council on the regional aspects of major policy issues and to supply management information
- Service enquiries attributable to nationally developed promotions and to provide literature
- Co-ordinate regional tourist information services as part of the national tourist information centre (TIC) network
- Maintain close liaison with planning authorities on policies affecting tourism
- Carry out a continuing domestic public relations campaign with the local authorities, the travel trade and the public within the region
- To create awareness of the need for tourism to be managed for the benefits of residents as well as tourists
- To promote tourism to the region both from other parts of the country and from overseas

Activity 16.3

Find out which regional tourist board your area falls into and what plans it has for future tourism development.

The role of local authorities

Key topics in this section

- **Reasons for public sector involvement in tourism**
- **Resource allocation**
- **Influences on local authority tourism policy**
- **Strategic planning**
- **Components of destination management**
- **'Best value' initiative**

Reasons for public sector involvement in tourism

Local authorities play a key role in the operation and development of UK tourism. Driven by the economic, social and environmental benefits that tourism can bring to an area, local councils throughout the UK are investing in tourism facilities and services, while at the same time spearheading the marketing of their destinations to British and overseas tourists. Local authorities also play an important role in minimising the negative impacts of tourism and contributing to sustainable tourism development. They use their resources to provide as wide a range of tourism facilities and services as finances will allow. In a typical area, this might include:

- ✪ **Promotional leaflets and brochures**
- ✪ **Parks and gardens**
- ✪ **Theatres**
- ✪ **Museums**
- ✪ **Tourist information centres (see Figure 16.6)**
- ✪ **Accommodation booking services**
- ✪ **Sports and leisure centres**
- ✪ **Outdoor activity centres**
- ✪ **Art and craft galleries**

Indeed, it could be argued that there are few local authority services that do not, in some way, contribute to an area's tourism industry, even refuse collection, buildings maintenance and planning control. Many councils support the establishment of local tourism groups and associations, which bring

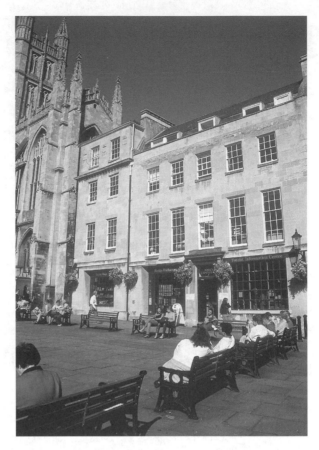

Figure 16.6 *Bath tourist information centre*
Courtesy of Bath Tourism Bureau

together the private and public sector. The Local Government Act of 1948 gave local authorities the powers to set up information and publicity services for tourists. This was reinforced by the Local Government Act 1972 which empowered them to publicise their areas for tourism and provide facilities for visitors.

Today, there are few local authorities in the UK that are not actively involved in some way with promoting their areas to tourists; places as diverse as Barnsley and Bolton, Aberystwyth and St Davids, St Andrews and Perth, and Enniskillen and Belfast, are all competing for a slice of the 'tourism pound'. The following industry example clearly demonstrates the economic impact that tourism has at local level.

Browse this website

www.doveruk.com

Industry example

Dover District, which includes the towns of Dover, Deal and Sandwich, and surrounding rural areas up to the boundaries of Folkestone, Canterbury and Ramsgate, is a popular tourist area. It derives considerable economic benefits from tourism, which, according to Dover District data, has led to the creation of 2,642 jobs in the area. The total value of tourism to the area is £80.3 million annually, made up of £33.5 million from visitors on day trips and £46.8 million from staying tourists.

Activity 16.4

Carry out some research to find out in what ways your local authority is involved in providing leisure and tourism facilities and services. Include any data on the economic impacts of tourism.

Resource allocation

The scale of involvement of local authorities in tourism is very variable, ranging from authorities with a single person given the responsibility for tourism promotion, to councils with separate tourism departments under a Director of Tourism. Some local authorities see tourism as a natural extension of their planning function and house their tourism officer and staff in this department. The more proactive authorities consider that tourism is an integral part of economic development and so assign individuals into this section. Still others view tourism, and particularly the marketing and promotion of tourism, as a PR activity that lends itself very well to their press and PR department. Irrespective of how tourism is organised within a particular local authority, it is clear that it will remain a vital and increasing part of the work of local councils in the future.

Local authorities in England and Wales are significant employers in their own right within the leisure and tourism sector. According to government figures for March 2000, in the region of 400,000 of the total of 1.8 million people employed in UK tourism work in libraries, museums, art galleries, sports and other recreational services.

Influences on local authority tourism policy

Local authorities are under pressure to provide the highest possible standards of facilities and services to their local population, within tight financial resources. There is no statutory (legal) duty on local authorities to provide the range of leisure and tourism facilities we see in most areas of the country today. They only have a legal duty to provide recreational opportunities through schools and libraries, but most go far beyond this and use their wide discretionary powers to provide the best possible leisure and tourism facilities within their local area. This discretionary provision does have its drawbacks, however, since in times of financial cutbacks it is often leisure and tourism that has its budget cut first.

Apart from financial influences on the provision of local authority tourism services, there is sometimes pressure from local communities to increase, decrease or modify tourism activities, for example diverting tourists away from particularly busy parts of an area to reduce congestion and inconvenience for local people.

Strategic planning

Planning for the future is a very important aspect of the work of local authorities in the UK. As well as making sure that current tourist activities benefit local areas, local authorities must also forecast likely future tourism trends and themes. Four common themes of strategic planning that are presently of interest to local authorities are:

1   **Sustainable tourism**
2   **Public-private sector partnerships**
3   **Raising quality**
4   **Regeneration**

Sustainable tourism

You will remember that in Unit 2 *Tourism development* we investigated the principles of sustainable tourism, the concept that has grown out of increased concern about the negative environmental and socio-cultural impacts of tourism. Sustainable tourism can be defined as tourism that meets the needs of the present without compromising the ability of future generations to meet their own needs. Local authorities have an important role to play in developing sustainable tourism in their areas, not least through the development of Local Agenda 21 strategies.

Private–public sector partnerships

There is general consensus across the UK tourism industry that partnership arrangements are the most effective way of achieving success for the industry. Partnerships and collaborative ventures can help to unite the wide range of interests throughout all sectors of the diverse tourism industry. A common partnership arrangement in tourism is when the private sector works in conjunction with the public sector on a wide range of issues, such as tourism policy formulation, infrastructure provision, the development of tourist facilities and amenities, marketing and promotion, and training. There are many examples of such partnership arrangements at all levels of the UK tourism industry, for example:

- ✪ **National tourist boards working collaboratively with tourism industry operators to develop attractions and facilities**
- ✪ **Regional tourist boards providing a range of services for their commercial members, including hoteliers, attractions operators and coach companies**
- ✪ **Local authorities co-ordinating the development of privately funded tourist facilities in their areas**

Partnership arrangements are also found *within* the private sector and the public sector of tourism. It is common for commercial operators to work together for mutual interest, for example hotels and tourist attractions creating joint products, tour operators contracting with accommodation providers and coach operators, and farm tourism enterprises undertaking joint purchasing and promotional schemes. Different levels of the public sector also work in partnership to pool resources for maximum effect; a local authority tourism department, for example, may work with its regional tourist board to develop new holiday packages.

Whatever the precise arrangements, effective partnerships offer a number of advantages, including:

- ✪ **Maximising the economic benefits of tourism**
- ✪ **Helping to minimise tourism's negative environmental and socio-cultural impacts**
- ✪ **Maximising the use of resources**
- ✪ **Spreading the risks of tourism development**

Collaborative arrangements between tourism industry partners in the same geographical area are particularly effective, for example when accommodation providers work with local tourist attractions for mutual benefit.

Raising quality

There is little doubt among the majority of tourism operators in the UK that the key to overall success in the industry is the raising of standards, i.e. standards of:

- ✪ **All types of tourist accommodation**
- ✪ **Visitor attractions**
- ✪ **Catering facilities**
- ✪ **Transportation**
- ✪ **Leisure and entertainment facilities**
- ✪ **Customer service**
- ✪ **Information services**

The national and regional tourist boards in the UK run voluntary accommodation inspection schemes and are striving for all tourism operators to sign up to these measures to help raise the quality of standards across the industry.

Regeneration

Tourism can often be the catalyst for the regeneration of derelict land or run-down parts of urban and rural areas. Tourism facilities and amenities can help to change the image of an area for the better, thereby encouraging further inward migration and investment. The tourism and leisure facilities developed along the Don Valley on the outskirts of Sheffield are a good example of this regeneration process.

Components of destination management

Local authorities that have responsibilities in tourism are involved in a process known as 'destination management', which includes:

- ✪ **Visitor management** – helping to control tourists and their vehicles to gain maximum benefit at minimum disruption to the local environment and communities
- ✪ **Provision of tourism services for all sectors of society** – local authorities have a duty to provide facilities and services for all sectors of their population, regardless of income, gender, race and ability/disability
- ✪ **Destination marketing** – local authorities play an important role in promoting their areas to potential visitors

✪ **Organising events** – regular or one-off events can bring considerable economic, cultural and social benefits for visitors and local people

'Best value' initiative

Since 1 April 2000, all local councils have been obliged to operate a new statutory duty known as 'best value'. 'Best value' requires all local authorities to:

> . . . secure continuous improvement in the way functions are carried out having regard to a combination of economy, efficiency and effectiveness

The 'best value' initiative's effect on the provision of local authority tourism will call for councils to measure the performance of their tourism services and explore the most cost-efficient and effective ways that these services can be delivered.

Browse this website

www.telford.gov.uk/
bestvalue/

Industry example

Telford & Wrekin Council's approach to implementing 'best value' is to review all its services under four criteria:

1 *Challenge* – the very purpose and need for the service and the way that it is delivered

2 *Compare* – performance with that of other unitary authorities and other providers to check efficiency and develop best practice

3 *Consult* – widely with service users and other appropriate stakeholders about the service and service standards

4 *Compete* – where appropriate, with other providers as a way of securing value for money

The Council has an extensive programme of consultation and service reviews to ensure that 'best value' really does make a difference to the community's quality of life.

How the public sector is funded

Key topics in this section

- **Introduction**
- **Taxation**
- **Special European and national funds**
- **National Lottery**
- **Commercial income**
- **Rationalisation**

Introduction

All public sector expenditure has to be paid for, whether it is wages for refuse workers, money for education or funds to produce a tourism brochure. The amount of funds available to a local authority will determine how much it can spend on tourism facilities and services.

Figure 16.7 shows the sources of local authority funding for tourism and how the money is distributed.

The figure also shows that a typical local authority tourism department receives funding from a number of sources and uses it to finance facilities and services for visitors. The main sources of funding are:

✪ **Taxation** – this will be a combination of local taxes (council tax and business rates) and national taxes from central government sources

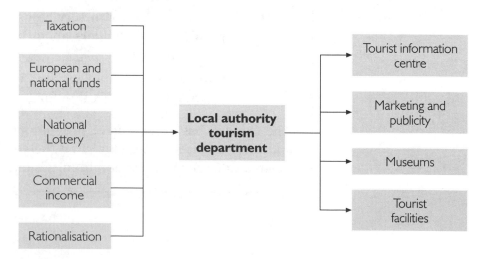

Figure 16.7 *Local authority funding for tourism*

- ✪ **Special European and national funds** – from time to time, funding is available from Europe and central government for projects to stimulate tourism development, e.g. the European Regional Development Fund (ERDF), European Social Fund (ESF) and the government's Single Regeneration Budget (see industry example below)

- ✪ **The National Lottery** – proceeds from the National Lottery are helping to fund local, national and regional tourism projects (see the industry example of the National Lottery on page 293)

- ✪ **Commercial income** – local authorities generate revenue from a number of sources to supplement their core funding, for example selling advertising space in tourism brochures, sponsorship and partnership funding

- ✪ **Rationalisation** – although not a source of income in the strict sense of the word, rationalisation, i.e. reducing the spending on some local authority services to allow additional funding on others, can free up additional funds for tourism

Industry example

The Single Regeneration Budget (SRB) provides funding to support regeneration initiatives in England carried out by local regeneration partnerships. Its priority is to enhance the quality of life of local people in areas of need by reducing the gap between deprived and other areas, and between different groups of people. The types of bid supported differ from region to region according to local circumstances, but they will include some or all of the following objectives:

- ★ Improve the employment prospects, education and skills of local people

- ★ Address social exclusion and improve opportunities for the disadvantaged

- ★ Promote sustainable regeneration, improve and protect the environment and infrastructure, including housing

- ★ Reduce crime and drug abuse and improve community safety

Tourism projects can be included in bids for SRB funding, often under the direction of private/public sector partnerships.

Browse this website

www.regeneration.detr.gov.uk

One very important point about local authority funding of tourism is that it is purely discretionary; in other words, the local authority does not have a duty to provide leisure and tourism services and facilities in the same way that it is duty bound to provide social services and education, for example. This discretionary nature of tourism funding makes it rather vulnerable, particularly in times of recession and economic stringency when the government is looking for further cuts in local authority budgets. Spending on tourism is likely to be one of the first areas to be cut because of its non-statutory status.

Activity
16.5

Carry out some research to find out how much your local authority is spending on tourism this year and what plans it has for future spending.

Destination management

Key topics in this section

- **Promotion**
- **Providing tourism services**
- **Product development**
- **Co-ordination**
- **Market research**
- **Different approaches to destination management**

Introduction

Destination management, which occurs at local, regional and national level, is designed to maximise the benefits of tourism to a destination while minimising tourism's negative impacts. Local authorities carry out a variety of destination management functions, including:

- ✪ **Promotion** – this is vital to the success of tourism and includes a range of techniques, including advertising, publications, public relations, staging events and attending exhibitions
- ✪ **Providing tourism services** – these range from providing tourist information centres (TICs), environmental maintenance, quality assurance, marketing and strategic planning
- ✪ **Product development** – as customers' requirements change, local authorities must develop new products and services, e.g. wet weather facilities, themed packages, programmes of events, cycling trails and walking routes
- ✪ **Co-ordination** – in order to maximise expertise and funding, local authorities often take the lead in co-ordinating tourism initiatives between the public, private and voluntary sectors
- ✪ **Market research** – is essential to keep abreast of customer needs, visitor attitude and competing destinations, e.g. by carrying out visitor surveys, focus group meetings and observation

Local authorities will place different emphases on these functions, depending on budgets and other local circumstances.

Industry example

The Waveney District Council area in Suffolk, centred on the coastal resort of Lowestoft, has developed a tourism strategy to develop its work in destination management. The strategy includes details of how the authority will progress its work in the key areas of:

★ Marketing and promotion

★ Tourism services

★ Product development

★ Co-ordination with other sectors

★ Market research

In terms of product development, for example, Waveney has highlighted the following initiatives:

★ Developing new products, e.g. trails

★ Extending the events programme

★ Supporting business development

★ Support to existing businesses

★ Encouraging major inward investment

★ Ensuring that all developments are sustainable and appropriate

Browse this website

www.waveney.
gov.uk

Choose a local authority that is involved in destination management. This could be a seaside resort, historic city, market town or a local authority covering a rural area. Carry out some research to discover the local authority's policy and practices on the following items of destination management:

1 Marketing and promotion

2 Tourism services

3 Product development

4 Co-ordination with other sectors

5 Market research

Using specific examples from your research, describe and evaluate the approach that the local authority takes in these five key areas.

Responding to other cultures

17

As international tourism continues to grow apace, so the need to appreciate the range of diverse and sometimes complex cultural traits of visitors increases. This unit introduces you to the cultural backgrounds, needs and expectations of visitors from a variety of world destinations so that you will feel confident when communicating with a range of visitors. You will learn about the different reasons for seeking the tourism experience, plus the religious and social influences on customer expectations. You will learn that an understanding, no matter how limited, of foreign languages will make overseas visitors feel more comfortable and welcome. You will also learn about the role of non-verbal communication in dealing with people from different cultures and the part played by codes of conduct in helping respect the environment and cultures of tourism destinations.

This unit is divided into five main areas:

- **Reasons for seeking the tourism experience**
- **Religious and social influences on customer expectations**
- **Language**
- **Non-verbal communication**
- **Codes of conduct**

We guide you through each of these areas using examples and case studies from the travel and tourism industry. At the beginning of each of these sections you will see a list of key topics to help you fully understand what you need to learn. Look out for the links to websites so that you can learn more about a particular travel and tourism company, organisation or topic.

Reasons for seeking the tourism experience

Key topics in this section

- **Tourist motivation**
- **The interdependency of tourism and culture**

Tourist motivation

As you learned in Unit 1 *Investigating travel and tourism*, tourists travel to destinations for a variety of reasons, including:

✪ **Visiting friends and relatives (known as VFR in the travel and tourism industry)**

✪ **Taking part in educational trips**

✪ **Conducting business**

✪ **Visiting religious centres**

✪ **Going on holiday or taking a short break**

✪ **Going to a concert**

✪ **Taking part in a sporting event or activity**

Precisely what motivates a person to travel to a particular place and for a specific reason is often difficult to understand. If we start from the standpoint that all individuals have a unique set of characteristics that determines their physical and psychological make-up, then the variety of influences on each person's reasons for travel is immense. Why, for example, will one person choose to visit Australia to visit the outback while another will be happy with a week's camping holiday in Norfolk?

Certain factors that influence tourism demand are outside the control of the individual. These factors are often referred to as *determinants*, while the influences that shape an individual's choice and over which they have a degree of control are termed *motivators*. The next two sections of this unit look at the determinants and motivators of travel and tourism in greater detail.

Travel determinants

Before an individual can take part in any type of tourist activity, whether for leisure, business or visiting friends and relatives, there are certain 'core' conditions that must be satisfied and which may limit a person's ability to travel. Having sufficient time available to travel is clearly a fundamental determinant of tourist travel. An individual must be able to spare the time to be away from home, work, study or other commitments for the duration of their trip. The introduction of paid holiday entitlements and increases in leisure time in the majority of western industrialised nations have contributed to the increased demand for tourism. It is clear, however, that patterns of tourism demand are changing, with a sharp rise in the popularity of short breaks at the expense of traditional long holidays. In addition to having sufficient time, a person must also be able to afford the cost of travel. Although there has been a gradual rise in income levels in western societies, there are clearly sections of the population whose income level does not permit spending on tourist travel. The income levels of many people living in the developing nations of the world are generally too low to allow them to travel internationally. As well as having sufficient time and money to travel, an individual must live under a political regime that allows its citizens freedom of movement within their own country and overseas. In the former Eastern Bloc states, prohibitions and restrictions on tourist travel were a common feature of the Communist regimes. In times of austerity, countries may limit the amount of foreign currency its citizens can spend abroad, sometimes to a level that makes international travel impossible to achieve. A fourth determinant of travel is the state of health of a prospective tourist; clearly, an individual who is incapacitated through serious illness or injury will be unable to undertake a tourist trip for whatever reason.

Travel motivators

Even when a person has satisfied the necessary determinants of tourist travel, there are complex psychological influences at work within the individual that will affect their demand for tourism. Major travel and tourism organisations invest large sums in market research in order to understand better these motivating factors that influence a tourist's choice and patterns of purchasing behaviour, in the hope of improving the products and service they offer their customers. Probably the most widely quoted work on motivation theory is that of Maslow, who developed the 'hierarchy of needs' (see Figure 17.1).

In Maslow's model there are five levels of needs that an individual seeks to satisfy, from physiological needs at the base of the pyramid to self-actualisation at the pinnacle. Maslow argues that individuals must satisfy certain physiological needs, such as shelter, warmth, water and food, and safety needs before moving on to the need for belonging and love, esteem and ultimately self-actualisation. Applying Maslow's hierarchy of needs to tourists' motivation to travel, it is clear that, depending on the particular circumstances of the individual, tourism can satisfy all levels of needs. A holidaymaker, for example, will choose accommodation, hospitality and travel arrangements that meet his or her physiological and safety needs. Holidays can certainly provide

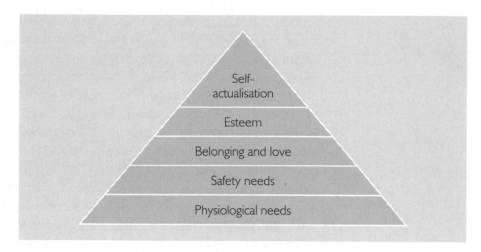

Figure 17.1 *Maslow's hierarchy of needs*

opportunities for developing social relationships, thereby contributing towards the need for belonging and love. Tourists sometimes use their travel experiences as a way of boosting their esteem among peers. Particular types of tourism-related experiences may also contribute to a person's achievement of self-actualisation or self-fulfilment, perhaps becoming spiritually enlightened or learning a new language while on holiday.

In attempting to understand the complexities of tourism motivators, it is clear that tourists' choices are influenced by a wide variety of factors, which, leaving aside the determinants of time, money, freedom to travel and health that have already been considered, include:

- ✪ **Education** – has a profound effect on individuals, not least in relation to their demand for travel and tourism, given the tendency for education to broaden the mind and stimulate the desire to travel

- ✪ **Stage in the life cycle** – tourism demand fluctuates in relation to a wide variety of life-cycle characteristics, such as age, family composition and domestic commitments

- ✪ **Fashions and fads** – destinations and tourist products go in and out of fashion

- ✪ **Personal mobility** – access to a private motor vehicle can open up greater tourism opportunities

- ✪ **Rural/urban residence** – urban dwellers may be motivated to seek the peace and solitude of rural areas for tourist travel, and vice versa

- ✪ **Race and gender** – cultural surroundings and societal stereotyping can influence the demand for tourism

- ✪ **Destination image** – the techniques used to create a favourable image of a destination and to promote it for tourism, and the methods used to communicate this promotional message to prospective tourists, will influence tourism demand

It is important to stress that none of these factors works in isolation, but rather each is part of a complex, interrelated mechanism that shapes an individual's motivation for travel. Moreover, the relative importance of each factor to an individual will change over time in response to internal and external influences.

The interdependency of tourism and culture

The global nature of travel and tourism, with people travelling to ever-distant and remote destinations, makes it almost impossible to separate tourism from culture. It is now relatively easy for a tourist to visit remote villages in the South American rain forest or take a weekend break in one of the many cultural cities of the world.

Tourism can have both positive and negative effects on the culture of a destination area, as the following two sections of this unit explain.

Positive cultural impacts of travel and tourism

Given that many of the reasons for visiting tourist destinations are concerned with social and cultural experiences, for example meeting new people and exploring cultural sites, the travel and tourism industry can be said to have positive impacts in this regard. Although the travel and tourism industry is often criticised for its negative social and cultural impacts on destination areas, it can have positive impacts, such as

- **Helping to preserve environmentally sensitive areas, e.g. the survival of African wildlife (see Figure 17.2)**
- **The revitalisation for visitors of neglected regions, e.g. dockland areas in many UK cities**
- **The rebirth of local arts, crafts and customs**
- **The staging of cultural events, e.g. the Proms and arts festivals**
- **The provision of community facilities**
- **The growth of religious tourism**
- **Refurbishment of local architecture**
- **Greater understanding between cultures**

At a local level, the provision of tourism facilities for the enjoyment of visitors gives local people the opportunity to improve the quality of their lives and to take part in community activities for the benefit of all. Also, by helping to maintain a clean and attractive environment for visitors, tourism can instil a sense of civic pride in local residents.

Figure 17.2 *Tourism can help conserve wildlife*
Courtesy of Ned Perry

Negative cultural impacts of travel and tourism

There is a general feeling among those with an interest in travel and tourism that the negative social and cultural impacts of tourism development are far more harmful in the long run than the environmental problems associated with the industry. This is based on the belief that many of the negative environmental impacts can be easily corrected with the right management and funding. The social and cultural problems, however, can be far more deep-rooted and may take generations to eradicate. Some of these problems are:

- **Overcrowding, which may cause a reduction in the quality of life for the 'host community', i.e. those living in the destination visited**
- **Traditional activities, e.g. farming and fishing, may lose labour to the seemingly more attractive jobs in travel and tourism**
- **Tourists' behaviour can distort local customs, e.g. the Anglicising of Ibiza and other Mediterranean holiday destinations**
- **Religious codes may be altered to adapt to the needs of visitors, e.g. Sunday opening of facilities**
- **Local languages may be lost through under-use**
- **Traditional crafts may be lost in favour of mass-produced souvenirs**

- ✪ Loss of communities, especially where tourists buy second homes in holiday areas
- ✪ Increase in crime rates, including public disturbances and burglaries

All concerned with tourism to overseas destinations – the tourist boards, travel agents, tour operators, airlines, hotel developers and tourists themselves – must work towards minimising tourism's negative impacts so that communities remain truly sustainable in the long term.

Industry example

Tourism Concern (see case study on page 332) is working for change in tourism and insists that tourism takes account of the rights and interests of those living in the world's tourist areas. It pursues campaigns to highlight injustices in tourism development, such as the following example taken from their website:

Safari parks such as the Maasai Mara have forced the Maasai themselves off their traditional cattle-grazing lands. Many have migrated to urban slums, or scratch a living selling souvenirs or posing for photos. Tourism Concern has been a facilitator, bringing together people from all sectors of tourism to formulate the accreditation and training of driver guides and a code for all tourists visiting the country. We also work closely with Maasai and other tribal communities who have been expelled from their ancestral lands to make way for wildlife/safari tourism.

Check out this website

www.tourismconcern.
org.uk

Activity 17.1

Gather information about the positive and negative cultural impacts of tourism in your local area. Work as part of a group to come up with some ideas as to how the positive impacts could be maximised and the negative impacts minimised.

Religious and social influences on customer expectations

Key topics in this section

- **Religious practices**
- **Social customs**
- **Dress**
- **Food and drink**
- **Gender issues**

Religion and social characteristics often provide good indicators of cultural identity and it is important that people working in the travel and tourism industry are able to appreciate these influences when dealing with visitors from abroad or working overseas. Table 17.1 shows some of the main religions and languages in a selection of countries that generate visitors to Britain.

Country	Main religions	Main languages
Australia	Christian	English
Belgium	Roman Catholic	French, Flemish
Canada	Christian	English, French
France	Roman Catholic	French
India	Hindu, Sikh, Muslim, Christian	Hindi, English
Ireland	Roman Catholic	English
Italy	Roman Catholic	Italian
Japan	Buddhist	Japanese
Middle East	Sunni Muslim (95%), Shia Muslim (5%)	Arabic (Iran – Farsi)
Netherlands	Roman Catholic, Dutch Reform	Dutch
South America	Roman Catholic	Spanish, Portuguese
USA	Christian	English
Germany	Protestant, Roman Catholic	German

Table 17.1 *Religions and languages of countries generating visitors to Britain*

Having an awareness of these characteristics helps people who work in travel and tourism to respond effectively to people from a variety of cultural, religious and ethnic backgrounds. Particular aspects that need special attention include:

- **Religious practices** – e.g. knowing the days of worship when in an overseas country, realising the significance of particular festivals in different religions, such as Ramadan for Muslims, when they are required to fast during the holy month, which can fall at any time of the year depending on the lunar calendar. During Ramadan all Muslims from the age of seven refrain from eating, drinking and smoking, between dawn and dusk. Saturday is the Sabbath for Jews, when they are all expected to refrain from work, travelling, using the telephone and handling money, among other restrictions.

- **Social customs** – e.g. how people are greeted. Staff who are giving directions or pointing something out to a Muslim woman should not touch her, even if this is done with the best of intentions, since this could be misinterpreted. Hindu women generally prefer not to shake hands when meeting new people.

- **Dress** – e.g. the need to cover heads, remove footwear, when formal attire is expected. Whatever their mode of dress, full 'hijab' with veil or a modified version of Western dress, the covering of Muslim women is because they are respected as mothers, wives and important contributors to society, not because they are second-class citizens. It is also felt to safeguard their respect and dignity. Middle Eastern women prefer black veils (chador) and may not cover their face (it is not essential). Tunisian women wear white and do cover their face. Hindu women often dress in traditional saris or loose-fitting trouser suits made of silk or satin with matching dupattas (long chiffon scarves). Sikh males wear turbans, distinguishing them from any other religious group.

- **Food and drink** – e.g. excluded foods, eating times, whether alcohol is permitted. No pork or pork products of any kind are eaten by Muslims, who eat Halal meat. Halal refers to the ritual slaughter of animals and the draining of their blood. Orthodox Jews do not eat pork or shellfish; meat should be Kosher, similar to Halal, and meat and dairy products should not be eaten together. Sikhs are vegetarian and do not drink or smoke. In the case of Hindus, beef is forbidden as the cow is considered a sacred animal. However, many Hindus are vegetarian and the vast majority do not drink alcohol, especially women. Alcohol is strictly forbidden for practising Muslims and Buddhists.

- **Gender** – e.g. the position of women in society. Although free to speak out and conduct their own affairs, many Hindu women leave decision making to the male members of the family.

You can see from the above that religious, social and cultural differences can be complex. The important point for staff working in travel and tourism is to appreciate these sorts of cultural characteristics and to be sensitive to the needs of visitors from overseas.

Language

Key topics in this section

- **The importance of an understanding of languages**
- **Basic foreign language phrases**

The importance of an understanding of languages

An understanding of other languages, no matter how limited, can often make overseas visitors feel more welcome and comfortable. Welcome, bienvenue, wilkommen or bienvenido, said in a warm and friendly manner in any language, makes visitors to a foreign country feel special and wanted. Often it is the simplest expressions – a greeting, small talk, being able to direct visitors or even making suggestions for visits – that can make all the difference when wanting to create a good impression and to show that we are making an effort. For over half the overseas visitors to Britain, English is not their first language. To succeed in the highly competitive travel and tourism industry, staff in the UK must be able to meet the expectations of foreign visitors. Communicating in their own language, even at a modest level of fluency, goes a long way towards achieving this.

Some of the circumstances in which a basic knowledge of a foreign language can help in travel and tourism include:

- ✪ **Welcoming people to this country**
- ✪ **Asking them about their origins**
- ✪ **Giving directions**
- ✪ **Advising on travel times**
- ✪ **Showing people around attractions and destinations**
- ✪ **Making reservations on behalf of the visitors**

Your language may not be fluent, but you will have shown the overseas visitor that you have made an effort on their behalf and most will appreciate this.

Industry example

English Heritage, with responsibility for over 400 historic properties in the nation's care, has long recognised the need to develop its foreign language provision for visitors and is doing what it can within funding constraints. As well as recruiting guides with fluency in foreign languages, foreign language publications have been produced, including:

★ Souvenir guides for Stonehenge and Dover Castle in French, German and Japanese

★ Free sheets giving basic site information in French, German, Japanese, Spanish, Italian and Dutch

★ Brief printed guides for selected sites in French, German and Italian

★ Foreign language audio tours

Foreign language material is provided according to the sites' profiles related to visits by overseas tourists.

Browse this website

www.english-heritage.org.uk

Basic foreign language phrases

The following is a list of basic phrases that are used in travel and tourism situations, with their French translations.

English	French
Good morning	Bonjour
Where is the station?	Où est la gare?
I live in England	J'habite en Angleterre
The church is near the hotel	L'église est près de l'hôtel
Where do you live?	Où habitez-vous?
The train arrives soon	Le train arrive bientôt
I would like to book a room with bathroom	Je voudrais réserver une chambre avec salle de bains
Where is the airport?	Où est l'aéroport?
What time is it?	Quelle heure est-il?
Where is the hotel?	Où est l'hôtel?
Do you have a room for 4 people?	Vous avez une chambre pour quatre personnes?

Where is the dining room?	Où est la salle à manger?
How much is it, please?	C'est combien, s'il vous plaît?
The bill, please	L'addition, s'il vous plaît
My name is Richard	Je m'appelle Richard
I'd like a coffee please	Je voudrais un café, s'il vous plaît

Activity 17.2

Working in pairs, practise pronouncing and learning these English/French phrases and using them in role play situations.

Activity 17.3

With the help of a phrase book and/or dictionary, translate the English phrases into the following languages:

★ Spanish

★ German

★ Italian

Practise the translated phrases with a colleague and try to learn as many as possible.

Industry example

Welcome Host International is a one-day training course offering an introduction to the language and culture of international visitors to Britain. Offered by regional tourist boards in the UK, the course aims to improve the skills and abilities of staff who deal with visitors from overseas. By the end of the day's training those who participate in the course will be able to:

1   Use words and phrases to meet, greet and inform visitors from overseas

2   Gain an understanding of some of the cultural differences between nationalities and know how these can be used to give assistance and advice to overseas visitors

3   Match the expectations of visitors to the facilities and services available regionally

The course includes sessions on the value of tourism to the UK, greeting people, opening conversations, helpful hints for dealing with visitors and information on the countries that generate visitors to Britain.

Browse this website

www.englishtourism.
org.uk

Non-verbal communication

Key topics in this section

- **Facial expressions**
- **Gestures**
- **Bodily posture**
- **Social space**
- **Eye contact**
- **Bodily contact**

Speech can be used in a number of different ways, but when contact is face-to-face, it is always supported and elaborated by non-verbal communication (NVC). You will have learned in Unit 5 *Customer service in travel and tourism* that NVC is the process by which we send and receive messages without the use of the spoken word. For example, we all use our eyes, hands and facial expressions to emphasise points and to confirm information we have received. When communicating with people from another country, whether in the UK or on a trip overseas, it is important to be aware that the use of certain expressions or gestures may be confusing and even offensive to them. Care must be taken in the use of body language, since there are a number of differences and distinctive characteristics in the body language of different nationalities and cultures. In certain tribes in India, for example, a nod of the head may mean 'no' rather than 'yes' and in certain parts of the world direct eye contact between men and women is considered socially unacceptable.

Our social relationships with one another, therefore, are based not only on spoken language but also on the unspoken language of the following:

- ✪ **Facial expressions**: The most welcoming of all facial expressions is the smile, which can put visitors from overseas at ease and show that you are interested in their welfare. Negative facial expressions are to be avoided.

- ✪ **Gestures**: We all make gestures with our bodies to reinforce a point, for example a wave of the hand to say goodbye or a 'thumbs up' to indicate that all is well. Care must be taken with gestures made to certain overseas visitors, e.g. western hand movements can sometimes be offensive to the Japanese, so it is advisable always to point with an open palm

- ✪ **Bodily posture**: In order to make sure that visitors can hear what you are saying, avoid covering your mouth with your hand while speaking.

In Japan, people are expected to bow upon meeting another person, according to seniority. However, Japanese people do not expect to see their customs replicated in the UK.

☺ **Social space**: Some nationalities are more 'tactile' than others. People from many Mediterranean and Latin countries, for example, indulge in much hand shaking and kissing when meeting people.

☺ **Eye contact**: As a general rule, eye contact is to be encouraged, since it helps people to communicate effectively. However, it is considered rude by some nationalities to make too much direct eye contact, for example men to Muslim women. For the same reason, eye contact is best kept to a minimum with the Japanese.

☺ **Bodily contact**: It is common for Spanish people to kiss on both cheeks on introduction, while the French and Italians have a tendency to shake hands more often than the British and to be kissed on both cheeks before departing. It is polite only to shake hands when a Japanese person has offered their hand first.

Activity 17.4

Observe a conversation between one pair of people who know each other well and one pair who are in a formal situation, for example a travel agency clerk serving a customer or a guest checking in to a hotel. Watch each person's body language and note the type of gestures made, both negative and positive. Discuss what you found with the rest of your group. You could also try this as a role play, where different members of your group take on the role of customer, travel agent, hotel receptionist, etc.

There are a number of examples of body language to avoid when working with any visitors, whether from the UK or overseas, for example:

☺ **Finger strumming and foot tapping shows impatience**

☺ **Arms folded across the chest suggests a defensive, 'closed' attitude**

☺ **Standing sideways to somebody, or with your back to them, can convey a disinterested attitude**

☺ **Pointing at the person you are talking to demonstrates aggression**

☺ **Nail biting can mean insecurity**

☺ **Hands on hips shows that you may be ready for confrontation!**

Codes of conduct

Key topics in this section

- **Responsible tourism**
- **Gender**
- **Dress**
- **Religion**
- **Tradition**

Responsible tourism

Responsible tourists follow codes of conduct, formal or informal, that display respect for the environment, tradition and cultures of destinations and the people who live there. This holds true in the UK as well as in overseas destinations. Compromise, confidence and common sense are seen as important attributes of responsible travel and tourism. Tourists should make every effort to observe social, religious and cultural customs and laws. As we have seen elsewhere in this unit, codes of conduct relate to a number of factors, including:

- ✪ **Gender**
- ✪ **Dress**
- ✪ **Religion**
- ✪ **Tradition**

Many codes of conduct stem from religious beliefs and great care must be taken in their observation. When travelling to overseas destinations, particularly those with strict religious and cultural origins, tourists must observe local traditions so as not to offend their hosts. Acceptable dress is an important consideration, for example shorts and skirts are considered offensive in some Muslim countries, as is topless bathing for women in some destinations.

Industry example

VSO (Voluntary Service Overseas) has initiated a campaign to highlight the negative impacts that global tourism can have on overseas destinations, particularly Third World countries, where much of the money generated by tourism may not reach local people nor benefit their communities. Called 'Worldwise', the VSO campaign demonstrates the problems that tourism can cause in developing nations:

The rapid development of tourism can devastate local communities and environments. We've all heard people talk about their latest holiday 'find', but they warn 'get there before it's spoilt'. Many of us have experienced that sense of loss when somewhere we loved for being idyllic has become commercialised or a concrete jungle. The fear is that the process will happen much quicker when nearly three times the number of people are travelling around the world by 2015.

The Worldwise campaign suggests the following action points in order to create a fairer travel and tourism industry:

★ If you are going on holiday to the developing world, visit VSO's on-line travel advice centre.

★ Travel agents should stock the Worldwise leaflet and insert a copy into ticket wallets or flight confirmation envelopes for their clients.

★ Tour operators should give their customers more information about the people and places they will be visiting, including advice on how they can visit locally-owned facilities and resorts. Tour operators should also develop a policy on how the holidays they provide could be of more benefit to the people living in their destination areas.

★ Hotels should start buying more goods and services locally, reduce imports and start environmental management programmes.

★ The UK government should recognise the contribution that international tourism can make in

continued

Browse this website

www.vso.org.uk/
campaign/tourism/
report.htm

continued

promoting development awareness among the UK public, and look into ways that tourism can be used to achieve this objective.

VSO believes that communities could benefit more from tourism, tourists could have more enjoyable holidays and the industry could have long-term security, but only if changes are made. If tourism is to be sustainable, it must be used to help communities move from poverty to prosperity.

The following case study investigates the work of Tourism Concern, an influential non-governmental organisation (NGO) that is concerned with the responsible development of tourism, particularly in developing nations of the world.

Case Study
Tourism Concern

▶ WHAT IS TOURISM CONCERN?

Tourism Concern is a membership organisation established in 1989 to bring together British people with an active concern for tourism's impact on community and environment, both in the UK and worldwide. The organisation is working for change in tourism and insists that tourism takes account of the rights and interests of those living in the world's tourist areas. Tourism Concern aims to look past the cosmetic 'green issues', such as recycling and energy conservation, to the way that tourism affects the people living in destination areas, their communities and their environments. It seeks to raise awareness of tourism's impacts, informs and influences decision-makers at all levels, and provides a comprehensive

continued

continued

information base. Through its membership network, global contacts and resource collection, Tourism Concern is a respected centre for advice and information on tourism's impacts on environment and culture.

▶ WHAT DOES TOURISM CONCERN STAND FOR?

Tourism Concern advocates:

- ★ Tourism that is just, yielding benefits that are fairly distributed
- ★ Tourism that is participatory, recognising the rights of residents to be involved in its development and management
- ★ Tourism that is sustainable, putting the long-term social and environmental health of holiday areas before short-term gain

▶ HOW IS TOURISM CONCERN ORGANISED?

Tourism Concern is made up of a voluntary membership body, led by an elected council, operating to a written constitution. It is supported by membership subscriptions, donations, grants and involvement in joint projects. Tourism Concern's current grant funders are:

- ★ The Joseph Rowntree Charitable Trust
- ★ Christian Aid
- ★ London Borough Grants Council
- ★ University of North London
- ★ Department for International Development
- ★ Network Foundation
- ★ VSO
- ★ Polden Puckham Charitable Foundation
- ★ CAFOD

There are links to a global network of like-minded organisations sharing information and occasional joint

continued

continued

action. Tourism Concern has a full-time co-ordinator, supported by part-time staff and volunteers. Its base is in north London.

► WHAT IS TOURISM CONCERN DOING?

★ *Campaigning* – to see that tourism is recognised by governments and development agencies as a key issue for the twenty-first century; to raise issues of injustice, like the harassment of those who speak out against developments in certain countries

★ *Networking* – to bring together different sectors to work on local and global projects such as the Himalayan Tourist Code, now distributed by the tourism industry, and Guidelines for Sustainable Tourism Development

★ *Informing* – the public, mounting exhibitions and providing literature to heighten awareness of tourism issues; providing speakers and information for the press, broadcasts and conferences

★ *Developing* – a resource base of information on the issues

★ *Educating* – by contributing to teaching resources on tourism's impact and exploring new ways to integrate tourism issues into education.

(Information courtesy of Tourism Concern).

Case study discussion points

Check out this website

www.tourismconcern.org.uk

1 How can Tourism Concern influence the development of tourist resorts and facilities that conform to the principles of sustainable development?

2 What factors will affect Tourism Concern's success in meeting its aims?

3 Do campaigning organisations like Tourism Concern have a role to play in regulating the tourism industry?

4 What measures can Tourism Concern implement to persuade governments of the need for planned tourism development?

Financial planning and control

18

In the highly competitive travel and tourism industry, planning and controlling finances is essential for survival and the long-term growth of enterprises. In this unit you will investigate how organisations control their flow of money in order to make sure that they are as profitable as possible, bills are paid when they are due and management can plan for the future with confidence. You will develop the skills and understanding that are necessary for dealing with basic financial matters in a travel and tourism organisation. In particular, you will learn about the importance of accounts in measuring the profitability of an organisation. You will also investigate how travel and tourism products and services are priced. The final part of the unit looks at the procedures used in producing budgets, including a cash flow forecast and a profit and loss account.

This unit is divided into three main areas:

- **Understanding accounts**
- **Pricing travel and tourism products and services**
- **Producing budgets**

We guide you through each of these areas using examples and case studies from the travel and tourism industry. At the beginning of each of these sections you will see a list of key topics to help you fully understand what you need to learn. Look out for the links to websites so that you can learn more about a particular travel and tourism company, organisation or topic.

Understanding accounts

Key topics in this section

- **The importance of understanding accounts**
- **Understanding cash flow, the profit and loss account and balance sheets**
- **Factors affecting the financial performance of a travel and tourism organisation**
- **Extracting information from the balance sheet and profit and loss account**
- **Interpreting accounts**

The importance of understanding accounts

Accurate and easily accessible accounts are the cornerstone of successful financial planning and control. Every travel and tourism enterprise, from the smallest bed and breakfast establishment to the largest international airline, needs to keep careful accounts or 'books' in order to:

1   **Keep track of how well the organisation is performing in terms of generating revenue and controlling costs**

2   **Meet the legal requirements to present audited accounts at the end of each trading year**

3   **Make sure that its selling, purchasing and payments transactions are free from error**

4   **Provide continuous feedback to management to help decision making**

5   **Form the source data from which the year end or final accounts are produced**

In travel and tourism organisations, even employees who are not directly concerned with financial planning and control need to understand the type of information provided by accounts, such as sales volumes, pricing, cash flow and profitability. The long-term success of any organisation relies on keeping control of money within the organisation and all employees contribute to this by making effective use of resources, maximising customer spending and encouraging new business.

Accounting methods used in the travel and tourism industry mirror closely those used by organisations in many other sectors of the UK economy. Financial accountants are bound by legislation contained in the various Companies' Acts concerning the method of presentation of financial data and the disclosure of certain information. As well as meeting the needs of shareholders, financial accounts include information required by the Inland Revenue and the Registrar of Companies. The accounts of all travel and tourism companies are subject to auditing, a technique that attempts to ensure that the financial information disclosed to shareholders and other interested parties is objective and fair.

Travel and tourism organisations in the public sector are also required by law to produce annual accounts. Under the Local Government Finance Act 1982, local authorities are required to produce Statements of Accounts, which include income and expenditure, summaries of capital expenditure, the consolidated balance sheet and the statement of sources of funds. With the development of 'contracted out' services, individual business units within local authorities, including leisure, travel and tourism facilities, are required to produce a separate annual report, prepared along the lines of commercial sector accounts. Many voluntary sector organisations also have to produce accounts to satisfy the requirements of the Charity Commission or the providers of National Lottery funding.

Understanding cash flow, the profit and loss account and balance sheets

All public limited companies (plcs), e.g. Airtours plc, Thomson Travel plc, British Airways plc and Virgin plc, produce a set of annual reports, which provide interested parties with details about business performance and company activities. Publicly funded and voluntary bodies, such as tourist boards, English Heritage, YHA and the National Trust, also produce financial reports so that anybody with an interest can investigate how effectively public money is being spent.

Financial accounting is concerned with the preparation of the financial information an organisation is required by law to produce. In the private sector, these statutory accounts comprise:

- ✪ **The cash flow statement**
- ✪ **The profit and loss account**
- ✪ **The balance sheet**

We will now look at each of these in greater detail.

The cash flow statement

The cash flow statement is a detailed record of cash flowing into and out of an organisation, usually on an annual basis. From this can be derived the monthly cash flow and, by adding together each month's figures, the organisation's cumulative cash position. Detailed cash flow management is critical to any travel and tourism organisation, in order to:

✪ **Be in a position to meet cash demands**

✪ **Ensure that maximum credit is being obtained**

✪ **Make sure that debtors are kept under tight control**

✪ **Determine when extra borrowing is needed**

Figure 18.1 gives an example of a summarised cash flow statement for a travel agency for a three-month trading period.

In the example, we can see that the cash flow statement identifies:

✪ **Cash inflows**: These will include capital from the sale of products or services, the start-up capital, loans obtained and income from other sources, such as rent from property and dividends received from shares. In the case of a travel agency, the main cash inflows will be made up of sales of holidays, flights, cruising, car hire, hotel reservations, travel insurance and other travel services.

✪ **Cash outflows**: These include all the expenses incurred in making the sales of products and services. Continuing with the travel agency example, these will include running costs such as wages, rent, postage, telephone, advertising and stationery, as well as interest and loan repayments.

✪ **Net cash flow**: By deducting total cash outflows from total cash inflows, the balance arrived at will show, on a monthly basis, the amount of cash forecast to be in the bank. For new businesses in travel and tourism, the operators can see immediately whether their efforts are likely to pay dividends.

	Jan (£000)	Feb (£000)	Mar (£000)
Cash at start	32	57	59
Total cash inflows	135	120	116
Total cash outflows	110	118	121
Net cash flow	+25	+2	−5
Cumulative cash	57	59	54

Figure 18.1   *Cash flow statement for a three-month trading period*

An organisation's cash flow statement provides a link between its profit and loss account and balance sheet. It forms part of the audited accounts and shows the funds that have entered the company, how they have been used and how any net surplus or deficiency in short- and long-term funds have been applied.

The cash flow statement will indicate the periods in the year when extra financing, in the form of an overdraft or loan, is required. This is particularly critical in the tourism industry, with its high degree of seasonal activity.

The profit and loss account

The information contained in the profit and loss account is probably the most important in managing and controlling the finances of a travel and tourism organisation. The profit and loss account, more precisely called the trading and profit and loss account, is a summary of all the income and expenditure of an organisation, over a given period of time, sometimes quarterly, half yearly or annually, depending on custom and practice. However, by law, companies must produce their final accounts at least once per year. In travel and tourism, profit and loss accounts are sometimes presented on a departmental basis, with, for example, costs and sales being shown separately for rooms, food and beverage in a hotel. Figure 18.2 shows the profit and loss account for a small country house hotel.

The figure is a typical profit and loss account, in that it starts with the total sales (turnover) for the year, from which is deducted a figure for the cost of sales to produce the gross profit. In this example the gross profit is £239,000. Expenses are deducted from the gross profit to produce the operating profit of £61,000. Finally, the net profit is calculated by deducting interest payments from the operating profit. All profit and loss accounts will show whether the organisation is carrying forward either a surplus or deficit into the next

Lakeview Country House Hotel Profit and Loss Account for the year ending 31/3/00	
	£000
SALES	
Rooms	120
Food and beverage	160
Other	24
TOTAL	304
Cost of sales	65
GROSS PROFIT	239
Expenses	178
OPERATING PROFIT	61
Interest	38
NET PROFIT (before tax)	23

Figure 18.2 *Profit and loss account for a small country house hotel*

accounting period, and are useful for comparing financial performance over different periods of time.

The purposes of a profit and loss account can be summarised as follows:

- ✪ **To indicate the success or failure of management policies in deploying available resources to generate profits. To achieve this, the profit and loss account should be read in conjunction with the balance sheet.**
- ✪ **To show the extent to which an organisation can cover its debt servicing costs, e.g. bank and loan interest, from the profits earned in the course of its day-to-day activities.**
- ✪ **To determine whether an organisation's goods and services are sufficiently popular to cover its necessary expenses, such as staff costs, rates, insurance and administration costs.**
- ✪ **To illustrate how an organisation's profits have been divided among claimants, such as external lenders, the Inland Revenue and the owners.**
- ✪ **To determine the extent to which profits are susceptible to erosion by rising costs.**
- ✪ **To give an impression of whether an organisation seeks a high turnover with low percentage profit margins, or a lower turnover with higher margins.**

Profitability is the ultimate objective of commercial travel and tourism enterprises. It is the management's responsibility to maximise profitability, which is usually the prime concern of the owners of the business and any shareholders it has. They will be particularly concerned that the return on their investment should be more than that available elsewhere, given the same or lower level of risk.

Activity
18.1

Research a range of annual reports of travel and tourism organisations and compare the financial data given in their profit and loss accounts. Compile a chart showing which have the highest turnover and calculate the increases or decreases in turnovers between current and past years.

Interpreting the profit and loss account

The results shown in an organisation's profit and loss account can be interpreted as follows:

- **By comparing the results against budgeted figures and analysing any variances (differences)**
- **By comparing the results against previous years' results and analysing differences**
- **By comparing the results against the performance of competitors**
- **By comparing the results with 'industry norms', i.e. how an organisation in the same sector would normally be expected to perform**

For example, the total achieved for room sales in the country house hotel example shown in Figure 18.2 may be lower than forecast in its budget. This could be due to an unrealistic budget figure or a decline in demand. Whatever the case, investigation should take place to determine the cause of the discrepancy.

Activity 18.2

Referring to the example of the profit and loss account for the country house hotel shown in Figure 18.2, and the information in the ratios chart (Figure 18.4 on page 349), calculate the gross profit ratio and the net profit ratio for the establishment.

The balance sheet

The balance sheet of a travel and tourism enterprise is a very important document. It is a statement of the assets, liabilities and capital of the organisation and summarises its financial position at a specified date, in other words a 'snapshot' of the financial health of the business on a particular day. Balance sheets are drawn up at least on an annual basis and often more frequently than this, depending on the financial systems of the organisation. An example of a balance sheet for a restaurant run by a young couple is given in Figure 18.3.

As Figure 18.3 shows, the balance sheet revolves around an organisation's assets and liabilities, the difference between the two being the working capital that it has available to use for day-to-day operations.

We will now explain some of the terminology used in the balance sheet example given in Figure 18.3:

- **Fixed assets**: These are items of a monetary value that have a long-term function and can be used repeatedly. Examples include land, buildings, vehicles, equipment and machinery. Fixed assets are not only

```
                     Balance Sheet for 'Seven Up' Restaurant
                          as at 31 December 2000
FIXED ASSETS                                    £              £

Lease on premises                            20,000
Fixtures and fittings                         8,500
Kitchen equipment                             4,900
Van                                           3,000         36,400

CURRENT ASSETS

Stock                                         2,400
Debtors                                       1,800
Bank                                          6,500
Cash                                            100
Total current assets                         10,800

CURRENT LIABILITIES

Creditors                                     2,900
Total current liabilities                     2,900

NET CURRENT ASSETS                                          7,900

TERM LOAN                                                  (3,000)
                                                           41,300
OWNER'S CAPITAL EMPLOYED

At start                                     12,500
Profit for period                            28,800
                                                           41,300
```

Figure 18.3 *Balance sheet for a restaurant*

useful in the running of an organisation, but can also be used as security for additional loans.

○ **Current assets**: These are items owned by an organisation, where the value is constantly changing, for example stock, debtors (those who owe you money) and cash. The balance of current assets over current liabilities is called the working capital.

○ **Current liabilities**: These are amounts owed to other businesses, where the amounts are constantly changing. Typical current liabilities are creditors (those to whom you owe money), overdrafts and dividends.

○ **Net current assets (working capital)**: This is the difference between the current assets and the current liabilities.

○ **Owner's capital employed**: This represents the money that the owner has put into the business either directly or indirectly by trading, making a profit and leaving some of the profit in the business.

The main purposes of a balance sheet can be summarised as follows:

- The organisation's ability to pay off outstanding debts can be assessed by comparing current assets with current liabilities

- It gives an opportunity to determine the extent to which an organisation is able to borrow further funds from external sources, without straining its capability to service its debts

- It illustrates the division of capital employed among outsiders, owners, proprietors and shareholders

- It allows an examination and analysis of the organisation's fixed assets to reveal whether assets are underutilised

- It provides evidence of management policies on subjective issues, such as the writing off of goodwill, the treatment of development costs and the expiry of fixed assets through depreciation

Activity 18.3

With reference to the balance sheet example given in Figure 18.3, calculate the working capital from the figures given.

Who uses financial accounts?

Various people, both inside and outside the organisation, will use accounting information to help determine how a travel and tourism enterprise is performing, including:

- **Owners**: All those who have invested, or are considering investing capital into a travel and tourism business, will be keen to assess profitability, liquidity and activity, in the past, present and future. How the organisation is performing is the responsibility of management and is, therefore, an assessment of how well they deploy their resources.

- **Shareholders and investment brokers**: Individuals and organisations that own shares in companies, as well as their advisers and brokers, will need access to accounts to check financial performance.

- **Managers**: All managers have a duty of stewardship, i.e. to report to the shareholders and to operate the organisation in their best interests. Effective managers in travel and tourism will monitor progress throughout the year, by comparing actual with budgeted results and taking steps to correct any problem areas.

- **Providers of finance**: Whether a banking institution in the private sector, or 'the public purse' in the public sector, providers of finance will be interested in how well an organisation can repay its debts, now and in the future.

- **Tax authorities**: The Inland Revenue and HM Customs and Excise will need to see accurate records for correct assessment of income tax and VAT.

Activity 18.4

Taking the examples of a voluntary sector organisation, such as the National Trust, and a private sector travel and tourism company, such as Airtours plc, compile a chart to show who would be likely to need to use the financial accounts of each organisation and for what purpose.

Factors affecting the financial performance of a travel and tourism organisation

The wide-ranging nature of the travel and tourism industry means that there will be many reasons why the financial performance of an organisation changes, for the better or the worse. External factors, outside the immediate control of the organisation, may include:

- **Seasonality**: Although a great deal of effort is channelled into extending the tourist season, many sectors of the UK travel and tourist industry operate on a seasonal basis only, rather than throughout the year. This will mean that there will be wide variations in cash flow over a 12-month period.

- **State of the economy**: In times of recession, levels of disposable income (the amount left over when essential expenses have been met) will be depressed, leading to reduced demand for some travel and tourism products and services. The reverse will be the case in boom times, with demand sometimes outstripping supply, thus forcing prices up.

- **Competitor activity**: A change in demand for a competitor's product or service, or an alteration in prices, may have an effect on the profitability of a travel and tourism organisation. For example, a 50 per cent reduction in the admission price for a major theme park is likely to reduce attendances at competitor attractions in the same locality.

- **Changes in tastes and fashions**: A particular tourist destination or resort can quickly come into, or go out of, fashion, making it difficult for some operators to forecast revenue. Organisations must be flexible enough to respond to sudden changes in demand.

- **Government legislation**: Unexpected changes in legislation, for example health and safety measures or changes in travel taxes, can have serious implications for an organisation's costs and revenues.

- **Industrial disputes**: Strikes, and other industrial action, can bring travel and tourism facilities to a halt, e.g. airports, ferries and rail services.

- **The weather**: A wet British summer can reduce the demand for UK holidays or affect the attendances at outdoor events and attractions.

Internal factors that may affect financial performance include:

- **Low sales volume**
- **Poor quality products**
- **Poor customer service**
- **Inappropriate pricing for products and services**
- **High levels of credit**
- **High levels of debt**
- **High fixed costs**
- **High variable costs**
- **Poor stock control**

The measures discussed later in this unit concerning the techniques to monitor an organisation's profitability and liquidity are designed to provide an early warning of any problems with these internal factors.

Extracting information from the balance sheet and profit and loss account

In today's highly competitive travel and tourism industry it is not enough merely to be able to understand a set of accounts. It is also necessary to be able to extract information from them to be able to answer such questions as:

- **How well is the business performing in terms of generating revenue and controlling costs?**
- **Has the business performed better than last year?**
- **Is the organisation as profitable as its competitors?**
- **Will the Inland Revenue be happy with the results?**

Potential investors in a travel and tourism company will want to examine the annual report and accounts to decide whether or not the enterprise is a good investment. In particular, they will study the financial information contained in the annual accounts to examine:

- ✪ **Turnover** – total revenue earned by the organisation
- ✪ **Gross profit** – turnover less direct costs
- ✪ **Net profit** – gross profit less indirect costs
- ✪ **Direct costs** – cost of sales or costs that can be directly attributed to the sales, e.g. stock or labour
- ✪ **Indirect costs** – overheads such as management salaries
- ✪ **Fixed assets** – items owned by the business and not intended to be sold on, e.g. vehicles
- ✪ **Current assets** – items that can be easily turned into cash, e.g. stock and debtors
- ✪ **Current liabilities** – debts that are due imminently
- ✪ **Long-term liabilities** – debts to be repaid over a longer time period
- ✪ **Capital** – original investment in the organisation

Investors may well be deciding between two or more travel and tourism companies as potential investments and will compare these measures to gauge the companies' prospects.

Activity 18.5

Study the financial information in the annual report of a public limited company (plc) in the travel and tourism industry. You could choose from a hotel chain, holiday company, transport operator, tourist attraction, airline, etc. From the information given in the annual report, extract the following information (refer to the above explanations of these terms to help you in this task):

Turnover, gross profit, operating profit (net profit), cost of sales, fixed assets, long-term liabilities, and capital and reserves.

You may find the information you need on a company's Internet website.

Interpreting accounts

The accounts of an organisation are an important source of information that enables the managers/owners and interested parties to examine and evaluate its financial performance. All travel and tourism organisations, regardless of which sector they operate in, are striving towards effective management and control, which should lead to a healthy profit and loss account and balance sheet. These statements, together with other performance indicators, should be used by managers to assess efficiency and indicate areas that may need adjustment to improve the overall outcome. It is common practice for organisations to develop ratios from the accounts, which can be used for performance appraisal.

Accounting ratios

Ratios tend to be the most common method by which financial information is interpreted, offering an easy way of comparing performance both within and between organisations. Comparisons between one year and another, between similar organisations in the same sector or comparisons with budgeted targets are much more useful than actual figures. It is important not to consider a single ratio in isolation or make decisions based on a single set of figures. It is much better to study a number of ratios in order to assess the state of health of the organisation. Also, the ratios themselves can only be as good as the financial information from which they are compiled; inaccuracies in the original data will result in ratios that give a false picture of performance.

It is possible to calculate many ratios from financial accounts. We will look at the most important under two main headings:

1   **Profitability**: This is a measure of the size of profit an organisation has made compared with previous years or throughout the year when comparing actual with budgeted results.

2   **Liquidity**: Sometimes called solvency, this is a measure of whether the organisation has sufficient funds to pay its debts when they fall due. Comparisons can be made between years to see whether liquidity is improving or declining, or whether the organisation is remaining in a solvent state when comparing actual with forecast.

We will now look at the ratios used to investigate profitability and liquidity in more detail.

Profitability

The most widely used indicator of the profitability of an organisation is based on the return on capital employed (ROCE), since it is meaningless to look at profitability without also analysing the resources that have been used to generate the profit. In simple terms, the ROCE is calculated as follows:

$$\text{Return on capital employed (\%)} = \frac{\text{Net profit}}{\text{Capital employed}} \times 100$$

This is known as the primary ratio. It has many variations, which can sometimes lead to a lack of consistency and distortion. In particular, there are a number of interpretations of resources or capital employed in a business.

The ratio can be used to compare the amount of profit made per £100 invested in the organisation. This could be useful to both investors and business operators, for example:

○ **Investors could compare the ROCE figure for a particular organisation with the return given by another company, or even a bank or building society investment account.**

○ **Sole traders and partnerships could compare the return with the amount they might get if they invested in a bank or building society. In comparing the two percentages, they may ask themselves whether the return from the business is good enough, taking into account the extra risk and work involved in running an enterprise.**

If we look at the information contained in the 'Seven Up' restaurant balance sheet example in Figure 18.3 (page 342), and we assume that the net profit (before tax) for the restaurant for the same trading period was £22,000, we can calculate the return on capital employed for the restaurant as follows:

Net profit (before tax) = £22,000
Capital employed = Fixed assets £36,400 + Current assets £10,800
= £47,200

By this method, the return on capital employed for the year 2000 is, therefore:

$$ROCE = \frac{£22,000}{£47,200} \times 100 = 46.6\%$$

This tells us that for every £100 that the owner has invested in the restaurant a profit of £46.60 has been made. This is a high figure for return on capital, but it must be remembered that the profit has to support the owners' personal financial requirements. Different organisations will have different methods of determining the figure for capital employed, but, whichever is chosen, the same basis should be used from one year to the next to produce consistency.

Other important profitability ratios used by travel and tourism organisations include:

○ **Gross profit percentage**: Sometimes referred to as the gross profit : sales ratio percentage, this will show how much profit the organisation is making as a percentage of sales. A fall in this ratio may be the result of increased competition, forcing a reduction in prices for facilities and services. The calculation is as follows:

$$\text{Gross profit \%} = \frac{\text{Gross profit}}{\text{Sales}} \times 100$$

○ **Net profit percentage**: Sometimes called the net profit : sales ratio, this will give a figure for profit (or loss) made per £ of income. The percentage profit on sales varies between different sectors, so it is essential to compare the ratio with similar businesses and also to make allowance for the prevailing economic conditions. It is calculated as follows:

$$\text{Net profit \%} = \frac{\text{Net profit (before tax)}}{\text{Sales}} \times 100$$

A summary of ratios used in the travel and tourism industry is shown in Figure 18.4.

Profitability Ratios	Calculation
Return on capital employed	$\dfrac{\text{Net profit}}{\text{Capital employed}}$
Gearing ratio	$\dfrac{\text{Fixed interest funds}}{\text{Equity funds}}$
Gross profit ratio	$\dfrac{\text{Gross profit}}{\text{Sales}} \times 100$
Net profit ratio	$\dfrac{\text{Net profit (before tax)}}{\text{Sales}} \times 100$
Solvency Ratios	
Debt collection period (days)	$\dfrac{\text{Trade debtors}}{\text{Annual credit sales}} \times 365$
Creditor payment period (days)	$\dfrac{\text{Trade creditors}}{\text{Annual credit purchases}} \times 365$
Operational Ratios	
Average room rate (£)	$\dfrac{\text{Net room sales income}}{\text{No. of rooms occupied}}$
Room occupancy (%)	$\dfrac{\text{No. of rooms occupied}}{\text{No. of rooms available}} \times 100$
Seat occupancy ratio (%)	$\dfrac{\text{No. of seats occupied}}{\text{No. of seats available}} \times 100$
Average spend per visitor (£)	$\dfrac{\text{Total revenue}}{\text{No. of visitors}}$
Marketing spend per visitor (£)	$\dfrac{\text{Marketing costs}}{\text{No. of visitors}}$

Figure 18.4 *Ratios used in the travel and tourism industry*

Liquidity

Liquidity is a measure of whether an organisation has sufficient funds to pay its debts when they fall due. In established travel and tourism companies, comparisons can be made between years to see whether liquidity is improving or declining, or whether the organisation is remaining in a solvent state when comparing actual with forecast results.

Two of the most important liquidity ratios are the current ratio and the acid test:

- **Current (or working capital) ratio**: This tells us the ratio between a company's readily available cash or near cash assets and its current liabilities. It is calculated as follows:

$$\text{Current ratio} = \frac{\text{Current assets}}{\text{Current liabilities}}$$

Using the example of the 'Seven Up' restaurant balance sheet again (see Figure 18.3), we can calculate the current ratio as follows:

$$\text{Current ratio} = \frac{10,800}{2,900} : 1 = 3.72 : 1$$

There is no ideal current ratio, but any figure in excess of 2 : 1 is considered healthy, although many companies will survive on a lesser figure than this. Just as important as the actual ratio figure is the consistency of ratios over time; any sudden change in a ratio gives cause for concern and should be investigated immediately.

- **Acid test (or liquid ratio)**: This is the relationship between what is owned by an organisation, where the value is constantly changing, and what it owes its creditors, where the amount is constantly changing. It is calculated as follows:

$$\text{Acid test} = \frac{\text{Current assets excluding stock}}{\text{Current liabilities}}$$

In the 'Seven Up' restaurant example (see Figure 18.3), we can calculate the acid test ratio as follows:

$$\text{Acid test} = \frac{£8,400}{£2,900} : 1 = 2.89 : 1$$

As a general rule, the acid test ratio should be in the region of 1 : 1. A figure much lower than this may indicate that the business will struggle to pay its debts on time. If it is very much higher than 1 : 1, the business may not be making best use of its funds.

Financial ratios in the public sector

Most public sector travel and tourism organisations, such as local authority tourism departments, museums and tourist information centres, are subsidised from either central or local government funds and are not normally expected to make a profit. However, it is still important to measure the ratio of income to expenditure in order to calculate to what extent the income from such items as ticket sales and admission charges can be offset against operating costs. The ratio, usually expressed as a percentage, is calculated as follows:

$$\frac{\text{Income}}{\text{Operating expenditure}} \times 100\%$$

Another useful ratio for public sector organisations is the level of subsidy per visitor or user, which is calculated as follows:

$$\frac{\text{Net operating expenditure}}{\text{Number of admissions}} : 1$$

This ratio can be applied to a whole range of leisure, travel and tourism facilities provided by local councils, including leisure centres, swimming pools, theatres, museums and entertainment venues.

A number of other primary ratios can be applied to public sector provision, including:

- ✪ **Staff costs : operating expenditure**
- ✪ **Bar gross profit : bar revenue**
- ✪ **Catering gross profit : catering revenue**
- ✪ **Income : number of admissions (to give spend per head)**
- ✪ **Bar income : number of admissions**
- ✪ **Catering income : number of admissions**

The number and range of secondary ratios that can be developed for public sector travel and tourism organisations is vast. It is important to calculate only those ratios that will contribute to the manager's decision-making process. From the expenditure point of view, common ratios that could prove useful include:

- ✪ **Energy costs : operating expenditure**
- ✪ **Marketing expenditure : total operating expenditure**
- ✪ **Cleaning costs : operating expenditure**

Ratios related to revenue include:

- ✪ **Bar income : total income**
- ✪ **Shop income : total income**
- ✪ **Catering income : total income**

It must be remembered that whether financial ratios are being applied in the private, public or voluntary sector, they are just one of the methods by which financial performance can be measured. Decisions taken on the basis of financial ratios alone will not produce the desired satisfactory outcome.

**Activity
18.6**

With the help of your tutor, arrange an interview
with the manager of a local public sector travel
and tourism facility to find out what financial and
operational ratios are used by management.

Pricing travel and tourism products and services

Key topics in this section

- **Introduction**
- **Types of costs in travel and tourism**
- **Fixed costs**
- **Variable costs**
- **Methods used to calculate prices for travel and tourism products and services**
- **Pricing strategies in travel and tourism**

Introduction

You will have learned in Unit 4 *Marketing travel and tourism* that calculating prices for travel and tourism products and services is a very complex task, involving a multitude of factors, including levels of demand, time of year, quality of facilities and, perhaps most important of all, the costs of providing the product or service. The final cost to a holidaymaker of a package holiday or hotel room, for example, will be based on the costs of supply, but will fluctuate according to location, facilities on offer, levels of demand, etc.

The competitive nature of the travel and tourism industry means that companies often operate a market-based pricing policy, adjusting their prices according to what their competitors are charging. Re-issuing brochures with revised prices is now commonplace among tour operators that are constantly checking competitors' prices and making adjustments to maintain their share of the market. Indeed, some holiday companies now distribute brochures with no prices in at all, asking customers to telephone or check the Internet for the latest prices.

Flexibility on prices is certainly here to stay, but this sort of market-based pricing is not always good news for the travel and tourism company. It makes it difficult for managers to forecast future sales volumes and often leads to very low profit margins.

In order to appreciate fully how travel and tourism products and services are priced you need to understand a little more about how costs are calculated, the subject of the next section of this unit.

Types of costs in travel and tourism

It is essential for managers in travel and tourism to have accurate, relevant and up-to-date information on the costs of running their organisation. Without this detailed information, they will not be in a position to appraise past performance and control future developments. The organisation's management information system (MIS) should be designed in such a way as to provide data on costs at regular intervals and in an appropriate format.

As well as having detailed cost data on which to base their management decisions, organisations and their personnel need to understand the different types of costs that they will encounter and their likely impact on organisational performance. Costs may be classified according to:

✪ **The nature of the costs (fixed and variable costs)**
✪ **The type of costs**
✪ **Function within the organisation**

Classification by nature (fixed and variable costs)

The nature of costs varies between those that remain constant despite changes in the level of activity (fixed costs) and those that alter in direct proportion to the volume of business generated (variable costs). Fixed costs for a museum, for example, would include rent, rates, insurance, interest charges and permanent staff costs, all of which stay the same regardless of how many people visit. The same museum's variable costs could include casual labour, telephone charges, postage, advertising and stationery, all of which will vary, depending on the level of use. Figure 18.5 shows the relationship of fixed, variable and total costs to output.

A third category of costs is semi-variable costs, which are made up of both a fixed and a variable element. Energy costs, telephone, Internet, telex and fax costs fall within this category, since there is usually a fixed charge for rental, with added usage charged thereafter.

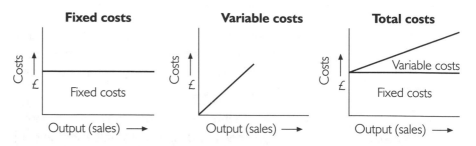

Figure 18.5 *The relationship of fixed, variable and total costs to output*

The costs incurred by the majority of travel and tourism organisations tend to be fixed rather than variable, given the high levels of overheads associated with many sectors of the industry, such as airlines, hotels and tour operating.

Classification by type

Costs can be classified into two types, direct and indirect. Direct costs are those that can be directly identified with the service or facility, for example the costs of hiring equipment and employing an extra instructor to run a series of health and fitness courses at a hotel's leisure facility. Indirect costs, also known as overheads, are those costs within an organisation that cannot be readily allocated to a specific function. Taking the example of the hotel's leisure facility organising the health and fitness courses, indirect costs would include the rent and rates for the centre, insurance and energy costs. In this example, it would not be easy to calculate an exact proportion of the overhead costs that should be allocated to the running of the courses.

Classification by function

This method groups costs on the basis of the functional department that incurs them, such as administration, sales, marketing and personnel. Each of these departments would have several cost centres, which are readily identifiable locations or functions against which costs can be charged. If we take the example of a large mass market tour operator, the expenditure incurred by its marketing department may be divided into the following cost centres:

- **Product development**
- **Customer services**
- **Brochure production**
- **Brochure distribution**
- **Photographic costs**
- **Market research**
- **Above-the-line activity (e.g. consumer and trade advertising)**
- **Below-the-line activity (e.g. sales promotions, PR, direct marketing)**
- **Agency sales support**
- **Agency marketing and merchandising**

Each cost centre will be allocated a cost code to ensure that all the costs it incurs are easily identifiable. In a local authority leisure centre, each of the main facilities and services, including the leisure pool, sports hall, outside pitches, health and fitness suite, restaurant/café, squash courts, vending and courses, will be independent cost centres, each with its own cost code.

Activity 18.7

While you are on work experience, find out if the organisation you are working for operates a system of cost centres. If so, make a list of the main cost centres identified.

Methods used to calculate prices for travel and tourism products and services

Organisations such as hotels, airlines and tour operators have a complex pricing system for all their products and services based on how much it costs to run them (known as unit costs) and the level of demand. In the travel and tourism industry, it is usual for prices to rise when demand is at its highest. For example, a two-week self-drive camping holiday in France for a family of four can cost more than £500 extra in the middle of August compared to the middle of September.

Activity 18.8

Working with a colleague, study some brochures and compare the prices of two family holidays (one in the UK and one abroad) at different times of the year. Make a chart of your findings and write a short explanation of why the prices vary throughout the year.

Once the unit costs of a product or service are known, it is then possible to begin to calculate a final selling price. The difference between the cost of supplying a product or service and its selling price is known as the profit margin or 'mark up'. There are three main methods of calculating prices, known as:

- ✪ **Absorption costing**
- ✪ **Marginal costing**
- ✪ **Activity-based costing**

We will now examine each of these in a little more detail.

Absorption costing

Absorption (or cost-plus) pricing is a pricing method that identifies all the *direct* costs of producing a product or service and adds to this an appropriate proportion of the overheads (*indirect*) costs of the organisation to arrive at the final price to charge, i.e.:

Price = Direct Costs + Proportion of Indirect Costs + Profit Margin

Absorption costing assumes that an organisation can calculate its indirect costs accurately, something that a large travel and tourism organisation may find difficult to do. Also, it does not allow for flexibility and any discounts or concessionary prices will directly affect the profit margin. This method of costing would normally be used for selling products such as souvenirs in tourist shops.

Marginal costing

Marginal costing (or contribution pricing) is a technique for setting prices for products and services on the basis that as long as the prices set cover the variable costs, then the product or service is making a contribution to the overheads (fixed costs) of the business. For example, if a hotel hired out its function room for a private party, only the variable costs, such as heating, lighting and wages for casual staff, would need to be covered in determining the price to charge.

Activity-based costing

This is a very flexible method of pricing that is being used increasingly in the travel and tourism industry. It looks at all costs, fixed and variable, and focuses on what drives them in order to arrive at a final price to charge. For example, if the hotel's function room used in the last example on marginal costing was hired out for a business conference, extra costs would be incurred and the price charged would be higher than when it was used for the private party. This means that, with activity-based costing, the prices charged more accurately reflect the true costs of the activity.

Pricing strategies in travel and tourism

From the many different pricing policies in use in travel and tourism, the following are some of the most common:

- ✪ **Skimming**: This is when a high price is charged initially for a new product that is unique and that attracts people who are willing to pay the high price for status reasons. The pricing of trips on the Orient Express train service is an example of market skimming.

○ **Penetration pricing**: This is used by organisations wanting to get into a new market where there are existing suppliers of the same product or service. The price will be set sufficiently low to persuade customers to switch their allegiance (sometimes known as a 'loss leader'). It is important that this pricing method is seen as a long-term strategy since customers will resent an early rise in price.

○ **Competitive pricing**: Sometimes referred to as 'the going rate', competitive pricing assumes that where products or services are similar, the organisation will charge the going rate, i.e. will match the price of competitors. This method often leads to very low margins and, in the long run, the collapse of some organisations, e.g. tour operators, who find their profitability is too low.

Activity 18.9

Examine the pricing structure of a local travel and tourism facility with which you are familiar. Analyse the factors that have influenced the prices charged and whether there is any evidence of skimming, penetration or competitive pricing.

Producing budgets

Key topics in this section

- **Introduction to budgeting**
- **What is a budget?**
- **Limitations on budgets**
- **Sales and expenditure budgets**
- **Producing a profit and loss forecast**
- **Producing a cash flow forecast**
- **Monitoring and controlling budgets**

Introduction to budgeting

Good management in travel and tourism involves not only reviewing past performance and the progress of current work, but also looking ahead to the future development of the organisation and the products and services it offers to its customers. The travel and tourism industry is constantly evolving, new technology is being introduced, customers are demanding better quality, and tastes and fashions are changing. To be successful in such a diverse and dynamic industry, private, public and voluntary sector organisations must identify and anticipate market changes and plan accordingly, both in the long term and short term. Budgeting helps them to do this by establishing future objectives and helping to manage cash flow. All travel and tourism organisations, however large or small, use budgets to ensure that there is enough money in the business to meet bills and other payments when they become due. Budgets can be set for a large facility such as a major tourist attraction or a one-off activity such as a summer fête.

What is a budget?

In simple terms, a budget is a forecast of likely income and outgoings over a given period of time. We all have to budget in our everyday lives, trying to balance our income, in the form of wages, salary or government benefits, against our living expenses, including rent, energy costs, taxation and costs for food and clothing. Another type of budget is the one presented by the Chancellor of the Exchequer every year to Parliament, setting out the income and expenditure plans of the government for the next 12-month period.

At the organisation level, a budget can be defined as:

✪ **A plan, quantified in financial terms, prepared and agreed in advance, showing the anticipated revenue and expenditure over a given time period**

The budget is the action plan for the coming financial period, which can be used to delegate responsibility to departmental managers or supervisors, leaving senior management to concentrate on investigating any major deviations from the plan. This delegation will mean that, in practice, a large travel and tourism organisation will have many different budget heads, i.e. a range of budgets that set out the financial responsibilities of each manager or supervisor. These detailed budgets will be consolidated into one master budget for the organisation, which will detail its overall short-term financial plan. The budget is the principal tool for allowing managers to co-ordinate and control the activities of their organisation. Performance is constantly monitored against the budget plans and feedback is an important part of the budgetary process.

Activity 18.10

With the help of your tutor, organise and carry out an interview with the manager or owner of a local travel and tourism facility and find out what budgets are used.

Limitations on budgets

Senior management teams in travel and tourism organisations are regularly faced with conflicting demands on the use of resources. The demand to improve or maintain services often conflicts with the need to minimise costs and keep within financial limits. Decisions on the use of resources have to be made at the time of preparing annual budgets. There are a number of questions that an organisation will need to consider, when determining its budgets and allocating its limited resources, including:

✪ **Is the information on which the budget decisions are made accurate?**

✪ **Is the information valid and reliable?**

✪ **How can the information be easily collected?**

✪ **Has the information been interpreted correctly?**

✪ **Does the organisation have the necessary staffing resources to be able to carry out the budgeting process effectively?**

- **Is there sufficient information on the external environment in which the organisation operates?**
- **Are the cost and revenue targets achievable and realistic?**
- **Are there sufficient staff benefits in place to reward achievement?**

The process of setting budgets needs to take place with the best information available at the time, but with built-in flexibility to allow for changes in circumstances.

Preparing a sales budget

This is normally the starting point for all budgets, since demand for travel and tourism products and services is often the overriding factor in determining success or failure of a business. In attempting to forecast its future sales pattern and volume, a travel and tourism organisation will need to take a number of important matters into account, including:

- **Past levels of sales, unless it is a new business just starting**
- **Market research**
- **The state of the economy**
- **Trend analysis, i.e. performance over past years**
- **Existing and potential competition**
- **The state of the market in which it is operating**

A high street travel agency, for example, will be concerned with a number of factors when producing its sales budget, for example:

- **Last year's sales figures**
- **Local competition from other agents**
- **Inflationary effects on its principals' product prices (i.e. the cost of package holidays, airline flights, car hire, etc.)**
- **Results of marketing and promotional activity**
- **The resources of its own agency staff, including training**
- **National trends in holiday bookings and destination choices**
- **The state of the local economy**

Figure 18.6 gives an example of a monthly sales budget schedule used in an independent travel agency.

The sales budget in Figure 18.6 allows the sales figures for 1999 to be used as a basis for forecasting likely sales in the same month in 2000. To the January 1999 figures is added an allowance for inflation in each of the product

Monthly sales budget				
Product Type	Value of sales January 1999 (actual)	Inflation allowance	Forecast share of market growth	Sales target January 2000 (budget)
Inclusive tours – Europe	32,000			
– Long haul	24,000			
– Domestic	3,600			
Scheduled air	7,800			
Flight only (charter)	20,000			
Cruising	18,500			
Car hire	1,800			
Hotel reservations	5,000			
Car ferries	6,800			
Miscellaneous	3,800			

Figure 18.6 *Sales budget schedule used in a typical independent travel agency*

categories plus any forecast growth in volume of sales, perhaps as a direct result of increased marketing and promotion or the closing of a competitor agency in the same locality. Monthly sales targets would be consolidated into a complete sales budget for the 12 month period.

Activity 18.11

Copy the travel agency sales budget shown in Figure 18.6 on to a sheet of paper and calculate the sales targets for January 2000 based on the following assumptions:

★ An inflation allowance of 2.1 per cent across all product categories

★ A 4 per cent market growth for all inclusive tours and car hire

★ A 3 per cent market growth for all remaining products

The expenditure budget

The expenditure budget shows the spending limits that must be adhered to so that an organisation as a whole, or an individual department, achieves its financial targets. It will include all the fixed and variable costs that are attributable over a given period of time, which could be annual or monthly. The example given in Figure 18.7 shows an expenditure budget schedule for an independent travel agency that chooses to budget on a quarterly basis.

Showing quarterly expenditure will allow management to rectify any variances in the budgeted and actual expenditure by taking the appropriate action.

The performance of the expenditure budget cannot be divorced from the figures contained in the sales budget and it is a matter of preference whether the two budgets are kept separate. Many organisations choose to

ITEM	1st Quarter		2nd Quarter		3rd Quarter		4th Quarter	
	Budget	Actual	Budget	Actual	Budget	Actual	Budget	Actual
Rent								
Rates – general								
– water								
Salaries and NI								
Casual labour								
Lighting								
Heating								
Telephone/fax								
Telex								
Prestel/Istel								
Postage								
Stationery								
Cleaning								
Insurance								
Travel – motoring								
– subsistence								
Maintenance								
Promotions								
Advertising								
Reference books								
Accounts charges								
Legal fees								
Bad debts								
Training								
Petty cash								
Miscellaneous								
Total								

Figure 18.7 *Expenditure budget used in an independent travel agency*

Item	Current month			Cumulative totals		
	Budget	Actual	Variance	Budget	Actual	Variance
Sales – product 1 – product 2 – product 3						
Total sales						
Expenditure – item 1 – item 2 – item 3 – item 4						
Total expenditure						
Gross profit (loss)						

Figure 18.8 *The structure of a combined sales and expenditure budget*

operate a combined sales and expenditure budget, as shown in the simplified example given in Figure 18.8, again modelled on an independent travel agency.

The combined budget allows for monthly figures and a cumulative total combining data from previous months. Any variations from the budgeted figures are included in the variance columns, which may contain actual figures or a percentage difference.

Activity 18.12

Working as a member of a group, and using the schedules in Figures 18.6 and 18.7 as a guide, produce a hypothetical sales budget and expenditure budget for a new small business in travel and tourism that you could set up in your own local area. Choose a business that you have some knowledge of and make the figures as realistic as possible. You could consider organising guided walks for visitors or perhaps a bike hire scheme or series of sports events for local people. Your tutor will be able to offer help and advice if you are stuck for an idea!

Producing a profit and loss forecast

We saw earlier in this unit that the profit and loss statement is perhaps the most important item of financial information for managing and controlling a travel and tourism organisation (page 339). You will remember that the profit and loss account is a summary of all the income and expenditure of an organisation, over a given period of time, sometimes quarterly, half yearly or annually, depending on custom and practice.

As its name implies, a profit and loss *forecast* is an estimate, based on all available data, of the expected profit (or loss) of an organisation over a given future time period. Anybody who is needing finance to start a travel and tourism business will need to draw up a profit and loss forecast to convince a bank manager that the project is viable in the short and long term. Travel and tourism businesses that are already in operation will also construct a profit and loss forecast to gauge their future financial performance. Of course, they have an advantage over a new business since they can look back at actual figures when calculating their forecast.

Figure 18.9 shows an extract from a profit and loss forecast schedule.

The profit and loss forecast schedule in Figure 18.9 shows that the figure for cost of goods sold (B) is deducted from total sales (A) to give the gross profit (C). From this figure, total overhead costs (E) are deducted to give the net profit before tax (F).

Activity 18.13

Continue to work in the group you set up for Activity 18.12 and complete the profit and loss forecast schedule shown in Figure 18.9 for your chosen business.

Producing a cash flow forecast

An essential financial item needed by any new travel and tourism business, and indeed one that is up and running, is the cash flow forecast. This is usually set down in a planning schedule that totals each month's projected flow of money into and out of the business. Put simply, a cash flow forecast is:

✪ **An estimate of an organisation's anticipated future cash inflows and outflows presented on a monthly basis**

Enter month		Budget	Actual	Budget	Actual
	Figures rounded to £s	**Budget**	**Actual**	**Budget**	**Actual**
1	**Sales** Home				
2	Export				
A	**Total Sales**				
3	**Direct Costs** Materials – purchases				
4	Wages and Salaries				
5	Stock changes (Increase/Decrease)				
B	**Cost of Goods Sold**				
C	**Gross Profit (A – B = C)**				
D	**Gross Profit as % of Sales** **(C + A × 100 = D)**				
6	**Overheads** Production				
7					
8					
9					
10					
11					
12	Selling and Distribution				
13					
14					
15					
16					
17					
18	Administration				
19					
20					
21					
22					
23					
24	Other Expenses				
25					
26					
27					
28					
29					
30	Finance Changes				
31	Depreciation				
E	**Total Overheads**				
F	**Net Profit Before Tax** **(C – E + F)**				
G	**Sales required to break even** **(E + D × 100 = G)**				

Note: The schedule normally spans twelve months.

Figure 18.9 *A profit and loss forecast schedule*

In travel and tourism organisations, cash *inflows* will include:

- **Payments received from clients for holidays and other travel products**
- **Injections of capital or personal investment into the business**
- **Money received from selling assets, e.g. surplus equipment, unwanted stock, etc.**

Cash *outflows* will be made up of:

- **Payments to principals, e.g. tour operators, hotels, airlines, etc.**
- **Salaries and wages for staff**
- **Rent, rates and associated premises/transport costs**
- **Money paid for advertising**
- **Legal and finance charges**
- **Tax payments**

Figure 18.10 shows an example of a cash flow forecast schedule.

The cash flow forecast schedule in Figure 18.10 indicates that figures for receipts and payments are the two main items that go to make up the forecast. From these, net cash flow and the closing bank balance can be calculated.

A cash flow forecast is essential to the smooth operation of a business since it:

- **Convinces potential lenders of finance (banks, friends, shareholders, etc.) that the business is viable**
- **Allows the management of an organisation to track actual against forecast cash inflows and outflows**
- **Enables an organisation to schedule its payments to creditors**
- **Makes it easier to plan for large items of expenditure**
- **Allows management to monitor sales turnover on a monthly basis**

Activity 18.14

Continue to work in the group you set up for Activity 18.12 and complete the monthly cash flow forecast schedule shown in Figure 18.10 for your chosen business over a full season of operation.

Enter month					
Figures rounded to £s		**Budget**	**Actual**	**Budget**	**Actual**
1	**Receipts** Sales (including VAT) – Cash				
2	– Debtors				
3	Other trading income				
4	Loans you have received				
5	New capital				
6	Selling of assets				
7	Other receipts				
a	Total receipts				
8	**Payments** Cash for goods you have bought				
9	Payments to creditors				
10	Owner or directors' withdrawals				
11	Wages and Salaries (net)				
12	PAYE/NI				
13	Capital items (for example) Equipment and vehicles				
14	Transport and packaging				
15	Rent or rates				
16	Services				
17	Loan repayments				
18	Hire or leasing repayments				
19	Interest				
20	Bank or finance charges				
21	Professional fees				
22	Advertising				
23	Insurance				
24					
25					
26	VAT				
27	Corporation Tax and so on				
28	Dividends				
b	Total payments				
c	Net cashflow (a – b)				
29	Opening bank balance				
d	Closing bank balance (c + Line 29)				

Note: Schedule normally extends for 12 months.

Figure 18.10 *A cash flow forecast schedule*

Monitoring and controlling budgets

Once budgets have been agreed and the mechanisms for recording the financial data are in place, it is necessary to introduce a monitoring and control process. Control is based on the concept of management by exception, i.e. the investigation of any items that deviate from the agreed budget. This is done by comparing the actual costs with the budgeted costs to identify any over- or under-expenditure. The differences are known as variances and their investigation is known as variance analysis. Variances may arise in any items of revenue or expenditure, including labour costs, sales figures and energy costs. Where actual costs are greater than budgeted costs, the term unfavourable or adverse is applied and where actual costs are below budget, the variance is favourable. The opposite is true of revenue variances, where favourable variances occur when the actual sales are above budget.

The aim of variance analysis is to highlight areas needing immediate attention. Minor variances from budget are common and are unlikely to require detailed analysis, but when the variance is large, either in percentage or monetary terms, the situation will need reviewing. Once a variance has been investigated and a cause identified, remedial action can be taken. For example, a visitor attraction that experiences a 10 per cent adverse variance in its admission income for a particular month will need to investigate the cause and put matters right immediately, if it is to achieve its annual budget targets. However, not all causes of variances from budget are capable of immediate solution. A permanent change in market demand, perhaps away from an existing type of home entertainment product that loses its appeal with the buying public, will force an organisation to feed the information back into its planning stage for alteration to projected sales figures. There must be a degree of flexibility in any budgetary planning system, which takes account of the fact that travel and tourism is a very dynamic industry.

A budget is generally broken down into shorter periods for control purposes. These are normally monthly but can be shorter or longer as the case demands. As well as a comparison of actual with budgeted figures, budgetary control often involves a comparison with data from the same period in the previous year. Whatever time period is agreed, managers will need a constant flow of financial information that they can use for control purposes. The combined sales and expenditure budget shown in Figure 18.8 includes columns for variances, which could be expressed in either percentage or monetary terms. Information presented in this tabular form may be supplemented by graphical presentation of the results, now made easier with the use of readily available graphics computer software. Figure 18.11 gives an example of the data contained in a monthly sales budget for a typical independent travel agency.

The presentation of information in this form provides a quick and easy way of identifying problem areas and is often an easier means of identifying budget

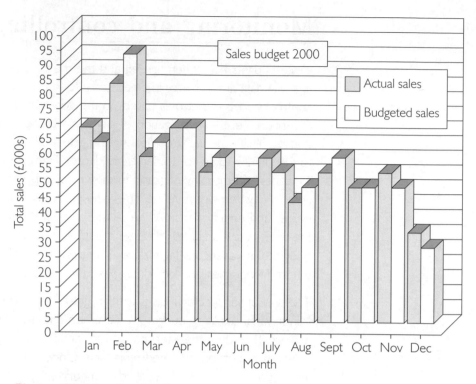

Figure 18.11 *Graphical representation of budget data*

variances. Graphical presentation should also be considered for comparing current year data with that from past years.

As well as comparing actual with budgeted results, the budget information can be used to measure performance of individual cost centres within the organisation.

Business systems in the travel and tourism industry

19

All travel and tourism organisations, whether commercial or in the public or voluntary sector, rely on systems to operate their enterprises efficiently and effectively. With the rapid growth in new technologies, many business systems used in the travel and tourism industry are now electronic or computer-based, although paper-based systems still have an important role to play. This unit introduces you to the wide range of business systems available to organisations in travel and tourism, including systems for customers, staff, financial accounting and health, safety and security. Anybody hoping to work in the travel and tourism industry needs to understand how these systems work, since they are likely to form a large part of a new entrant's day-to-day responsibilities. You will also investigate the evaluation of business systems and methods, as well as learning about how the quality of business systems is measured.

This unit is divided into eight main areas:

- **Business systems**
- **Evaluating suitable business systems and methods**
- **How the quality of business systems is measured**
- **Systems for customers**
- **Systems for staff**
- **Systems for financial accounting**
- **Systems for health, safety and security**
- **Methods used to operate business systems**

We guide you through each of these areas using examples and case studies from the travel and tourism industry. At the beginning of each of these sections you will see a list of key topics to help you fully understand what you need to learn. Look out for the links to websites so that you can learn more about a particular travel and tourism company, organisation or topic.

Business systems

Key topics in this section

- **Introduction – what are business systems?**
- **Functions of business systems**

Introduction – what are business systems?

It is important for travel and tourism organisations to have operating systems that are effective, reliable and efficient. Any system that supports an organisation in achieving its business objectives can be considered a 'business system', for example:

- ✪ **The procedures that are followed for handling customer complaints**
- ✪ **The process by which holidays are sold to customers (see industry example below)**
- ✪ **The techniques that are used to monitor sales income and costs**
- ✪ **The procedures followed when checking in guests to a hotel**
- ✪ **The procedure that is followed in a visitor attraction to ensure high standards of health, safety and security**
- ✪ **The processes that are followed in designing a new holiday brochure**

Since no two travel and tourism organisations operate in exactly the same way, it follows that a business system will be unique to an individual organisation. There are, however, similarities in systems across organisations, e.g. two tour operators may use the same accounting software to manage their finances, but the results will be specific to each individual business.

The following industry example gives you an idea of the different systems used when booking a package holiday through a travel agent.

Industry example
Business systems for package holiday bookings

The starting point for a package holiday booking will be when a client makes contact with a travel agent, either in person, by telephone, fax or e-mail (see Figure 19.1).

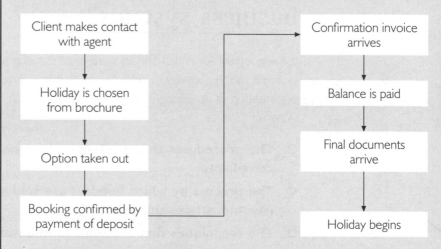

Figure 19.1   *Stages in the booking of a package holiday*

If the client has a definite departure date, holiday company and resort in mind, the agent will quickly be able to check availability on the agency's computer system. If there is availability, the booking can proceed. If not, or if the client is unsure about which resort to choose, some further advice and help will be needed from the agent. The tour operators' reservation systems are designed to be able to search by date, resort, hotel, type of holiday, etc., so the client's needs should be satisfied eventually. Once the holiday is chosen, the agent takes out an option, giving the client the chance to think about the choice before committing himself or herself. The option will be entered into the computer system and normally lasts for 24 hours, after which time it automatically lapses and the holiday is put on sale again. If the client makes contact with the

continued

continued

agent within the 24 hours and pays a deposit, then the booking is confirmed. The client will be issued with a receipt for the deposit payment and a new file will be started in the agency.

Normally within two weeks of making the booking, a written confirmation invoice will be sent direct from the tour operator, giving precise details of the clients travelling, the booked holiday, travel details and any special requirements. The balance is normally paid eight weeks before departure, but if the holiday is booked within eight weeks of departure the full amount must be paid at booking. Two to three weeks before the holiday starts, final tickets and documentation are received by the agent and passed to the client.

This industry example shows us that there is a wide range of business systems used in the travel and tourism industry, which can be categorised as follows:

- ✪ **Administration systems**: These are designed to ensure the smooth running of an organisation, e.g. payroll, payments to suppliers, ordering of supplies, etc.

- ✪ **Communication systems**: Concerned with dealing with people inside and outside an organisation, e.g. handling customer complaints, inter-departmental meetings, telephone systems, etc.

- ✪ **Information processing systems**: Designed to make sure that information is made available speedily and accurately, e.g. a customer database, spreadsheets showing sales and expenditure forecasts, an organisation's Internet site, a computer reservation system (CRS) or global distribution system (GDS) such as Galileo, Sabre or Worldspan, etc.

Browse these websites

www.galileo.com

www.sabre.com

www.worldspan.com

Functions of business systems

Travel and tourism organisations use a number of business systems on a day-to-day basis. These systems have three basic functions:

1 **To conduct business on a regular basis, e.g. handling admission charges in a tourist attraction or taking payments for holidays**

2 **To manage information and maintain records, e.g. accounts or customer records**

3 **To support management decision taking, e.g. planning the future direction of a business or forecasting sales for future months and years**

Such systems influence all aspects of an organisation's operation, from legal requirements and financial planning, to customer service, sales and marketing. Above all, a business system will help an organisation achieve its objective, whether this is maximising profits or meeting wider social or community aims.

Activity 19.1

Working with a colleague, draw up a list of the business systems you would expect to see in a typical travel agency, under the following headings:

1 Administration systems

2 Communication systems

3 Information processing systems

Against each of your systems (e.g. taking payments, interviewing staff, producing accounts, etc.), write down any items of equipment associated with the system, e.g. computer, mobile telephone, etc.

The concept of 'front office' and 'back office'

It is common for travel and tourism organisations to divide their business functions into 'front office' and 'back office', developing systems in support of each. In simple terms, the 'front office' (sometimes referred to as 'front of house') refers to the reception area of any travel and tourism facility, the point at which the customer first makes contact with the organisation. The 'back office' (also known as 'back of house') refers to the organisation's functions that take place behind the scenes, for example accounting, maintenance and stock control, which the customer is unlikely to be aware of. There must always be a strong link between front and back offices for the organisation's business systems to be truly effective; for example, when a guest books into a hotel at reception (the 'front office'), information must be conveyed, possibly manually but more likely via a computer system, to the other departments that need to know, such as housekeeping, accounts, food and beverage, laundry, marketing, etc.

The concept of front and back office is widespread in the travel and tourism industry. Hotels operate on this basis, as do many leisure/sports centres, travel agencies, visitor attractions, transport companies, catering outlets, entertainment venues and tourist information centres. The division into front and back office allows management to focus resources on particular functions and train staff in these areas. The selection and training of staff to work in the 'front office' is particularly important, since it provides the visitor with his or her first impressions of the organisation. Staff with an understanding of customer needs and expectations and who are committed to providing excellence in customer service should be chosen to work in this high profile area. The environment in which the 'front office' is positioned also needs to be carefully planned, and should provide a clean, warm, efficient, welcoming and friendly atmosphere.

Examples of the different functions carried out by front and back office staff in travel and tourism organisations are shown in Figure 19.2.

 Activity 19.2

While on work experience, list the front office and back office functions that take place in the organisation. Explain the linkages between the two.

Front Office Functions	Back Office Functions
Welcoming visitors	Cash and credit control
Taking bookings	Accounting
Selling services	Membership systems
Providing information	Stock control
Handling cash, cheques, cards	Maintenance
Controlling entry	Marketing and publicity
Promoting services	Analysis of management data
Answering enquiries	Staff training
Issuing equipment	Personnel
Maintaining records	Health and safety
Passing information to back office	Food preparation

Figure 19.2 *Front and back office functions in travel and tourism*

Evaluating suitable business systems and methods

Key topics in this section

● **Introduction**

● **Factors to be considered when evaluating business systems**

Introduction

In the travel and tourism industry, nothing stays the same for long! Organisations, both large and small, constantly monitor their activities to make sure that their business systems remain effective. Evaluation of a business system will indicate any strengths and weaknesses; it is part of management's role in an organisation to reduce weaknesses to a minimum while at the same time building on the strengths of the business systems. Many organisations develop measures of effectiveness to help with the evaluation, as shown in Table 19.1.

Administrative function	Measure of effectiveness
Credit control	Are customers paying within an agreed period of time?
Recruitment	Is the rate of staff turnover acceptable?
Budgetary control	Are figures accurate and produced on time?
Customer care	Is the number of complaints within an acceptable limit?
Marketing	Is competition activity regularly monitored?

Table 19.1 *Measures used to evaluate the effectiveness of business systems*

Depending on the size of the travel and tourism organisation, the measures shown in Table 19.1 may be carried out by staff from different departments. If this is the case, it is important that the evaluation of the business systems is co-ordinated throughout the organisation, ideally under one senior member of staff with responsibility for overall quality systems and standards.

Factors to be considered when evaluating business systems

Travel and tourism organisations investigate a variety of factors when evaluating their business systems, including:

- **Value for money**: All travel and tourism organisations must strive to make the best use of their available financial resources by choosing business systems that offer the best value for money.

- **Fitness for purpose**: This means choosing a business system that does what it is designed to do! All too often, particularly with computers, travel and tourism organisations are persuaded to buy systems that are not always fit for purpose.

- **Accuracy**: Systems must offer high levels of accuracy, especially when dealing with finances, e.g. payroll systems for staff salaries and wages, accounts software, etc.

- **Efficiency**: Any business system must be efficient, both in terms of the organisation's and its customers' needs, e.g. a specialist holiday call centre operation must offer an efficient service to its customers.

- **Ease of use**: It is little use having a state-of-the-art business system if nobody knows how to use it! The skill in designing business systems, whether computer-based, electronic or paper-based, is to keep things simple.

- **Security**: All business systems need to be secure, particularly those dealing with sensitive information, e.g. sales figures, personnel records, customer databases, etc.

- **Legal requirements**: Depending on the nature of the travel and tourism organisation, business systems may have to comply with a variety of legal requirements, e.g. employment legislation, health and safety regulations, publication of accounts, the Data Protection Act (see page 399), etc.

How the quality of business systems is measured

Key topics in this section

- **Introduction – quality in business systems**
- **Quality systems concerned with the whole organisation**
- **Quality systems used in specific sectors of the travel and tourism industry**

Introduction – quality in business systems

There is no doubt that 'quality' is one of the 'buzz words' in travel and tourism in the new millennium. All sorts of travel and tourism organisations, be they in the private, public or voluntary sectors, have pledged their commitment to introducing or enhancing the quality of the products, services and facilities they offer their customers. In an increasingly competitive environment, it makes good business sense to review an organisation's systems to see if any improvements can be made to the levels of customer service and quality of products on offer.

Some travel and tourism organisations have sought external recognition of their activities, either by gaining certification under the British Standard (BS) 5750 (see page 385), now more generally referred to as ISO 9000 or BS EN ISO 9000, or by implementing the 'Investor in People' initiative (see page 383). Others operate very well without the need to register formally for recognition, based on the fact that management has practised a customer-centred approach for many years. Whether or not external recognition is sought, the main purpose of implementing quality standards in travel and tourism is the same, namely to ensure that all business systems are fully documented and audited, so as to ensure high standards of quality at all times.

**Activity
19.3**

Carry out some research on local and national travel and tourism organisations to find out what policies they have on quality in their organisations.

What do we mean by 'quality'?

In the travel and tourism industry, quality is synonymous with satisfying customer needs; in other words, the introduction of any quality system or set of quality standards into an organisation must place the customer as the focus of all activity. This is borne out by the International Standards Organisation (ISO), which defines quality as:

> *The totality of features and characteristics of a product or service that bear on its ability to satisfy stated or implied needs.*

Looking at this definition in a little more detail, it assumes that an organisation will have knowledge of the needs of its customers. You will have learned from units on your course that all travel and tourism organisations have a wide range of customers, all with varying needs. Detailed market research is needed to identify customers and their needs, before the specific features and characteristics of products and services can be developed.

Industry example

The English Tourism Council (ETC) was established in July 1999 as the successor to the English Tourist Board. The ETC's mission is to:

> *. . . drive forward the quality, competitiveness and wise growth of England's tourism, by providing intelligence, setting standards, creating partnerships and ensuring coherence.*

In terms of *quality*, the ETC understands that, although England's tourism industry is one of the most successful in the world, consumers' demands change all the time and that a successful industry must continually strive to improve the quality of the tourism experience. The ETC is committed to increasing standards in accommodation and service quality across the industry.

Browse this website

www.englishtourism.org.uk

Quality systems concerned with the whole organisation

Quality systems concerned with the whole organisation include:

- ✪ **Quality control and quality management**
- ✪ **Total quality management (TQM)**
- ✪ **Investor in People (IIP)**
- ✪ **BS5750/ISO9000**

We will now look at each of these in greater detail.

Quality control and quality management

Quality control is concerned with monitoring product and service quality by identifying and addressing quality problems through checking and inspection. A holiday company, for example, will regularly invite feedback from customers on the quality of accommodation, flights and representatives, by carrying out questionnaire surveys. Quality management, on the other hand, is a wider concept that attempts to make sure that standards of product and service quality are right first time every time.

Total quality management (TQM)

While quality control and quality management are important concepts, the development of total quality management (TQM) takes quality assurance one stage further by establishing a management philosophy and systems throughout an organisation, which recognise that customer needs and the achievement of organisational objectives are inseparable. The development of TQM in an organisation is a longer-term goal when compared to the introduction of a quality standards system such as BS EN ISO 9000 (see below); some would say that the implementation of BS EN ISO 9000 is merely a step (albeit a large step) along the road to total quality management.

Those who advocate a TQM approach consider that it has a number of benefits to any travel and tourism organisation, including:

- ✪ **Increased profitability**
- ✪ **Increased competitiveness**
- ✪ **Closer relationships with customers**
- ✪ **Committed management and staff**
- ✪ **Closer relationships with suppliers and contractors**
- ✪ **Improved measurement of quality performance**
- ✪ **Improved decision making by management**

To be successful, the implementation of a TQM culture in an organisation will necessitate increased resources and prolonged staff training and management commitment.

Investor in People (IIP)

Investor in People is the national quality standard in the UK for effective investment in the training and development of people to achieve organisational objectives. Organisations, large and small, in all sectors of the economy, have achieved the standard or are working towards Investor in People. The standard provides a framework for improving business performance and competitiveness, through a planned approach to setting and communicating objectives and developing people to meet these goals. In other words, what people can do and are motivated to do in an organisation matches what the organisation needs them to do to be successful.

The Investor in People standard is a cyclical process based on four principles:

1 **Commitment**: to develop all employees to achieve organisational goals and objectives.

2 **Review**: of training and development needs regularly in the context of the organisation.

3 **Action**: to meet identified training and development needs throughout people's employment.

4 **Evaluation**: of the outcomes of training and development for individuals and the organisation, as a basis for continuous improvement.

These principles are summarised in the diagram shown in Figure 19.3.

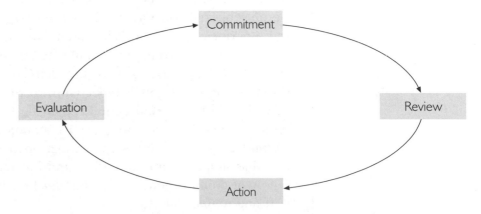

Figure 19.3 *The key principles of the Investor in People standard*

The practical benefits of working towards and achieving a standard such as Investor in People include:

- ✪ **Reduced costs and wastage**
- ✪ **Improved productivity and profitability**
- ✪ **Enhanced product and service quality**
- ✪ **Improved staff motivation**
- ✪ **Enhanced customer satisfaction**
- ✪ **Public recognition**
- ✪ **Competitive advantage**

To become an Investor in People, everyone working for an organisation must be committed to achieving the standard; senior management, union representatives and all employee groups must play an active part in the process. The length of time needed to achieve the standard ranges between 6 and 18 months, depending on the size of the task.

Industry example

In the travel and tourism industry, one of the first companies to achieve the Investor in People standard was De Vere Hotels Ltd, which was unusual in that it received IIP for the whole of its chain of 25 hotels in the UK rather than for just one specific establishment. The award followed an assessment of its staff development programmes involving every member of staff in the hotels and at head office. The training needs of each individual member of staff were assessed, agreed targets were set and a performance appraisal system was implemented to monitor and reward achievements. It was implemented in all the Group's hotels from the Belfry in the West Midlands, home of golf's Ryder Cup, to the recently refurbished Oulton Hall near Leeds. All De Vere staff have been involved in developing quality standards manuals and attend frequent training sessions. An open management style has helped communication and has led to a high degree of commitment to the standard on the part of both staff and management.

BS5750/ISO9000

This is a quality standard (also known as BS EN ISO9000) that aims to ensure consistently high levels of product and service delivery in an organisation. Initially developed for manufacturing industry, this British Standard (BS) is now increasingly applied to service industries, including travel and tourism.

The decision by an organisation to introduce a quality standard such as BS5750/ISO9000 should not be entered into lightly. It should be seen as a long-term initiative, rather than a process that will bring quick rewards. The comprehensive nature of such a standard will focus on:

- **Determining the needs of the customer**
- **Defining the quality of service required to meet these needs**
- **Planning how the level of service will be delivered**
- **Deciding who will deliver the agreed level of service and when**
- **Delivering the level of service to the customer**
- **Monitoring to ensure that the agreed level of service has been achieved**

The aim with a quality assurance system such as BS5750/ISO9000 is to ensure consistent levels of service delivery. Every employee, whether senior management, full-time or part-time staff, has a role to play in making sure that the service is delivered right first time every time. BS5750/ISO9000 requires the pulling together of the various strands of a travel and tourism operation into one 'book of rules'. It will involve the re-examination of what is already written down and committing to paper that which is operated 'by custom and practice'. Figure 19.4 shows the five steps to implementing a quality standards system such as BS5750/ISO9000.

Step one involves giving employees an understanding of the importance of quality and customer service, while at the same time undertaking market research to determine customer needs and requirements. Step two, understanding the organisation's role, tries to answer such questions as 'why is the job done?', 'where is the job done?', 'who does what and why?', and 'when is the job done?'. Once this understanding has been achieved, the job of documenting and developing the system can begin (step three). This may start with the preparation of straightforward operations manuals and ultimately develop into a full quality system for which external certification may be sought. Step four, embedding the system, will involve further training and clarification of roles, together with a clear explanation of the procedures and practices of all employees. Whether or not external certification is being sought, it is good practice to set up internal monitoring procedures to make sure that the system is maintained, updated and amended.

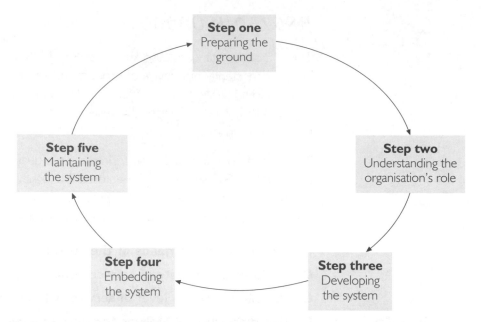

Figure 19.4 *The five steps in implementing a quality standards system*

Quality systems used in specific sectors of the travel and tourism industry

Specific sectors of the travel and tourism industry have developed quality systems to meet their own specific circumstances. These include:

- **Resort classifications**: Tour operators will sometimes categorise resorts according to their suitability for different client groups, e.g. families, couples and groups

- **Accommodation grading and classification systems**: For example, the Thomson Holidays 'T' ratings shown in the company's brochures (see industry example below), countries' official classifications (usually 'star' ratings) and the new English Tourism Council quality ratings, represented by 'Star' and 'Diamond' symbols (see Figure 19.5)

- **Charter Marks**: The government introduced a series of Charter Marks in the 1990s for public sector organisations, including local authority leisure and tourism departments that provide excellent service to their customers

- **Industry award schemes**: Commercial organisations sometimes establish award schemes to reward their best employees or favourite

Browse this website

www.
englishtourism.
org.uk

Figure 19.5 *The new ETC Hotel and Guest Accommodation ratings*
Courtesy of the English Tourism Council

Browse this website for details of the Tourism for Tomorrow awards

www.britishairways.com/tourism/

companies, e.g. the *Travel Trade Gazette* awards and the Tourism for Tomorrow awards sponsored by British Airways

❍ **Customer charters**: Organisations that are committed to giving their customers the best possible products and service sometimes produce a customer charter (see Figure 19.6) to demonstrate their commitment

Customer Service Charter

Price Guarantee

Should the hotel or another Short Break operator offer a like for like package cheaper to you directly we will refund the difference. Of course, once we have confirmed your booking we will not change the price of your holiday.

Customer Satisfaction

In the unlikely event you experience a problem and have cause to make a written complaint, we will respond within 14 days of receipt. If we do not you will be entitled to a £10 Leisure Break Voucher.

Service

We are at your service 7 days a week, 8am - 11pm. In the rare circumstance of you receiving poor or discourteous service from any member of our staff, we would welcome you bringing this to the attention of one of our directors and we will send you a £10 Leisure Break Voucher.

Meeting your every need

Should your first choice of break not be available we promise to offer you an appropriate alternative. Don't forget that you can make a reservation right up to the last minute – even on your chosen date of travel.

Ticket Despatch

All tickets and travel documents will be despatched to you the same day for bookings made before 13.00 hrs or for bookings made after 13.00 hrs the next working day.

Peace of mind

Your rooms will still be secured in the event of your late arrival at a hotel.

Enjoy your stay

Figure 19.6 *Superbreak's customer service charter*
Superbreak brochure 2000–01, courtesy of Superbreak mini-holidays, York, UK

Industry example

Thomson has devised its 'T' ratings to avoid the complication of trying to compare properties against different local ratings in overseas destinations. The ratings are based on the company's annual appraisals and the views of customers when they complete end-of-season customer satisfaction questionnaires (CSQs). Hotels and apartments are rated from '2T' for standard, good value, no-frills accommodation, to '5T' for those offering more comfort and a wider range of facilities.

Browse this website

www.thomson-holidays.com

Activity 19.4

Carry out some research on the Tourism for Tomorrow awards to discover why they were set up and the names of some recent award winners. You might like to start by looking at the website of British Airways www.british-airways.com, one of the main sponsors of the awards.

Systems for customers

Key topics in this section

- **Introduction**
- **Customer records**
- **Booking/reservation systems**
- **Ticketing systems**
- **Customer complaints and feedback**
- **Customer correspondence, communication and information**

Introduction

We saw in Unit 5 *Customer service in travel and tourism* that customers are the most important part of any organisation. Put simply, without customers there would be no business! It follows, therefore, that all travel and tourism organisations must have excellent business systems in place to be able to offer customers a high standard of service, in such areas as

- ✪ **Customer records**
- ✪ **Booking/reservation systems**
- ✪ **Ticketing systems**
- ✪ **Customer complaints and feedback**
- ✪ **Customer correspondence**

Each of these topics is covered in greater detail in the following sections of this unit.

Customer records

You will have learned from Unit 5 *Customer service in travel and tourism* that an effective travel and tourism organisation must have detailed information about its customers in order to be able to provide them with the facilities and services they want, and to do so with attention to their desire for a good standard of customer service. A computerised business system is invaluable for providing such information on customers and can help highlight under-exploited opportunities or areas of an organisation that need more promotion. A theatre's database, for example, may indicate that residents of a particular area of a city do not visit the theatre in anything like the same proportions as those who live in other areas. The management may investigate why this is so, and may feel it worthwhile to mount a publicity campaign in the under-represented area in order to increase attendance.

Booking/reservation systems

Booking and reservation systems used in travel and tourism can be either manual or computerised. Many organisations that formerly used manual systems have transferred their data onto computers, because of the greater speed and storage capacity they offer. If we think of the example of a computerised booking system in a hotel's fitness suite, it will need to be able to handle a range of different types of bookings, including bookings from individuals and club bookings, which may be in advance or on a casual admission basis. Hire of equipment and bookings for particular facilities, e.g. pool and fitness equipment, will also be logged into the computer.

Smaller travel and tourism operators may choose to adopt a manual system that meets their particular needs. An example of an advance booking sheet for a small hotel that uses a manual booking system is shown in Figure 19.7.

In Figure 19.7, the room numbers are entered in the left-hand column, while the days of the month run along the top of the chart. When a customer makes a booking in advance, it is a simple matter to complete the appropriate square or squares on the chart.

Activity 19.5

While on work experience, carry out an in-depth investigation of the operation of your placement's booking/reservation system(s) and make suggestions for improvements.

Advance Booking Chart

Room No.	1	2	3	4	5	6	7	8	9	10	11	12	13	14	15	16	17	18	19	20	21	22	23	24	25	26	27	28	29	30	31

Figure 19.7 *An advance booking chart for a small hotel*

Industry example
Best Western central reservations system (CRS)

▶ THE ROLE OF THE CRS

The CRS at Best Western's Central Office can handle
enquiries and bookings for all Best Western hotels in the
UK. All international reservations, i.e. those for a UK
client who requires an overseas hotel, are made by the
reservations office in Dublin. CRS supports Best Western's
sales and marketing efforts by providing the most
important point of contact for clients from all over the
world and ensures that enquiries are turned into actual
bookings using the information provided by the
consortium's members.

▶ THE RESERVATIONS SYSTEMS

Best Western has some of the most advanced reservations
systems in the hotel industry with sophisticated links to
all the airline global distribution systems (GDS) and
the Internet. At Central Office, there are three airline
terminals, SABRE, Amadeus and Galileo, and a help desk
facility to provide assistance to travel agents when trying
to book Best Western hotels and to help member hotels
understand the complexities of airline transactions in more
detail. There is also access to Best Western International
systems, with the ability to update its database and the
Internet from Central Office.

▶ HORNET – THE DOMESTIC CRS FOR BEST WESTERN GREAT BRITAIN

All domestic UK reservations taken by the CRS are
processed by a system called HORNET, one of the most
advanced reservation systems in the world in terms of
technology and flexibility. Rooms are sold on a declining
inventory basis and can be booked at any rate. Bookings

continued

continued

made via this system will come through to member hotels at any of the various rate levels, such as:

★ Rack rates

★ Standard and superior corporate rates

★ Standard and superior preferred rates

★ Negotiated rates for standard and superior room types for commercial companies

★ Getaway Breaks packages and promotional rates

★ Promotional rates as a result of public relations activity, e.g. newspaper advertising campaigns

★ Car tour programme rates

HORNET is a very flexible system and offers great opportunities for members to be able to market their hotels via CRS and sell the last room available at a moment's notice.

THE INTERNET

Anyone with a connection to the Internet is able to make reservations on-line for member hotels by visiting the Best Western International website. Best Western was one of the first global hotel brands to provide an on-line booking facility via the Internet.

AIRLINE SYSTEMS

All of the major travel agents, including American Express and Thomas Cook, use airline GDS systems to make hotel reservations as well as booking flights and car hire. There are approximately 500,000 terminals around the world and when an enquiry is made availability is displayed. A booking can be made and confirmation is given within seconds with a confirmation number.

Browse this website

www.bestwestern.com

A hotel receptionist will generally ask guests to complete a registration card when checking in (see Figure 19.8).

```
                                                      Registration Card

CASTLE VIEW HOTEL

Name:                                    Account:
Address:                                 Address:



Overseas Visitors                   Arrival Date:
Nationality:                        Departure Date:
Passport No:                        No. of Nights:        Room Type:
Issued at:                          No. of Guests         Room No:
Destination:                        Payment Method:       Room Rate:

Hotel Res. No:                      Credit A/C No:

Vehicle Reg. No:                    Signature.................................................
```

Figure 19.8   *A hotel guest registration card*

Ticketing systems

Like many business systems used in travel and tourism organisations, ticketing can be either manual or computerised. It is quite rare nowadays to find ticketing systems that are totally manually operated. If not fully computerised, many organisations will at least print their tickets with the help of a computer system and are likely to keep ticket records on a computer. New technology is changing the way that tickets are sold and distributed. Bookings for hotels, airlines, car hire, events and a variety of other travel and tourism products and services can now be made 'on-line' using the Internet. Indeed, some companies operate 'ticketless' transactions, where all bookings are made electronically and no ticket is issued to the customer at all; the low-cost airline easyJet is a good example of this.

Browse this website

www.easyjet.com

Customer complaints and feedback

Unit 5 *Customer service in travel and tourism* showed us that even organisations with the highest standards of customer service will have to deal with customer complaints from time to time. Travel and tourism organisations must have systems in place to handle complaints efficiently, with all members of staff fully trained to deal with difficult situations. You will remember that it is important to stay calm when handling a customer's complaint and to seek help if a situation begins to get out of hand, as the following industry example demonstrates.

Industry example

Lunn Poly, one of the UK's biggest travel agency chains, offers the following advice on how to deal with a client who comes into an agency with a complaint.

★ Always use a calm and steady tone, which should encourage the customer to adopt a more communicative manner.

★ Try to get the customer to sit down.

★ Listen to the customer's complaint.

★ Apologise that the customer is upset and disappointed.

★ Summarise back to the customer what is understood to be their problem and explain what action will be taken.

★ Tell the customer when they can expect to hear from the agency again.

★ If a customer is particularly abusive, staff should not try to deal with them alone. Call the shop manager and contact the police immediately if a client becomes aggressive.

★ Staff who have dealt with a tricky customer should inform their manager and/or their head office immediately so they can be prepared for a formal complaint.

Browse this website

www.lunn-poly.co.uk

Feedback from customers on their attitudes to a particular travel and tourism organisation or product can be gathered either informally or formally. Informal feedback is often spontaneous, making it just as valuable as information that is given in a more formal manner. Indeed, many would say that a customer is more likely to reveal his or her true feelings and attitudes in an unprompted chat with a member of staff, than when that same member of staff is carrying out a questionnaire survey of users. Informal feedback can take many forms, including:

✪ **A remark to a holiday representative about the poor standard of the food in a resort hotel**

- ✪ **A member of staff overhearing customers praising the standard of service received at a holiday centre**
- ✪ **A child heard complaining to his father about the length of time they are having to queue for a ride at a theme park**

It is important that management establish a system by which both formal and informal feedback is collected and monitored. Surveys, questionnaire interviews, observation and customer comment cards are just a few of the techniques that can be used. We are all well aware of the influence that unhappy customers can have on the image of an organisation and thereby its success. We all like to talk about our travel and tourism experiences, which, if negative, can spread very quickly by 'word of mouth'. This powerful mechanism can also be beneficial for those organisations that have provided an excellent standard of service.

Many travel and tourism operators now have regular staff meetings at which employees are invited to share any informal feedback that they have picked up. They are also encouraged to record comments from customers on specially designed feedback forms, so that management can monitor the situation to see if corrective action is needed in any areas.

Customer correspondence, communication and information

When communicating with customers, it is important to have in place business systems that offer a speedy and reliable service. Whether communication is by letter, telephone, fax or e-mail, customers expect a response within a reasonable period of time. A key point is always to do what you have told a customer you will do! So if you have promised to return a telephone call or send a brochure, for example, you must make sure that it is done.

Systems for staff

Key topics in this section

- **Introduction**
- **Work records**
- **Recruitment and selection**
- **Personnel records**
- **Disciplinary and grievance**
- **Appraisal and staff development**
- **Induction and training**
- **Consultation and communication**
- **The Data Protection Act**

Introduction

In large travel and tourism organisations, systems for dealing with staff matters are usually handled by the personnel or human resources (HR) department (Unit 20 *Human resources in the travel and tourism industry* has more detail on HR systems and procedures). Regardless of the size of an organisation, it will need to carry out structured procedures for the appointment of staff, their training, appraisal and welfare while at work. These procedures will vary between organisations, but are likely to focus on:

- ✪ **Work records** – e.g. job title, grade, holiday entitlement and salary/wages structure for staff in the organisation
- ✪ **Recruitment and selection** – e.g. interview guidelines, screening procedures, etc.
- ✪ **Personnel records** – e.g. accident and sickness records, references, personal details such as address, date of birth, bank account number, etc.
- ✪ **Disciplinary and grievance** – e.g. procedures for disciplining staff and records of staff interviews concerning grievances
- ✪ **Appraisal and staff development** – e.g. records of any staff appraisal interviews and action plans
- ✪ **Induction and training** – e.g. systems for inducting new staff and procedures for further staff training
- ✪ **Consultation and communication** – e.g. copies of all communication between members of staff and the organisation

In smaller travel and tourism organisations, information on employees may be stored and updated manually. If only a small number of staff are employed, this system will prove to be quite adequate. Larger organisations, however, are likely to use a computerised personnel records system, with the benefits of greater storage capacity, speed of use and accessibility to many staff at the same time. Information on employees that is held on computer, however, does fall within the scope of the Data Protection Act 1984 and 1998, which provides new rights for individuals and demands good practice from those who hold personal data on individuals. We look at the Act in more detail in the next section of this unit.

The Data Protection Act 1984 and 1998

Since 10 May 1986, all organisations that hold personal data about individuals on automated systems have been required to register with the Data Protection Registrar and to comply with the Data Protection Act (DPA). The exact definition of an 'automated system' is open to debate, but in general terms, information held on computer falls within the scope of the Act and, under the terms of the 1984 Act, that which is processed manually does not. Indeed, some organisations have chosen to store certain data on manual systems in order that it is not covered by the DPA. However, the 1998 Data Protection Act widens the scope of the 1984 Act by stating that a significant amount of data held manually is now covered within the legislation. The Act seeks to regulate the way in which data is gathered, stored and disclosed to third parties.

The 1984 Act established eight Data Protection Principles with which data users must comply (data users are defined as individuals, corporations or other agencies that control the automatic processing of data). The eight principles, which in reality are a set of points of good practice to which data users should aspire, are as follows:

1   **That the information held on computer shall be obtained and processed fairly and lawfully. Data would be said to have been obtained unfairly if the provider was deceived or misled about the purpose for which the information was being obtained.**

2   **That personal data shall be held only for one or more specified and lawful purposes. A contravention of this particular principle would, for example, be when an organisation holds personal information for staff training purposes but chooses to use it for the selection of staff for redundancy.**

3   **That data shall not be disclosed to persons other than those named in the registration document, nor for any other**

purpose than that registered under the Act. A tour operator, for example, which collects information on its customers to offer them discounted holidays, cannot then sell the data to another company without contravening this principle.

4   That personal data held for any purpose or purposes shall be adequate, relevant and not excessive in relation to the registered purpose. An organisation that holds data unrelated to the purpose for which it is registered, or is clearly holding far more than is needed to satisfy the purpose, will be in breach of this principle.

5   That personal data shall be accurate and updated as and when necessary. If an organisation, for example, holds a list of customers who have exceeded their annual credit limit, but the organisation makes no attempt to update the list when further payments are made, it is likely to be considered as having contravened this principle.

6   That personal information held for any purpose or purposes shall not be kept for longer than is necessary. For example, a travel agency that holds a prize draw and uses a computer to store the names and addresses of those entering should destroy this data at the end of the promotion.

7   That an individual shall be entitled, at reasonable intervals and without undue delay or expense, to know whether information is held on him or her and to have access to any data that does exist; also to have any data corrected or erased as appropriate.

8   That the data user shall take reasonable security measures to guard against unauthorised access to, alteration, disclosure, accidental loss or destruction of the personal data.

Under the Act, individuals who have data held on them have a range of rights in civil law, including:

✪   **Rights of access to the data**

✪   **Rights to compensation for inaccuracy of data**

✪   **Rights to compensation for loss, destruction or unauthorised disclosure of data**

✪   **Rights to apply to have any inaccuracies in the data rectified and, in certain circumstances, rights to have the information erased**

New Data Protection legislation came into force on 1 March 2000 with the implementation of the Data Protection Act 1998, which updates and reinforces the Data Protection Principles established in the 1984 Act and includes data held manually for the first time.

Systems for financial accounting

Key topics in this section

- **Sales records**
- **Stock control and purchasing**
- **Staff payroll systems**
- **Customer accounts**
- **Customer payment**

Sales records

Accurate recording of sales volumes and sales revenue is an essential component of an effective financial system. As we saw in Unit 18 *Financial planning and control*, managing cash flow is vital to the success of many travel and tourism organisations. Systems for recording sales can be manual but are increasingly computer-based nowadays.

Stock control and purchasing

Although travel and tourism is a service industry, providing 'experiences' rather than 'products', there are a number of areas where it is necessary to undertake some form of stock control. These include:

- ✪ **Catering outlets**
- ✪ **Bars**
- ✪ **Retail units**

Travel and tourism facilities often generate healthy extra revenue, sometimes known as 'secondary spend', from the sale of food, drinks, souvenirs, equipment and clothing, all of which will need careful control of stock. Stock control is a broad term, covering:

- ✪ **Storage**
- ✪ **Recording of stock levels**
- ✪ **Stocktaking**
- ✪ **Withdrawing stock**

Careful attention to stock control is particularly important in the case of food, which will deteriorate in quality if not stored in the right conditions. Holding

Bar stock control sheet

Product	Opening stock	Stock received	Closing stock	Amount sold	Price	Cash value
Keg beers						
Bitter						
Lager						
Guinness						
Best Bitter						
Bottled beers						
Newcastle Brown						
Grolsch						
Stella Artois						
San Miguel						
Manns Brown						
Guinness						
Spirits						
Whisky						
Brandy						
Gin						
Vodka						
Bacardi						
Rum						
Cinzano						
Mixers						
Coke						
Tonic						
Ginger Ale						
Cordial						

Total sales
Cash taken
Under/over

Figure 19.9 *A stock control sheet as used in a bar*

too much stock of any sort is wasteful, since it ties up money unnecessarily and takes up valuable space. Records will be needed for all receipts of stock and stock issues (see Figure 19.9).

Staff payroll systems

It is a fact of life that everybody expects and wants to be paid on time! Travel and tourism organisations need to operate efficient payroll systems to keep their staff happy. It is more and more common for payroll to be a computer-based operation in the travel and tourism industry, with software automatically calculating deductions for tax and national insurance contributions.

Customer accounts

Accuracy is important when establishing a system for monitoring customer accounts. A computer-based system will automatically print invoices and payment reminder letters when a period of credit is exceeded.

Customer payment

Cash is the lifeblood of any travel and tourism organisation. As such, it requires very strict control to record its movement through the organisation and to provide a check against negligence and fraud (see examples of a credit note and payment slip used in a hotel in Figures 19.10 and 19.11 respectively).

It is essential that all members of staff are aware of the importance of cash, and that money, in its various forms, is credited to the organisation's bank account with safety and without any undue delay. A daily receipts summary, similar to that shown in Figure 19.12, will help keep track of cash takings.

Figure 19.12 also shows that 'cash' received by the hotel will not consist only of coins and notes. Most travel and tourism businesses will receive payment by one or more of the following methods:

- **Bank notes and coins**
- **Cheques and postal orders**
- **Credit cards, debit cards and charge cards**
- **Direct debits and standing orders**
- **Banker's drafts and certified cheques**
- **Travellers' cheques**

REBATE CREDIT   Date...
HLO549A
                                       Name..

                                       Room ....

EXPLANATION	CODE No.	£	p

Dept Signature...................................   Accounts..............................

Figure 19.10   *Credit note used in a hotel*

PAID OUT   DATE...

                                       NAME..

                                       ROOM..

EXPLANATION	CODE No.	£	p
RECEIVED BY:			
	TOTAL		

AUTHORISED BY ....

HLO 561

Figure 19.11   *Customer payment slip used in a hotel*

Maesmawr Hall Hotel
Daily receipts summary

W/E	Monday	Tuesday	Wednesday	Thursday	Friday	Saturday	Sunday	Total
Accom/Room hire								
Restaurant								
Lounge bar								
Wines								
Bar Meals								
Functions Food								
Functions Wines								
Functions Bar								
Telephone								
Miscellaneous								
Deposits								
Total								

Figure 19.12 *Daily receipts summary as used in a hotel*
Courtesy of Maesmawr Hall Hotel

```
┌─────────────────────────────────────────┐
│          Mountainside Arts Centre        │
├─────────────────────────────────────────┤
│             Tel: (0123) 45613            │
│                                          │
│  Date: _____  │
│  Received from: _____ │
│                 _____  │
│                                          │
│                                          │
│  For: _____  │
│       _____  │
│       _____  │
│                                          │
│                                          │
│  Amount: £ _____   │
│                                          │
│  Signed: _____  │
│             VAT Reg. no. 263 7633 25     │
└─────────────────────────────────────────┘
```

Figure 19.13 *An example of a receipt used in an arts centre*

Although it is becoming a little unfashionable to carry coins and notes, there are still a lot of people who wouldn't think of using anything else. Cash is the main payment method in many travel and tourism facilities, such as visitor attractions, leisure centres, museums, catering outlets and sports venues. It is usual practice to issue a receipt immediately for cash transactions, which acts as proof of purchase (see Figure 19.13). Cash paid into a bank account does not need 'clearing' and is immediately credited to the organisation's account.

Accepting cheques is a very common method of payment in many travel and tourism organisations. Once paid into a bank account, it will take a minimum of three working days for the cheque to be processed, during which time it remains 'uncleared'; clearing is the process of passing the cheque to the customer's bank, debiting their account and crediting your own. Staff should always ask for a cheque guarantee card to be presented; most will honour cheques up to the value of £50, although it is becoming increasingly common to see £100 cheque guarantee cards in use. Cheques for values in excess of that quoted on the card should not normally be accepted; it is safer to ask the customer to provide another form of payment.

Credit cards are widespread in hotels, restaurants and other catering outlets, and for booking holidays and flights. The two most common cards in use in Britain are Mastercard and Visa, used on a whole range of credit cards offered by banks, building societies and even car manufacturers (Vauxhall and Ford have recently introduced credit cards). For the customer, credit cards are a very convenient way of making payment, since they can be used for postal and telephone bookings, as well as payment in person. They offer an interest-free period subject to certain conditions. Debit cards, such as Switch and Delta, should not be confused with credit cards, since they have a completely different function. A debit card is used in place of a cheque, with the holder's bank account being debited within three working days. Charge cards, such as American Express and Diners Club, offer no extended credit facility, as with credit cards. Their use in travel and tourism facilities is mainly by business and corporate customers.

A banker's draft or certified cheque will be used when payment is required immediately and there is no time to go through the normal clearing process. Some people will pay a large amount by a certified cheque issued by their building society. Banker's drafts are an easy way of accepting payment in a foreign currency.

Travellers' cheques may be used for payment in hotels and restaurants by overseas visitors. Care should be taken to ensure that the cheques are not already countersigned before they are presented for payment.

Whichever method of payment is accepted, and depending on the policy of the individual organisation, the stages that the payment will go through are as follows:

1 **Payment received by the leisure or tourism facility**
2 **Receipt issued to customer (see Figure 19.13)**

CASHIERS REPORT

DATE................................ CASHIER ....

DUTY ....

ACTUAL BANK ACCOUNT AT CLOSE OF PLAY		CONTENTS OF ENVELOPE	£	p
Notes £50		Notes £50		
£20		£20		
£10		£10		
£5		£5		
£1		£1		
Coins £1		Coins £1		
50p		50p		
20p		20p		
10p		10p		
5p		5p		
2p		2p		
1p		1p		
		CHEQUES – LIST ENCLOSED		
		FOREIGN CURRENCIES COUNTRY–AMOUNT–RATE		
		U.S.		
DUE FROM GENERAL CASH				
TOTAL BANK				
		TOTAL AMOUNT ENCLOSED		
		NET AMOUNT DUE		
		OVER (SHORT)		
		DIFFERENCE RETURNABLE		

Figure 19.14 *A cashier's report envelope*

3   Entry made on daily cash summary sheet (see Figure 19.12)

4   Receipts and summary sheets reconciled (see example of cashier's report envelope in Figure 19.14)

5   Bank paying-in slips completed

6   Monies paid into the bank account

7   Paying-in slips stamped by bank

Systems for health, safety and security

Key topics in this section

- **Introduction**
- **Complying with relevant legislation**
- **Emergency procedures**
- **First aid provision**
- **Security of people and premises**
- **Reporting systems**

Introduction

A basic function of all organisations involved with the travel and tourism industry is to provide a safe and secure environment for staff to work in, and for visitors to enjoy. The wide-ranging nature of travel and tourism means that each industry sector has its own particular requirements in terms of systems for health, safety and security. For example:

✪ **Many indoor entertainment complexes are very large and often cater for the needs of hundreds, if not thousands, of people at any one time. Cinemas, theatres, sports stadia and indoor arenas must put health and safety at the top of their list of priorities.**

✪ **The managers and staff of hotels and other types of accommodation have a number of health and safety concerns that must be addressed, e.g. the storage and handling of food, and ensuring safe means of escape in case of fire.**

✪ **Tourist attractions, especially theme parks with complex 'rides', have to be aware of dangers to both staff and visitors from machinery and electrical installations.**

✪ **Holiday centres will offer a range of sports activities that can, if not properly supervised, expose the participants and spectators to potential risks. Centres that offer swimming and other water-based attractions need to be especially aware of health and safety requirements.**

✪ **Outdoor activity centres that cater for the needs of both young and old must ensure that staff are fully trained in**

- supervising potentially dangerous activities, such as rock-climbing, watersports and fell-walking.

✪ **Transport operators, including airlines, coach companies, ferry and cruise operators and car hire firms, have a duty to ensure that their vehicles and equipment are safely maintained and that all staff are capable of carrying out emergency procedures when necessary.**

Health and safety is not just the concern of the private sector in travel and tourism; it is just as applicable to both the public and voluntary sectors, as this extract from the *National Trust Handbook* indicates:

The Trust endeavours to provide a healthy and safe environment for visitors at its properties as far as is reasonably practicable, and to ensure that the activities of its staff and contractors working on Trust properties do not in any way jeopardise the health and safety of visitors. You can help the Trust by observing all notices and signs relating to this subject during your visit, by following any instructions given by Trust staff, by ensuring that children are properly supervised and by wearing appropriate clothing and footwear at outdoor properties.

Activity 19.6

While on work experience, carry out an investigation into the health, safety and security policies of your placement agency and list the ways in which the policies are put into practice.

Complying with relevant legislation

There is a variety of legislation that imposes certain duties on the management and staff of leisure and tourism facilities in relation to health and safety issues. For anybody considering working in, or already involved with, the travel and tourism industry at whatever level, it is important to be aware of the ever-increasing impact of health and safety legislation.

To begin with, there is a common law duty of care, under which each citizen owes a duty to all others who may be affected by his or her activities. If a person takes insufficient care in relation to another citizen, and that person suffers damage as a result, the injured party may begin an action in the civil court to reclaim damages. However, this civil law only comes into action after damage has been suffered. Although the outcomes of civil cases have given the courts many opportunities to create precedents that guide the conduct of similar occurrences in the future, the civil law has always been considered an inappropriate instrument in the area of accident prevention. The advent of the Health and Safety at Work, etc. Act 1974 changed all this.

Health and Safety at Work, etc. Act 1974

The Health and Safety at Work, etc. Act (HSW Act) was introduced to provide the legislative framework to promote, stimulate and encourage high standards of health and safety at work.

Contents of the Act

The HSW Act is an enabling measure superimposed over existing health and safety legislation. In addition to placing duties of a general nature on employers, manufacturers, employees, the self-employed and others, the Act provides wide powers for the making of regulations. Part I of the Act, the part that concerns travel and tourism organisations the most, aims to:

- **Secure the health, safety and welfare of people at work**
- **Protect other people against risks to health or safety arising from the activities of people at work**
- **Control the storage and use of dangerous substances, e.g. chemicals, and prevent their unlawful use**
- **Control the emission into the atmosphere of noxious or offensive substances from premises**

Scope of the Act

All 'persons at work', whether employees, employers or self-employed, are covered by the Act, with the exception of domestic servants in private households. About 8 million people who were not covered by previous health and safety legislation, such as the self-employed and those employed in education, health services, the leisure, travel and tourism industries and in some parts of the transport industry, are now protected.

The HSW Act aims gradually to replace existing health and safety requirements by revised and updated provisions, which take the form of regulations and approved codes of practice prepared in consultation with industry. Regulations relating to health and safety matters are usually made by the appropriate government minister on the advice of the Health and Safety Commission. In reality, most regulations are made by the Secretary of State for Employment. Codes of practice have a special legal status. Although they are not statutory requirements, they may be used in criminal proceedings on health and safety issues, as evidence that the statutory requirements have been contravened.

Duties of employers

It is the duty of every employer to safeguard, so far as is reasonably practicable, the health, safety and welfare of all those in his or her employment. This duty is extended to others who may be affected by the operation of the facility, e.g. contractors, visitors and members of the general public. In practice the employer must have specific regard for the following:

1 **To provide plant and equipment that is not a risk to health**

2 **To ensure that work systems and practices are safe**

3 **To ensure that the work environment is regularly monitored in respect of health and safety requirements**

4 **To provide safe storage for substances that could pose a threat to safety and ensure their safe use**

5 **To provide a written statement of safety policy and bring it to the notice of employees (applies only to those employing five or more staff)**

6 **To provide adequate information and training for all staff in matters relating to health and safety.**

Duties of employees

Employees have a duty under the HSW Act to:

✪ **Take reasonable care to avoid injury to themselves or to others by their work activities**

✪ **To co-operate with their employers and other agencies to ensure that the requirements of the Act are carried out**

✪ **Not to interfere with or misuse anything provided to protect their health, safety and welfare under the Act**

Enforcement of the HSW Act

The Act established the Health and Safety Commission (HSC) and the Health and Safety Executive (HSE) both to publicise the need for safety at work and to begin prosecutions for breaches of the Act. The HSC is responsible to the Secretary of State for Employment for taking the necessary steps to secure the health, welfare and safety of people at work and also to protect the public against risks to health and safety arising out of a work situation. The HSE is the operating arm of the HSC and is responsible for enforcing the legislation under the HSW Act. HSE appoints and controls teams of inspectors who have wide powers to enter premises and examine records and staff to check that the Act is being complied with. Inspectors can also make enquiries into accidents that have occurred at places of employment. This covers accidents, not only to employees themselves, but also to visitors and would include, for example, people using sports centres and other leisure and tourism facilities.

If an inspector discovers a contravention of one of the provisions of the HSW Act or any of the earlier legislation that is still in force, he or she can take one of several courses of action:

1   The inspector can issue a prohibition notice if there is a high risk of serious personal injury. This effectively stops the activity in question until the specified action to remedy the situation has been completed. The notice can be served either on the person undertaking the activity or the person in control of it.

2   An alternative course of action would be to issue an improvement notice if there is a contravention of any of the requirements of the Act. This notice gives a time limit for compliance with the relevant contravention.

3   Over and above the issuing of either a prohibition notice, an improvement notice or both, any person found contravening the Act or any of its regulations may be prosecuted.

4   The inspector has powers to seize, render harmless or destroy any substance or article considered to be the cause of imminent danger or serious personal injury.

Industry example

Alton Towers has the following health and safety codes that it must abide by:

★ Fairgrounds and Amusement Parks Guidance on Safe Practice

★ The Health and Safety at Work, etc. Act 1974

★ The Management of Health and Safety at Work Regulations 1992

★ The Provision and Use of Work Equipment Regulations 1992

★ The Disability Discrimination Act 1995

Browse these websites

www.alton-towers.co.uk

www.altontowers.com

European Union (EU) directives on health and safety

Six new sets of health and safety at work regulations came into force at the beginning of 1993. They apply to almost all kinds of work activity, including travel and tourism, and, like the health and safety laws we already have, they place duties on employers to protect:

- ✪ **Their employees**
- ✪ **Other people, including members of the public, who may be affected by the work being carried out**

These UK regulations are needed to implement six European Union (EU) directives on health and safety at work. They are also part of a continuing modernisation of existing UK law. The directives are part of the EU's programme of action on health and safety, which is an essential ingredient in the move towards a single European market. Most of the duties in the regulations are not completely new, but clarify what is already in current health and safety law. Any travel and tourism organisation, which is already complying with the HSW Act and the regulations linked with it, should not find the new regulations at all daunting. A number of old and out-of-date laws have been repealed by the new regulations.

What do the regulations cover?

The new regulations cover:

- ✪ **Health and safety management**
- ✪ **Work equipment safety**
- ✪ **Manual handling of loads**
- ✪ **Workplace conditions**
- ✪ **Personal protective equipment**
- ✪ **Display screen equipment**

Health and safety management

The Management of Health and Safety at Work Regulations 1992 set out broad general duties that apply to almost all work activities in Great Britain and offshore. The regulations make more explicit what is already required of employers under the HSW Act and are principally aimed at encouraging them to take a more systematic approach to dealing with health and safety matters. In general terms, the regulations require employers to:

1 **Systematically assess the risks to the health and safety of employees and anyone else affected by the work activity, e.g. visitors, spectators and contractors. Employers with five or more employees will need to record their findings by drawing up a *risk assessment*.**

2 **Put into practice the measures outlined in the risk assessment. This will involve planning, organisation, control, monitoring and review; in other words, the management of health and safety.**

3 **Appoint competent people to help devise and apply the measures.**

4 **Set up emergency procedures.**

5 **Provide employees with information about health and safety.**

6 **Co-operate with other employers who may share the same work site.**

7 **Provide adequate training for employees in health and safety.**

8 **Provide temporary workers with particular health and safety information to meet their needs.**

Work equipment safety

The Provision and Use of Work Equipment Regulations are designed to pull together and tidy up the laws governing equipment used at work. Instead of piecemeal legislation covering particular kinds of equipment in different industries, they:

○ **Place general duties on employers**

○ **List minimum requirements for work equipment to deal with selected hazards whatever the industry**

'Work equipment' is broadly defined to include everything from a hand tool, through machines of all kinds, to a complete plant such as a leisure centre or indoor arena. The regulations include both general duties placed on employers and specific requirements to which they must adhere to. General duties require employers to:

○ **Make sure that equipment is suitable for its intended use**

○ **Take into account the working conditions and hazards in the workplace when selecting equipment**

○ **Ensure that equipment is adequately maintained**

○ **Give adequate instruction, information and training**

○ **Provide equipment that conforms with EC product safety directives**

The specific requirements of these regulations cover such items as the guarding of dangerous parts of machinery, stability of equipment, warnings and markings, to name but a few.

Manual handling of loads

The incorrect handling of loads causes large numbers of injuries and can result in pain, time off work and sometimes permanent disablement. The Manual Handling Operations Regulations came into force on 1 January 1993 and replace patchy, old-fashioned and largely ineffective laws with a modern, ergonomic approach to the problem.

They apply to any manual handling operations that may cause injury at work. Such operations should have been identified by the risk assessment carried out under the Management of Health and Safety at Work Regulations 1992.

Employers have to take three key steps:

1 **Avoid hazardous manual handling operations where reasonably practicable**

2 **Assess adequately any hazardous operations that cannot be avoided**

3 **Reduce the risk of injury as far as is reasonably practicable**

The regulations are backed up by general guidance that can help to identify the more serious risks within any work situation.

Workplace conditions

The Workplace (Health, Safety and Welfare) Regulations 1992 replace a total of 38 pieces of old law, making safety in the workplace a much easier topic to understand and making it clear what is expected of employers.

The regulations set general requirements in four broad areas.

1 **Working environment**
  - ✪ **Temperature in indoor workplaces**
  - ✪ **Ventilation**
  - ✪ **Lighting**
  - ✪ **Room dimensions and space**
  - ✪ **Suitability of workstations and seating**

2 **Safety**
  - ✪ **Safe passage of pedestrians and vehicles**
  - ✪ **Safe opening, closing and cleaning of windows and skylights**
  - ✪ **Use of safety materials in transparent doors and partitions**
  - ✪ **Safety devices on doors, gates and escalators**
  - ✪ **Construction and maintenance of floors**

3 **Facilities**
  - ✪ **Toilets**
  - ✪ **Washing, eating and changing facilities**
  - ✪ **Clothing storage**
  - ✪ **Drinking water**
  - ✪ **Rest areas, including arrangements to protect people from the discomfort of tobacco smoke**
  - ✪ **Rest facilities for pregnant women and nursing mothers**

4   **Housekeeping**

- ✪ **Maintenance of workplace, equipment and facilities**
- ✪ **Cleanliness**
- ✪ **Removal of waste materials**

Employers must ensure that any workplace within their control complies with the regulations. Existing workplaces had until 1996 to be brought up to scratch.

Activity 19.7

While on work experience, carry out a simple audit of how well the facility meets the four general requirements of the Workplace (Health, Safety and Welfare) Regulations 1992.

Personal protective equipment (PPE)

The Personal Protective Equipment at Work (PPE) Regulations 1992 replace parts of over 20 old pieces of law. PPE includes most types of protective clothing, and equipment such as eye, foot and head protection, safety harnesses, life jackets and high visibility clothing. Employers must supply PPE free of charge to their employees, and have a duty to:

- ✪ **Make sure that the PPE issued is suitable for the risk involved**
- ✪ **Maintain, clean and replace PPE**
- ✪ **Provide storage for PPE when it is not being used**
- ✪ **Ensure that PPE is properly used**
- ✪ **Give training, instruction and information to staff on the use and care of PPE**

Display screen equipment

Unlike some of the other regulations described above, the Health and Safety (Display Screen Equipment) Regulations do not replace old legislation but cover a new area of work activity for the first time. Work with display screens is not generally high risk, but it can lead to muscular and other physical problems, eye fatigue and mental stress. Problems of this kind can be overcome by good ergonomic design of equipment, furniture, the working environment and tasks performed.

Under these regulations, employers have a duty to:

- ✪ **Assess display screen equipment workstations and reduce risks that are discovered**
- ✪ **Make sure that workstations satisfy minimum requirements**
- ✪ **Plan display screen equipment work so that there are breaks or changes of activity**
- ✪ **Provide information and training for display screen equipment users**

Display screen equipment users are also entitled to appropriate eye and eyesight tests by an optician or doctor, and to special spectacles if they are needed and normal ones cannot be used. It is the employer's responsibility to provide tests and special spectacles if needed.

Emergency procedures

All travel and tourism organisations must ensure that they have adequate emergency procedures to follow in the event of an incident of any kind. Depending on the nature of the organisation, this could be an accident to staff or visitors, a fire, a bomb warning or a vehicle crash. Relevant staff must be fully trained in supervising the evacuation of people from buildings and vehicles.

First aid provision

First aid refers to treatment that can be carried out immediately at the scene of an accident, prior to the emergency services arriving. The Health and Safety at Work, etc. Act and its associated regulations, in particular the Health and Safety (First Aid Regulations) 1981, place a duty on employers to provide adequate first aid for both employees and non-employees, which in the case of travel and tourism would include guests, visitors, spectators, customers and contractors. Every travel and tourism organisation must have a sufficient number of first aiders, suitably qualified in first aid and able to decide if further professional help is required.

Security of people and premises

Customers who use travel and tourism facilities, and the staff who serve them, have a right to feel confident that they and their possessions, together with the premises they are occupying, are safe and secure.

Security of people

When looking at the wide range of security concerns confronting the industry, the welfare of people must be the prime concern for all travel and tourism organisations. 'People' will include:

- **Staff**
- **Visitors (invited or uninvited)**
- **Others (contractors, etc.)**

All employers have a legal duty under the Health and Safety at Work, etc. Act 1974 to ensure the health, safety and welfare at work of their staff (see page 411). There are many health and safety risks and hazards that may confront staff working in travel and tourism, but providing a safe working environment that is free from any violence is becoming an increasingly important concern for employers. The Health and Safety Executive working definition of violence is:

> *Any incident in which an employee is abused, threatened or assaulted by a member of the public in cirumstances arising out of the course of his or her employment. (HSE 1992)*

Being a service industry involving a high degree of contact between staff and customers, those working in travel and tourism can expect to encounter uncomfortable and sometimes violent incidents during the course of their work. Verbal abuse and threatening behaviour are the most common types of incident. Physical attacks are comparatively rare.

Both employers and employees have an interest in reducing violence in the workplace. For employers, violence can lead to low morale and a poor image for the organisation, making it difficult to recruit and retain staff. It can also mean extra costs, with absenteeism, higher insurance premiums and possible compensation payments. For employees, violence can cause pain, suffering and even disability or death. Physical attacks are obviously dangerous but serious or persistent verbal abuse or threats can also damage employees' health through anxiety and stress.

The HSE recommends the following seven-point plan to tackle violence in the workplace:

- **Step one**: Find out if there is a problem. It may seem obvious, but many employers are not aware of a problem until they ask staff directly.
- **Step two**: Record all incidents. By using a simple report form (see Figure 19.16 on page 425 in 'Reporting systems' section), an organisation can begin to build up a picture of the problem.
- **Step three**: Classify all incidents. Incidents that involve serious injury will be easy to classify, but those involving, for example, verbal abuse will need careful discussion with the staff involved.

- ✪ **Step four**: Search for preventative measures. The way jobs are carried out can help reduce the risk of violence. For example, if a travel and tourism organisation needs its staff to work late, it should arrange for them either to have a safe place to park their car or provide transport home; many nightclubs and pubs do this already, particularly for female staff. Changing from using cash to accepting cheques, credit cards or tokens can help reduce attempted thefts.

- ✪ **Step five**: Decide what to do. A mixture of measures usually works best, and particularly if the employees are fully involved in deciding what needs to be done. It is often a question of striking a balance between the fears of the staff and the needs of the public. For example, many busy tourist attractions provide entertainment for customers who are forced to queue to get in. This helps to diffuse what can sometimes turn into a threatening situation for staff on duty.

- ✪ **Step six**: Put measures into practice. Whatever measures are decided upon, the policy for dealing with violence should be included in the organisation's safety policy statement, so that all employees are aware of it.

- ✪ **Step seven**: Check that the measures work. It is important to check how well the measures are working. If the problem persists, it may be necessary to go back and repeat steps two and three.

It may be that violence among customers is identified as a problem for an organisation. Similar steps to those above can be put in place to help deal with this situation.

Browse these websites

www.alton-towers.co.uk

www.altontowers.com

Industry example

Alton Towers has its own security department and health and safety department, which are jointly responsible for the safety and welfare of both guests and staff. There are 30 security staff who are responsible for looking after Alton Towers 24 hours a day, 7 days a week and 365 days a year. To help them do this effectively, most areas of the park are covered by 37 close circuit television (CCTV) cameras, which are closely monitored from a central control room.

Security of premises

Security of property in travel and tourism involves:

- ✪ **The fabric of the building itself, including fitments**
- ✪ **The contents of the building**

Security of buildings

Buildings used for travel and tourism purposes can be under many different types of threat. One of the most obvious and costly is robbery, but other threats include wanton damage, often carried out by youths, and daubing with graffiti. There are some fundamental rules for securing any type of property, including:

- **Fitting security locks to doors and windows, and window bars to high-risk areas such as equipment stores and bar areas**
- **Using closed circuit television (CCTV) or employing security personnel to monitor large areas including car parks and staff and public entrances and exits**
- **Installing invisible beams and pressure pads in passageways and entrances to activate alarms**
- **Fitting intruder alarms which, for large organisations, should be capable of alerting a central monitoring station that operates 24 hours a day**
- **Introducing card access control using PIN systems to identify which parts of a building are for staff access only**
- **Installing security lighting, particularly in high-risk areas**

Security of the contents of the building

The contents of any travel and tourism facility that are potentially at risk could be:

- **Equipment, e.g. computers, sports equipment, catering equipment, furniture, museum artefacts, etc.**
- **Stock, e.g. wines, beers and spirits, food, sports clothing, etc.**
- **The personal possessions of the staff**
- **The personal possessions of the customers**
- **The personal possessions of any other people, such as contractors, who are on-site**

Most visitors will expect a facility to guard their possessions in exchange for a ticket, whether or not any payment is involved. This service is all part of making the visitor relaxed and in a better mood to enjoy their experience, whether it is a game of squash or a visit to an art gallery. Where visitors are not allowed to take possessions with them for security reasons, e.g. cameras are not allowed in certain museums and at certain events, secure storage must be provided by the travel and tourism operator.

Some of the techniques mentioned under 'security of buildings' above will help protect equipment and possessions inside the building. Over and above these technical measures, all staff must be vigilant and alert at all times to suspicious characters and circumstances. As well as ensuring a pleasant experience for all visitors, it is the job of staff and management to safeguard visitors' possessions. In particular, staff should look out for people behaving in a suspicious manner, for example:

✪ **A customer who cannot provide proof of identity or who is hesitant when questioned in suspicious circumstances**

✪ **A customer who loiters for long periods of time or who seems unusually interested in what everyone else is doing**

✪ **Members of a group in a restaurant or other eating place leaving one-by-one, with the intention of not paying the bill**

✪ **People taking a particular interest in cars or other vehicles parked on-site**

✪ **Sudden disturbances between two or more customers, who may be trying to create a distraction to cover theft by an accomplice**

✪ **Guests in accommodation bringing empty suitcases into their rooms, perhaps with a view to removing stolen items from the establishment**

Activity 19.8

While on work experience, carry out an investigation to find out what measures are in place to deal with the security of staff and customers and their possessions.

Reporting systems

We saw earlier in this unit that the Management of Health and Safety at Work Regulations 1992 required employers with five or more employees to, amongst other things, systematically assess the risks to the health and safety of employees and anyone else affected by the work activity, e.g. visitors, spectators and contractors, by carrying out a risk assessment. The aim of the assessment is to identify potential risks and put measures in place to prevent them becoming incidents. Figure 19.15 shows a risk assessment form used for a travel and tourism event.

If an incident does occur in a travel and tourism organisation, it is important that all details are logged in order to satisfy internal and external procedures, which could include the local authority, Health and Safety Executive (HSE),

Travel and tourism event
RISK ASSESSMENT FORM

Organisation ....
Title of event ....
Location of event ....
Date of event ....
Date inspection conducted ....
Conducted by (name) ....
Time conducted ....

Topic	Requires attention Y/N	Comments
General environment • Lighting adequate • Heating adequate • Cleanliness • Condition of floors • Condition of steps • Condition of seating • Traffic management • Waste disposal • Signage		
Hygiene • Condition of toilets • Cleanliness of eating places • Food storage facilities • Condition of work area		
Protective clothing (where appropriate) Provision and condition of: • Safety footwear • Eye protection • Hearing protection • Respirators • Gloves • Safety headgear • Overalls		
Machinery • Location suitable • Guarding adequate • Suitable stop mechanism • Noise level • Storage of fuels		
First aid • Contents of First Aid boxes • Sufficient appointed First Aiders • Location of First Aid points • Briefing of First Aiders		

Figure 19.15 *A risk assessment form*

Topic	Requires attention Y/N	Comments
Fire • Appropriate fire fighting equipment • Extinguishers clearly visible • Fire exit routes marked and unobstructed • Fire alarm testing • Special fire hazards • Clear routes for emergency vehicles		
Electrical • Condition of wiring • Access to isolators • Equipment tested and approved • Wiring and appliances weatherproof		
Safety training • Routine procedures in operation • Any special training requirements		
Storage of dangerous substances • In accordance with COSHH regulations		
Additional comments		
Summary of action to be taken		

Figure 19.15   (cont'd)

emergency services and insurance companies. Figure 19.16 shows a typical incident report form.

In order to minimise the likelihood of equipment failure leading to incidents, it is important for travel and tourism organisations to have rigorous systems for the cleaning and maintenance of buildings and equipment. The importance of maintaining the fabric of a travel and tourism facility goes well beyond the routine tasks associated with keeping the weather out. With visitors now demanding high quality standards, a facility that is poorly maintained or not cleaned on a regular basis will not be able to compete effectively with those organisations that give cleaning and maintenance a high priority. The image of a facility and its management is closely linked to its physical appearance. Add to this the fact that legislation demands a healthy and safe environment for both staff and visitors, plus the fact that a poorly maintained building will decrease in value, and it is not surprising that the cleaning and maintenance of travel and tourism facilities has taken on greater importance of late.

The maintenance of facilities can be either routine or corrective. Work that is carried out as a matter of routine is often referred to as planned

Sunway Travel Ltd.		
date of incident	day of week	time

EMPLOYEE

name   address
job/grade
department
what activity were you engaged in at the time of the incident?

DETAILS OF ASSAILANT(S)	WITNESS(ES)
name(s) address(es) age male/female other details	name(s) address(es) age male/female other details

WHAT HAPPENED

give an account of the incident, including any relevant events leading to the incident

OUTCOME

Injury? Verbal abuse? Anti-social behaviour? Damage to personal/other property?
                                            time lost
                                        legal action?

DETAILS OF LOCATION OF INCIDENT

provide sketch if possible

any other relevant information

Figure 19.16   *A typical incident report form*

maintenance, while corrective maintenance involves tasks carried out in response to an emergency or failure of equipment or services. It is expected that by adopting a policy of planned maintenance, carried out at pre-determined intervals and according to prescribed criteria, an organisation will reduce the probability of the failure of systems or equipment and hence the need for corrective maintenance.

The normal cleaning routine of the facility should be part of the programme of planned preventative maintenance. Any minor defects should be reported to the appropriate authority and remedial action carried out. However, as well as this day-to-day activity, there also needs to be a systematic inspection of essential equipment and systems on a regular basis. Managers or supervisors should also implement frequent inspections of all parts of the facility, recording the findings on a report form (see Figure 19.17).

It makes good sense to carry out a programme of planned inspection and maintenance of equipment and facilities, for a number of reasons, including:

- ✪ **It is a cost-effective exercise, since preventative measures can save on costly major works in the future**
- ✪ **It will provide a healthy and safe environment for staff and customers**
- ✪ **It will ensure all areas are cleaned on a regular basis**
- ✪ **It will reduce the incidence of failure of equipment and systems**

Cleaning and maintenance inspection report				
Name of Facility				
Area inspected	Date	Time	Comments/action required	Inspection carried out by

Figure 19.17 *Inspection report form*

Methods used to operate business systems

Key topics in this section

- **Introduction**
- **Computer-based methods**
- **Electronic methods**
- **Paper-based methods**

Introduction

Travel and tourism organisations use a wide range of methods to enable them to operate their business systems effectively. These include computer-based, electronic and paper-based methods. A number of factors, including the size of an enterprise, location, operating costs and levels of staff training, will influence the choice of method. In reality, most travel and tourism organisations use a combination of all three methods.

Computer-based methods

The principal reason for installing a computer-based business system is that it will increase the efficiency and improve the effectiveness of the organisation in which it is operated. More specific reasons for choosing a computer system will vary between the different sectors of the travel and tourism industry, but could include:

✪ **As a means of expanding the organisation**: A small company may wish to expand its number of customers but realises that its manual system will not be able to cope with the extra information.

✪ **To make better use of staff resources**: It is unlikely that a computerised business system will actually reduce the number of employees once it is introduced, but it will enable the same number of people to do much more, thus improving staff efficiency.

✪ **As a way of accessing a remote database**: A travel and tourism organisation may introduce a computer system so that it can gain access to data from other sources. Staff in a travel agency, for example, will be able to access information and make bookings with tour operators and airlines directly via a computer link. In the same way, a public sector leisure centre may set up a direct link with its local authority mainframe computer in order to transfer and process data.

✪ **In order to provide a better standard of service to its customers**: A computer system is likely to speed up the processing of such items as bookings, membership details, cash handling, credit transfers, invoicing, letters and mailing of publicity materials, as well as freeing staff to concentrate on delivering high standards of customer service.

✪ **To provide information for management purposes**, which is regular, accurate, reliable and in a form which is easily understood.

Browse these websites

www.alton-towers.co.uk

www.altontowers.com

Industry example
Computer systems at Alton Towers

Around three million people a year are welcomed to Alton Towers, the UK's number one theme park. With such a large number of visitors, it is important that the managers of the theme park have access to detailed information on matters such as visitor numbers, costs, staffing, income and marketing. The attraction uses more than 200 terminals and PCs throughout the business, handling data concerning finance, admissions, marketing, merchandising and catering. The park's catering function has benefited from the most recent system installation. Catering accounts for 400 of the 700 peak season workforce within retail, with 76 outlets generating in excess of £6.5 million during the 32-week season.

Personal and networked computers

Larger travel and tourism organisations need the greater speed and capacity offered by mainframe computers and networked systems. In addition to these large-scale, integrated computer management information systems, which can handle complex data management functions, the use of microcomputers has grown rapidly in the travel and tourism industries in recent years. It is becoming increasingly common to find these personal computers (PCs) not only on the desks of administrative staff but also on the desks of the managers themselves. Modern business computers, most of which conform to the standards established by the IBM personal computer, will run word processing, spreadsheets, database and DTP (desk-top publishing) programs, depending on the type of software used. Smaller travel and tourism organisations are able to provide acceptable levels of management information based solely on the use of PCs. Laptop PCs are particularly useful for staff whose job takes them away from their office. With the correct software, a laptop can carry out exactly the same functions as an office-based PC, with the added bonus of portability.

Word processing

This is the most common form of information processing found in today's travel and tourism organisations. Computers loaded with word processing software, such as Microsoft Word or WordPerfect, have all but replaced typewriters in the production of textual information. Letters, reports, memoranda and other types of written communication can be quickly, accurately and professionally produced on a word processor. They can be stored in the machine's memory (on the 'hard disk') or on floppy disks, allowing amendments and deletions at a later date. Word processing software offers many features that can be used in the production of documents, including:

- **Tables, graphics and images can be incorporated into the text**
- **Text can be enhanced using such features as underlining, emboldening, varying font sizes and styles, italics, etc.**
- **Blocks of text can be moved within a document and between documents**
- **'Mailmerge' allows personalised letters to be produced quickly and accurately by combining a standard letter with a list of names and addresses**
- **Spelling and grammar can be checked with most word processing software**
- **Words and phrases can be searched for and either removed or replaced with an alternative**

Word processing software enables organisations of whatever size to produce high quality documents, particularly when using a laser or ink jet printer. Small travel and tourism organisations often find that a standard word processing package is all they need to carry out a wide range of routine administrative tasks, from producing simple promotional materials to writing detailed reports and feasibility studies incorporating graphics and charts.

Databases

Databases are collections of files, data and records, stored on a computer-based system. The many sectors found within the travel and tourism industry mean that databases are used extensively in many different situations, for example:

- ✪ **A tour operator will hold details of its agents on a database, including sales details**
- ✪ **A hotel will maintain a database of its customers, for financial and promotional purposes**
- ✪ **A health and fitness club will hold details of its members on a database, including names, addresses and telephone numbers**
- ✪ **The owner of a gift shop will have a database of all his or her suppliers**
- ✪ **A conference organiser will hold details of his or her clients on a database**

The main advantage of using a computerised database, such as Microsoft's Access, is that once data has been entered onto the system, it can be retrieved, amended or sorted much more quickly than using a manual database. Also, searches of the database can be made for specific purposes, for example the names of all those living in a particular region or taking a holiday in a particular destination.

In addition to offering a search facility, a computerised database can also:

- ✪ **Sort records numerically, alphabetically or in date order**
- ✪ **Carry out numerical calculations, e.g. total sales of a particular product in a specified month**
- ✪ **Export data, e.g. the names and addresses of a travel agent's clients could be transferred to a word processing file to use the mailmerge function**

It is important for travel and tourism organisations to remember that information stored on computer falls within the scope and regulation of the Data Protection Act, giving rights to those whose details are held on the system (see page 399 for more detail on the Data Protection Act)

Activity 19.9

Research the travel and tourism companies operating in your local area and put the information onto a database for future reference.

Spreadsheets

A spreadsheet is a very useful and powerful computer application that can be used to perform a range of numerical calculations. It can carry out simple arithmetical calculations, such as percentages and additions, and proceed to more complex automated calculations and analyses.

Spreadsheets are found in both large and small travel and tourism organisations, and are used extensively for providing accounting information, such as cash flow forecasts, budget projections and tax returns. In its simplest form, a spreadsheet is little more than a grid consisting of a number of horizontal rows and vertical columns, into which data is written. Spreadsheets are particularly useful for a process known as 'sensitivity analysis', when the outcome of alterations to one or more elements of a spreadsheet will automatically be calculated by the programme. For example, a tourist attraction may have used a spreadsheet to calculate its total potential income for the forthcoming season, based on an admission price of £2.75 for adults. With a spreadsheet program, it is a simple matter to calculate the effect on total income of a reduction of 25p in the admission price.

Another very useful function of a database is that graphs and tables can be produced directly from information held on the database.

Desktop publishing

Desktop publishing, or DTP as it is sometimes known, is a sophisticated word processing system that is capable of producing very high quality documents from a standard PC. A desktop publishing system, such as Corel Draw or Aldus Pagemaker, provides its user with the means to produce a document with a number of features, including:

- **A range of typefaces and text styles**
- **Incorporation of pictures and other images by a process known as 'scanning'**
- **The ability to reduce and enlarge images and text**

DTP enables smaller travel and tourism organisations to produce very professional documents at a reasonable price, including sales leaflets, information sheets, direct mail packages, posters and other point-of-sale materials.

Internet, intranet and extranet

The Internet is an interactive system of networked computer databases, which offers users a wealth of information via the World Wide Web (www). Travel and tourism organisations can use the Internet to gather data, publicise their services and sell their products. Use of the Internet is revolutionising the distribution and sale of holidays and other travel products. An intranet is a network of computer-based information whose use is restricted to selected individuals within an organisation, e.g. the staff in an airline reservation office. An extranet is similar to an intranet, except that it can be accessed remotely by selected individuals, e.g. sales managers of the airline working away from their office base.

Browse this website

www.thomascook.
co.uk

Industry example

Thomas Cook is currently installing up to 2,500 new PCs in its branches in preparation for the creation of a private on-line information and booking service for its agents. The new PCs will allow agents to use a variety of Internet-based technologies. The company is looking to create an intranet that would allow agents to search for travel information and make on-line bookings, rather than allow unfettered use of the Internet.

Global distribution systems (GDS)

Browse these GDS websites

www.sabre.com

www.worldspan.
com

www.galileo.com

Global distribution systems (GDS) are computerised reservation systems developed by the world's major airlines to sell flights and a wide range of other travel-related services, including accommodation, car hire, event tickets and other transport services. They are a 'one-stop shop' for the traveller, who can make all necessary travel arrangements through an agent using one of the GDS systems anywhere in the world. Sabre, Worldspan and Galileo are three of the most widely used systems.

E-mail

E-mail (electronic mail) is revolutionising the travel and tourism industry, from both the customers' and management's perspective. Customers can now e-mail their information and advice requests to a wide range of organisations in travel and tourism, including:

- **National tourist boards**
- **Activity holiday companies**
- **Tourist resorts in the UK**
- **Airlines**
- **Ferry companies**
- **Hotels and other accommodation providers**

E-mail is especially suitable for customers wanting information from destinations or travel companies overseas, since it offers a speedy service on a global scale.

From the business perspective, e-mail can increase staff efficiency and effectiveness, allowing virtually instant communication within a company or with colleagues working away from their normal base. Documents and images can be attached to e-mails and distributed to relevant colleagues. It is important for organisations to remember that customers generally expect a faster reply to their e-mail enquiries when compared with a more traditional postal or telephone enquiry. It is essential, therefore, that any travel and tourism company offering an e-mail enquiry service is able to respond to enquiries within a reasonable time.

CD-ROM and DVD

Some of the information used by travel and tourism companies is available on CD-ROM (compact disc read-only memory) and DVD (digital video disc), for example travel directories, atlases and destination information.

Touch-screen technology

Electronic point-of-sale (EPOS) systems are being introduced in ever-increasing numbers to many leisure sector premises, especially pubs, clubs, bars and fast-food outlets. The only way the customer is likely to know that a facility has an EPOS system is when the staff use their 'touchpads' or 'scatterpads', the small touch-sensitive panels located behind the bar or counter, sometimes on the cash register itself. The benefits of EPOS to a travel and tourism organisation are:

1   **It gives the management control over cash transactions**

2   **It improves stock control**

3   **It frees staff to concentrate on improving customer care, rather than having to calculate prices and issue bills**

As well as performing all the normal functions of an electronic cash register, an EPOS system will log all transactions with time, date, items served, cost, method of payment and the member of staff who dealt with the customer. This not only reduces the possibility of fraud by staff, but also allows management to introduce incentives for staff who are meeting or exceeding their sales targets. The system will also mean that the busiest times can be better anticipated and allow better management of staff generally. The detailed management information given by EPOS will mean that stock levels can be monitored more closely, enabling the outlet to hold much smaller levels than would otherwise be the case, thus reducing overheads and improving cash flow.

Carry out a small-scale survey of establishments in your area that use an EPOS system. Indicate the function that the EPOS fulfils.

Electronic methods

There have been huge advances in electronic communications systems in recent years in the leisure and tourism industries. Based on the premise that electronic systems will be faster and more efficient than paper-based alternatives, worldwide communications are now available to all organisations, regardless of their size of operation. The 'electronic office' is now a reality, with many organisations having introduced computer systems and electronic equipment to communicate internally and externally. Some of the most important electronic communication methods include:

- ✪ **Integrated services digital network (ISDN)**: This is a sophisticated system developed by British Telecom that makes use of cable technology to transfer signals, allowing services such as video conferencing, desktop conferencing and data transfer to be offered.

- ✪ **Mobile telephones**: The use of 'mobiles' has grown dramatically in recent years, not least in all sectors of the travel and tourism industry.

- ✪ **Fax transmissions**: The number of fax (facsimile) transmissions has grown dramatically in the past five years. Like the photocopier before it, many travel and tourism organisations can't think how they managed before the fax machine was invented! They combine the speed of the telephone with the accuracy of the printed word, and are, therefore, particularly suited to the work of travel agents, tour operators and airlines, who often operate across different time zones. Systems combining fax, telephone, copier and answering machine are now within the reach of large and small travel and tourism organisations.

- ✪ **Display panels and departure boards**: Electronic systems have now all but replaced manual boards in airports and train stations.

- ✪ **Audio guides**: These are an alternative to a 'real' guide and are useful in that they can operate in a number of different languages.

- ✪ **Paging systems**: As with mobile telephones, pagers are used extensively in travel and tourism, particularly in large facilities such as tourist attractions and airports.

- ✪ **Intercom**: This is a useful way of communicating over relatively short distances.

- **Public address (PA)**: This is useful at events when information needs to be transmitted to large numbers of people at the same time.
- **Video conferencing**: This saves the time and expense of travelling for a meeting. Instead, the parties communicate with each other via a video link.

Paper-based methods

There are many different paper-based methods that a travel and tourism organisation can use to liaise with people internally and externally. The principal advantage of written communication is that it provides a permanent record of what took place, which can be stored for future reference. Other advantages of paper-based methods are that:

- **They enable complex information to be sent, e.g. statistical data**
- **They can serve as a reminder to those in receipt of the communication**
- **The quality of presentation can be altered to appeal to different audiences, e.g. the quality of headed notepaper and use of colour**
- **They provide evidence of confirmation of a previous discussion, e.g. the list of names of the passengers on an airline flight**
- **People located at a distance can communicate effectively, e.g. a memo sent to an overseas representative of a holiday firm working in Majorca**

Some of the most common types of written communication methods used in travel and tourism organisations include:

- **Letters**
- **Memoranda**
- **Promotional materials**
- **Reports**
- **Documentation for meetings**
- **Annual reports**
- **Advertisements**
- **Questionnaires**
- **Timetables**

Letters

The letter is the most commonly used type of external written communication. The reasons for sending a letter are many and varied, depending on the nature of the organisation. Typical situations when a letter may be sent include the following:

✪ **Letter to a job applicant to confirm interview details**

✪ **Letter to a customer thanking her for praising the standard of service received in a hotel**

✪ **Letter to a professional body confirming details of a forthcoming joint training seminar**

✪ **Letter of complaint to a supplier for non-delivery of goods**

✪ **Sales letter sent to all customers on an organisation's database**

With the advent of information processing technology, letters with a high standard of presentation can now be generated by most travel and tourism organisations, whatever their size. The presentation and content of a letter is important, since it gives the receiver an impression of the quality of the organisation sending it; a letter with many spelling and grammatical mistakes, printed on poor quality paper with an old printer ribbon, does little to enhance the reputation of an organisation.

Activity 19.11

Draft a letter that could be used by the marketing department of a large tour operator to send to its existing clients informing them of the launch of a new holiday brochure.

Memoranda

A memorandum (often shortened to memo) is commonly used within an organisation in place of a formal letter. It may be used for a number of reasons, including:

✪ **To confirm a verbal conversation**

✪ **To ask for information**

✪ **To remind a colleague of something**

✪ **To pass on instructions**

Figure 19.18 shows the layout of a memo used in a holiday company.

> **GLOBAL ACTIVITY TOURS**
> **MEMORANDUM**
>
> To: All staff
> From: John Tansley, Assistant Manager
> Date: 2 February 2001
> Ref: T101
> Subject: Staff Training
>
> Please note that there will be a one-day customer care training seminar for all staff on Monday 19 February 2001 starting at 0930 hrs in the meeting room FR5. The subject of the seminar is 'identifying customer needs'. A copy of the programme for the day is attached.
>
> I look forward to seeing you all.

Figure 19.18   *Memorandum used in a holiday company*

Promotional materials

Brochures, leaflets, posters and other promotional items have a vital role to play in all travel and tourism organisations. Industries like travel and tourism, mainly concerned with selling 'intangible' products and services, rely heavily on promotional materials to persuade customers to buy. A tour operator will produce brochures to inform potential customers of its holidays, leisure centres print leaflets to attract customers to their facilities, and a hotel will produce brochures and leaflets for business and leisure clients. You will have learned from studying Unit 4 *Marketing travel and tourism* that brochures, leaflets and other promotional items are often based on the AIDA principle, to attract *attention*, maintain *interest*, create a *desire* and trigger *action* on the part of the customer.

Reports

Written reports are used extensively in travel and tourism organisations for a number of reasons, including:

- ✪ **To present statistical information**
- ✪ **To investigate the feasibility of a new development, product or service**
- ✪ **To recommend changes to the management or staff structure**
- ✪ **To meet legal requirements, e.g. a limited company must publish an annual report and accounts**
- ✪ **To investigate a disciplinary matter involving staff**

A report should follow a logical sequence and structure, depending on its purpose. A typical structure is as follows:

1   **Terms of reference**: This should state why the report was written, for whom it was undertaken, what it will aim to achieve and the date by which it is to be completed.

2   **Procedure**: This part of the report should indicate how the information for the report was obtained, e.g. secondary research and/or primary research methods.

3   **Findings**: This section is the largest in the report and will give the results of the investigations. It is likely that there will be a number of subdivisions within this section.

4   **Conclusions**: This will be a summary of the main points found in the course of the investigation.

5   **Recommendations**: This section will outline suggested courses of action, based on the findings and conclusion.

6   **Bibliography and sources of information**: Although not always included, this section will indicate the main sources consulted during the investigation and may help to confirm the validity and credibility of the report.

Documentation for meetings

Part of the process of ensuring that meetings are effective and do not waste valuable management and staff time is a structured approach to their administration. Written communication in relation to a meeting should include:

✪ **Written notice of the meeting**: This will be sent out in advance of the meeting, giving the date, time and venue. The notice may also include a closing date by which items for the agenda should be submitted.

✪ **Agenda**: This is the list of items to be discussed at the meeting. It is helpful if it is distributed in advance of the meeting, but may be given out on the day. Figure 19.19 gives an example of a combined notice of meeting and agenda.

✪ **Minutes**: These are a written record of what was discussed at the meeting, usually compiled by the secretary and sent out to members who attended as well as those who were absent. At the next meeting, the minutes will be discussed and agreed as a true record of events.

Annual reports

It is a legal requirement for limited companies to publish an annual report and accounts for their shareholders. Large travel and tourism companies, such as Airtours, British Airways and Thomas Cook, produce glossy annual reports to contribute towards their image building. Public sector organisations, including

Northbridge Sports Hall Committee
Notice of meeting

Please note that the next meeting of the above committee will take place at 7.30pm on Friday 9 February 2001 in committee room 2 at Northbridge District Council offices.

The agenda is as follows.
1   Apologies for absence.
2   Minutes of the last meeting (previously circulated).
3   Matters arising from the minutes.
4   Secretary's report.
5   Implications of National Lottery funding
6   Any other business.
7   Date of next meeting.

David Oxenbury
Secretary

Figure 19.19   *Combined notice of meeting and agenda*

the national tourist boards, National Trust, BTA, Countryside Commission and Arts Council, also produce annual reports to give interested parties details of their activities and achievements. Many annual reports are made available in libraries for the public to consult.

Activity 19.12

Do some research in your own school or college library, as well as public libraries nearby, to find out which annual reports of travel and tourism organisations are available.

Advertisements

Advertising plays an important role in the travel and tourism industry. Written advertisements, in newspapers and magazines, inform people of services and products, with the aim of persuading them to buy. Travel and tourism organisations may choose to design their own advertisements or buy in the services of an advertising agency.

Questionnaires

Questionnaires are usually made available in paper-based format, although e-mail questionnaires are beginning to be used by some travel and tourism organisations.

Timetables

Leisure and tourism organisations involved with transportation need to inform their travellers of the times of travel. This is usually done by publishing a timetable, listing arrival and departure points and times. Companies that produce timetables include the airlines, airports, bus companies, private rail operators, tram operators and tour operators.

Human resources in the travel and tourism industry

20

It is a common remark that travel and tourism is very much a 'people business', but it's true! It is often said that people, sometimes referred to as human resources, are the most important part of any organisation, whether it operates in the private, public or voluntary sector. This is particularly so in travel and tourism, where members of staff play a crucial role in providing services to the travelling public. In this unit, you will explore the practical application of human resources in the travel and tourism industry, starting with a definition of human resources management and an investigation into how organisations plan their staffing needs. You will also learn about recruitment and selection in travel and tourism, including legal and ethical aspects of working in the industry. The unit concludes with a description of the techniques used to motivate staff.

This unit is divided into five main areas:

- **Human resource management (HRM)**
- **Human resource planning**
- **Recruitment and selection**
- **Employment issues**
- **Motivating staff**

We guide you through each of these areas using examples and case studies from the travel and tourism industry. At the beginning of each of these sections you will see a list of key topics to help you fully understand what you need to learn. Look out for the links to websites so that you can learn more about a particular travel and tourism company, organisation or topic.

Key topics in this section

- **Introduction – what is human resource management?**
- **Workforce planning**
- **Equal opportunities provision**
- **Recruitment and training**
- **Employee appraisal and motivation**
- **Remuneration**
- **Measuring personal effectiveness**

Introduction – what is human resource management?

Human resource management (HRM) is the activity that deals with all aspects of an organisation's staff, their recruitment, deployment, training, development, support and relationships with their employer. More than the mechanistic approach of personnel management, HRM is a more all-embracing concept to signal that an organisation is taking a more long-term view of all aspects of employing, empowering, supporting and rewarding its employees. HRM is concerned with achieving a balance between the ambitions of the individual member of staff and the returns to the organisation. It is crucial that this balance is achieved, particularly since staff costs typically make up more than three-quarters of all the costs of a travel and tourism business.

An effective HRM strategy in a travel and tourism organisation aims to achieve a number of important aims, including:

- **Efficient allocation of all staff in clearly defined roles with no staff shortages**
- **Staff with appropriate skills for their job roles**
- **Low levels of staff turnover**
- **Low levels of absenteeism**
- **Respect for legal and moral aspects of employment**
- **A highly motivated workforce**
- **An open and participative management style**

There are many factors that influence HRM in travel and tourism organisations, including:

- **Workforce planning**
- **Equal opportunities provision**
- **Recruitment and training**
- **Employee appraisal and motivation**
- **Remuneration**
- **Measuring personal effectiveness**

We will now investigate each of these in more detail.

Workforce planning

In a volatile industry like travel and tourism, which is constantly developing and innovating to meet changing customer requirements, the task of planning future staff needs is no easy matter. In such a competitive environment, however, the need to have just the right number of suitable employees becomes even more important; too few members of staff and the organisation may not be able to meet customer needs, too many and efficiency will not be maximised. Workforce planning gives an organisation the opportunity to look at existing staffing levels and to forecast the mix of human resources it will need in the future.

Although travel and tourism organisations vary greatly in size, it is possible to identify a number of stages that any organisation will need to go through in order to draw up its workforce plan. These are:

- **An examination of the organisation's strategic plan (this indicates the future direction of the organisation)**
- **Consideration of existing staff resources in the context of the strategic plan**
- **An estimate of any likely future changes in the supply of labour**
- **The likely demand in the organisation for staff in the future**
- **Development of the future human resources 'mix'**

Later in this section, we look at many of the influences on human resource planning (see page 448).

Equal opportunities provision

There has been a steady growth in recent years in the number of travel and tourism organisations that publicly announce that they are 'equal opportunities employers', or that they are 'working towards equality of opportunity'. Hotels, local authority tourism departments, tour operators, airlines, visitor attractions and voluntary sector providers, to name but a few, have all followed this trend in order to enhance their image, thereby attracting and retaining the best possible staff. However, in the same way that an organisation may say that it is 'committed to customer care', there must be a firm organisational policy that puts the words into action and proves that a commitment to equal opportunities for its workforce is more than just a statement of good intent.

Such a policy should include:

- **A clear statement that the organisation will avoid all forms of discrimination in its employment practices**
- **A statement that it will take steps to outlaw discrimination if, or when, it is found to occur**
- **What the policy means in terms of recruitment, selection, training and promotion of staff**
- **How the policy will be monitored and evaluated**
- **Who will be responsible for managing the implementation of the policy**

An equal opportunities policy that includes each of these elements, and is implemented with the full support of both management and staff, will go a long way towards allowing employees to achieve their full potential without the fear of being held back by prejudice or discrimination. Figure 20.1 shows a typical equal opportunities policy statement of a large travel and tourism company.

The four most common types of discrimination that employees, or those seeking employment, in travel and tourism are likely to encounter are:

- **Discrimination on the grounds of race**
- **Sex (or gender) discrimination**
- **Discrimination related to equal pay**
- **Discrimination on the grounds of disability**

We investigate each of these later when investigating employment issues in travel and tourism (see page 471).

EQUAL OPPORTUNITIES POLICY

This recruitment policy must be seen to abide by and take an active role in maintaining and improving the following Equal Opportunities Policy:

The Company is committed to a policy of treating all its employees and job applicants equally. No employee or potential employee shall receive less favourable treatment or consideration on the grounds of disability, sexual orientation, race, colour, religion, nationality, ethnic origin, sex or marital status, or, as such, will be disadvantaged by any conditions of employment or requirements of the Company that cannot be justified as necessary on operational grounds.

Every senior executive and member of management, and all employees, are instructed that:

1   There should be no discrimination on account of disability, race, colour, religion, ethnic minority, sex, marital status, or sexual orientation.

2   The Company will appoint, train, develop and promote on the basis of merit and ability alone.

3   All employees have personal responsibility for the practical application of the Company's Equal Opportunities Policy, which exends to the treatment of employees and customers.

4   Special responsibility for the practical application of the Company's Equal Opportunities Policy falls upon managers and supervisors involved in the recruitment, selection, promotion and training of employees.

5   The Company's grievance procedure is available to any employee who believes that he/she may have been unfairly discriminated against. The grievance should be directed through line management in the first instance. Should the issue remain unresolved the Group Personnel Department should be consulted.

6   Disciplinary action will be taken against any employee who is proven to have committed an act of unlawful discrimination. Discriminatory conduct and sexual or racial harassment may be treated as gross misconduct and will result in *summary* dismissal.

7   In the case of any doubt or concern about the application of the policy in any particular instance, any member of staff should consult the Group Personnel Department.

Figure 20.1   *A typical equal opportunities policy statement*

Recruitment and training

Recruitment and staff training are at the heart of human resource management in travel and tourism. Organisations want to find the best people to fill their vacancies, whether they come from within or outside. Training should be viewed as an investment in the most important resource of the organisation, its staff (Figure 20.2).

Later in this unit (see page 460) we will investigate the recruitment and selection process in travel and tourism. The section on motivating staff considers staff development and training in more depth (see page 494).

Figure 20.2 *Staff are the most important part of any organisation*
© Unijet Travel Limited

Employee appraisal and motivation

These two issues are covered in the final section of this unit on motivating staff (see page 483).

Remuneration

If you were to ask a group of people why they go to work, the chances are that nine out of ten of them would say 'to earn money to pay the bills'. We all need money to buy food and clothes, and to provide a roof over our heads. Although surveys taken of British people show that, by and large, most workers are not very happy in their jobs, working in the travel and tourism industry is very appealing to a great many people. They are attracted by the fact that it is very much 'a people industry', where interaction with customers and clients is an essential part of the job. Many jobs in travel and tourism sound very glamorous and involve travel, working in the open air and are, in some cases, an extension of a sport or hobby. It is little wonder that there has been such a dramatic growth in the number of travel and tourism courses on offer at colleges, universities and even in schools to prepare people, young and old, for working in this dynamic industry.

While the travel and tourism industry reflects a very positive image to those seeking employment, it does have something of an image problem when it comes to levels of pay and remuneration. Travel and tourism is generally perceived as a low wage industry, with a high proportion of unskilled and often temporary jobs. Travel and tourism is still a very new sector that is working hard to develop career structures and qualifications that will project a more professional image at the start of the new millennium. Many people who work in travel and tourism are willing, in the short term, to put up with low pay, which they consider is compensated by the travel opportunities, freedom and rapid promotion that many sectors of the industry can offer.

Measuring personal effectiveness

Whereas managers use appraisal to investigate staff performance and to agree future work objectives with their employees, individual members of staff can also monitor their own personal effectiveness by, for example, setting work and training goals, completing self-study packages and keeping abreast of industry developments. We look in greater detail at appraisal later in this unit (see page 486).

Human resource planning

Key topics in this section

- **External influences on human resource planning**
- **Internal influences on human resource planning**

External influences on human resource planning

The economic climate

The state of the economy has a great bearing on the uptake of holidays and other travel products. In simple terms, if people are in work and have a good standard of living, they will be able to afford to take a holiday, or even a number of holidays or short breaks. This is sometimes referred to as 'the feel good factor'. This extra demand for holidays influences the staffing levels of travel and tourism organisations. For example, when the economy is in a healthy state, i.e. low unemployment, low interest rates and good wage rates, demand for travel and tourism products and services will be high, meaning that organisations will need to be fully staffed in order to serve the travelling public. When the economic climate is poor, sometimes called being in recession, people will find it harder to afford holidays and, hence, staff may be laid off or have their working hours cut.

Consumer trends

Successful travel and tourism organisations are constantly monitoring consumer trends in order to be able to offer their customers the right products and services. Recent trends in the travel and tourism industry include:

- ✪ **Demand for high quality accommodation and other facilities**
- ✪ **Growth in the popularity of long-haul destinations, e.g. the Caribbean, Australia, USA, the Far East and South Africa**
- ✪ **Growth in activity and special interest holidays and breaks**
- ✪ **Increasing use of the Internet to gather information and make bookings**
- ✪ **Growth in the use of low-cost airline services, such as Ryanair, Go, Buzz and easyJet**

○ **Demand for 'all-inclusive' holidays, where all food, accommodation, drinks, sporting activities and entertainment are included in the cost of the holiday**

Organisations must use market research in order to discover, and even try to forecast, consumer trends.

Employment trends

There are currently some 1.8 million people employed in the UK travel and tourism industry. Figures from the Department for Culture, Media and Sport (DCMS) show that, since 1980, tourism-related employment has increased by over 40 per cent in the UK, whereas the total in all jobs has risen only marginally. While employment has grown in all sectors of the travel and tourism industry, the most marked increase is in restaurants and cafés where employment has more than doubled.

Browse this website

www.culture.gov.uk

The main sectors of the travel and tourism industry, and the numbers employed in March 2000, are as follows:

○ **Bars, pubs, clubs, etc.**	**459,500**
○ **Restaurants, cafés, etc.**	**419,900**
○ **Sporting activities**	**360,000**
○ **Hotels and other accommodation**	**349,600**
○ **Travel agencies, tour operators**	**113,200**
○ **Libraries, museums, etc.**	**79,100**

Between 1995 and 2000, tourism-related employment grew by 12 per cent across Britain. A breakdown of tourism employment in selected regions shows the following growth rates:

○ **South-east England**	**+ 23 per cent**
○ **London**	**+ 20 per cent**
○ **East Anglia**	**+ 20 per cent**
○ **North-west England**	**+ 10 per cent**
○ **Wales**	**+ 7 per cent**
○ **Yorkshire & Humberside**	**+ 6 per cent**

In line with many other sectors of industry in the UK, there has been a general move in recent years away from permanent contracts for workers in travel and tourism towards short-term contracts and casual working. The growth in these temporary contracts has been seen by many organisations as a cost-saving exercise in difficult economic circumstances. The wages bill is by far the biggest cost for the majority of travel and tourism organisations, and is, therefore, a prime target for cost-cutting. While temporary contracts make sense for the employer, they are not always in the best interests of employees, who may lose out in terms of job security and career progression. Temporary contracts have a specific finish date included in their terms, and are common in hotel work and any tourism employment that is seasonal. It is becoming common to find sub-contractors providing the cleaning, catering and grounds maintenance services in travel and tourism organisations in both the private and public sectors, in order to save the costs of employing permanent staff.

The state of the industry

The general health of the travel and tourism industry has a marked effect on human resource planning. When the industry is buoyant, with numbers of visitors and holidaymakers on the increase, staff numbers will need to remain high to meet customer demand for facilities and holidays. The reverse will be the case when the industry is in recession. Investment in travel and tourism also provides short-term employment for building contractors, who may be called upon to work on a variety of projects, from building hotels and new tourist attractions to landscaping and environmental enhancement.

Skills shortages

Browse this website

www.culture.gov.uk

The government is committed to raising the general skill level of the UK workforce, through training and development. The travel and tourism industry suffers from particular skills shortages, especially in customer service, languages and ICT (information and communication technology). The government's new tourism strategy *Tomorrow's Tourism* suggests ways in which these skills shortages can be overcome.

Location issues

In general, people do not like to have to travel too far to work, not only because of the extra expense of a long journey but also from the point of view of the time taken to travel to and from work every day. The location of an organisation has to be suitable not only for customers but for staff as well. Travel and tourism facilities located in towns and cities can be convenient for staff, as long as public transport services are good or on-site parking is provided. Facilities in the countryside, such as tourist attractions and country house hotels, may well need to provide transport in order to attract and retain staff.

Competition for employees

By now, you will have gathered that travel and tourism is a very competitive industry, with many private sector companies attempting to increase their share of the market. One way they do this is by attracting the best staff, sometimes by offering somebody working for a rival company a better salary or remuneration package. For senior positions, staff are sometimes 'head hunted', i.e. they are approached, usually by an agency, to see if they are considering a change of career. Organisations must offer their employees adequate pay, good conditions of employment and future career progression if they are to retain them.

Internal influences on human resources planning

Responding to consumer trends

Consumer tastes change rapidly in the travel and tourism industry. Organisations need to recruit and retain staff who can respond to changes in consumer tastes and fashions by developing new products and services. This may not always mean that a new employee will have worked previously in the travel and tourism industry. In senior positions, it is quite common to recruit new staff from other industry sectors, including retail and banking.

Staff turnover

Staff turnover is the frequency with which members of staff leave an organisation. It can be calculated as follows:

$$\frac{\text{Number of staff leaving} - \text{Unavoidable departures}}{\text{Average number employed}} \times 100$$

Using this formula, if 12 members of staff leave a travel and tourism organisation during the course of a year, and 2 more leave because their contracts come to an end (unavoidable departures), the staff turnover for the year will be:

$$12 - 2 = \frac{10}{100} \times 100 = 10 \text{ per cent}$$

Most organisations will wish to keep their staff turnover to a minimum, but not to the point where no staff leave, since this will stifle innovation and creativity. In order to improve its employee retention rate, an organisation will focus on a number of areas, including:

- ✪ **Improving its recruitment and selection process**
- ✪ **Introducing training courses for staff**
- ✪ **Improving pay and working conditions**
- ✪ **Improving the working environment for staff**

- ✪ **Improving career progression for staff**
- ✪ **Introducing job rotation and job enlargement (see page 495)**

Organisations are loathe to see an employee depart voluntarily, since they have invested heavily in their personal and professional development.

Sickness rates and absenteeism

Many of the areas discussed in the last section to improve staff retention rates may also help to reduce sickness rates and absenteeism.

Activity 20.1

Working with a colleague, discuss how you would go about reducing high staff sickness rates and absenteeism in a travel and tourism organisation.

Organisational structures, staff roles and responsibilities

Management decision making and the day-to-day operations of any travel and tourism enterprise take place within its organisational structure. All but the very smallest of organisations will need a clearly defined structure, in order to:

- ✪ **Define the lines of communication between one part of the organisation and another**
- ✪ **Identify the channels of communication between individuals working in the organisation**
- ✪ **Define the sources of authority, decision making and responsibility within the organisation**
- ✪ **Clarify job activities, relationships and responsibilities**
- ✪ **Co-ordinate the organisation's activities to help achieve its objectives**
- ✪ **Identify the pattern of control for the benefit of internal and external parties**

In small travel and tourism enterprises, the organisational structure is likely to be simpler, with matters such as the allocation of tasks, definition of responsibility and authority, and relationships between members of staff being carried out on an informal basis. Nonetheless, all travel and tourism organisations, of whatever size or type, will need some form of structure so that duplication of effort is minimised and staff efforts and interactions are co-ordinated effectively.

Types of organisational structures

Hierarchical structures

Sometimes called pyramid structures, hierarchical structures are characterised by a small number of senior decision makers at the top of the organisation who control its activities and resources. Decisions flow downwards from the top, affecting a succession of layers of employees lower down the organisation chart. Ultimate power and responsibility lie with the senior staff; conversely, the lower down the organisation chart a member of staff is located, the less influence he or she will have on the organisation as a whole. Figure 20.3 shows the organisation chart for a typical local authority leisure centre, showing the hierarchical structure.

Centralised versus decentralised

Many organisations with hierarchical structures are very centralised, with power and decision making resting with a small number of powerful

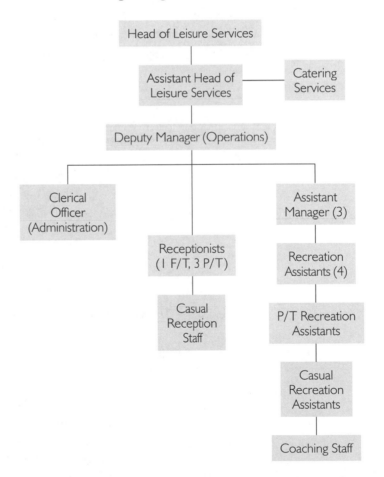

Figure 20.3 *Organisational structure of a local authority leisure centre*

individuals, below which are many tiers of management. Sometimes referred to as 'steep pyramids' (see Figure 20.4), such organisations are sometimes criticised for being too bureaucratic, with decisions having to pass through a number of channels for confirmation, thus hindering the speedy resolution of problems.

Another common criticism of a centralised structure is that senior management can seem very remote from the workforce and out of touch with their everyday concerns and problems. Advocates of a centralised organisational structure would say that it has the advantage of promoting a clear corporate image for the organisation and easier implementation of common policies across very large businesses.

The shortcomings of a centralised approach have led many travel and tourism organisations to consider an alternative strategy, namely decentralisation, where there are fewer layers of bureaucracy within the organisation, resulting in faster decision making, better communication, more senior management involvement in day-to-day activities and a positive effect on staff motivation and morale. Sometimes referred to as the 'flat pyramid', an example of this type of structure is given in Figure 20.5.

The degree of centralisation or decentralisation within an organisation will be a function of its size, the sector in which it operates, its geographical location, the adopted management style and the quality of its staff.

Figure 20.4 *The steep pyramid structure*

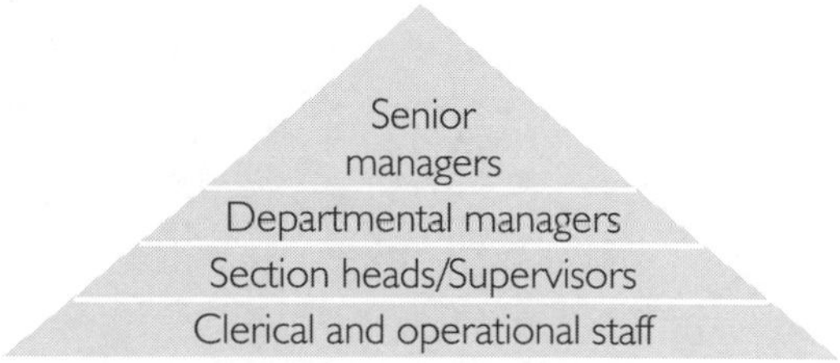

Figure 20.5 *The flat pyramid structure*

Line and staff structures

We have seen that a typical hierarchical structure within a travel and tourism organisation consists of a number of tiers, through which responsibility, power and authority are delegated. This process is known as line management, where each employee knows to whom he or she is responsible and from whom instructions should be taken.

As travel and tourism organisations become more complex, the range of activities and functions carried out increases. The line management structure may then be supplemented by specialists who provide an advisory function through all departments of the organisation. Common 'staff' functions include:

✪ **Personnel**

✪ **Marketing and external communications**

✪ **Accounting and finance**

✪ **Research and development**

✪ **Administration**

✪ **Maintenance and security**

✪ **Health and safety**

Generally speaking, a 'staff' relationship describes the liaison between other employees in the organisation who are not part of the direct line of authority.

Matrix structures

Most large organisations in the travel and tourism industry will operate a mixture of both line and 'staff' structures, commonly referred to as a matrix structure. Figure 20.6 gives a diagrammatic representation of how a part of a matrix structure operates in an outbound mass market tour operator.

The example in Figure 20.6 shows that line relationships, where the reservations manager, for example, has responsibility for activities in his or her department, can be combined with 'staff' relationships, for example personnel, to provide an integrated and co-ordinated structure. This structure can, however, present difficulties, with friction developing between line and staff managers. Another disadvantage of the matrix structure is the blurring of lines of responsibility, lack of accountability and lengthier decision-making processes.

Functional structures

Some large travel and tourism organisations choose to develop their organisational structure on the basis of the principal functions carried out by the organisation. Figure 20.7 shows this type of functional structure as found in a typical national tourist organisation.

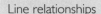
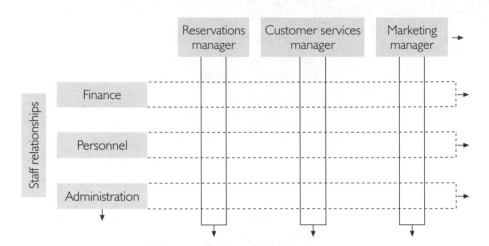

Figure 20.6   *Part of a matrix structure in a mass market tour operator*

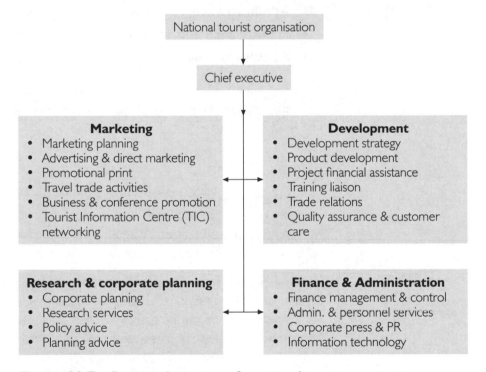

Figure 20.7   *Functional structure of a national tourist organisation*

Departmental structures

It makes sense for many travel and tourism organisations to group certain functions and activities under a particular manager and develop their organisational structure on this basis. If we take the example of a typical mass market outbound tour operator, it will have a main UK head office, regional offices and overseas offices. The UK head office will be organised on a departmental basis in order to carry out the following functions:

- **Marketing**: Staff employed in the marketing department will be responsible for planning and developing products, which will be aimed at particular segments of the market. They will focus on the selection of resorts, choice of accommodation and selection of regional UK departure airports. Typical segments of the market include:
  - Singles
  - Families
  - Couples without children
  - Disabled travellers
  - Groups
  - Business travellers
  - Youth market
  - Elderly travellers

- **Research**: A great deal of background research is undertaken to ensure that the products have the best chance of meeting their sales potential. Sources of research data include:
  - Internal sales data
  - External sales data (available from commercial sources)
  - Analysis of competitors' programmes
  - Analysis of customer comment questionnaires
  - Financial analysis

- **Contracting**: Once the structure of the programme is finalised, staff in the contracts department will negotiate with accommodation providers over the number of beds and names of accommodations required.

- **Flights**: Teams working on different programmes and products liaise with the flight or aviation department over how many seats they will need, which regional airports are to be used and whether day or night flights are required. The flight department must make optimum use of its resources.

- **Brochure production**: The brochure is the most visible part of the marketing process. Teams working in the marketing department will work with brochure production staff to finalise design, copy and photographs. A lot of brochure printing takes place outside the UK to save on costs.

- **Brochure distribution**: Sales staff will make decisions about how many brochures are required and to which travel agents they will be distributed.

- **Promotion**: Marketing staff will plan and co-ordinate a range of activities, including advertising, direct mail, sales promotion and PR (public relations).

- **Reservations**: Systems are developed by computer operations personnel and sales staff are fully briefed on the features of products included in the brochure.

- **Agency sales support**: Sales representatives will regularly visit agencies and offer product training and POS (point-of-sale) materials, such as posters and window displays.
- **Administration**: The administration department is responsible for producing invoices, receiving payments and issuing tickets and other documentation.
- **Customer services**: This department will be responsible for handling complaints and queries from agents and members of the public. They will try to ensure that all matters are dealt with quickly and efficiently in order to retain goodwill.

The overseas office of a major tour operator will be responsible for:

- **Feeding back to head office any formal or informal research findings**
- **Organising transfers to and from the accommodation and airport**
- **Arranging and selling excursions and other 'extras' such as car hire**
- **Finalising contracts with hoteliers and transport operators**
- **The well-being, training and deployment of representatives**
- **The handling of complaints and emergencies**

Activity 20.2

Working in a small team, try to find out the organisational structure of a local travel and tourism organisation. Present your findings as an organisation chart.

Recruitment and selection

Key topics in this section

- **Introduction**
- **Reasons for recruitment and selection**
- **The recruitment and selection process**

Introduction

Good employees are the backbone of any organisation in the service sector, and particularly in travel and tourism where they are an integral part of the 'experience' that the customers are buying. But how can you be sure of getting the best people for the job? A thorough approach to recruitment and selection, paying attention to detail and allowing enough time to see the process through to its completion, will pay dividends to the organisation, and in particular will go a long way towards reducing the high levels of staff turnover that are found in some sectors of travel and tourism. Management time spent on recruitment should be regarded as a wise investment for the future; all too often, more time and attention is given to choosing a new computer system than to selecting the most important resource that the organisation has – its staff!

Reasons for recruitment and selection

In the dynamic world of travel and tourism nothing stays the same for long, including the staffing of an organisation. Companies have to recruit new staff from time to time for a number of reasons, including:

- ✪ **Changing market and financial pressures** – e.g. a company that decides to diversify into a different sector of the travel and tourism industry will need to review its staffing and make adjustments as necessary. An organisation that is experiencing poor sales revenues may need to shed staff to cut costs.
- ✪ **Business start-up or growth** – e.g. a completely new travel and tourism enterprise will need to recruit staff to run the operation, in the same way that an existing company that is expanding its operation will need to increase staff numbers.
- ✪ **Changing job roles** – changes in an organisation's operations, perhaps from having a head office based sales force to a travelling sales force, will trigger changes to the job roles of existing staff.

✪ **Staff promotion, resignation or retirement** – all organisations will need to recruit internally and externally to compensate for these sorts of staff movements.

Travel and tourism enterprises need to remain flexible and competitive. In terms of their human resources, they do this by employing a combination of permanent, fixed-term, full-time, part-time, casual, contract and seasonal workers. Each of these modes of employment offers different conditions of service, which can affect a member of staff's working methods and loyalty to an organisation.

The recruitment and selection process

Factors such as the fall in the number of young people available for work, the number of employees who no longer see a post as 'a job for life' and the general skill shortages within the UK workforce mean that the task of selecting staff can no longer be left to chance. While there will always be mistakes made when it comes to employing people, a systematic and objective approach to the process of recruitment and selection is likely to achieve the objective of getting the best person for the job.

The recruitment and selection process is shown in diagrammatic form in Figure 20.8.

Once the need for a new member of staff has been identified, Figure 20.8 shows that the recruitment and selection process consists of seven inter-related stages, which we will now look at in more detail.

Job analysis

Whenever a vacancy arises, whether it is to replace an employee who is leaving or if it is a new post, there needs to be a thorough analysis of what the job entails. If it is an existing post to be filled, simply finding a set of old job details and reproducing them without considering if they are still relevant is not good enough. The dynamic nature of the travel and tourism industry is such that an approach of this sort will not achieve the desired objective of filling the post with the best candidate. Information to be included in the job analysis can be obtained from the existing postholder, previous records, other members of staff, competitor organisations and by direct observation of members of staff.

Job description

Having completed a job analysis a job description can then be compiled, detailing the content of the job and areas of responsibility. A typical job description is likely to include:

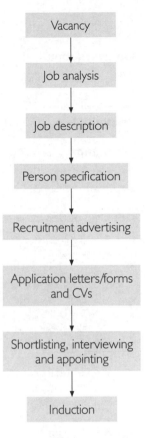

Figure 20.8 *The recruitment and selection process in travel and tourism*

- ✪ **Title of the post** – including grade, post number, department/section, location, etc.

- ✪ **Summary of the job** – outlining the key objectives of the post

- ✪ **Responsibilities** – clarifying the position in the organisational structure, detailing to whom responsible and for whom responsible

- ✪ **Detailed duties** – a list of all the relevant duties attached to the post

- ✪ **Conditions of employment** – general information on salary/wage, holiday entitlement, hours of work, pension arrangements, welfare and social facilities, trade union membership arrangements, training, etc.

- ✪ **Date it was written** – this is important because duties and responsibilities may change over time

Figure 20.9 shows an example of a typical job description for a travel clerk in a city centre branch of a travel agency chain.

The job description will be sent out to potential candidates together with an application form and further details as appropriate.

Sundown Travel PLC

Job description

Title of post: Travel clerk
Post no: TC/9/00
Location: Anytown branch
Responsible to: Branch manager

Job summary

To work with the branch manager and other staff to provide previous and current clients with a first-class standard of service in meeting all their travel needs.

Detailed duties

1   Advising clients on the details and availability of a range of holidays and other travel products.
2   Liaising regularly with travel principals in the process of selling holiday products.
3   Issuing tickets and other travel documentation.
4   Maintaining brochure stocks, window displays and other promotional activities.
5   Carrying out the range of duties by telephone, computer, VDU, direct contact, fax, telex, courier and post.
6   Handling cash and completing non-cash transactions.
7   Keeping up to date with the latest holiday and travel products through training and personal development.
8   Helping to maintain a safe, friendly and welcoming environment for staff, customers and other callers.
9   Other duties as detailed by the branch manager or other nominated senior staff member.

Special conditions

- Hours of work will be from 9 am to 5.30 pm, five days per week.
- Saturday working is compulsory, with a weekday off in lieu.
- Staff are expected to work overtime by arrangement at busy periods of the year.
- Some evening work will be necessary.
- Salary is in accordance with the company's standard pay scales.
- The post carries a holiday entitlement of 20 days per year.
- On- and off-the-job training will be provided for the postholder.

Dated: 1 October 2000

Figure 20.9   *Job description for the post of a travel clerk*

Person specification

At the same time as they are compiling a job description, many organisations will also draw up a person specification, sometimes called a job specification, which provides a blueprint of the 'ideal' person for the job in terms of skills, character, previous experience and qualifications. Figure 20.10 gives an example of a person specification for an Assistant Events Officer post with a voluntary sector organisation.

As well as indicating the type of experience and skills that the successful candidate will need to demonstrate, the example of the person specification

JOB KNOWLEDGE, SKILLS & EXPERIENCE	AF	I	RP	WE
Experience required				
Working as a team member with groups of people either in the voluntary or commercial sector	x	x		
Planning, organising and managing projects	x	x		
Skills required				
Good communication skills including listening skills and the ability to give accurate information and clear instructions	x	x	x	x
The ability to write letters and reports	x	x		x
Interpersonal skills including the sensitivity to respond to different people and situations appropriately and the ability to deal with the public in a tactful and diplomatic manner	x	x	x	x
Good organisational and planning skills including the ability to prioritise and to manage his/her own time	x	x		
Ability to work under pressure and to meet deadlines	x	x		
Sound administrative skills and attention to detail including the ability to set up and maintain accurate filing systems	x	x		
Willingness to undertake routine and mundane tasks		x		
Good personal presentation		x		

KEY
AF Assessed from Application Form
I   Assessed at Interview
RP Assessed by Role Play
WE Assessed by Writing Exercise

Figure 20.10 *Person specification for the post of Assistant Events Officer*

shown in Figure 20.10 also shows how the extent to which the candidate meets the criteria will be assessed. In this case, the criteria will be assessed from the application form, at interview, by role play and by means of a writing exercise. Some person specifications divide the qualities, experience and skills sought into those that are 'essential' and those that are 'desirable'. When drawing up a person specification, organisations must be careful not to introduce bias either in favour of, or against, one particular section of society. Discrimination on the grounds of sex, race and disability is covered by legislation under the Sex Discrimination Act, the Race Relations Act and the Disability Discrimination Act respectively, each of which is investigated in greater detail later in this unit.

Recruitment advertising

Once the job specification and person specification have been finalised, the task of finding suitable applicants can begin in earnest. The task may focus solely on internal candidates or may be opened up to outside applicants. The process can be carried out entirely in-house or may be partly or wholly delegated to an outside recruitment agency. In travel and tourism, agencies tend to be used either for very senior appointments, e.g. Director of Marketing or Head of Flight Operations, or in situations where jobs are becoming hard to fill, notably some posts in the hotel and accommodation sector. Recruitment agencies specialising in travel and tourism advertise their services in the relevant trade newspapers and journals. Although advertising is often used to seek out suitable applicants, there are other recruitment channels, as the following list demonstrates:

✪ **Advertisements in local, regional and national newspapers, e.g. the *Guardian* has appointments covering the arts, marketing, tourism, environment and countryside**

✪ **Advertisements in trade journals and magazines, e.g. *Leisure Management, Leisure Opportunities, Attractions Management, Travel Weekly, Travel Trade Gazette, Caterer and Hotelkeeper*, to name but a few**

✪ **Employment agencies**

✪ **Job centres**

✪ **Links with universities, colleges and schools**

✪ **A 'trawl' through any speculative applications held on file**

✪ **Advertisements in internal staff newsletters or equivalent**

✪ **Vacancies circulated by professional bodies, e.g. ILAM (Institute of Leisure and Amenity Management), Tourism Society, Institute of Travel and Tourism, etc.**

Application letters/forms and CVs

It is common for commercial travel and tourism organisations to ask for a CV (curriculum vitae) and covering letter from prospective candidates, rather than sending out a job application form. However, the public and voluntary sectors of the industry generally prefer completed application forms to CVs. Some organisations will immediately reject an application if the applicant has sent a CV in place of a completed application form.

Letters of application

Whether you are completing an application form or sending a CV, you will need to include a covering letter. A typical letter would include the following information:

✪ **Why you are applying for the job**

✪ **What contribution you could make to the organisation**

- Achieved
- Planned
- Created
- Established
- Developed
- Introduced
- Completed
- Set up
- Finished
- Reorganised

Figure 20.11 *'Action' words to use in application letters, CVs and application forms*

✪ **Your skills and achievements you consider to be relevant to the post**

✪ **The capabilities you have developed through education, training and leisure activities**

In writing your letter you should be positive at all times, including the kind of 'action' words shown in Figure 20.11, which can also be included in your CV and any application forms you complete.

It goes without saying that your letter should not include spelling mistakes or grammatical errors! It should be to the point, look uncluttered and be presented in a professional manner. Unless requested to apply in your own handwriting, it is usual to have your letter typed or word processed.

Application forms

Some employers prefer candidates to complete an application form for a job, rather than accepting CVs. Figure 20.12 gives an example of a typical application form for employment.

You will see that the form includes much of the same information that is found in a CV.

Activity 20.3

Make a copy of the application form in Figure 20.12 and complete it as if you were applying for your first job after leaving school or college. You can choose the particular post that you are applying for, but make sure it is at the appropriate level for your skills and experience.

CVs

A curriculum vitae (CV) is a structured, written statement of a person's career history that has one simple aim, namely to get you a job interview! A CV can

Application for Employment

Strictly Confidential

Position applied for _____

Date free to take up appointment _____

Personal details

Surname _____ First name(s) _____

Mr/Mrs/Miss/Ms _____ Age _____ Date of birth _____

Nationality _____ Marital status _____

Telephone (home) _____ (work) _____

Do you own a car? _____ Do you have a current driving licence? _____

Education

School, college, university	From	To	Qualifications obtained
_____	_____	_____	_____
_____	_____	_____	_____
_____	_____	_____	_____

Present and past employment

Name and address of employer	From	To	Job titles and duties
_____	_____	_____	_____
_____	_____	_____	_____
_____	_____	_____	_____

Explain why you have applied for this job (continue on separate sheet if necessary)

References

Please provide contact details for two referees

1 Name _____   2 Name _____

  Address _____   Address _____

  _____   _____

  _____ Tel _____   _____ Tel _____

  Relationship to you _____   Relationship to you _____

Signed _____ Date _____

Figure 20.12 *Application form for employment*

be used in place of a completed application form when applying for a specific job or can be sent speculatively to employers to persuade them to invite you for interview.

The precise format you choose for your CV is up to you. Remember that your CV is a reflection of you. The CV is more than just a 'selling' document; it must be a 'marketing' document, i.e. one that matches your skills and experience to the needs of the employer. Whatever format you choose,

- Name
- Address
- Telephone number
- Age
- Date of birth
- Nationality
- Education to date
- Academic and vocational qualifications
- Employment history (most recent first)
- Skills
- Notable achievements
- Interests
- Names and addresses of referees

Figure 20.13 *Minimum information that should be included in a CV*

whether it is a CV that focuses on your skills and achievements or one that emphasises your academic and employment credentials, there is certain basic information that must be included (see Figure 20.13).

It is unlikely that you will get the CV right at the first attempt and you may need several drafts. Writing it on a computer will help with this, since you can make and save alterations as necessary. Remember also that your CV is dynamic; it needs updating at regular intervals throughout your personal and professional development to reflect new skills acquired, qualifications gained, etc.

When you are happy with your CV, you may wish to review it by answering the following questions:

✪ **Does it look good? Is it well laid out, with a professional appearance?**

✪ **Will the first half-page immediately gain the reader's interest?**

✪ **Does it include all your vital selling points?**

✪ **Are the benefits of your achievements noted?**

✪ **Are there any discussion openers for interviews?**

✪ **If it is more than two pages, will the reader's effort be rewarded?**

✪ **Is the contact information clear?**

It may be sensible at this stage to show your CV to a friend or colleague to see if they agree that it does you justice.

Activity 20.4

Based on the information given in Figure 20.13, write your own CV using a word processing package. Write a covering letter in your own handwriting that you could include when sending your CV to a variety of travel and tourism employers looking for a job.

Shortlisting, interviewing and appointing

If the job description and person specification have been carefully prepared, and any advertisements, if used, are written in a clear and precise manner, the organisation is likely to keep the number of unsuitable applications to a minimum. The initial sift of application forms, letters or CVs will concentrate on matching the candidates' qualifications, experience and skills to the previously prepared person specification. This process will end with the drawing up of a shortlist of suitable candidates who will be invited to take part in the next stage of the recruitment process. This will usually take the form of an interview, either one-to-one or in front of a panel, at which the candidate will be given the opportunity of expanding on his or her written application and will be able to learn a little more about the people and the organisation that he or she is hoping to work for. The candidate will also be asked questions during the interview and may be asked to carry out tasks, such as operating a computer or using a telephone. Some organisations use other selection methods, including written tests and personality questionnaires.

Interviewing

Although often criticised for being too subjective, the interview is usually the central component of the selection process for any job in travel and tourism. It has two basic aims:

- **To give the organisation the opportunity to meet candidates face-to-face and find out more detail about the applicants and their achievements to date**
- **To give the candidates the chance to formulate their assessment of what the job entails and the people that they will be working for and with**

Much of the criticism levelled at interviewing as a way of selecting staff is that it is by its very nature personal and, therefore, open to bias on the part of those carrying it out. In order to make the interview as objective as possible, it needs to be carefully planned in advance, with each candidate being asked exactly the same set of questions. In this way, candidates' responses can be more accurately compared and evaluated. There are a number of 'golden rules' in interviewing, including:

- ✪ **Draw up an agreed list of questions in advance of the interview.**
- ✪ **Take brief notes during the interview, as it is very easy to mistake one candidate for another, particularly if several are being interviewed on the same day.**
- ✪ **Invite the interviewees to take notes if they wish.**
- ✪ **Get the interviewee to expand on the information contained in the application form or CV.**
- ✪ **Be alert to the interviewees' strengths and weaknesses.**
- ✪ **Ask open questions which invite an answer other than 'yes' or 'no'.**
- ✪ **Ask for information on future career plans. A question often used at interview is 'where do you see yourself in x years' time?'**
- ✪ **Give applicants plenty of opportunity to reveal all relevant information and ask any questions.**
- ✪ **Avoid asking personal questions.**

There are occasions when, after having carried out the painstaking task of interviewing several candidates, the interview panel does not consider that any of the applicants is suitable for the job. This should not necessarily be seen as a failure of the selection process, but rather the fact that the process has worked well, even though no suitable candidate has been found. On these occasions, the organisation may decide to re-interview a selection of candidates or start the whole process again by seeking new applications.

Activity 20.5

Working with a partner, conduct a mock interview for the post of a marketing assistant in a small company specialising in organising walking holidays in Scotland. One of you should play the role of the interviewer (the managing director of the company) and the other the interviewee. After the interview, swap roles. Keep notes of how each 'interviewee' performed and compile a list of positive and negative points for future reference.

Appointment

If the interviewer or interview panel are sure that a suitable person has been found, a formal written offer of appointment can be made, subject to satisfactory references and possibly a medical examination. The successful candidate will be invited to reply in writing that he or she accepts the offer of the job. Once this letter of acceptance is received, those candidates who were unsuccessful should be informed of the decision as a matter of courtesy and to maintain the organisation's professional image.

Induction

It is vital to maintain the momentum of the recruitment process by providing the successful candidate with a structured induction to the organisation. An induction programme should be designed to help new members of staff familiarise themselves with their new environment, to settle easily into their new jobs and to establish good working relationships with other members of staff. Induction is particularly important in those sectors of the travel and tourism industry which have a higher than average staff turnover, since it can help to build relationships over the crucial first few months of a new appointment.

A comprehensive induction programme should include the following details:

- **Brief information on the scope and importance of the travel and tourism industry**
- **The structure, aims and philosophy of the organisation**
- **The main features of the job with an indication of lines of responsibility**
- **The principal conditions of employment**
- **An introduction to work colleagues**
- **A tour of the facilities**
- **Rules on dress, personal appearance, eating, drinking, smoking, etc.**
- **Health, safety and security procedures**
- **Staff representation, including trade union membership and trade associations**
- **Social and welfare facilities**
- **Training and personal development opportunities**

Some organisations identify an existing member of staff to help the new person to settle into their new surroundings, a process known as mentoring. The mentor plays an important role in the induction process, which, if planned well and carried out with enthusiasm, will give the new employee an early opportunity of becoming an effective and valued member of the team.

Employment issues

Key topics in this section

- **Race, sex and disability discrimination**
- **Equal pay**
- **Minimum wage and maximum working hours**
- **Contracts of employment**
- **Hours of work and annual leave**
- **Disciplinary and grievance procedures**
- **Redundancy and dismissal**
- **Health and safety of employees**
- **Maternity, paternity and sickness benefits**

Race, sex and disability discrimination

Legislation to protect individuals from discrimination on the grounds of race, gender and disability is contained in the following Acts:

- ✪ **Race Relations Act 1976**
- ✪ **Sex Discrimination Act 1986**
- ✪ **Disability Discrimination Act 1995**

We will now look at each of these laws in more detail.

Race Relations Act 1976

Britain is a multi-cultural and multi-ethnic society where people of all races live and work together and have the right to use their leisure time as they choose. When it comes to employing staff, the Race Relations Act 1976 states that it is illegal to discriminate against anybody on the grounds of race by treating them less favourably in areas such as recruitment, training and promotion. Any employer who does so is guilty of direct discrimination. An example of a breach of the Act involving direct racial discrimination would be an advertisement for the post of a tourist information centre manager which stated that the post was 'considered unsuitable for those of African descent'. Indirect discrimination is also unlawful under the Race Relations Act, and is when a condition is imposed on all staff, but is clearly more difficult for certain staff to comply with, on account of their race or creed. If a visitor attraction, for example, made it a condition of appointment that all staff must work on a Sunday, but an employee of a particular creed was unable to fulfil this requirement on religious grounds, he or she may be able to claim indirect racial discrimination by the employer.

Sex Discrimination Act 1986

The Sex Discrimination Act (SDA) was introduced in 1975 to outlaw discrimination on the grounds of whether a person is male or female. The SDA applies to both males and females, and makes sex discrimination unlawful in:

- ✪ **Employment**
- ✪ **Vocational training**
- ✪ **Education**
- ✪ **The provision of goods, facilities and services**
- ✪ **Housing**

Employers must not discriminate on the basis of a person's gender by treating them less favourably when it comes to recruitment, training and promotion. The distinction between direct and indirect discrimination also applies to sex discrimination. An example of direct discrimination would be to advertise for an assistant in a local museum and state that it was only suitable for female applicants. Indirect discrimination on the grounds of sex would include an airline setting an unnecessary minimum height requirement of 1.8 metres for the post of steward or stewardess; clearly such a requirement would favour male applicants and discriminate against females who wished to apply.

There are certain circumstances when discrimination on the grounds of race or sex is allowable under the law, if employers can show that there is a genuine occupational qualification that demands that the applicant must be of a particular sex or race. There are many occasions in travel and tourism when these exceptions need to be used, including:

- ✪ **Where a job involves personal contact with one sex or another and may lead to embarrassing or compromising situations, e.g. an advertisement for an attendant to work in the male changing room at a leisure centre could legally ask for male applicants only**
- ✪ **Where staff of a particular race are needed to provide authenticity, e.g. an Indian craft shop set within a theme park may wish to recruit only Indian workers to provide an authentic atmosphere**

- ✪ **Where an actress or entertainer is playing the part of a woman, for example, and the essential nature of the job would be materially different if it was carried out by a man**

Disability Discrimination Act 1995

The Disability Discrimination Act 1995 (DDA) introduces, over a period of time, new laws and measures aimed at ending the discrimination faced by many people with disabilities. It gives disabled people new rights in:

- ✪ **Employment**
- ✪ **Access to goods, facilities and services**
- ✪ **The management, buying or renting of property**

The Act defines 'disability' as:

> A physical or mental impairment which has a substantial and long-term adverse effect on a person's ability to carry out normal day-to-day activities.

In April 2000 the Disability Rights Commission was set up with the following duties:

- ✪ **To work towards the elimination of discrimination against disabled people**
- ✪ **To promote the equalisation of opportunities for disabled people**
- ✪ **To encourage good practice in the treatment of disabled people**
- ✪ **To keep under review the working of the Disability Discrimination Act 1995**

The Act relates to all areas of employment, including recruitment, terms and conditions of service, arrangements made for people who become disabled (or who have a disability which worsens), pensions, dismissal and all aspects of promotion, transfer, training or receipt of other employment benefits.

The following fall outside the scope of the DDA:

- ✪ **Employers with fewer than 15 (full- or part-time) employees**
- ✪ **Prison officers, fire fighters, members of a police force**
- ✪ **Employees who work wholly or mainly outside Great Britain**
- ✪ **Members of the armed forces**
- ✪ **People who work on board ships, aircraft and hovercraft**

Browse this website

www.disability.
gov.uk

Although they fall outside the scope of the Act, businesses employing fewer than 15 people may wish, as good practice, to ensure that their present employment arrangements do not discriminate against staff with disabilities.

Equal pay

The Equal Pay Act was introduced in 1970 to abolish discrimination between men and women in pay and other terms of their contracts of employment. It was amended in 1983 to give all workers the right to equal pay for work of equal value, when:

- ✪ **The work being carried out by both male and female employees is the same or broadly similar; the technical term for this is 'like work'. A female hotel receptionist should be paid the same as a male colleague, for example.**
- ✪ **The work of employees undertaking different jobs is of 'equal value'; for example, a hostess employed by an inter-city coach company may argue that her job is of equal value to an airline stewardess and she should, therefore, receive similar pay.**
- ✪ **A job evaluation study (JES) has been carried out and two jobs have been rated as 'equivalent' in terms of the demands made under various headings, including skills, decision making, effort, etc.**

Employees who feel that they should be receiving equal pay can apply to an industrial tribunal at any time during their employment, or up to six months after leaving.

Minimum wage

The National Minimum Wage Act 1998 provides powers to implement a statutory minimum wage. It became law throughout the UK on 1 April 1999, when the rates were as follows:

- ✪ **A general minimum wage level of £3.60/hour (this rose to £3.70/hour on 1 October 2000)**
- ✪ **A minimum level of £3.20/hour for 18–21-year-olds**
- ✪ **A minimum level of £3.20/hour for workers of 22 years and over for six months after starting a new job with a new employer, if they are receiving accredited training**

The national minimum wage does not apply to:

- ✪ **The genuinely self-employed**
- ✪ **Volunteers**
- ✪ **People less than 18 years of age**
- ✪ **Apprentices over 18 but under 26 in the first 12 months of their apprenticeships**

- **Members of the armed forces**
- **People working and living as part of a family, e.g. au pairs**

Maximum working hours

The Working Time Regulations came into force in the UK on 1 October 1998. The Regulations implement the European Working Time Directive and parts of the Young Workers Directive that relate to the working time of adolescent workers (workers above the minimum school leaving age but under 18). The basic rights and protections that the Regulations provide are:

- **A limit of an average of 48 hours per week that a worker can be required to work (although workers can choose to work more if they want)**
- **A limit of an average of 8 hours work in 24 that night workers can be required to work**
- **A right for night workers to receive free health assessments**
- **A right to 11 hours rest per day**
- **A right to a day off each week**
- **A right to an in-work rest break if the working day is longer than six hours**
- **A right to four weeks' paid leave each year**

When the Working Time Directive was adopted in 1993, a number of sectors were excluded from its scope because the Commission and member states agreed that these sectors would require their own special rules. These excluded sectors were road, rail, air, inland waterway and lake transport, sea fishing, 'other work at sea' (essentially offshore oil and gas exploitation) and the activities of doctors in training. Those working in the excluded sectors are therefore not currently covered by the existing UK Working Time Regulations which came into force in October 1998, although discussions have taken place about special conditions for these excluded sectors.

Contracts of employment

An employment contract is a written document that sets out the terms and conditions under which a member of staff is expected to work. Most travel and tourism organisations will want to give every member of staff a written statement that gives details about the job, rates of pay, holiday entitlement, etc. If such points are not clarified in writing, there may be disputes at a later date about what was agreed at the time when the employee started the job.

By law, all employers are required to give employees, except those taken on for less than a month, a written statement of their main terms and conditions of employment within two months of taking on the employee (or if at an earlier stage the employee is required to work abroad for a period of more than one month, the statement must be given before he or she leaves). Particulars of the following must be included in the statement:

✪ **The names of the employer and the employee**

✪ **Job title or brief job description**

✪ **The date when the employment (and, if different, the period of continuous employment) began**

✪ **Wages or salary and the intervals at which they are to be paid**

✪ **Hours of work**

✪ **Holiday entitlement**

✪ **Entitlement to sick leave and sick pay**

✪ **Pensions entitlement**

✪ **Entitlement of the employer and the employee to notice of termination of employment**

✪ **Where it is not permanent, the period for which the employment is expected to continue, or, if it is for a fixed term, the date when it is to end**

✪ **Place of work**

✪ **Existence of any collective agreements that directly affect the employee's terms and conditions of employment**

The written statement must also include a note giving details of the employer's disciplinary rules and grievance procedures, although employers with fewer than 20 employees need give only the contact name for raising a grievance.

Activity 20.6

Working as a member of a small team, write a draft contract of employment for an assistant manager in either a tourist information centre or a local travel agency.

Hours of work and annual leave

These topics are discussed in detail in the section on maximum working hours on page 475.

Disciplinary and grievance procedures

Most employees in travel and tourism who are given clear guidance as to the standards of work and conduct expected of them will be motivated and professional enough to exercise effective self-discipline and work well with a minimum of supervision. However, it is sometimes necessary for management to take action to deal with those employees whose behaviour, work performance or absenteeism is giving cause for concern. Minor problems of this nature are best dealt with informally by the employee's immediate supervisor in the first instance, but for serious or more persistent problems, it will be necessary to implement the organisation's formal disciplinary procedures.

In any travel and tourism organisation, it is essential for the management to follow the disciplinary procedures to the letter, so as to ensure fairness for the employee and to reduce the likelihood of a claim for unfair dismissal being brought at an industrial tribunal. Such claims can be very costly, both in terms of staff time devoted to contesting the case and any financial settlement that may arise. Unless the problem is one of gross misconduct, which could include such matters as being drunk on duty, theft or fraud, assault, causing damage to company property or the misuse of equipment, dismissal should be regarded as the final stage of the procedure and is only considered after formal warnings and other sanctions have failed to solve the problem. Other sanctions available to management include demotion, suspension without pay and loss of promotion opportunities.

In order to be fair to all concerned, the disciplinary procedure must follow the rules of natural justice, which state that:

○ **Individuals must be told of the complaints against them**
○ **They must be given the opportunity to state their case**
○ **They must be given the right to be accompanied by a representative of their choice**
○ **Nobody should act as 'prosecutor' and 'judge' in the same case**
○ **They must be told clearly of the outcome of the proceedings**
○ **They must be given the opportunity to appeal against any decision**

It is essential that written records are kept at all stages of the disciplinary procedure. In cases of inadequate performance, the employee must be given the chance to improve and must be offered suitable training and possibly the chance to be transferred to a less demanding job. In arriving at any decision following a disciplinary hearing, it is necessary to take into account factors such as age, length of service, previous employment record and domestic circumstances.

Redundancy

Redundancy is defined as dismissal of an employee wholly or partly due to:

1   **The fact that an employer has ceased, or intends to cease, to carry on the business for the purposes of which the employee was employed, or has ceased, or intends to cease, to carry on that business in the place where the employee was so employed.**

2   **The fact that the requirements of that business for employees to carry out work of a particular kind, or to carry out work of a particular kind in the place where they were so employed, have ceased or diminished, or are expected to cease or diminish.**

In simple terms, redundancy is dismissal caused by an employer's need to cut jobs, move the place of work or close down completely. Redundancy can be a very painful process for both employers and employees. For the employers, it can be seen as the ultimate sign of failure, after what is often a long struggle for survival. For employees, it means the loss of a job that they may have held for many years, with all the financial and emotional repercussions that this entails. In travel and tourism, one of the biggest collapses in recent times was that of the International Leisure Group (ILG), best known for its Intasun brand, with the loss of many thousands of jobs. Less publicised, although no less tragic, are the daily redundancies of employees working in all sectors of travel and tourism, as their employers cut back on staffing levels in order to remain competitive.

Redundancy payments

Any employee who is made redundant cannot accuse an employer of unfair dismissal but may be entitled to compensation under the State Redundancy Payments Scheme. Claims for redundancy payments can only be made by employees over the age of 18 and under 65 years of age. The number of hours worked for the employer is also important in deciding whether an employee is eligible; those who work less than eight hours per week are not entitled to any redundancy payments, those who work between eight and 16 hours per week cannot claim unless they have worked for more than five years, and employees who work more than 16 hours each week can claim redundancy payments as long as they have worked for the same employer for two years or more. The amount that any individual receives will depend on the number of years' service for the employer and how much he or she earns.

As well as access to redundancy funds, some employees who face redundancy have the right to be given time off to look for another job without loss of pay.

Dismissal

An employer can dismiss an employee at any time, although a period of notice must normally be given. Employees have the right not to be unfairly dismissed, but a dismissal will be lawful provided that it is for a fair reason and that the employer has acted reasonably in all the circumstances. Dismissal is defined as:

- **The termination of an employee's contract by his or her employer either with or without notice**
- **Where a fixed term contract comes to an end and is not renewed**
- **Where the employee is entitled to terminate the contract without notice by reason of the employer's conduct (constructive dismissal)**

There are occasions in all industries, and travel and tourism is no exception, when the dismissal of an employee can cause problems that may end up being resolved by way of an arbitration scheme or an industrial tribunal. There are provisions in the Employment Protection Act 1978, as amended by the Employment Act 1989, concerning the protection of employees who feel that they have been unfairly dismissed. Under present law, not all workers can claim for unfair dismissal. Those excluded are:

- **Employees over the age of 65, or the normal retirement age of their organisation if this is lower**
- **Those who work for less than 16 hours per week**
- **Staff who have been with their employer for less than two years**

What constitutes fair and unfair dismissal?

A dismissal is fair if the following two conditions are both met. Firstly, the main reason for the dismissal must be one of the following:

- **The employee is unable or unqualified to do the job**
- **The employee's conduct is unacceptable, e.g. a poor attendance record**

- ✪ **A legal requirement prevents the employee from continuing to do the job, e.g. a coach driver who is disqualified from driving for 12 months following a prosecution for dangerous driving**
- ✪ **Redundancy**
- ✪ **Some other substantial reason**

Secondly, the employer must act reasonably in deciding to dismiss the employee rather than, for example, taking another form of disciplinary action. What is reasonable will depend on the circumstances and on the size and resources of the employer's business.

There are a number of reasons for which it is automatically unfair to dismiss an employee, including:

- ✪ **Being a trade union member**
- ✪ **Being pregnant or taking maternity leave**
- ✪ **Taking, or seeking to take, parental leave**
- ✪ **Taking, or seeking to take, time off for dependants**
- ✪ **Refusing (in certain circumstances) to do shop or betting work on a Sunday**

The most common reasons for employees to be dismissed include misconduct, a lack of capability to do the job properly, absenteeism, redundancy, ill health or a legal restriction which makes continued employment impossible. Any reason that does not fall into one of these categories will be regarded as 'unfair' by an industrial tribunal. While there are many instances when the dismissal of a member of staff by an employer is wholly justified, for example when a hotel porter continues to arrive at work under the influence of drink after repeated written and verbal warnings, there are occasions when employees are dismissed unfairly. Even if an employer is sure that the reason for dismissal is fair, there is a further requirement that states that the dismissal must be reasonable, must take the individual's circumstances into account and that the manner of dismissal must be fair, e.g. warnings must be given to the employee before the decision to dismiss him or her is made.

Any employee who is eligible to claim unfair dismissal must do so by complaining to an industrial tribunal within three months of the date the employment was terminated. If the tribunal is satisfied that the dismissal was indeed unfair, it can propose three possible remedies:

1   **The employee can have his or her job back**
2   **The employee can take another job with the same organisation, but not necessarily on the same terms and conditions**
3   **The employee can choose compensation made up of a basic amount that is calculated in the same way as a redundancy payment, plus an amount to cover loss of earnings**

Health and safety

The basis of British health and safety law is the Health and Safety at Work, etc. Act 1974. The Act sets out the general duties that employers have towards employees and members of the public, and employees have to themselves and to each other. These duties are qualified in the Act by the principle of 'so far as is reasonably practicable'. In other words, the degree of risk in a particular job or workplace needs to be balanced against the time, trouble, cost and physical difficulty of taking measures to avoid or reduce the risk. What the law requires is what good management and common sense would lead employers to do anyway, i.e. to look at what the risks are and take sensible measures to tackle them.

The Management of Health and Safety at Work Regulations 1992 make more explicit what employers are required to do to manage health and safety under the Health and Safety at Work Act. Under the Regulations, the main requirement on employers is to carry out a risk assessment. Employers with five or more employees need to record the significant findings of the risk assessment.

Maternity, paternity and sickness benefits

It is unlawful to dismiss a pregnant employee, or single her out for redundancy, for reasons connected with her pregnancy or maternity. In addition, every pregnant employee who has given her employer proper notification of her pregnancy is entitled to:

- ✪ **Reasonable time off with pay for antenatal care**
- ✪ **18 weeks' ordinary maternity leave**
- ✪ **All her normal terms and conditions of employment, except wages or salary, while she is on ordinary maternity leave**
- ✪ **Suspension from work on full pay if there is an unavoidable health and safety risk to her as a new or expectant mother and suitable alternative work cannot be found**

In addition, pregnant employees who have completed one year's service or more with their employer, by the beginning of the 11th week before the week the baby is due, are entitled to a period of additional maternity absence. Many pregnant women will also be entitled to Statutory Maternity Pay.

The Employment Relations Act 1999 gives a new right to parental leave for all employees who have completed one year's service with their employer. It allows parents with children born or adopted on or after 15 December 1999 to take parental leave to care for that child. The right applies to mothers and fathers and to a person who has obtained formal parental responsibility for a child under the Children Act or its Scottish equivalent. Key elements of parental leave which apply in every case are as follows:

- **13 weeks' parental leave for each child**
- **The employee's rights to take the leave until the child's fifth birthday or until five years have elapsed following placement in the case of adoption**
- **Parents of disabled children are able to use their leave over a longer time period, up to the child's 18th birthday**
- **The employee remains employed while on parental leave**

At the end of parental leave an employee is guaranteed the right to return to the same job as before, or, if that is not practicable, a similar job which has the same or better status, terms and conditions as the old job; where the leave taken is for a period of four weeks or less, the employee is entitled to go back to the same job.

Motivating staff

Key topics in this section

- **Introduction**
- **Management style**
- **Staff appraisal**
- **Staff development and training**
- **Job rotation and job enlargement**
- **Team working**
- **Remuneration, performance-related pay and other incentives**
- **The working environment**

Introduction

We have seen in earlier units that many travel and tourism employees are unskilled, sometimes low-paid and often called upon to work unsocial hours. It is a fact of life that people employed in travel and tourism are often asked to work at the very time when most people are at leisure. Add to these factors the stress and commitment that high levels of direct contact with customers generate and we can begin to see the challenges that face managers when it comes to motivating their staff. The motivation to work well is usually related to job satisfaction, a complex issue that depends on many inter-linking factors, such as the working environment, attitude of senior management, co-operation with colleagues, pay and reward systems, terms of employment, recognition of achievements, personal circumstances, status, etc.

Travel and tourism organisations that put people first and treat staff motivation as a high priority are likely to be rewarded with employees who:

- ✪ **Attend work regularly**
- ✪ **Display high morale**
- ✪ **Project a good company image**
- ✪ **Are happy at their work**
- ✪ **Give a high level of customer service**
- ✪ **Achieve greater productivity**
- ✪ **Are motivated to achieve**
- ✪ **Work well individually and as members of teams**

Above all, an employee needs to feel a valued part of an organisation, recognised for his or her achievements and managed by senior staff who provide a supportive and effective environment. With all of these points in place, staff motivation will be high and the organisation will be in excellent shape to achieve its aims.

Types of motivation

Various theorists have analysed motivation theory and have concluded that motivation can be divided into two types:

1   **Intrinsic motivators**

2   **Extrinsic motivators**

Intrinsic motivators are those factors that are internal to an individual and are influenced by his or her feelings and emotions. Factors which give us internal satisfaction, a warm glow inside and a sense of emotional well-being include being awarded greater responsibility, a line manager saying thank you for doing a job well and a respected colleague asking for help and advice.

Extrinsic motivators are factors that are external to the individual, i.e. those that can be altered or given to an employee. Examples of this include money, 'perks' and improved working conditions. Powerful motivators are the possibility of a financial bonus or perhaps a new office with new furniture and administrative assistance.

Motivation theory tends to show that, on the whole, intrinsic motivators are the key to attracting a member of staff and retaining them. The theories show that these motivators are at a higher level. Money and bright new things are fine but they don't tend to give as much satisfaction, in the long term, as praise, trust and responsibility. Also, it is unlikely that the real level of pay an employee receives, or working conditions, will go on improving significantly year and after year. For example, it is difficult to improve the working conditions of an employee once they are in a large new office with all the necessary state-of-the-art equipment.

Management style

Different management styles will not only affect the day-to-day operation of an organisation, but will also have an important role to play in motivating staff. In travel and tourism organisations, management styles vary enormously. They can be categorised as follows:

✪   **Style one – Passive management**: The passive manager will do the bare minimum in any given situation, will generally resist change and will operate with an unhealthy degree of 'slackness'.

- **Style two – Committee management**: Committee managers will tend to steer a middle course on most matters and will try to remain popular with all members of staff. They will avoid open conflict and praise achievement, almost to the point of flattery.

- **Style three – Administrative management**: This style of management will be carried out by the person who likes to 'do everything by the book'. The administrative manager will tend to be conscientious rather than innovative and will develop systems within an organisation to handle most procedures and operations.

- **Style four – Aggressive management**: The aggressive manager is generally not a good listener but will request that everything is done his or her way, often without recourse to staff discussion. He or she will give the impression of not worrying unduly about creating conflict within an organisation.

- **Style five – Motivational management**: The motivational manager will agree goals with members of staff and will expect them to perform well and achieve their aims. He or she will be supportive if staff are experiencing difficulties in their work. The motivational manager will consult widely with members of staff and make clear who is responsible for what.

When it comes to selecting which is the most effective management style within a travel and tourism organisation, most people would agree (except perhaps those that exhibit styles 1 to 4!) that style five, motivational management, is likely to achieve the most positive outcome. Displaying a management style that is 'open' rather than defensive, supportive rather than destructive, criticises in a positive rather than negative fashion, is assertive rather than aggressive, praises rather than undermines staff achievement and advocates good communication, is far more likely to result in a high degree of staff motivation.

Activity 20.7

Working as a member of a team of six, set up a meeting to discuss the introduction of a new computer system in a tourist information centre. Five members of the team should play the role of managers, each adopting one of the five management styles shown above. The sixth person should act as an observer, taking notes on the discussion and reporting back at the end of the meeting. The team should conclude the activity by agreeing which management style was the most effective.

Staff appraisal

The main function of staff appraisal, sometimes referred to as staff development review, is to give an employee and his or her immediate superior the opportunity to discuss current performance and to agree a working plan for the future, in relation to specific targets and objectives. The appraisal, usually taking the form of an interview between the two parties, is also likely to highlight training needs for the individual that will have time and cost implications for management. Some travel and tourism organisations, particularly in the commercial sector of the industry, use the staff appraisal process to determine what level of bonus or performance-related pay the employee should receive. Others prefer to keep the two issues quite separate.

Staff appraisal has been widely used in private sector travel and tourism companies for many years. More recently, in response to the 'privatising' of many local authority leisure and tourism services, the public sector has begun to introduce the concept of appraisal of staff performance as part of a wider process of increasing efficiency and competitiveness.

In order to be of maximum benefit to any travel and tourism organisation, whether it is in the private or public sector, an effective system of staff appraisal needs:

- **Careful preparation by both the supervisor/manager and the employee**
- **A procedure that is clearly understood by both parties**
- **A well-designed appraisal form with space for comments by both parties**
- **An appraisal interview that is structured, but flexible enough to incorporate new ideas and developments**
- **An objective, written summary of the key points of the interview and agreed future targets and plans**
- **Feedback from employee and supervisor/manager on the effectiveness of the process**
- **An informal yet 'business like' atmosphere**

Figures 20.14 to 20.19 inclusive show examples of the paperwork that is used when an employee is taking part in an appraisal interview. Such an interview is a process by which managers and staff can hold a discussion, in a non-threatening environment, about all aspects of the member of staff's work performance and any subsequent training and development needs.

PRIVATE & CONFIDENTIAL

STAFF APPRAISAL & DEVELOPMENT PROGRAMME

EMPLOYEE PREPARATION FOR APPRAISAL INTERVIEW

This document forms an integral part of your development programme within the company. In its simplest form, appraisal involves your immediate line manager or supervisor discussing with you your present performance in the job and giving you guidance on future performance and how to develop your potential within the company.

The occasion on which your appraiser discusses these points with you is also an opportunity for you to raise with them any matters associated with your work in the company. During your discussion, you and your appraiser will have an opportunity to resolve any points of disagreement and record conclusions reached. All this is designed to allow you to develop your own particular abilities with the overall objective of agreeing a joint performance development plan for the next 12 months.

It is strongly recommended that you familiarise yourself with the content of this appraisal form and record your own thoughts and ideas prior to the actual appraisal interview. Your appraiser will also be making notes as part of their preparation for the interview.

Please read your job summary and ensure that you fully understand what is expected of you in the performance of your job.

Distribution:
Appraisee   *Personnel*
Appraiser
Appraiser's Line Manager

EMPLOYEE'S NAME

LOCATION

DATE OF JOINING THE COMPANY

JOB TITLE

DATE APPOINTED TO CURRENT JOB

DATE OF LAST APPRAISAL

APPRAISED BY

APPRAISAL INTERVIEW DETAILS

DATE OF INTERVIEW

TIME OF INTERVIEW

VENUE

APPRAISER'S NAME

TITLE

Figure 20.14 *Staff appraisal and development programme sheet one*

PRIVATE & CONFIDENTIAL   STAFF APPRAISAL & DEVELOPMENT PROGRAMME

To assist you in obtaining the maximum benefit from this programme, you are asked to give consideration to the following questions making a note of your thoughts and ideas prior to the interview. Your appraiser will be making similar notes and you will be discussing both sets of comments during the appraisal interview.

1.	Having read your job summary, in which aspects of the job do you feel you have achieved significant success? What has made you successful in these areas?
2.	What progress have you made in relation to the objectives set at your previous appraisal?
3.	In what areas of your job have you experienced difficulties or what has restricted you from meeting your stated objectives?
4.	What can you do yourself to improve any areas of job performance or conduct?
5.	What can your immediate supervisor/manager/department head/company do to improve any areas of your job performance or conduct?
6.	What training or experience would help you to develop your career: a) Now? b) Future?
7.	How do you see your future development within the company?
8.	List any suggestions/ideas that you consider would improve your own department and the company in general.
9.	Please read the latest training manual and consider your training needs for the next 12 months.

Figure 20.15 *Staff appraisal and development programme sheet two*

SHEET THREE

STAFF APPRAISAL & DEVELOPMENT PROGRAMME

INTERVIEW RECORD

Summary of points discussed, conclusions reached and actions agreed at the interview.

Employee's name _____
Location _____
Date _____

Figure 20.16 *Staff appraisal and development programme sheet three*

MOTIVATING STAFF   489

STAFF APPRAISAL & DEVELOPMENT PROGRAMME

Employee's name _____
Location _____
Date _____

SKILL ASSESSMENT

SKILL	OUTSTANDING	VERY GOOD	GOOD	AVERAGE	REQUIRES IMPROVEMENT
ADMINISTRATION					
ATTITUDE					
COMMUNICATION					
QUALITY/ACCURACY OF WORK					
QUANTITY OF WORK					
TIME MANAGEMENT					
COMPETENCE					
DECISION MAKING					
KNOWLEDGE OF POLICIES AND PROCEDURES					
INTERNAL/EXTERNAL CUSTOMER CARE					
TEAM WORK					
DEPENDABILITY					

Figure 20.17 *Staff appraisal and development programme sheet four*

PRIVATE & CONFIDENTIAL

SHEET FIVE

STAFF APPRAISAL & DEVELOPMENT PROGRAMME

ACTION PLAN

APPRAISEE NAME	LOCATION		DATE

KEY AREAS IDENTIFIED FOR ACTION	AGREED ACTION/OBJECTIVES	TARGET DATE	REVIEW DATE

SIGNED _____ APPRAISEE   SIGNED _____ APPRAISER   DATE _____

Figure 20.18 *Staff appraisal and development programme sheet five*

PRIVATE & CONFIDENTIAL

STAFF APPRAISAL & DEVELOPMENT PROGRAMME

DEVELOPMENT/TRAINING NEEDS IDENTIFICATION

APPRAISEE NAME | LOCATION | DATE

COURSES LISTED IN COMPANY TRAINING PROGRAMME

PREFERRED DATE	COURSE CODE	NAME OF COURSE	DURATION	LOCATION

ALL TRAINING NEEDS NOT MET BY COMPANY TRAINING PROGRAMME

TARGET DATE	DEVELOPMENT/TRAINING REQUIRED	LOCATION PREFERRED

AUTHORISED BY:

Figure 20.19 *Staff appraisal and development programme sheet six*

Activity 20.8

Using the staff appraisal and development forms in Figures 20.14 to 20.19 as a guide, role play an appraisal interview for a tour operator's marketing assistant who has been in post for six months. You should take the role of the marketing assistant's line manager (appraiser) and another member of your group should take the role of the marketing assistant (appraisee). When you have completed the interview, swap roles and carry out an interview for another travel and tourism job.

Most organisations recognise the benefits of introducing a staff appraisal system, although it can have one or two drawbacks if not carefully planned. The benefits include:

○ **Assisting in meeting organisational objectives**
○ **Helping managers improve the effectiveness of their staff**
○ **Assisting the employee to identify his or her role in the organisation**
○ **Improving communication between staff and management**
○ **Building commitment and loyalty**
○ **Helping managers understand better the jobs that their staff carry out**
○ **Identifying training and personal development needs**

Because staff appraisal is understandably a very sensitive issue, introducing such a scheme without a supportive and positive approach on the part of management and employees can sometimes lead to problems. There is often a great deal of uncertainty and suspicion surrounding the process when appraisal is linked to pay and bonuses, which is why many organisations choose to treat the two issues separately. Managers and supervisors must be aware of the importance of confidentiality in the whole process in order to gain the confidence of their staff. Management must also be careful not to raise expectations in their staff which cannot be met, for example promising staff training opportunities that fail to materialise. If staff appraisal is well planned and has the commitment of management and employees, it can be a very useful tool for improving performance and helping to meet overall organisational objectives.

Staff development and training

There can be little doubt that a well-trained workforce is any travel and tourism organisation's greatest asset. Offering opportunities for training and development increases staff morale and motivation, which in turn feed through into increased efficiency, productivity and output. In short, training can:

- ✪ **Increase profitability and efficiency**
- ✪ **Improve customer service**
- ✪ **Reduce staff turnover**
- ✪ **Increase flexibility**
- ✪ **Trigger innovation and new ideas**
- ✪ **Reduce costs**

Training needs analysis

A logical starting point for any travel and tourism organisation wanting to introduce, or improve, training for staff is to implement a training needs analysis (TNA). A TNA is an auditing process that aims to identify:

1 **The current level of technical and management skills within the organisation**

2 **The required level of technical and management skills needed to be an effective organisation**

3 **Any shortfall or surplus in the level of technical and management skills**

If a shortfall is identified, which is often the case with organisations in the travel and tourism industry, many of which have generally under-invested in training for their staff, the TNA should make recommendations on the action necessary to bridge the training gap. TNAs can be carried out by staff within the organisation or by employing outside consultants who specialise in the field. Either way, the senior management must give their full commitment to the initiative, since it may require additional resources over a long period of time. A fully planned and costed staff training plan is not a 'quick fix' solution, but one which will take time to achieve its aims. The TNA may well identify the need for increasing the level of technical and management skills through a mixture of on-the-job and off-the-job training.

On-the-job training

As its name implies, on-the-job training is when employees gain and develop their skills and knowledge while carrying out their normal everyday duties.

Many jobs in travel and tourism are ideally suited to this type of 'hands on' training, for example operating a VDU in a travel agency, working in the plant room of a leisure centre, training to be a chef in a restaurant or hotel and working behind the counter in a tourist information centre, to name but a few. On-the-job training often leads to qualifications such as National Vocational Qualifications (NVQs) and SVQs in Scotland, both of which give employees credit for competence-based training related to the world of work.

Off-the-job training

Training that takes place away from the normal place of work is sometimes preferred by staff and employers as a way of achieving a specific training objective. Some travel and tourism organisations make extensive use of 'day release' courses offered by local colleges and private training providers, often leading to industry-related vocational qualifications. Evening classes are also popular in sectors such as travel and leisure centre management. Some organisations encourage their senior staff to work towards management and supervisory qualifications, either by the traditional route of going on a course, or perhaps by following a distance-learning programme based around home study and a small amount of tutorial support. Many organisations have found that extra training in the areas of customer care, ICT and foreign languages is particularly beneficial for staff working in travel and tourism.

Job rotation and job enlargement

Job enlargement is the practice of increasing the scope and variety of a job and the range of tasks that a person is responsible for carrying out. A public relations assistant for a large tour operator, for example, whose job usually consists of writing press releases, may be given the job of organising a familiarisation visit for a group of travel journalists. While job enlargement can be useful for a person's career development, it should not be seen as a type of cheap labour, e.g. getting junior staff to carry out tasks that are usually done by more senior, higher paid employees. However, if managed as part of an individual's personal and professional development, job enlargement can give added job satisfaction.

Job rotation is a type of job enlargement, with an employee's work tasks being alternated over a period of time, so as to relieve the monotony of mundane tasks and to expose employees to the work of other departments or individuals in their organisation. Job rotation should be seen as an important part of staff training and development, allowing employees to gain useful transferable skills.

Team working

You will have learned the importance of team working when studying Unit 6 *Travel and tourism in action*. Effective teamwork brings benefits both to the organisation that sets up the team and to the individual team members. Benefits to the organisation will vary depending on its size, structure and culture, but are likely to include:

✪ **Increased efficiency** – an example of this could be that an effective team working in the information department of a national tourist office will be able to handle more enquiries from customers

✪ **Increased sales** – a teamwork approach to selling holiday insurance by telephone is likely to yield increased sales when compared with the same activity carried out individually

✪ **Less staff conflict** – a team that is trained to take responsibility for its own work and decision making is likely to be better at resolving its own internal problems, thus saving valuable management time

✪ **Reduced absenteeism** – staff who see themselves as valued members of a team are likely to be more content and take less time off work

✪ **Increased loyalty** – teamwork instills a sense of loyalty and commitment into members of staff

✪ **A more creative workforce** – team members are more likely to come forward with ideas for improving work practices, reducing costs or increasing efficiency

✪ **A happier workforce** – teamwork allows individuals to work to their full potential and feel good about themselves and their work

Above all, management is keen to see that by establishing a team to carry out a task, they are getting more than just 'the sum of the parts'. For example, three waiters who previously worked individually in a restaurant, and were able to service eight tables each per shift, would be expected to service more than 3 × 8 tables per shift when working as a team.

Benefits to individual team members may include:

✪ **An enhanced sense of their worth within the organisation**
✪ **The ability to use their talents to the full**
✪ **Increased status within the organisation**
✪ **The chance to be innovative and creative**
✪ **Increased rewards for their work made possible as a result of greater efficiency, e.g. a productivity bonus or extra 'perks'**
✪ **The support of other team members**
✪ **More job satisfaction**

Remuneration, performance-related pay and other incentives

We will now consider the many types of remuneration available to staff working in the travel and tourism industry, including:

- ✪ **Salary and wage structures**
- ✪ **Incentive schemes**
- ✪ **Pensions**

Salary and wage structures

Many people who work in travel and tourism will be expected to work unsocial hours. The very nature of the industry means that it is necessary to work during the times that are normally associated with 'leisure', often at evenings and weekends. Staff working in hotels, visitor attractions, bars, restaurants, airports, etc. will all be affected by this work pattern. By way of compensation for working these unsocial hours, the employees may be paid a shift allowance in addition to their normal basic pay.

Depending on which sector of travel and tourism we are dealing with, the basic pay may be fixed solely by the employer, by the employer in consultation with a trade union or workers' association, or by a wages council (the hotel and catering sector has its own wages council). The 'going rate' for any job will depend on many factors, such as:

- ✪ **The supply of suitable people who could do the job**
- ✪ **The skills demanded**
- ✪ **The qualifications necessary to secure the job**
- ✪ **The level of responsibility**
- ✪ **The part of the country in which the job is located (jobs in the south-east of England often attract an extra payment known as a London 'weighting')**
- ✪ **The degree of danger or risk involved with the job**
- ✪ **The experience of those applying for the job**

Some travel and tourism organisations prefer to pay their existing employees overtime rather than take on new members of staff when extra work becomes available. The sorts of occasions when overtime may be paid include:

- ✪ **To cover for staff illness and short-term absence**
- ✪ **To be employed for a special event that is not part of the normal work programme**

- **To put in extra hours in response to a heavy demand on the organisation, e.g. a reservations assistant for a tour operator may work overtime in the peak booking period or a tourist information centre assistant may work extra hours over a Bank Holiday weekend**
- **To carry out a survey of users of facilities**
- **To write up an important report or complete a tender application**

Activity 20.9

Research local and national job advertisements and draw up a chart of specific jobs in travel and tourism, with the salaries and benefits each offers.

Incentive schemes

In addition to basic pay, many travel and tourism organisations offer their employees other incentives in order to encourage or reward performance, such as:

- **Commission payments**
- **Bonuses**
- **Profit-sharing schemes**
- **'Perks' and fringe benefits**

Commission payments

Commission is usually associated with sales staff who can increase their earnings by increasing the amount they sell. A commission is a payment that is usually made in addition to a basic salary, although there are occasions when a job is 'commission only' with no basic pay at all. The commission may be a lump sum paid when a certain target is reached, or, more usually, a percentage of the value of the sales. The payment of commission occurs in many sectors of the travel and tourism industry, including:

- **Counter staff in a travel agency who receive extra payments according to the number of holidays and other products sold**
- **An area sales manager for an airline who earns commission based on the value of flights sold by her sales team**
- **A conference executive who receives part of his salary as commission based on the number of conference bed-nights sold by his company**

Commission is a very good incentive for the employee to work hard and achieve pre-determined work targets.

Bonuses

It is common in the travel and tourism industry to pay staff a bonus at certain times of the year or in appreciation of the hard work and effort on the part of the employees in relation to a particular campaign or project. Hotel workers may receive a bonus at Christmas, overseas representatives may be paid a bonus by their tour operator at the end of the summer or winter season and a manager of a major tourist attraction may receive a bonus for a particularly successful year. Bonus payments are not normally linked to the productivity or performance of an individual member of staff but are one-off payments that will vary from time to time.

Profit-sharing schemes

As its name implies, a profit-sharing scheme is when an employee receives an extra payment in addition to his or her basic salary, which is related to the profitability of the organisation. For example, a 10 per cent increase in profits over a 12-month period may result in an employee receiving a bonus which is equivalent to an extra 10 per cent of his or her annual salary. When an organisation is not generating any profits, perhaps because it has only just begun trading or is struggling to maintain its share of the market, the bonus will not usually be paid, although it is rare for staff to be asked to take a cut in pay in this situation.

'Perks' and fringe benefits

We have seen that many employees working in travel and tourism are attracted to the industry by the glamour that is often associated with the industry and by the 'perks' that many positions can offer. 'Perks' are very common in travel and tourism, and are seen as a way of supplementing a sometimes low basic wage or salary. One of the most widespread fringe benefits is the right to buy or use facilities and services either free or at discounted prices, for example:

- **Free use of swimming pool and sports facilities for staff working in a leisure centre**
- **Discounted flights for travel agents, tour operators and airline personnel**
- **Free rail travel for train company staff and their families**
- **Free entrance to visitor attractions for staff and their guests**
- **Discounted rates at hotels in the same chain for employees**

There may be certain restrictions on when staff can take advantage of these 'perks'; Center Parcs, for example, insist that employees can only use the facilities when they are off-duty, a ruling that is widespread throughout all sectors of the travel and tourism industry.

Other benefits to staff in travel and tourism include discounts at selected stores, subsidised canteen services, free uniforms, private health insurance, company vehicles and free shares in the company, to name but a few.

Staff working in travel agencies are offered many types of incentives by tour operators, airlines, car hire firms, coach operators, etc., to encourage them to sell their particular product. One of the most common is to give sales staff gift vouchers from major high street stores in return for selling a particular number of holiday packages or a certain value of airline flights, for example. By using this technique, sales representatives are able to influence counter staff and hopefully increase sales for their company.

Pensions

Most travel and tourism organisations will want to help their staff in later life and will offer pension facilities that will give their permanent employees an extra income when they retire. This benefit will be in addition to the normal state retirement pension. Pension arrangements will vary greatly between one organisation and another, as well as between individuals doing the same job. This is why some organisations offer free financial and pre-retirement planning for their employees, to ensure that they receive the best possible pension benefits at retirement. Public sector travel and tourism employees are likely to be members of a local authority pension scheme, which, within certain parameters, can be transferred from one public sector organisation to another, without loss of benefits.

Pensions can be either contributory, when the member of staff pays a certain amount towards the pension, or non-contributory, when all pension payments are made by the employer. Even with a contributory pension scheme, it is likely that the employer will make some contribution towards payments. There has been a steady growth in recent years of private pensions as a tax-efficient way of supplementing an existing pension.

The working environment

Members of staff function best when they are provided with a well-designed and well-equipped working environment. The nature of many travel and tourism organisations will mean that the work environment for staff is the facility itself, e.g. a hotel, museum, aircraft or outdoor activity centre. Working in close proximity to colleagues in these situations, with few physical barriers, can mean that staff who work in teams perform particularly well and that a tremendous team spirit is built up. Team leaders need to be aware, however, of the potential pressures and conflicts that can arise in such circumstances and be prepared to take whatever action is necessary to manage the situation. As well as being well designed and well equipped, the working environment must comply with relevant health and safety legislation.

Access to the necessary equipment and technology is an important aspect of working in travel and tourism today. Depending on the type of organisation, staff may need access to:

- **Specialist computer software, e.g. for a CRS (central reservations system)**
- **Technical equipment, e.g. specialist ovens for kitchen staff**
- **Communications equipment, e.g. fax machine, telex, telephones, audio-visual aids, etc.**
- **The use of vehicles for transporting people and equipment**

Given the right level of equipment, staff will feel comfortable about having sufficient resources to do the job they have been set.

Index

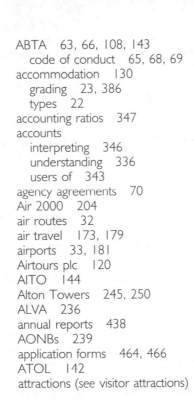